MW00478562

# Counseling Fathers

## The Routledge Series on Counseling and Psychotherapy with Boys and Men

### SERIES EDITOR

**Mark S. Kiselica**
The College of New Jersey

### ADVISORY BOARD

**Deryl Bailey**
University of Georgia

**Chris Blazina**
University of Houston

**J. Manuel Casas**
University of California,
Santa Barbara

**Matt Englar-Carlson**
California State University,
Fullerton

**Ann Fischer**
Southern Illinois University,
Carbondale

**David Lisak**
University of Massachusetts Boston

**William Liu**
University of Iowa

**James O'Neil**
University of Connecticut

**Steve Wester**
University of Wisconsin–Milwaukee

### VOLUMES IN THIS SERIES

### FORTHCOMING

# Counseling Fathers

EDITED BY
Chen Z. Oren and
Dora Chase Oren

Routledge
Taylor & Francis Group
New York   London

Routledge
Taylor & Francis Group
270 Madison Avenue
New York, NY 10016

Routledge
Taylor & Francis Group
27 Church Road
Hove, East Sussex BN3 2FA

© 2010 by Taylor and Francis Group, LLC
Routledge is an imprint of Taylor & Francis Group, an Informa business

Printed in the United States of America on acid-free paper
10 9 8 7 6 5 4 3 2 1

International Standard Book Number: 978-0-415-98864-3 (Paperback)

For permission to photocopy or use material electronically from this work, please access www.copyright.com (http://www.copyright.com/) or contact the Copyright Clearance Center, Inc. (CCC), 222 Rosewood Drive, Danvers, MA 01923, 978-750-8400. CCC is a not-for-profit organization that provides licenses and registration for a variety of users. For organizations that have been granted a photocopy license by the CCC, a separate system of payment has been arranged.

**Trademark Notice:** Product or corporate names may be trademarks or registered trademarks, and are used only for identification and explanation without intent to infringe.

**Library of Congress Cataloging-in-Publication Data**

Oren, Chen Z.
    Counseling fathers / Chen Z. Oren and Dora Chase Oren.
        p. cm.
    Includes index.
    ISBN 978-0-415-98864-3 (pbk. : alk. paper)
    1. Counseling. 2. Fathers and daughters. 3. Fathers and sons. 4. Parent and child. I. Oren, Dora Chase. II. Title.

    BF636.6.O74 2009
    155.6'462--dc22                                                    2009001381

**Visit the Taylor & Francis Web site at**
**http://www.taylorandfrancis.com**

**and the Routledge Web site at**
**http://www.routledgementalhealth.com**

*In memory of my parents, Yecheskel and Dvora Opochinsky,
who did not get to meet my wife and kids—wish you were here.
To Steve and Elinor Fienberg, my new parents—thank you.*

*To my wife, Dora,
my kids, Yoni and Emma,
Elizabeth and Hannah.*

*And for all the fathers who try to do the best they can.*

**CZO**

*For Steve, Chen, and Eric—the fathers in my life.*

**DCO**

# Contents

# Series Foreword

One of my goals for the Routledge Series on Counseling and Psychotherapy with Boys and Men has been to support the publication of books by highly respected scholars that would address the needs of neglected populations of boys and men. So, I was ecstatic when I learned that Dr. Chen Oren and Dr. Dora Chase Oren—two national authorities on fatherhood issues—were interested in editing a volume on fathers whose challenges and concerns warrant the increased attention of mental health professionals.

It will come as no surprise to many readers of this book that Drs. Oren and Oren have assembled an impressive team of colleagues to produce *Counseling Fathers*, which is the third volume in this series. For the past several years, Drs. Oren and Oren and their students have been a consistent presence at numerous professional conferences, presenting the findings of their research about the needs of fathers and how practitioners can help them. Through their ongoing work on the subject, Drs. Oren and Oren have developed a network of counselors, marriage and family therapists, psychologists, and social workers interested in supporting fathers in the important roles they play in their families and their communities. To my great pleasure, a dedicated subgroup from this network pulled their informative ideas together in this volume. What will be surprising to some readers, however, is that until recently, fathers have been neglected and viewed with disdain by scholars and helping professionals, which is why this book is so badly needed. Many behavioral scientists prior to the 1960s and 1970s assumed that fathers were relatively unimportant in the development of their children (Cabrera, Tamis-LeMonda, Bradley, Hofferth, & Lamb, 2000). In addition, for decades the literature on fatherhood was dominated by a deficit perspective that overemphasized the inadequacy of men to be effective parents (Hawkins & Dollahite, 1997a). Due in large part to this deficit point of view, services for fathers were lacking (Kiselica, 2008). As Hawkins and Dollahite (1997a) have pointed out, "when scholars and practitioners approach their work with fathers from a deficit paradigm, they are likely to find inadequate role performance" (p. 3), overlook good fathers, and fail to see the potential of men to care for their children.

As a positive alternative to the deficit perspective on fathers, a new generation of social scientists and clinicians has constructed the generative fatherhood model, which emphasizes the many ways that fathers care for the next generation and strength-based approaches to supporting men in their role as fathers (see Brotherson & White, 2007; Fagan & Hawkins, 2001; Hawkins & Dollahite, 1997b; Lamb, 2003; Snarey, 1993). In *Counseling Fathers*, Drs. Oren and Oren and their esteemed colleagues have situated themselves within the generative fatherhood tradition by examining numerous theoretical, cultural, and developmental issues pertaining to work with fathers and by describing strength-based interventions with several special populations of fathers. In short, *Counseling Fathers* helps us to understand the complex contexts in which men become fathers, the challenges they face during the transition to parenthood and the in years following the birth of their children, and the many ways practitioners can identify and utilize male strengths to help men be loving, engaged fathers.

I thank Drs. Oren and Oren and their colleagues for adding *Counseling Fathers* to this series, and I look forward to the positive influence their work will have on the practice of counseling, psychotherapy, and social service with fathers.

**Mark S. Kiselica, Series Editor**
The Routledge Series on Counseling and
Psychotherapy with Boys and Men
The College of New Jersey
January 2009

# REFERENCES

Brotherson, S. E., & White, J. M. (2007). *Why father's count: The importance of fathers and their involvement with children.* Harriman, TN: Men's Studies Press.

Cabrera, N. J., Tamis-LeMonda, C. S., Bradley, R. H., Hofferth, S., & Lamb, M. E. (2000). Fatherhood in the twenty-first century. *Child Development, 71,* 127–136.

Fagan, J., & Hawkins, A. J. (Eds.). (2001). *Clinical and educational interventions with fathers.* New York: The Haworth Clinical Practice Press.

Hawkins, A. J, & Dollahite, D. C. (1997a). Beyond the role-inadequacy perspective of fathering. In A. J. Hawkins & D. C. Dollahite (Eds.), *Generative fathering: Beyond deficit perspectives* (pp. 3–16). Thousand Oaks, CA: Sage.

Hawkins, A. J, & Dollahite, D. C. (Eds.) (1997b). *Generative fathering: Beyond deficit perspectives.* Thousand Oaks, CA: Sage.

Kiselica, M. S. (2008). *When boys become parents: Adolescent fatherhood in America.* New Brunswick, NJ: Rutgers University Press.

Lamb, M. E. (Ed.). (2003). *The father's role in child development* (4th ed.). New York: Wiley.

Snarey, J. (1993). *How fathers care for the next generation: A four-decade study.* Cambridge, MA: Harvard University Press.

# *Foreword*

JOSEPH H. PLECK

Fathers today face significant challenges. In a Pew Research Center (2007) national survey, about three-fifths of adult men and women said that they think it is harder to be a father now than it was 20 or 30 years ago. And how well does the public think today's fathers are doing in the face of this increased "paternal challenge"? Of women in the survey, 56% said today's dads are doing as good a job or a better job raising their kids compared with fathers a generation ago. Intriguingly, married working mothers' assessments of fathers' performance were especially positive: 72% of those working at least part-time and raising young children said dads today are doing as good a job or better.

But here's the rub: Among fathers themselves, there is a crisis of paternal self-confidence. Only 41% of men in the Pew survey thought contemporary fathers are doing better or even as well as fathers in the past. A clear majority of men (55%) said today's dads are actually doing a worse job.

The need for this important book lies precisely in the intersection of today's increased paternal challenges and the rising crisis in paternal self-confidence. Practitioners can use this book as a guide for clinical work and interventions to help fathers from diverse groups become the kinds of fathers they want to be. Researchers will benefit from the future directions it identifies for further exploration of today's paternal challenges, and ways both to remediate the researchers and to transform the challenges into positive growth and resilience.

From the viewpoint of someone who began working on fathering in the 1970s, the way that the "landscape" of fatherhood, both scholarly and culturally, has changed over the last four decades is remarkable. When I started out, "fatherhood research" meant research on the consequences of father absence. Through the early 1970s, it seemed that in psychological theory, fathers were considered absolutely towering figures in child development, but towering only by their absence, not by their presence. Of course, a father did not have to be nonresident to be absent. In my clinical internship in 1970 at a major Boston psychiatric hospital, having a weak, passive father was so commonplace in case histories that it might as well have been preprinted on the patient history form. Someone involved in the 1991 film *Hot Shots*, a parody of *Top Gun*, must have heard about this: A psychiatrist in the film, after interviewing the main character, pilot Topper Harley, enters the diagnosis in Harley's case file using a stamp, "Paternal Conflict Syndrome (P.C.S.)."

Besides father absence, other aspects of paternal behavior and children's relationships with their fathers gradually began to be studied in the 1970s and early 1980s, such as fathers' roles in children's cognitive, social, and moral development; fathers' interaction style; and infant attachment to fathers. However, at that time no formal construct existed that addressed how large a part fathers play in the care and socialization of their children—in simple terms, how much fathers *do* as parents. No existing construct had yet been developed that captured emerging concerns about whether fathers were "doing enough" with their children, and from the perspective of the adolescent and young adult, whether his or her father is "really there for me."

In the mid-1980s my colleagues Michael Lamb, James Levine, and I formulated the concept of "father involvement." The involvement construct is now so deeply embedded in contemporary thinking about fatherhood that it may be surprising to many to realize how recent this concept actually is, and how controversial it has been.

Like most new constructs in the social sciences, the involvement concept soon came in for its share of criticism. Didn't the concept imply a "maternal template?" A deficit perspective on fathers? A feminist-oriented assumption that there should be equity in parenting? Didn't it ignore fathers' thoughts and feelings? Devalue fathers' economic support for their children? Wasn't the concept based on the experience of only White middle-class fathers, therefore defining fathering in a way that makes fathers of minorities and of lower socioeconomic status appear deficient? (For an analysis of these critiques and my evaluation, see Pleck & Stueve, 2001.) Also, isn't the idea that father involvement is increasing only "media hype"? (For recent U.S. and European data indicating otherwise, see Pleck & Masciadrelli, 2004.)

In my view, these "father involvement wars" of the 1990s reflecting the intense debates about these questions are now over. The good news is that everyone won. That is, the engagement, accessibility, and responsibility components in the Lamb-Pleck-Levine formulation of involvement continue to be studied. Paternal warmth, support, control/monitoring, and other cognitions and affects not included in the original formulation are also receiving increasing attention, and economic support is now clearly recognized as an aspect of fathering. Researchers still do vary in how they operationally define involvement. Some have broadened the concept of involvement to include cognitions, affects, and economic support, and other investigators have found value in maintaining the original focus on engagement, accessibility, and responsibility while studying other aspects of fathering as additional dimensions. What is important is not resolving a theoretical debate about what the term "involvement" *should* include, but that these latter dimensions are being increasingly investigated as important components of fathering, whether considered as aspects of involvement or not.

Today, as reflected in this book and elsewhere, fatherhood research and practice have entered a new era. This new period is marked especially by the recognition that fathering occurs in multiple contexts that can be profoundly different from each other. Chapters in this volume cover a wide range of these contexts, including many cutting-edge ones not discussed in other recent compendia. Of course, no single collection can cover all possible topics and groups, because this would require including not only all the ones previously recognized, but also all the others emerging more recently. Just to keep them in mind, some of the other father groups that could not be addressed here but are receiving increasing attention include stepfathers, incarcerated fathers, cohabiting biological fathers (who are surprisingly numerous), "fragile family" fathers, and of course the very large group of nonresident fathers.

A particularly notable way in which this book fosters today's new era of fatherhood research and practice is its attention to the ways that fathering is embedded in and intertwined with masculinity. It has been perhaps commonplace to say that fathering is gendered. This important framing leads to focusing on differences *between* men and women—certainly worthwhile. But to say, more pointedly, that fathering is intrinsically linked to issues of masculinity is a further conceptual step that the field is only now beginning to take. This next step, reflected in this volume's chapters, necessarily gives more attention to variations *among* men in their parenting. In bringing the masculinity perspective to fatherhood, one of this book's special contributions is its mix of authors, a mix that includes some of the founding, long-time contributors to the psychological study of men and masculinity as well as important new voices.

## REFERENCES

Pew Research Center. (2007). Being Dad may be tougher these days, but working Moms are among their biggest fans. Retrieved July 26, 2008, from http://pewsocialtrends.org/pubs/510/fathers-day

Pleck, J. H., & Masciadrelli, B. (2004). Paternal involvement in U.S. residential fathers: Levels, sources, and consequences. In M. E. Lamb (Ed.), *The role of the father in child development*, 4th ed (pp. 222–271). New York: Wiley.

Pleck, J. H., & Stueve, J. L. (2001). Time and paternal involvement. In K. Daly (Ed.), *Minding the time in family experience: Emerging perspectives and issues* (pp. 205–226). Oxford, UK: Elsevier Science.

# Preface
## Counseling Diverse Populations of Fathers

### DORA CHASE OREN AND CHEN Z. OREN

With almost 60 million fathers today in the United States (U.S. Census Bureau [USCB], 2001), it is critical for mental health providers and educators to give thoughtful consideration to how fathers are counseled. The increased immigration and diversification of the U.S. population (Cabrera, Tamis-Lemonda, Bradley, Hofferth, & Lamb, 2000; Coley, 2001; Lamb, 2004) have significantly impacted fathers' roles and experiences. Mental health providers' increased knowledge and understanding of diverse fathers' experiences, background, and world views set the stage for more effective counseling.

By 2007, the United States had experienced an explosion in interest about fathers. President George W. Bush prioritized increasing fathers' involvement as the 12th most important key policy (U.S. Government, 2001). Landmark legislation and public policy were established to ensure child support, including the Personal Responsibility and Work Opportunity Reconciliation Act of 1996 (P.L. 104-193; Curran, 2003). Programs such as DADS Family Project (Cornille, Barlow, & Cleveland, 2005) and the National Fatherhood Initiative (National Fatherhood Initiative, 2006) were developed to help fathers gain mastery and expertise in their roles as parents. Recent trade books such as *The Father Book: Being a Good Dad in the 21st Century* (Cohen, 2001) and *The Expectant Father* (Brott & Ash, 2001) as well as ubiquitous articles such as "Moms Knows Best, but It's Time for Guys to Get More Into the Game" (*Detroit Times*, December 17, 2006) and "Unwed Fathers Fight for Babies Placed for Adoption by Mothers" (*New York Times*, March 19, 2006) highlight the current significant attention paid to fathers. Almost three-quarters of the U.S. population believe that fatherlessness is the most significant family or social problem facing America (National Center for Fathering, 1999).

Mental health providers and researchers recognize the growing public attention to fathers and have increased efforts to study and address fathers. Some of the broad issues identified include changes in family structure (Curran, 2003; Marsiglio, 1995) and male gender roles (Fagan & Hawkins, 2001; Marsiglio, Day, & Lamb, 2000). Other research areas have included child support and noncustodial fathers (Curran, 2003; O'Donnell, Johnson, D'Aunno, & Thornton, 2005); nontraditional households including gay fathers, single fathers, and stepfathers; and the transition to fatherhood (Condon, Boyce, & Corkindale, 2004; Draper, 2003; Zelkowitz & Milet, 1997). King, Harris, and Heard (2004) noted that ethnicity and race are related to fathers' patterns of involvement with their children. Experiences become more complex within minority groups who have their own definitions of successful fatherhood/fathering (Lamb, 2004), unique challenges and accomplishments, and particular norms for appropriate affective expression (Fagan & Hawkins, 2001; Sue & Sue, 2007). Today's mental health providers can more effectively counsel fathers by viewing them not only in terms of their influence on children, but also on a broader scope that incorporates the father's individual experiences. The sheer enormity in numbers and types of fathers is remarkable:

In 2000, there were over 25 million fathers who were part of a traditional married-couple family with children under 18 (USCB, 2001).

Children who were part of the "postwar generation" could expect to grow up with two biological parents who were married to each other. Eighty percent did. Today, only about half of children will spend their entire childhood in their families of origin (USCB, 1997).

Over 2 million households include children living in nontraditional family structures. Approximately 1.9 million include opposite sex unmarried couples; 96,000 are female partners, and 66,000 are male partners (USCB, 2001).

While the number of single mothers remained constant over the 3-year period from 1988 to 2001, the number of single fathers grew 25% to over 2 million in 1998, which represents an increase of 50% since 1990 (Brown, 2000). In 2000, single-father families jumped to one in six of single-parent families (USCB, 2001).

The number of stay-at-home fathers, while modest, continues to grow. In 2005, there were an estimated 5.8 million stay-at-home parents: 5.6 million mothers and 143,000 fathers (USCB, 2001).

Despite the growth in single-father households, the United States is the world leader in families without fathers (Klinger, 1998).

Culture is associated with types of family structure. Over half of African American children, almost a third of Hispanic children, and 20% of White children live in single-parent homes (USCB, 1997).

The current demographic landscape of the United States illustrates the importance of not only training mental health providers to understand a father's experiences, but also the timeliness of addressing the differences and similarities of the many types of fathers.

The approval of the Guidelines on Multicultural Education, Training, Research, Practice, and Organizational Change for Psychologists by the American Psychological Association was a milestone event in the diversity training of some mental health providers (Arredondo & Perez, 2006). One area of multicultural competency includes a counselor's knowledge and understanding of a client's world view, culture, and background to increase rapport and promote successful treatment outcome (Sue & Sue, 2007). Multicultural competencies are an important construct for mental health providers to understand to be effective in helping culturally diverse populations (Fuertes et al., 2006).

The U.S. census data suggest that the diverse groups of fathers addressed in this book continue to increase, with more Asian American and Hispanic fathers, teen fathers, older fathers, stay-at-home fathers, gay fathers, and the like than ever before (USCB, 1997, 2001). Several researchers have called attention to the need to focus more research on these diverse groups of fathers and to develop clinical applications (Andrews, Luckey, Bolden, Whiting-Fickling, & Lind, 2004; Coley, 2001; Fagan & Hawkins, 2001). The growing need to study underrepresented fathers in child development has been highlighted by the recent changes in welfare reforms, child support, paternity establishment, immigration, and child custody (Lamb, 2004). Although scholarly attention has begun to focus on ethnic and special groups of fathers in child development (Lamb, 2004), limited focus has been given to the counseling of these fathers (Fagan & Hawkins, 2001).

This book is designed to bridge the gap between fathers and professional helpers. The two main foci of this book, the application of working with different ethnicities of fathers and with diverse subpopulations of fathers, represent a unique pairing that adds to the understanding of counseling fathers. The intent is to highlight some of the United States' common ethnic/racial groups of fathers (Caucasian, African American, Asian American, and Hispanic) as well as specific populations of fathers, such as religious fathers, stay-at-home fathers, gay fathers, and others. It is beyond the scope of this book to examine each type or category of father; the selected populations represent a consideration of both cultural and distinct experiences. Similar to any type of counseling, there are many different ways to help fathers. The authors draw from theory, research, and clinical experiences to highlight some effective ways to provide counseling to different populations of fathers.

The focus of this current text is on fathers' multilayered experiences rather than an emphasis on fathers' involvement with their children and within their families. The importance of looking at both ethnicity and specific groups highlights the focus of multiculturalism that considers the experience of different populations and is not limited to race or ethnicity (Leach & Carlton, 1997; Pope-Davis, Liu, Toporek, & Brittan-Powell, 2001). The common goal throughout the following chapters is to provide practitioners with ways to integrate fathers' needs and experiences to provide competent, informed, and effective counseling.

## ORGANIZATION

This book is organized into three sections. The first section looks at the historical underpinnings of the new fatherhood movement and examines two avenues to consider when counseling fathers. The second and third sections provide in-depth discussions of fathers across ethnicities and within specific populations. The chapters in these two sections begin with foundational material of the particular group being examined, including background and historical information, followed by some of the world views and challenges that specific populations will bring to counseling. The editors asked each author to include the strengths that these fathers bring to counseling, as these positive attributes can be capitalized to enhance counseling and deepen interventions. Each chapter also explores approaches or models to work effectively with the respective population of fathers. Vignettes and case examples are included throughout the chapters to illustrate the suggested approaches and interventions.

Section 1, Historical Perspectives and Current Directions, begins with an introductory chapter by Ronald F. Levant and David J. Wimer. The chapter combines a personal as well as scholarly perspective in providing a brief historical overview of changes in family structure, gender roles, and counseling and their impact on the emergence of the new father role. In Chapter 2, Chen Z. Oren, Matt Englar-Carlson, Mark A. Stevens, and Dora Chase Oren explore a strength-based perspective to working with fathers. The chapter reviews the literature on positive fathering, introduces a five-stage strength-based model, and concludes with a clinical case example illustrating the use of the model. In Chapter 3, James M. O'Neil and Melissa L. Lujan explain how to apply gender role conflict theory and research as an assessment paradigm to counsel fathers. It discusses the effects of gender role socialization on fathers, including the roles of masculinity ideology and norms, the roles of diversity and acculturation, and the father-wound concept. Diagnostic schema are presented to help counselors assess fathers and guide interventions.

Section 2, Counseling Fathers Across Ethnic Groups, highlights four predominant ethnic groups within the United States. For this text, Latino, Asian American, African American, and Caucasian fathers are examined to identify the impact of ethnicity on the fathering experience and how to work effectively with these fathers in counseling. The section begins with Joseph M. Cervantes examining the experiences of Hispanic fathers based on the application of relevant concepts, such as machismo, and areas of particular relevance, such as acculturation, family structure, spirituality, and gender roles. The chapter provides suggestions for culturally sensitive interventions and approaches to counsel Hispanic fathers. In Chapter 5, Atsuko Seto, Kent W. Becker, and Nirupma Narang focus on counseling fathers of Asian descent. This chapter addresses the essence of fatherhood of Asian American men from social, cultural, and historical perspectives. The authors focus on the six largest ethnic groups defined in the 2000 U.S. Census that includes Chinese, Filipino, Indian, Vietnamese, Korean, and Japanese fathers. Counseling approaches and techniques that are respectful to fathers of Asian cultural backgrounds are provided. In Chapter 6, Anderson J. Franklin looks at the challenges of Black fathers who are engaged and present in the lives of their children but contend with overwhelming negative associations from public beliefs about the absent Black father. The chapter discusses the role of employment and wage earning in self-esteem and self-efficacy of the present Black father. Further, the chapter shows how these challenges create a particular form of role strain that is another side of invisibility of a Black man. In Chapter 7, Jesse Owen and Jon Glass describe a theoretical framework to assist mental health practitioners to work with Caucasian fathers. The chapter examines the multifaceted privilege many Caucasian fathers experience, with consideration given to socioeconomic status. The authors draw from a systems approach to espouse a variety of clinically relevant conceptualizations and intervention strategies to promote father identity, communication, and family role balance.

Section 3, Counseling Specific Populations of Fathers, focuses on working with fathers from different world views, life stages, and experiences. In Chapter 8, John M. Robertson explores ways in which religious commitment influences fathering behavior. The chapter notes how counselors can offer a father an opportunity to express his views about how religion informs various aspects of his role as a father (e.g., disciplinary strategies, appropriate gender role behavior for children, distribution of house and child-care activities). The chapter offers guidelines for counselors who wish not only to respect a man's religious heritage, but also to provide effective research-supported interventions. In Chapter 9, Rod Berger discusses clinical approaches to working with first-time fathers and the importance of examining these fathers' internal experiences. This chapter provides a historical context of first-time fathers in relation to social norms and research findings. The chapter concludes with suggestions for appropriate clinical and psychoeducational interventions with first-time fathers. In Chapter 10, Aaron B. Rochlen and Ryan A. McKelly review two studies that provide a rich, detailed, and personal view of the daily lives, challenges, and self-concepts of stay-at-home fathers (SAHFs). These studies not only discuss the struggles such men face, but also illustrate the joys of being a SAHF. The chapter concludes with practice-based suggestions for working therapeutically with SAHFs.

In Chapter 11, Ferdinand Arcinue and Judy L. Prince discuss the myths and stereotypes surrounding young fathers and the necessity for counselors to assess their own attitudes and beliefs about these young fathers. The chapter focuses on a strength-based perspective and developmental considerations to help teen fathers in counseling. In Chapter 12, Daniel J. Alonzo discusses the limited research, counseling interventions, and resources for gay fathers. With a focus on application, a variety of key issues involving gay fatherhood is addressed, including adoption and custody issues, the coming-out process, parenting and family structure, and step-family issues. This chapter concludes with interventions and resources for counselors to use when working with gay fathers. In Chapter 13, Rory Remer, Neil Massoth, Gwendolyn Pugh Crumpton, Chen Z. Oren, and Dora Chase Oren look at the underexamined population of older fathers. The chapter integrates recent gerontological literature on treating older men and gender-sensitive methods to develop an approach for counseling older fathers.

## CONCLUSION

With the increased societal focus on fathering and the heightened attention paid to diversity and multiculturalism, it is the editors' hope that this book will provide a timely contribution to the area of counseling fathers. Though some texts have examined fathers' roles within the family, this book focuses on ways to counsel fathers that are mindful of a father's broader internal and external experiences. Mental health providers and educators can more readily provide effective services to fathers by knowing particular themes, strengths, and challenges, as well as specific interventions that can enhance counseling. Throughout this book, theory, research, clinical interventions, and case examples are integrated to shed light on the process of counseling some of the many types of fathers who seek services.

## REFERENCES

Andrews, A. B., Luckey, I., Bolden, E., Whiting-Fickling, J., & Lind, K. A. (2004). Public perceptions about father involvement: Results of a statewide household survey. *Journal of Family Issues, 25*(5), 603–633.

Arredondo, P., & Perez, P. (2006). Historical perspectives on the multicultural guidelines and contemporary applications. *Professional Psychology: Research and Practice, 37*(1), 1–5.

Brott, A. A., & Ash, J. (2001). *The expectant father: Facts, tips, and advice for dads-to-be.* New York: Abbeville.

Brown, B. V. (2000). The single-father family: Demographic, economic, and public transfer use characteristics. *Marriage & Family Review, 29*(3), 203–220.

Cabrera, N. J., Tamis-Lemonda, C. S., Bradley, R. H., Hofferth, S., & Lamb, M.E. (2000). Fatherhood in the twenty-first century. *Child Development, 71*(1), 127–136.

Cohen, D. (2001). *The father book: Being a good dad in the 21st century.* New York: John Wiley.

Coley, R. L. (2001). (In)visible men: Emerging research on low-income, unmarried, and minority fathers. *American Psychologist, 56*(2), 743–753.

Condon, J. T., Boyce, P., & Corkindale, C. J. (2004). The first-time fathers study: A prospective study of the mental health and wellbeing of men during the transition to parenthood. *Australian and New Zealand Journal of Psychiatry, 38,* 56–64.

Cornille, T. A., Barlow, L. O., & Cleveland, A. D. (2005). DADS family project: An experiential group approach to support fathers in their relationships with their children. *Social Work With Groups, 28*(2), 41–57.

Curran, L. (2003). Social work and fathers: Child support and fathering programs. *Social Work, 48*(2), 219–227.

Draper, J. (2003). Men's passage to fatherhood: An analysis of the contemporary relevance of transition theory. *Nursing Inquiry, 10,* 66–78.

Fagan, J., & Hawkins, A. J. (2001). *Clinical and educational interventions with fathers.* New York: Haworth.

Fuertes, J. N., Stracuzzi, T. I., Bennett, J., Scheinholtz, J., Mislowack, A., Hersh, M., & Cheng, D. (2006). Therapist multicultural competency: A study of therapy dyads. *Psychotherapy: Theory, Research, Practice, Training, 43*(4), 480–490.

King, V., Harris, K. M., Heard, H. E. (2004). Racial and ethnic diversity in nonresident father involvement. *Journal of Marriage and Family, 66,* 1–21.

Klinger, R. (1998). What can be done about absentee fathers? *USA Today* (Society for the Advancement of Education). Retrieved on November 1, 2006, from http://findarticles.com/p/articles/mi_m1272/is_n2638_v127/ai_20954306%20-%2030k%20-

Lamb, M. E. (2004). *The role of the father in child development* (4th ed). Hoboken, NJ: John Wiley.

Leach, M. M., & Carlton, M. A. (1997). Toward defining a multicultural training philosophy. In D. B. Pope-Davis & H. L. K. Coleman (Eds.), *Multicultural counseling competencies: Assessment, education and training, and supervision* (pp. 184–208). Thousand Oaks, CA: Sage.

Marsigilo, W. (1995). *Fatherhood: Contemporary theory, research and social policy.* Thousand Oaks, CA: Sage.

Marsigilo, W., Day, R. D., & Lamb, M. E. (2000). Exploring fatherhood diversity: Implications for conceptualizing father involvement. *Marriage and Family Review, 29*(4), 269–293.

National Center for Fathering. (1999). *Fathering in America poll.* Retrieved on November 15, 2006, from http://www.fathers.com/research/1999 Gallup FathAmerica.html

National Fatherhood Initiative. (2006). *A guide to strengthening fatherhood in your community: Moving from inspiration to implementation.* Gaithersburg, MD: Author.

O'Donnell, J. M., Johnson, W. E., D'Aunno, L. E, & Thornton, H. L. (2005). Fathers in child welfare: Caseworkers' perspectives. *Child Welfare, 84*(3), 387–410.

Pope-Davis D. B., Liu, W. M, Toporek, R. L., & Brittan-Powell, C. S. (2001). What's missing from multicultural research: Review, introspection, and recommendation. *Cultural Diversity and Ethnic Minority Psychology, 7*(2), 121–138.

Sue, D. W., & Sue, D. (2007). *Counseling the culturally diverse: Theory and practice* (5th ed.). New York: John Wiley & Sons.

U.S. Census Bureau. (1997). *Statistical Abstract of the United States: 1997.* Washington, DC: Author.

U.S. Census Bureau. (2001). *Statistical Abstract of the United States: 2001.* Washington, DC: Author.

U.S. Government. (2001*). Blueprint for new beginnings: A responsible budget for America's priorities.* Retrieved December 10, 2006, from http://www.whitehouse.gov/news/usbudget/blueprint/budtoc.html

Zelkowitz, P., & Milet, T. H. (1997). Stress and support as related to postpartum paternal mental health and perceptions of the infant. *Infant Mental Health Journal, 18,* 424–435.

# *Acknowledgments*

This book is about counseling diverse populations of fathers. It is also about developing a balanced perspective of fathers' challenges and strengths. The limited resources on clinical work and interventions with different types of fathers inspired the need for and the format of this book, yet also created some challenges for the different chapters. Almost without exception, the chapter authors integrated foundational theory from counseling, diversity, and the psychology of men to inform the work of counseling fathers. We want to thank all of the authors who contributed to this book for stepping up to the plate and consistently delivering thoughtful and comprehensive chapters. Thanks for your openness to feedback, the numerous hours you spent writing and revising, and your creativity and dedication. This book could not have happened without you.

How is a book born? This book would have not come to fruition without the trust of Mark Stevens and Mark Kiselica. Our friend and colleague Mark Stevens suggested to Mark Kiselica that Chen write a book for Kiselica's series, *Counseling and Psychotherapy with Boys and Men*. From an idea to a reality, we owe special acknowledgment to each of them. Mark Kiselica was a role model in the truest sense in editing, providing feedback, and negotiating difficult situations, always with warmth, support, wisdom, and professionalism. Thank you for your mentoring; we value our friendship with you. Mark A. Stevens, in a genuine, calm, and creative way, helped us to focus, to remember what is important, and to balance life's responsibilities. Thanks for your support and friendship throughout this process.

We also would like to acknowledge our parents. Chen's parents have both passed away and did not meet his wife or have a chance to spoil his children. They are particularly missed at these times of accomplishment and joy. Dora's parents, Steve and Elinor Fienberg, gave 110% to support our work on this book. We want to thank Elinor for her attention to detail and willingness to do the same task 15 different times. Her availability, sensibility, and kindness were cornerstones for our work. Steve was always willing to share his perspectives and give us his consistently valuable suggestions. Thank you both for all of the support.

Our children, Elizabeth, Hannah, Yoni, and Emma, deserve gratitude and appreciation. Each of them adds meaning and purpose to our lives and deepens our sense of family. In many ways this book is about and for our children. Thanks for babysitting the younger ones, for giving us time to work, for eating cup-of-soups for dinner, and for the tears and smiles you put on our faces.

We would like to thank Phillips Graduate Institute, the clinical psychology doctoral program's faculty and students, and the president, Lisa Porché-Burke. Thank you for your understanding, support, and time to work on this project. We would also like to thank Andrea, Linda, and the rest of the PGI library for accommodating and helping us get articles and books on a short notice.

Thanks to our friends who gave us support on this project: Jennifer and Henry Chiu, Sari and Mitch Cicurel, Evan Guston, Michelle and Jeff Nakamura, Nicole Seeley, Brinell and Jonathan Slocumb, and Christine M. Staples-Smith.

Finally, we would like to thank the staff at Routledge who has made this book a reality. Special thanks to Dana Bliss. Dana's communication skills, prompt responses, support, and guidance were instrumental and deeply appreciated. We would also like to thank Chris Tominich, Charlotte Roh, Kenya Pierre, and Robert Sims for their help.

We would like also to individually acknowledge those family, friends, colleagues, and others who made this project possible.

DCO –

Dad, your dependability, encouragement, insight, and friendship were particularly meaningful on this project. Thank you for much more than I can say. Mom, it would be tough to overstate the importance of your help with this book. On this project and on countless ones before, you have always been my ace in the hole. A daughter is not often asked to reflect on fathers. For me, this exercise has shone light on my own father, and my mother as well, and revealed the integrity and strengths of each of my parents. Thanks to you both for your unwavering support and commitment to our family. I also want to recognize my brothers and their wives, Joe and Jackie Fienberg and Andrew and Jill Fienberg, and to thank them for creating a pretty amazing extended family. To my nieces and nephews, Michael, Caroline, Sadie, and Moe, we appreciate being included on your journeys.

To Eric Chase, thank you for your friendship and for your love of our daughters. To Maria Zagorski, my college buddy and lifelong friend who continues to inspire. Dr. Prager, thank you for your trust and motivation. Katherine Yardley, I appreciate the endless discussions and your wisdom. To Laura Forsyth, Sharon Manakas, and the entire staff at the Moorpark College Student Health Center, you are the best! Your commitment to our students creates a remarkable center. Thank you for your generosity of spirit.

Most of all, I want to acknowledge my husband. Chen, you make all things possible. Thank you for dreaming and for making dreams come true. How lovely it is to share life with you.

CZO –

My father encouraged me to be independent and to get as much education as possible. He would want to see this day. Thanks to my abba for doing the best he could as a father. My mother died when I was 6 years old. I was always told that she was a special, caring, and devoted mother who loved her mischievous son. Her spirit and love are always felt. Both of my parents would have been proud of this book.

I would like to recognize Dora's parents, Steve and Elinor Fienberg. You welcomed me into your family with much grace and respect. Thanks for all your professional support along the way. More important, you are an inspiration of how to be good and positive grandparents. So, this is my public opportunity to thank you for being great parents and grandparents and to call you Mom and Dad.

I would like to recognize my family, who has deeply influenced who I have become. Bat-Sheva and Barry, thank you for helping raise me and being there in difficult times. David and Lisa, for your unconditional support and ongoing sense of family. To my nephews, Nicole, Debbie, Daniel, Lauren, and Neil.

To my two mentors, Joan Rosenberg and Mark Stevens: In your own way, you both inspired me to become the psychologist, professional, scholar, and man that I am. Joan, thank you for taking me to my first American Psychological Association conference, transferring your clinical knowledge, opening your home at times of need, teaching me how to teach, and helping me get my first job. Thanks for your friendship. Mark, from a teacher to a supervisor to a friend, thanks for your belief and trust. Thanks for introducing me to Division 51; getting me jobs; getting me into biking; riding the MS bike ride; all the holiday parties; the Dodgers, Lakers, USC, and UCLA games; and the Vegas trips and Esalen retreats. I am looking forward to our continued friendship.

To all my lifelong friends, Itai, Ety, Noam and Noam, Galit, Raphy, Ferd, and all my other childhood friends in Israel whom I spent my days with shooting hoops, scoring goals, and listening to music. You were my extended family at all times. Who knew...

Dora, I could not have done this without you! My wife, mother of our children, friend, co-editor, and life partner. Thanks for trusting me and agreeing to co-edit this book with me in this busy period of our lives. This was a journey and process that will be hard to forget. Your strengths, optimism, and hard work are commendable. I respect your courage, dedication, and integrity. Co-editing this book with you reflects for me the true meaning of teamwork on a personal and professional level. Thank you for attending to the little details and capturing the explicit and implicit meaning of each idea, thought, sentence, and word. You have a special talent helping others to express what they intend and to become who they want to be. Thanks for sacrificing your time to complete this project (and many others) and to still find the time to let me ride, take care of all the kids, work, and become a competent psychologist. You are a model mom. You are an amazing woman.

Finally, we want to acknowledge all the fathers who are trying to do the right thing. Fatherhood is one of the most challenging and fulfilling tasks you will ever have. This book is to recognize your trials and successes. Our hope is that this text will raise the awareness of fathers, their needs, their experiences, and their strengths.

# About the Editors

**Chen Z. Oren, PhD,** professor in the Clinical Psychology Doctoral Program at Phillips Graduate Institute in Encino, California, completed his master's degree in marriage, family, and child counseling and doctoral degree in counseling psychology from the Department of Counseling Psychology at the University of Southern California (USC). Dr. Oren received the Paul F. Bloland Award for the Distinguished Scientist–Practitioner Student in the Counseling Psychology department at USC.

Dr. Oren is a member of Division 51, the Society for the Psychological Study of Men and Masculinity, of the American Psychological Association and currently serves as the division treasurer. He is a reviewer for the APA journal *Psychology of Men and Masculinity*. Dr. Oren has presented at national and international conferences in the area of counseling and training (supervision, sport psychology, and men) and has been in numerous consultation and outreach programs for university and community mental health centers. Dr. Oren was a member on the organizing committee for the 2007 National Psychotherapy with Men Conference.

Dr. Oren is a psychologist in private practice and works with a diverse clientele of couples and individuals. His areas of specialty include diversity, men's issues, and sports psychology. He has worked extensively with men in community and private practice settings. Dr. Oren is also trained in conducting men's groups.

As professor, Dr. Oren teaches clinical and diversity-related classes. He is the chair of the Diversity Laboratory course, which introduces doctoral students to the different areas of diversity and focuses on awareness of students' biases and stereotypes. He also teaches sex and gender role classes that focus on men's and women's issues. Dr. Oren has two incredible children and is stepfather to two amazing teenagers. In his little bit of free time, he enjoys sports and biking.

**Dora Chase Oren, PhD,** received her master's degree in developmental psychology from Columbia University in New York and her doctorate in clinical psychology from California School of Professional Psychology, Los Angeles. Dr. Oren is an editor with work that includes editing clinical psychology doctoral projects and dissertations, nonfiction books, and professional texts. Dr. Oren is adjunct faculty at Phillips Graduate Institute in Encino, California, as well as an adjunct professor at other local graduate programs. She is the instructor for clinical psychology doctoral students in human sexuality as well as in her specialty area, developmental psychology. In her life span/child development courses, historical theory is integrated with current research, particularly as it concerns more modern views of male and female development and the often overlooked role of the father in child development. She also teaches professional writing courses for psychology graduate students. Dr. Oren provides mental health services to community college students in her work at Moorpark College. She is the lucky mother of four amazing children.

# Contributors

**Daniel J. Alonzo, PsyD,** is core faculty at Phillips Graduate Institute in Encino, California. As a licensed marriage and family therapist for 18 years, he has specialized in GLBT (gay, lesbian, bisexual and transgender/transsexual) mental health, human sexuality, and gay male psychosocial development over the life span. In addition to his private practice, he conducts trainings and workshops in mental health challenges facing GLBT couples and families.

**Ferdinand Arcinue, PhD,** is currently a faculty member at California State University at Long Beach where he is a psychologist in the Division of Student Services. He earned his doctorate in counseling psychology from the University of Southern California and a master's from New York University. Dr. Arcinue specializes in men's and Asian American psychology.

**Kent William Becker, PhD,** is a licensed marriage and family therapist (LMFT) and a licensed professional counselor (LPC) with a Doctorate of Education in counselor education and supervision. Dr. Becker is an associate professor of counselor education at the University of Wyoming and the director of the Wyoming SAGE Photovoice Project, an advocacy initiative that serves youth with mental health needs and their families.

**Rod Berger, PsyD,** recently worked with children and their families at the Vanderbilt University Medical Center in the Division of Community Psychiatry. Currently, Dr. Berger is a senior consultant for the ALOC Group, executing leadership development programs for Vanderbilt University's Owen Graduate School of Management. He co-hosts a national radio show on gender issues called "He Said She Said with Dr. Rod and Christie."

**Joseph M. Cervantes, PhD,** received his doctorate in community-clinical psychology from the University of Nebraska-Lincoln in 1977. He is a professor in the Department of Counseling at California State University, Fullerton, and maintains an independent forensic practice in child, adolescent, and family psychology. He holds diplomates in both clinical and family psychology from the American Board of Professional Psychology and is licensed in the states of California and Hawaii. Dr. Cervantes's research interests are in the relatedness of cultural diversity and indigenous spirituality. He has served on the editorial board for the journal *Professional Psychology: Research and Practice* and currently serves as consulting editor for *Cultural Diversity and Ethnic Minority Psychology* and *Journal of Education and Latinos.* Dr. Cervantes also currently serves as the Ethics Chair for the Orange County Psychological Association. He is past president for the National Latina/o Psychological Association, and past Chair, Committee on Ethnic Minority Affairs (CEMA), American Psychological Association.

**Gwendolyn Pugh Crumpton, MS,** received her master's in child and family development from the University of Georgia in 2004. She is currently pursuing a PhD in counseling psychology at the University of Kentucky. She is a certified child life specialist and a disability and child activist. Her research interests include social support and empowerment of families of children with disabilities, parenting, family systems, and multicultural approaches to research and therapy. She is also an Algernon Sydney Sullivan Award Recipient.

**Matt Englar-Carlson, PhD,** is an associate professor of counseling at the California State University at Fullerton. Dr. Englar-Carlson co-edited the books *In the Room with Men: A Casebook of Therapeutic Change* (2006) and *Counseling Troubled Boys* (2008) and is co-editor of the upcoming book series *Theories of Psychotherapy* to be published by the American Psychological Association. Dr. Englar-Carlson has worked with boys and adult males in schools, community settings, work sites, and university settings. He lives in Huntington Beach, California, with his wife and two children.

**Anderson J. Franklin, PhD,** is the Honorable David S. Nelson Professor of Psychology and Education in the Department of Counseling, Developmental and Educational Psychology at Boston College Lynch School of Education and professor emeritus of The City University of New York. He is a psychotherapist in private practice, having a specialty with African American males. He is a member of the Committee on Ethnic Minority Affairs of the American Psychological Association and past president of The Society for the Psychological Study of Ethnic and Minority Issues, a division of the American Psychological Association. He is a recipient of the Distinguished Psychologist award from the Association of Black

Psychologists. His research focuses on developing his theory of the invisibility syndrome in Black males and studying resilience and psychological well-being in African-Americans. This included collaboration on a City College of New York/Memorial Sloan Kettering Cancer Center Partnership study investigating colon cancer screening for African-Americans. He lectures and consults with a variety of domestic and international organizations on program development and diversity issues. He is co-author with Dr. Nancy Boyd-Franklin of *Boys into Men: Raising Our African American Teenage Sons*, published by Dutton. His last book is *From Brotherhood to Manhood: How Black Men Rescue Their Relationships and Dreams From the Invisibility Syndrome*, published by John Wiley & Sons, which was placed on *Essence* magazine's best-seller list.

**Jon Glass, MeD,** is a doctoral candidate in counseling psychology at Gannon Univeristy. He has worked with children, adolescents, and families in a broad range of mental health and educational settings. His research and clinical interests include family and multicultural issues, as well as developmental and health psychology. Mr. Glass is currently working on a study examining the relationship between ethnic identity, acculturation, and fathers' involvement with their children.

**Ronald F. Levant, EdD, ABPP,** was the 2005 president of the American Psychological Association. He earned his BA from the University of California, Berkeley, and his EdD from Harvard University. He is dean and professor of psychology, Buchtel College of Arts and Sciences, The University of Akron. Dr. Levant has authored, co-authored, edited, or co-edited 14 books and more than 175 peer-reviewed journal articles and book chapters. One of Levant's contributions is in helping to pioneer the new psychology of men. He has developed theory and conducted research programs investigating fathering, masculinity and femininity ideology in multicultural perspective, and normative male alexithymia. He was also the co-founder and first president of APA Division 51 (the Society for the Psychological Study of Men and Masculinity). His books include *Between Father and Child* (1991, Penguin), *Masculinity, Reconstructed* (1995, Dutton), *A New Psychology of Men* (1995, Basic Books), *Men and Sex: New Psychological Perspectives* (1997, John Wiley & Sons) and *New Psychotherapies for Men* (1998, John Wiley & Sons).

**Melissa L. Luján, MA,** received her BA in human development from California State University, Long Beach, and her master's degree in human development and family studies from the University of Connecticut. Her research interests relate to men, masculinity, violence prevention, and the positive aspects of being male.

**Neil Massoth, PhD,** received his doctoral degree at Washington University in 1966. He has been a professor of clinical psychology at Fairleigh Dickinson University for more than 40 years. His private practice emphasis is on men's issues, particularly adjustment to physical injury. He has conducted extensive research with men's issues. Dr. Massoth's current research areas are male identity, ego development, and relationship to political ideology.

**Ryan McKelley, PhD,** is an assistant professor of clinical/counseling psychology at the University of Wisconsin—La Crosse. His clinical and research interests involve gender role socialization and men's issues in help-seeking, including publications on men in nontraditional roles (e.g., stay-at-home fathers), the marketing of mental health services, and alternative interventions to traditional therapy (e.g., the practice of coaching).

**Nirupma Narang, MA,** is a school counselor at West Windsor-Plainsboro High School South (WWPHSS) in Princeton Junction, New Jersey. She received her master's degree in school counseling from The College of New Jersey and holds a national certified counselor (NCC) credential. Ms. Narang is originally from India and moved to the United States in 1982. Ms. Narang works with a diverse population at WWPHSS that largely includes Asian American students and their families. Further, she is a member of the Diversity Committee at her school district with a goal of promoting understanding and appreciation of diverse populations among faculty.

**James M. O'Neil, PhD,** is professor of educational psychology and family studies in the Neag School of Education at the University of Connecticut and in private practice in South Windsor, Connecticut. He is one of the founding members of the Society for the Psychological Study of Men and Masculinity (Division 51 of APA). He has spent much of his career encouraging research on men's gender role conflict. The Gender Role Conflict Research Web page (http//web.uconn.edu/joneil/) summarizes the 250 empirical studies completed on men's gender role conflict in 24 informational files.

**Jesse Owen, PhD,** is a psychologist and assistant professor at the University of Louisville Education and Counseling Psychology Department. His research interests include interventions for individuals and families, cultural competency, and relationship decision making. He also directs a coparenting program with high-conflict couples struggling with child custody disputes.

**Joseph H. Pleck, PhD,** is a professor of human development and family studies at the University of Illinois at Urbana Champaign. With Michael

Lamb, he originated the contemporary concept of paternal involvement, one of the most fundamental constructs in current research on fathering, and also developed the widely used "four factor" model of the sources of paternal involvement (motivation, skills, support, facilitating institutions). He has published over 50 articles and chapters on fatherhood and fathering, on a wide range of topics including fathers' time use, the influence of work schedules on fatherhood, paternity leave, identity theory approaches to father involvement, the influence of mother involvement on father involvement, immigrant fathers, and the history of U.S. fatherhood. Dr. Pleck is also a founding member of the NICHD (National Institute of Child Health and Human Development) Transition to Fatherhood Research Network. His 1997 and 2004 review chapters in *The Role of the Father in Child Development* are the most frequently cited syntheses of research and theory in the field of father involvement. He also serves as editor of *Fathering: A Journal of Research, Theory, and Practice About Men as Fathers.*

**Judith L. Prince, PsyD,** is a clinical psychologist in Southern California. Dr. Prince earned a master's degree in counseling psychology from Loyola Marymount University, followed by a doctorate in clinical psychology from the California School of Professional Psychology. With a background in community mental health, Dr. Prince joined the faculty of California State University, Long Beach, in 2001 where she works as a staff psychologist providing direct clinical services to students. Dr. Prince has extensive experience working with young adults on a broad range of issues, with relationship concerns being a primary area of focus.

**Rory Remer, PhD,** received his doctorate in counseling and research methodology from the University of Colorado in 1972. He has taught counseling psychology at the University of Kentucky for over 30 years. An ABE-TEP, Fellow of ASGPP, licensed psychologist, and ABPP in Family Psychology, Dr. Remer has research interests that include interpersonal communication modeling, multicultural perceptions and interactions, rape prevention, gerontology, and dynamical family systems research methodology. Dr. Remer won a Fulbright to study in Taiwan during 2002–2003.

**John M. Robertson, PhD,** received his doctorate in counseling psychology from the University of California at Santa Barbara, with an internship at the Department of Medicine and Surgery at the Veterans Administration Medical Center in Sepulveda, California. He also has a doctoral degree from the School of Theology at Claremont, where his focus was on issues of common academic interest to the disciplines of ethics, communication theory, and religious studies. For many years, Dr. Robertson held teaching and clinical positions at Kansas State University and the

University of Kansas. A licensed psychologist, he currently is Director of Psychological Services for the Professional Renewal Center, a day treatment clinic for impaired professionals in the medical, legal, and corporate fields. He a past president of the Society for the Psychological Study of Men and Masculinity, a division of the American Psychological Association. He has authored more than 30 articles and book chapters on the psychological concerns of men, including a dozen original research articles published in peer-reviewed psychology journals.

**Aaron B. Rochlen, PhD,** is a psychologist and an associate professor in counseling psychology at the University of Texas at Austin. Dr. Rochlen is currently the president elect of Division 51, the Society for the Psychological Study of Men and Masculinity, of the American Psychological Association. Dr. Rochlen has conducted several studies on men in nontraditional work/home roles including his recent work on stay-at-home fathers. His other publications have been in the areas of marketing mental health to men, men and depression, alternative approaches to counseling, and the use of technology in counseling and psychotherapy. His work can be reviewed at: http://aaronrochlen.edb.utexas.edu/ar.html.

**Atsuko Seto, PhD,** is an assistant professor in the Department of Counselor Education at The College of New Jersey. Dr. Seto received her doctorate in counselor education and supervision from the University of Wyoming and holds credentials as a licensed professional counselor (LPC) and a national certified counselor (NCC). Dr. Seto has worked with an Asian American and Pacific Islanders student association as an advisor and has coordinated campus events to promote Asian cultural heritage. Her scholarly work includes counseling Japanese women, Japanese immigrant families, and cross-national couples.

**Mark A. Stevens, PhD,** is the director of the University Counseling Services at California State University Northridge (CSUN). His latest edited book with Matt Englar-Carlson, *In the Room with Men: A Casebook of Therapeutic Change* (2006), was published by the American Psychological Association. Dr. Stevens is also the featured therapist in an APA-produced video (2003) *Psychotherapy with Men.* Dr. Stevens is a Fellow of the American Psychological Association and is a past president of APA Division 51, the Society for the Psychological Study of Men and Masculinity. He recently was honored with the outstanding researcher of the year from the American Psychological Association. Mark is married to Jawai and a proud parent of three adult children, Jamie, Jeremy, and Shawn.

**David J. Wimer, PhD,** was the 2004–2005 chair of The Society for the Teaching of Psychology's Graduate Student Teaching Association (GSTA). He received his BA in psychology and English literature from

Ithaca College, his MA in social psychology from Miami University (Ohio), and his PhD in counseling psychology from The University of Akron in 2008. In 2006, he received an Outstanding Doctoral Student award from The University of Akron's College of Education. At this early phase of his career he has authored or co-authored eight articles and book chapters on the new psychology of men, the teaching of psychology, and the psychology of humor.

# *Historical Perspectives and Current Directions*

# 1

# *The New Fathering Movement*

RONALD F. LEVANT AND DAVID J. WIMER

This chapter takes a recent historical perspective and examines the emergence of the new father role, also known as the involved or nurturing father, which began around 1975 in the United States and became prominent on the national scene in the 1980s. The first author was a participant in the movement that created this new area of research and clinical practice. Thus, we will discuss this movement, in part from the first author's own experiences that include serving as the Director of the Boston University Fatherhood Project from 1983 to 1988. We will discuss the social changes in the 1960s and 1970s that led to the new father role. We will also consider data on paid work, family work, and free time that suggest that men have not fully adopted the new father role, and data on changes in divorce patterns that suggest there may continue to be a "crisis of connection" between men and women. Finally, we will consider how counselors have in the past and might in the future address these matters.

## THE NEW FATHERING MOVEMENT:
## A PERSONAL PERSPECTIVE

In the mid-1970s, the first author was a young assistant professor in counseling psychology at Boston University who was considered an expert on family therapy. During this time, he also struggled on a personal level with the role of the divorced father. He visited his daughter in New York on weekends, and she lived with him during several summers. It was hard for him to imagine being an involved father because he did not have much to draw on from his memories of his own father, whose idea of spending time with his sons always involved work, like having his sons mow the lawn while he supervised.

These extended visits with his daughter did not always go smoothly. He lived with a sense of fraudulence, often thinking to himself: "How can you pretend to be an expert on parenting when you are so inept in your own life as father?" Like most men, he kept his sense of inadequacy to himself for fear of violating the traditional male norms of self-reliance and invulnerability. He thus deprived himself of the experience of learning that other fathers struggled with this role.

In the late 1970s, the film *Kramer vs. Kramer* resulted in a major epiphany in his life. He saw himself in the character portrayed by Dustin Hoffman and realized, for the first time, that he was not alone. His focus started to shift from a sense of personal inadequacy to a realization that his struggles might be inherent in the larger-scale change going on in the lives of men. Fathers were starting to take on roles vastly different from that of their own fathers and for which they had received little, if any, preparation. He researched the question of what resources existed for fathers who wanted to be fully involved, effective parents of their children. The answer was, Nothing. Echoing Michael Lamb (1979), he concluded that the father was the forgotten parent and that parent education was synonymous with mother education.

This series of events became the proverbial "fork in the road" in his life. He found his academic interest in parenting waning and became much more invested in fathering. This shift led to the founding of the Boston University Fatherhood Project in 1983, which was a research, service, and training program designed to enhance fathers' involvement in family life. With the help of bright young doctoral students, he turned to the task of designing psychoeducational parenting programs for men (Levant & Doyle, 1983; Levant & Kelly, 1989).

Along with colleagues, such as Joseph Pleck and James Levine, Levant participated in developing a revolutionary new concept of fathering that emphasized the father's ability to play an "expressive" role in the family, rather than being limited to an "instrumental" role (Parsons & Bales, 1955). Levant and others viewed the father as capable of providing even the most intimate type of nurturance for his children from infancy onward. These pioneers envisioned a new father role that went far beyond the elements of the traditional father role as good provider, supporter of the children's mother, and chief disciplinarian, and accumulated data that showed that men could be involved, nurturing parents (Lamb, 1981; Levant, Slattery, Loiselle, Sawyer-Smith, & Schneider, 1990; Parke, 1979; Pruett, 1987). They also actively advocated for the new father role. For example, Levant and Pleck served on the steering committee for the Greater Boston Fatherhood Forum in 1984.

This event drew a lot of media attention because it featured the former U.S. Senator Paul Tsongas, who had recently resigned his Senate seat when diagnosed with cancer, making a statement (seen at the time as a radical departure from traditional norms) that he was not resigning because of his health, but rather because he wanted to spend more time with his family.

Levant (1992; Levant & Kopecky, 1995) went even further, arguing that the traditional view of fathers' roles as helping their sons become more "masculine" deserved serious scrutiny. Premised on an essentialistic philosophy, such a notion encourages fathers to engage in behaviors that empirical research has shown play an important role in socializing young boys to conform to the norms of traditional masculinity. We are referring to data such as those showing that traditional fathers begin to take an active interest in their children after the thirteenth month of life (Lamb, 1979) and from that point on socialize their toddler sons and daughters along gender-stereotyped lines (Lamb, Owen, & Chase-Lansdale, 1979; Siegal, 1987), which includes expressing disapproval to sons who engage in gender atypical play (Langlois & Downs, 1980). Recent longitudinal research confirms these findings, demonstrating that paternal responses to sons (emotion socialization) were associated with a 50% decrease in sons' expressions of sadness and anxiety from preschool to early school-age (Chaplin, Cole, & Zahn-Waxler, 2005). Levant has long been critical of the idea that fathers should reproduce masculinity in their sons. Instead, he argues that the endorsement of and conformity to traditional masculine norms is not essential to being a healthy male, but rather is a social construction and not entirely benign at that. Levant and Richmond (2007, p. 142) reviewed the literature and concluded that the endorsement of traditional masculinity ideology was found to be associated with a range of problematic individual and relational variables, "including reluctance to discuss condom use with partners, fear of intimacy, lower relationship satisfaction, more negative beliefs about the fathers' role and lower paternal participation in child care, negative attitudes toward racial diversity and women's equality, attitudes conducive to sexual harassment, self reports of sexual aggression, lower forgiveness of racial discrimination, alexithymia and related constructs, and reluctance to seek psychological help."

## SOCIAL CHANGES THAT LED TO THE NEW FATHER ROLE

The women's movement of the late 1960s and 1970s produced enormous changes in women's roles, particularly with regard to women's dramatically increased participation in the workplace. To grasp the magnitude of these changes, consider that there has been a 500% rise in the employment of mothers of small children since the 1950s. Twelve percent of mothers with children under the age of 6 were employed in

1950, whereas 60% were employed in 2000 (Bureau of Labor Statistics, 2000). Currently, less than 10% of American families fit the traditional model of breadwinner husband/homemaker wife with children (Fraad, 2001), and the percentage for families of lower socioeconomic status and families of different ethnicities has always been lower than the overall percentage because these families have never conformed to the traditional family structure (Baca Zinn & Eitzen, 1996).

Coincident with this change in workforce participation was women's dramatically increased participation in higher education. In 2006, women earned approximately 51% of all doctoral degrees in the United States, representing an increase from 39% in 1995, 34% in 1985, and only 22% in 1975 (Hoffer et al., 2007). In addition, 2006 was the first time in U.S. history in which women were awarded more doctorates than men across every racial/ethnic minority group. The enrollment of women in undergraduate education has increased dramatically since 1960. As of 2003, women as a whole made up 58% of all students enrolled in undergraduate institutions, compared with only 38% in 1960 (National Center for Education Statistics, 2006). As with doctoral degrees, more women receive bachelor's degrees than men across all racial/ethnic minority groups. In 2003, 67% of all undergraduate degrees awarded to African Americans were awarded to women. This trend was consistent for American Indians (63%), Latin Americans (61%), and Asian Americans (55%).

Thus, women have been living with major changes in the construction of their gender roles for almost 50 years. They have moved from a sole emphasis on the family, and many now juggle career and family concerns (including spouse, child, and elder care, in many cases), although juggling work and family has likely always been the case for women of different ethnicities (Baca Zinn & Eitzen, 1996). In making this shift, they have combined traditional feminine norms such as love, family, and caring for others with newer norms such as independence, career, and defining themselves through their own accomplishments.

It was in this context that the new father role developed. Some men saw the compelling need to co-parent with their working wives and willingly chose to do so by taking either the "morning shift" (getting the children dressed, fed, and off to day care or school) or the "evening shift" (picking up the kids, starting dinner, and settling the children into their evening routines), but as we document below, the new father role has not yet been universally adopted. Although there has been an increase in men's openness to relationships and much greater participation in the emotional and domestic arenas (c.f. Silverstein, Auerbach, & Levant, 2002), many men cling to the older definitions that emphasize work and individual accomplishment over emotional intimacy and family involvement. Masculinity plays an important role in this. Using path analysis, Bonney, Kelley, and Levant (1999) found that the endorsement of traditional masculinity ideology directly influenced (as an unmediated relationship) both maternal and paternal beliefs about the father's role, and indirectly influenced men's participation in child care (through its effect on maternal and paternal beliefs about the father's role).

## RESISTANCE TO THE NEW FATHER ROLE

It is puzzling that many men have resisted change in their role definitions in light of the loss of the "good provider" role. Many men are in fact no longer the good providers for their families that fathers have traditionally been and that many men expect themselves to be. With the majority of adult women in the work force, very few men are sole providers and most are coproviders. This has been documented repeatedly, for example, in the study conducted by the Families and Work Institute (1995) that found 55% of employed women provide half or more of the household income. In addition, 73% of American companies have women in senior or top-level positions (Bond, Galinsky, Kim, & Brownfield, 2005). Finally, there has been an erosion of wages for men over the last 30 years that has challenged the ability of men to be the sole family provider (Levy, 1995).

The good-provider role has been such an important part of the definition of what it means to be a man that one would think its loss would impel an immediate search for alternatives. Although some men are actively involved in constructing new definitions of being a man that do not require devotion to work, others seem to be caught up in denial. For example, we know men whose wives work full-time, but who still consider themselves their family's provider, and they justify this attitude by rationalizing that they make more money, could make more money, or are more committed than their wives to providing for the family.

The obvious candidate to replace the good provider is the "good family man," the husband who shares child care and housework, as well as provision, with his wife, which would include the new father role. However, men have not flocked to this new role. Although some think that contemporary culture has embraced the idea of the nurturing father (LaRossa, 1989), there have not been major changes in corporate and government family policies supportive of men's full involvement in family life. Until President Clinton's Fatherhood Initiative in 1995, researchers and policymakers focused on the father's role of provider (Cabrera & Peters, 2000). The Fatherhood Initiative sparked interest in a more comprehensive study of the father's role, and researchers are now starting to understand better the impact that fathers can have on the cognitive, moral, and social development of their children (Lamb, 1981, 2004; Pleck & Pleck, 1997). However, the research sparked by the Fatherhood Initiative also revealed many barriers to overcome. One major barrier is that men themselves have not fully embraced this new good family man role, judging from studies on the division of household labor.

## The Division of Household Labor

In the middle and late 1960s, large-scale time-budget studies indicated that husbands' participation in family work (both child care and housework) was quite low (1.1 to 1.6 hours/day) compared with that of their wives (7.6 to 8.1 hours/day for housewives and 4.0 to 4.8 hours/day for employed wives), and that husbands tended to increase their participation only slightly (0.1 hour/day) in response to their wives' employment (Robinson, 1977; Walker & Woods, 1976). Juster and Stafford (1985) found a 20% increase in the amount of time husbands put into family work over the period 1965–1981. Douthitt (1989) found additional increases in the amount of time that husbands put into family work during the 1980s. Although Berardo, Shehan, and Leslie (1987) found the type of family work men engaged in shifted from yard and car work to child care and meal preparation, in the area of child care, fathers still tended to rely on their wives to assign tasks rather than taking responsibility for the care (Van Egeren, 2004). Data from 1988 indicate that the amount of time husbands spend in family work is only about 38% of the total, and access to free time is a major area of inequality, in which fathers have approximately 20% more free time than mothers (Sayer, 2005). The failure of men to share family work equally with their wives continues the "second shift" identified by Hochschild (1989). Hence, it is clear that inequities remain, owing to some men's unwillingness to accept responsibility for family work. This may be contributing to the continuing "crisis of connection" between men and women (Levant, 1996), which can be seen in the contemporary patterns of divorce.

## The Increasing Fragility of Marriage

As is well known, the divorce rate more than doubled between 1965 and 1979. Divorce rates are measured in terms of numbers of occurrences per 1,000 members of the population. The rate had been roughly in the 2 per 1,000 range since World War II, and had risen slightly to 2.3 per 1,000 by 1965. But then, fueled by changes in women's work roles and the development of no-fault divorce laws, the divorce revolution occurred, and the rate skyrocketed to 5.4 per 1,000 in 1979.

The conventional wisdom has been that the divorce rate has been moderating since 1980. However, demographic research by Martin and Bumpass (1989) indicates there was an initial decline in the rate, followed by a rather dramatic increase. Whereas Cherlin (1981) projected that 50% of all marriages will end in divorce, Martin and Bumpass (1989) projected that 67% of all marriages will end in divorce. Although this latter figure has subsequently been viewed as an overestimate, Bumpass (1990, p. 485) suggested that "60% may be closer to the mark." While caution is warranted, as there is disagreement and even controversy over how divorce rates are calculated (Hurley, 1995), more recent estimates hover around the 50% mark (Bramlett & Mosher, 2002; Faust & McKibben, 1999). Know, however, that this number is for the U.S. population as a whole, and divorce rates are different for various racial and ethnic groups. For example, Peterson (2000) reported that the divorce rate is approximately 2% higher for African American married couples than for European American married couples. Not all ethnic groups experience relatively high divorce rates, however. For example, although the specific number was not reported, Smith (2006) mentioned that Asian American married couples experience a much lower rate of divorce than any other racial or ethnic group in the United States. In sum, even accounting for the easing of divorce laws beginning in the 1970s, the consistently high divorce rate among most racial and ethnic groups suggests that all is not well in Eden and that the genders are having trouble staying connected.

We are also finding that two-thirds of all divorces are initiated by women (Brinig & Allen, 2000). Comparable figures from earlier periods are not available, and thus we cannot state with confidence how much this has actually changed over time. However, it is reasonable to assume that more women are initiating divorce now as compared with earlier times, if only because of the dramatic changes in their work roles that make them less financially dependent on men.

In our view, women's increasing willingness to leave marriages is related to attitude changes. Basically, women want a better deal. Women are now much less willing to shelve their own needs while "adapting" to meet the needs of the men in their lives (McMullin, 2005). They have been on their gender-role journeys for most of their adult lives, and they really *are* tired of waiting for men to catch up and join them on an equal plane, although Black women may have become tired of this much earlier than White women (Baca Zinn & Eitzen, 1996). Thus, women would appreciate men becoming more proactive in their marriages by contributing equally to household labor and child rearing. There is some evidence that this would also benefit the men themselves by providing a stronger connection to their wives and children (Barnett, Davidson, & Marshall, 1991; Barnett, Marshall, & Pleck, 1991). Fathers with nontraditional gender ideologies are more likely to accomplish this (Bulanda, 2004; see also Bonney, Kelly, & Levant, 1999), so counselors could help fathers in families experiencing such marital conflicts to examine their views of gender roles.

## WHY DON'T MEN DO MORE?

Why don't men do more? The first author has argued elsewhere (Levant, 1990) that one of the major reasons men do not participate more in child care is that of skill deficits, deficits that could be remedied through fatherhood education. But this is clearly not the whole story. When the first author sits in the treatment room with parents who are in conflict about this issue, it is not too difficult to discern in some fathers the plaintiff voice of a little boy who feels he should not have to do all this women's work and who feels entitled to leave this job to his wife.

## The Male Socialization Ordeal and Its Consequences

Here we come up against some of the consequences of the traditional masculine socialization process. One aspect of this process that likely interferes with men doing an equal share of parenting or housework is known as the "male code," a set of socially constructed and socially rein-forced rules delineating how "real" men should behave (Brannon, 1985), also know as traditional masculinity ideology. One rule is "no sissy stuff," or the idea that men should avoid demonstrating stereotypically femi-nine behavior. This rule may delineate that men should not do an equal amount of parenting or housework because those roles have traditionally been associated with femininity. Another rule is known as "the sturdy oak," which delineates that men should never reveal weakness, including the display of emotion. This rule may interfere with men's being equally engaged in parenting, because adept parenting involves being emotion-ally connected with a child (Bee & Boyd, 2007). Men are strongly rein-forced for following these male code rules because those who do not tend to experience *discrepancy strain*, which is psychological distress brought on by failing to live up to the cultural ideal of masculinity (Pleck, 1995). However, men who do follow these rules tend to experience *dysfunction strain*, or distress created by fulfilling the socially constructed rules of masculinity. This distress can be experienced by both a man and those close to him, and inferior parenting and a lack of participation in house-work are two prime examples of dysfunction strain.

Another aspect of the traditional masculine socialization process is the normative developmental traumas that occur during the separation-individuation phase of early childhood, which have been discussed in detail elsewhere (Levant, 1992, 2001; Levant & Kopecky, 1995; Pol-lack, 1995). Here we will provide a brief summary. In the separation-individuation phase of early childhood, boys are thought to be required to give up their dependence on their mothers much earlier than are girls. The loss of the holding environment, which robs boys of the tran-quillity of childhood, is thought to have three major consequences:

1. *Defensive Autonomy*: As traditionally reared boys grow up, yearn-ings for maternal closeness and attachment bring up fears of losing their sense of separateness and their male identity. Consequently, some adult men feel much safer being alone than being close to another person.
2. *Unconscious Dependence on Women*: The yearnings for maternal attachment never completely go away, but go underground in the form of often unconscious, certainly unacknowledged, depen-dence on women that some men experience.

3. *Destructive Entitlement:* The loss of the holding environment is never acknowledged, much less mourned, leaving some men vulnerable to developing "destructive entitlement" (Boszormenyi-Nagy & Ulrich, 1981), a feeling that people in one's adult life are required to make up for these losses.

These consequences of traditional male socialization may have the following results: Some men feel more comfortable working than participating in family life (due to defensive autonomy); some men depend on their wives to meet a considerable number of their needs (due to unconscious dependence); and some men expect their wives to care for their needs without any requirement for reciprocity on their part (due to destructive entitlement). Men who suffer from these problems may need to undertake significant emotional work to resolve them. Counselors working with families can help such men do this work.

## Toward Change

There are compelling reasons to do this emotional work, reasons that include not only men's overloaded wives and the fragility of their marriages, but also their children (Silverstein, 1996). It is of the utmost importance for fathers to get deeply involved in rearing their children so that their sons will not grow up with the same skill deficits and emotional problems, and their daughters can derive the benefits of parenting from their fathers.

It is also important for the fathers themselves. We are not only referring to the obvious notions that if men do the emotional work, then they will function better in life; or that if men put their overriding commitments to work in better perspective, then they would experience a more balanced life and less work stress; or that if men are open to it, fatherhood provides a golden opportunity for men to heal their hearts. We are also referring to studies that indicate that both psychological distress and physical illness may be related to the quality of men's family roles. Gottman (1991) found that husbands who do housework have better health. Barnett, Marshall, and Pleck (1991) found the quality of men's marital role and parental role are both significant predictors of men's psychological distress. Barnett, Davidson, and Marshall (1991) found the quality of men's parental role, but not that of their marital role, was a significant predictor of men's physical health.

## CLINICAL WORK WITH FATHERS: PAST AND PRESENT

Very little scholarship was published on clinical work with fathers until the late 1970s (Dreyfus, 1979), reflecting the fact that fathers had long been an afterthought in the mental health field. The sparse scholarship that exists can be traced to the 1950s (Le Camus & Frascarolo,

2003). This early work tended to take a stereotypical and traditional view of fathers and their role as provider and authority figure. The early articles also tended to focus on group psychotherapy, as group therapy has been the preferred treatment method for fathers, and this trend seems to continue today (Gregg, 1994). The early clinical work emanated from a psychodynamic perspective (Grunebaum, 1962), but later a cognitive-behavioral perspective emerged, with a focus on homework and the dissemination of information about resources, an approach that still guides recent work (Tedder & Scherman, 1987). Thus, the theoretical underpinnings of clinical work with fathers paralleled overall trends in the mental health field.

Another early trend was that fathers tended to present for counseling to treat their emotionally disturbed children rather than to seek help for themselves (Marcus, 1956). A shift seemed to occur in the treatment of fathers around the late 1970s, as the traditional role of fathers started to change (Gelman, 1978). Clinicians began recognizing the importance of fathers developing a more nurturing approach to child rearing (Tedder & Scherman, 1987), and this recognition of the importance of a nurturing approach evolved in the 1990s and beyond (Fagan & Hawkins, 2001). Dollahite and Hawkins (1998) discussed a contemporary approach known as *generative fathering*, which is defined as "fathering that meets the needs of children by working to create and maintain a developing ethical relationship with them" (p. 111). In other words, fathers have an ethical obligation to care for and contribute to the next generation by meeting the needs of their children to the best of their ability.

In regard to specific interventions and treatment, Hallowitz and Stephens (1959) suggested that the mental health professional identify with the fathers in a therapy group, with the aim of restoring their self-esteem. Grunebaum (1962) discussed clinical problems that typically arise in group therapy with fathers. The first was that fathers did not seek counseling for themselves, and thus it was difficult to engage them in the group. This problem continues to this day (Walters, Tasker, & Bichard, 2001). Second, Grunebaum (1962) found that some men in the group tended to become hostile during the middle phase of counseling, when the group started becoming closer, perhaps because the fathers felt threatened by the prospect of intimacy with other men. Later, Dreyfus (1979) argued that counseling divorced fathers typically involves four phases. Phase I involves crisis intervention and occurs when the father initially presents for counseling. Phase II involves examining losses, including the loss of children and the loss of a home. Phase III involves confronting the realities of the impact the divorce has on the father and the children. Finally, Phase IV involves examining the meaning of being a father and the specific type of father the client is. More recently, Wall and Levy (1994) outlined assessment and treatment guidelines for mental health professionals working with fathers. They recommend working in concert with other service providers and engaging in interventions that address multiple levels of the father's life. They also recommend fostering nurturance and helping the father to find nurturing, nontraditional male role models.

As for the present and future, a major challenge that still exists for mental health professionals working with fathers is engaging fathers in clinical work (Walters et al., 2001). Fathers tend to present for family counseling or support groups reluctantly, if they present at all. Wall and Levy (1994) suggest that therapists can alleviate this problem by reframing treatment as "consultation" or "planning sessions" and by creating a more "male friendly" environment by having sports magazines and so forth available in the office.

## Counseling Fathers From Diverse Groups

Not all fathers are created equal. The experiences and counseling needs of parents from different ethnic and racial backgrounds vary both between and within cultures (Kiselica & Pfaller, 1993). Kiselica (1999) mentioned several factors that counselors should be aware of when working with fathers from diverse groups. One is the importance of addressing institutional barriers that stem from racism. Counselors and service providers should utilize an ecological systems framework in which service providers target change efforts at the dynamic interaction between the father and society. Regarding adolescent Black fathers, there is inherent danger in aiming change efforts only at the individual level and viewing an adolescent, ethnically diverse father as a deviant in need of rehabilitation. Another issue is that Black fathers, and especially young Black fathers, typically want help with practical concerns, such as finding employment or learning parenting skills (Hendricks, 1988). Finally, it is crucial for mental health professionals to consider that each racial-ethnic group is itself internally diverse, and racial-ethnic minorities are as different from one another as they are from the dominant culture (Mirande, 1991). Thus, the multicultural counseling competencies (Sue, Arredondo, & McDavis, 1992) may provide a helpful guidepost for mental health professionals working with fathers from diverse groups.

## FUTURE DIRECTIONS

Fathers started to become more actively involved in child rearing in the late 1970s and 1980s (Levant et al., 1990). However, the progress has been slow, as fathers still only do approximately 40% of family work and have approximately 20% more free time than mothers (Sayer, 2005), even though a majority of women provide half or more of household income (Families and Work Institute, 1995). Thus, the "second shift" (Hochschild, 1989) still exists for women. A future direction is for scholarship such as this book and the research reviewed in this chapter to increase awareness of these continuing inequalities and, in turn, to increase the engagement of fathers. There is a big difference between fathers who contribute to family work begrudgingly because their part- ners asked them to and fathers who are proactively engaged in family work of their own volition. A goal is that fathers will someday willingly contribute an equal amount of family work and be just as engaged in child rearing as mothers.

A second future direction is the increasing influence of the generative fathering movement (Dollahite & Hawkins, 1998). This movement's growing dominance in the literature will likely shape how fathers are viewed in the future. An example of this increasing influence is the recent publishing of *Why Fathers Count: The Importance of Fathers and Their Involvement With Children* (Brotherson & White, 2007), by Men's Studies Press (an important wing of the American Men's Studies Association). In essence, the central thesis of the generative fathering movement is that mental health professionals must move away from a deficit perspective of fathers and consider the many strengths and contributions of fathers to their children, families, and society. Alan Hawkins and David Dollahite have published works on the emerging generative fathering model (Dollahite, Hawkins, & Brotherson, 1996) and an important historical critique of the deficit viewpoint (Hawkins & Dollahite, 1996). Other scholars have discussed generative fatherhood among Latinos (Hernandez, 2002), Dakota Native Americans (White, Godfrey, & Iron-Moccasin, 2006), and African Americans (Conner & White, 2006). Finally, Kiselica, Englar-Carlson, Horne, and Fisher (2008) have suggested how promoting generative fathering can enhance the development of boys. These works point toward a new way of look- ing at fathers, helping boys to think about fatherhood in a healthy way, and helping fathers with their parenting challenges.

A third future direction is that older fathers, nonresident fathers, and fathers raising children they did not sire are three growing popula- tions who will need increased attention from mental health profession- als. Regarding older fathers, the National Center for Health Statistics indicates that more men are delaying fatherhood until their 30s and 40s, while the percentage of younger fathers has been on the decline (Tejada-Vera & Sutton, 2008). Thus, an increasing number of men are beginning their fatherhood duties at an older age. In the future, prac- titioners and researchers must be prepared to meet the needs of these older fathers by figuring out how the needs of older fathers differ from those of men who become fathers in their 20s.

Recall that approximately 50% of all U.S. marriages end in divorce (Bramlett & Mosher, 2002). This relatively large number of divorces has resulted and will continue to result in a growing number of fathers who are not residing with their biological children. These nonresident fathers are not only growing in numbers, but are also over-represented among the poor. The Urban Institute (2006) recently reported that 2.6 million nonresident fathers, representing about 23% of all nonresident fathers, have incomes below the poverty line. These poor, nonresident fathers tend to face significant barriers to successful fatherhood and overall adjustment, including employment difficulties, high levels of stress, lack of English language skills, housing instability, transportation difficulties, substance abuse problems, and antisocial behavior. An important implication of this trend is that practitioners must be knowledgeable about effective ways to assist these nonresident fathers with problems such as coping with living away from their children, dealing with repeated separations from children, visitation problems, and establishing traditions in the father's home. Model interventions for men from fragile families are a key to assisting nonresident fathers with their difficult life circumstances. For example, the widely acclaimed Texas Fragile Families Initiative (Romo, Bellamy, & Coleman, 2004) successfully served a high percentage of low-income, nonresident, younger fathers.

Another development related to divorce and remarriage was mentioned by Hofferth (2006, p. 53): "Children today are increasingly likely to live in two-parent families in which they are not the biological children of the mother's new partner." In other words, nonbiological fathers are playing an increasing role in the lives of children. There are many challenges facing fathers raising children they did not sire. For example, children being raised by a nonbiological father consistently show higher levels of behavioral problems than children being raised by two biological parents (Amato & Rivera, 1999). Thus, nonbiological fathers may raise children who are more difficult to parent. An example of how counselors may assist these men is by motivating them to invest time and resources in the nonbiological child, as this has been shown to improve the behavior of children and the relationship between children and their nonbiological fathers (Fragile Families & Child Wellbeing, 2000). In brief, there will be an increasing need in the future to understand the challenges of and provide interventions for nonbiological fathers.

A fourth future direction is the positive movement to support fathers in both the private and public sectors. It is important for mental health professionals who work with men to be aware of the resources these sources of support can provide to assist us in our efforts to help men. Earlier in this chapter we alluded to the Federal Fatherhood Initiative that was started by the Clinton administration (Cabrera & Peters, 2000) and is still going strong. Another example of a source of support for fathers is the National Fatherhood Initiative, which is a nonprofit organization dedicated to helping men be good fathers (National Fatherhood Initiative, n.d.). The National Fatherhood Initiative has several curricula focused on fatherhood, and some are geared toward neglected populations such as incarcerated fathers. The federal government has also made important policy changes that support fathers, and it offers numerous grants that fund services for fathers, such as Responsible Fatherhood Grants from the Administration for Children and Families (Federal Grants Wire, n.d.). In short, there seems to be an increasing public awareness of the need to support fathers.

Finally, a fifth future direction involves measurement. Researchers must reconsider how to measure father involvement, assess the impact of fathers on children, and evaluate the impact of father programs on men and their children. Day and Lamb (2004) argued that more refined measures of father involvement can enhance the insight and impact of both scholars and policymakers. Day and Lamb also stressed the need for researchers to use a variety of research methods (both quantitative and qualitative) and designs (experimental, quasi-experimental, survey, observational, and interview) to provide the broadest and most accurate view of the involvement and influence of men in families. An example of a future trend in the measurement of father involvement is the narrative approach discussed by Pleck and Stueve (2004) and Dollahite (2004).

## SUMMARY

To summarize and conclude, the goal of this chapter was to provide a brief overview of the historical background and development of the new fatherhood movement in the United States. This chapter examined the emergence of the nurturing father in the mid 1970s, discussing the social changes in the 1960s and 1970s that led to the new father role. We examined, in turn, data on paid work, family work, and free time that suggest that men have not fully adopted the new father role, and data on changes in divorce patterns that suggest there may continue to be a "crisis of connection" between men and women. We subsequently considered how counselors might address these matters with their clients and the likely advantages of doing so, and provided a brief history of counseling fathers. Finally, we concluded the chapter with speculation about the future of the new fatherhood movement.

## REFERENCES

Amato, P.R., & Rivera, F. (1999). Parental divorce and the well-being of children: A meta-analysis. *Psychological Bulletin, 110*, 26–46.

Baca Zinn, M., & Eitzen, S. (1996). *Diversity in families* (4th Ed.). New York: Harper Collins.

Barnett, R.C., Davidson, H., & Marshall, N. (1991). Physical symptoms and the interplay of work and family roles. *Health Psychology, 10*, 94–101.

Barnett, R.C., Marshall, N., & Pleck, J. (1991). Men's multiple roles and their relationship to men's psychological distress. *Journal of Marriage and the Family, 54*, 348–367.

Bee, H., & Boyd, D. (2007). *The developing child* (11th Ed.). New York: Pearson/ Allyn & Bacon.

Berardo, D.H., Shehan, L.L., Leslie, G.R. (1987). A residue of tradition: Jobs, careers and spouse time in housework. *Journal of Marriage and the Family, 49*, 381–390.

Bond, J.T., Galinsky, E., Kim, S.S., & Brownfield, E. (2005). *Families & Work Institute's 2005 National Study of Employers.* Retrieved March 22, 2008, from http://familiesandwork.org/site/research/reports/2005nse.pdf

Bonney, J.F., Kelley, M. L., & Levant, R. F. (1999). A model of fathers' behavioral involvement in child care. *Journal of Family Psychology, 13,* 401–415.

Boszormenyi-Nagy, I., & Ulrich, D.N. (1981). Contextual family therapy. In A.S. Gurman & D.P. Kniskern (Eds.) *Handbook of family therapy* (pp. 159–186). New York: Brunner/Mazel.

Bramlett, M.D., & Mosher, W.D. (2002). Cohabitation, marriage, divorce, & remarriage in the United States. *Vital Health Statistics, 22(23).* Retrieved March 22, 2008, from http://www.cdc.gov/nchs/data/series/sr_23/sr23_022.pdf

Brannon, R. (1985). A scale for measuring attitudes about masculinity. In A. Sargent (Ed.), *Beyond sex roles* (pp. 110–116). St. Paul, MN: West.

Brinig, M.F., & Allen, D.W. (2000). These boots are made for walking: Why most divorce filers are women. *American Law and Economics Review, 2,* 126–169.

Brotherson, S.E., & White, J.M. (2007). *Why fathers count: The importance of fathers and their involvement with children.* Harriman, TN: Men's Studies Press.

Bulanda, R.E. (2004). Paternal involvement with children: The influence of gender ideologies. *Journal of Marriage and Family, 66,* 40–45.

Bumpass, L.L. (1990). What's happening to the family? Interactions between demographic and institutional change. *Demography, 27,* 483–498.

Bureau of Labor Statistics. (2000). *Employment characteristics of families in 1999.* Retrieved September 17, 2007, from ftp://146.142.4.23/pub/news.release/History/famee.06152000

Cabrera, N., & Peters, H.E. (2000). Public policies and father involvement. *Marriage and Family Review, 29,* 295–314.

Chaplin, T.M., Cole, P.M., & Zahn-Waxler, C. (2005). Parental socialization of emotional expression: Gender differences and relations to child adjustment. *Emotion, 5,* 80–88.

Cherlin, A. (1981). *Marriage, divorce, remarriage.* Cambridge, MA: Harvard University Press.

Conner, M.E., & White, J.L. (2006). *Black fathers: An invisible presence in America.* Mahwah, NJ: Erlbaum.

Day, R.D., & Lamb, M.E. (Eds.). (2004). *Conceptualizing and measuring father involvement.* Mahwah, NJ: Erlbaum.

Dollahite, D.C. (2004). A narrative approach to exploring responsible involvement of fathers with their special-needs children. In R.D. Day & M.E. Lamb (Eds.), *Conceptualizing and measuring father involvement* (pp. 109–128). Mahwah, NJ: Erlbaum.

Dollahite, D.C., & Hawkins, A.J. (1998). A conceptual ethic of generative fathering. *The Journal of Men's Studies, 7(1),* 109–132.

Dollahite, D.C., Hawkins, A.J., & Brotherson, S.E. (1996). Father work: A conceptual ethic of fathering as generative work. In A.J. Hawkins & D.C. Dollahite (Eds.), *Generative fathering: Beyond deficit perspectives* (pp. 17–35). Thousand Oaks, CA: Sage.

Douthitt, R.A. (1989). The division of labor within homes: Have gender roles changed? *Sex Roles, 20,* 693–704.

Dreyfus, E.A. (1979). Counseling the divorced father. *Journal of Marital and Family Therapy, 5(4),* 79–85.

Fagan, J., & Hawkins, A.J. (2001). Introduction. In J. Fagan & A.J. Hawkins (Eds.), *Clinical and educational interventions with fathers* (pp. 1–19). Binghamton, NY: Haworth Clinical Practice Press.

Families and Work Institute (1995). Women: The new providers. *Whirlpool Foundation Study Part One.* New York.

Faust, K.A., & McKibben, J.N. (1999). Marital dissolution: Divorce, separation, annulment, and widowhood. In M.B. Sussman, S.K. Steinmetz, & G.W. Peterson (Eds.). *Handbook of marriage and the family* (2nd ed. pp. 475–499). New York: Plenium Press.

Federal Grants Wire. (n.d.). Healthy marriage promotion and responsible fatherhood grants. Retrieved September 20, 2008, from http://www.federalgrantswire.com/healthy-marriage-promotion-and-responsible-fatherhood-grants.html

Fraad, H. (2001). Whither (wither) the family? *Journal of Psychohistory, 28,* 334–342.

Fragile Families and Child Wellbeing. (2000). Dispelling myths about unmarried fathers. *Fragile Families Research Brief No. 1.* Princeton, NJ: Bendheim-Thoman Center for Research on Child Wellbeing.

Gelman, D. (1978). How men are changing. *Newsweek,* January 16: 52–56, 59–61.

Gottman, J. (1991). Predicting the longitudinal course of marriages. *Journal of Marital and Family Therapy, 17,* 3–7.

Gregg, C. (1994). Group work with single fathers. *Journal for Specialists in Group Work, 19,* 95–101.

Grunebaum, H. (1962). Group psychotherapy of fathers: Problems of technique. *British Journal of Medical Psychology, 35,* 147–154.

Hallowitz, E., & Stephens, B. (1959). Group therapy with fathers. *Social Casework, 40,* 183–192.

Hawkins, A.J., & Dollahite, D.C. (1996). Beyond the role inadequacy perspective of fathering. In A.J. Hawkins & D.C. Dollahite (Eds.), *Generative fathering: Beyond deficit perspectives* (pp. 3–16). Thousand Oaks, CA: Sage.

Hendricks, L.E. (1988). Outreach with teenage fathers: A preliminary report on three ethnic groups. *Adolescence, 23,* 711–720.

Hernandez, R. (2002). *Father work in the crossfire: Chicano teen fathers struggling to take care of business* (p. 14). (Report No. JSRI-WP-58). East Lansing, MI: Michigan State University, Julian Samora Research Institute. (ERIC Document Reproduction Services No. ED 471 926)

Hochschild, A. (1989). *The second shift.* New York: Avon Books.

Hoffer, T.B., Welch, V. Jr., Webber, K., Williams, K., Lisek, B., Hess, M., Loew, D, & Guzman-Barron, I. (2007). *Doctorate Recipients from United States Universities: Summary Report 2006.* Chicago: National Opinion Research Center.

Hofferth, S.L. (2006). Residential father, family type and child well being: Investment versus selection. *Demography, 43,* 53–77.

Hurley, D. (1995, April 19). Divorce rate: It's not what you think. *The New York Times.* Retrieved September 17, 2007, from http://www.divorcerateform.org/nyt05.html

Juster, F.T., & Stafford, F.P. (1985). *Time, goods, and well-being.* Ann Arbor, MI: Institute for Social Research.

Kiselica, M.S. (1999). Counseling teen fathers. In A.M. Horne & M.S. Kiselica (Eds.), *Handbook of counseling boys and adolescent males: A practitioner's guide* (pp. 179–197). Thousand Oaks, CA: Sage.

Kiselica, M.S., Englar-Carlson, M., Horne, A.M., & Fisher, M. (2008). A positive psychology perspective on helping boys. In M.S. Kiselica, M. Englar-Carlson, & A.M. Horne (Eds.), *Counseling troubled boys: A guidebook for practitioners* (pp. 31–48). New York: Routledge.

Kiselica, M.S., & Pfaller, J.P. (1993). Helping teenage parents: The independent and collaborative roles of counselor educators and school counselors. *Journal of Counseling and Development, 72,* 42–48.

Lamb, M.E. (1979). Paternal influences and the father's role: A personal perspective. *American Psychologist, 43,* 938–943.

Lamb, M.E. (1981). *The role of the father in child development (2nd Ed.).* New York: Wiley.

Lamb, M.E. (2004). *The role of the father in child development (4th Ed.).* New York: Wiley.

Lamb, M.E., Owen, M.J., & Chase-Lansdale, L. (1979). The father daughter relationship: Past, present, and future. In C.B. Knopp & M. Kirkpatrick (Eds.) *Becoming female.* New York: Plenum.

Langlois, J.H., & Downs, A.C. (1980). Mother, fathers, and peers as socialization agents of sex-typed play behaviors in young children. *Child Development, 51,* 1217–1247.

LaRossa, R. (1989, Spring). Fatherhood and social change. *Men's Studies Review,* 6(2), 1–9.

Le Camus, J., & Frascarolo, F. (2003). Introduction of the special issue on fatherhood. *European Journal of Psychology of Education, 18,* 95–99.

Levant, R.F. (1990). Coping with the new father role. In D. Moore & F. Leafgren (Eds.) *Problem solving strategies and interventions for men in conflict* (pp. 81–94). Alexandria, VA: American Association for Counseling and Development.

Levant, R.F. (1992). Toward the reconstruction of masculinity. *Journal of Family Psychology, 5,* 379–402.

Levant, R. (1996). The crisis of connection between men and women. *Journal of Men's Studies, 5,* 1–12.

Levant, R.F. (2001). Desperately seeking language: Understanding, assessing and treating normative male alexithymia. In G.R. Brooks and G. Good (Eds). *The new handbook of counseling and psychotherapy for men.* (Vol. 1, pp. 424–443). San Francisco: Jossey-Bass.

Levant, R.F. & Doyle, G.F. (1983). An evaluation of a parent education program for fathers of school-aged children. *Family Relations, 32,* 29–37.

Levant, R.F., & Kelly, J. (1989). *Between father and child.* New York: Viking.

Levant, R. & Kopecky, G. (1995). *Masculinity reconstructed.* New York: Dutton.

Levant, R.F., & Richmond., K. (2007). A review of research on masculinity ideologies using the Male Role Norms Inventory. *Journal of Men's Studies,* 15, 130–146.

Levant, R., Slattery, S., Loiselle, J., Sawyer-Smith, V., & Schneider, R. (1990). Non-traditional paternal behavior with school-aged daughters. A discriminant analysis of cognitive, attitudinal, behavioral, time use, and demographic variables. *Australian Journal of Marriage and the Family, 11,* 28–35.

Levy, F. (1995). Incomes and income inequality. In R. Farley (Ed.), *State of the union: America in the 1990s* (pp. 1–58). New York: Russell Sage Foundation

Marcus, I.M. (1956). Psychoanalytic group therapy with fathers of emotionally disturbed preschool children. *International Journal of Group Psychotherapy, 6,* 61–79.

Martin, T.C., & Bumpass, L. (1989). Recent trends in marital disruption. *Demography, 26,* 37–51.

McMullin, J.A. (2005). Patterns of paid and unpaid work: The influence of power, social context, and family background. *Canadian Journal on Aging, 24,* 225–236.

Mirande, A. (1991). Ethnicity and fatherhood. In F.W. Bozett & S.M. Hanson (Eds.), *Fatherhood & families in cultural context* (pp. 53–82). New York: Springer.

National Center for Education Statistics. (2006). Digest of education statistics. Retrieved September 17, 2007, from http://www.nces.ed.gov/programs/digest/d97/d97t184.asp

National Fatherhood Initiative. (n.d.). Retrieved September 20, 2008, from http://www.fatherhood.org

Parke, R.D. (1979). Perspectives on father-infant interaction. In J.D. Osofsky (Ed.). Handbook of infant development. New York: Wiley.

Parsons, T., & Bales, R.F. (1955). *Family, socialization and interaction processes.* New York: The Free Press.

Peterson, K.S. (2000, March 7). Black couples stay the course. *USA Today.* Retrieved June 26, 2008, from http://www.divorcereform.org/mel/rdivorceblack.html

Pleck, J.H. (1995). The gender role strain paradigm: An update. In R.F. Levant & W.S. Pollack (Eds.), *A new psychology of men* (pp. 11–32). New York: Basic Books.

Pleck, E.H., & Pleck, J.H. (1997). Fatherhood ideals in the United States: Historical dimensions. In M.E. Lamb (Ed.), The role of the father in child development, 3rd ed. (pp. 33–48). New York: Wiley.

Pleck, J.H., & Stueve, J.L. (2004). Narrative approach to paternal identity: The importance of parental identity: "Conjointness." In R.D. Day & M.E. Lamb (Eds.), *Conceptualizing and measuring father involvement* (pp. 83–108). Mahwah, NJ: Erlbaum.

Pollack, W.S. (1995). No man is an island: Toward a new psychoanalytic psychology of men. In R.F. Levant & W.S. Pollack (Eds.), *A New Psychology of Men* (pp. 33–67). New York: Basic Books.

Pruett, K.D. (1987). *The nurturing father.* New York: Warner Books.

Robinson, J. (1977). *How Americans use time: A social-psychological analysis.* New York: Praeger.

Romo, C., Bellamy, J., & Coleman, M.T. (2004). *TFF final evaluation report.* Austin, TX: Texas Fragile Families Initiative.

Sayer, L.C. (2005). Gender, time, and inequality: Trends in women's and men's paid work, unpaid work and free time. *Social Forces, 84,* 285–303.

Siegal, M. (1987). Are sons and daughters treated more differently by fathers than by mothers? *Developmental Review, 7,* 183–209.

Silverstein, L. (1996). Fathering is a feminist issue. *Psychology of Women Quarterly, 20,* 3–37.

Silverstein, L.B., Auerbach, C.F., & Levant, R.F. (2002). Contemporary fathers reconstructing masculinity: Clinical implications of gender role strain. *Professional Psychology: Research and Practice, 33,* 361–369.

Smith, D. (2006, September 17). *The American Divorce.* Retrieved June 27, 2008, from http://ezinearticles.com/?The-American-Divorce&id=301525

Sue, D.W., Arredondo, P., & McDavis, R.J. (1992). Multicultural counseling competencies and standards: A call to the profession. *Journal of Multicultural Counseling & Development, 20,* 64–89.

Tedder, S., & Scherman, A. (1987). Counseling single fathers. In M. Scher, M. Stevens, G. Good, & G.A. Eichenfield (Eds.), *Handbook of Counseling & Psychotherapy with Men* (pp. 265–277). Newbury Park, CA: Sage.

Tejada-Vera, B., & Sutton, P.D. (2008). Births, marriages, divorces, and deaths: Provisional data for 2007. *National Vital Statistics Reports, 56(21).*

Urban Institute. (2006). *2006 Annual Report.* Retrieved September 20, 2008, from http://www.urban.org/annualreport/home.html

Van Egeren, L.A. (2004). The development of the co-parenting relationship over the transition to parenthood. *Infant Medical Health Journal, 25,* 453–477.

Walker, K., & Woods, M. (1976). *Time use: A measure of household production of goods and services.* Washington, DC: American Home Economics.

Wall, J.C., & Levy, A.J. (1994). Treatment of noncustodial fathers: Gender issues and clinical dilemmas. *Child and Adolescent Social Work Journal, 11,* 295–313.

Walters, J., Tasker, F., & Bichard, S. (2001). 'Too busy?' Fathers' attendance for family appointments. *Journal of Family Therapy, 23,* 3–20.

White, J.M., Godfrey, J., & Iron-Moccasin, B. (2006). American Indian fathering in the Dakota Nation: Use of Akicita as fatherhood standard. *Fathering, 4,* 49–69.

# 2

# *Counseling Fathers from a Strength-Based Perspective*

CHEN Z. OREN, MATT ENGLAR-CARLSON,
MARK A. STEVENS, AND DORA CHASE OREN

### MY FATHER'S HANDS

Held the warmth of a newborn baby
Wiped away the tears of a broken heart
Helped heal all the cuts and bruises
Made as many meals as a famous chef
Clapped louder than any parent in the stands
Have driven more miles for softball than a business trip
Patted the back of a victorious champion
Have been hurt more times by softballs than anything else
Always crossed when they were angry
Held more than a thousand coffee cups
But most important, my father's hands
Have been and always will be there for me.

The first author of this chapter wondered how to begin a discussion of positive fathering. As it often happens, clients inspire us in different ways. Recently, one of my clients came to his weekly session holding a picture frame in his hand. He spent the first few minutes updating me about his week. As we were ready to delve deeper into an issue, he asked to show me the picture frame. With much pride and red eyes he read "My Father's Hands," a poem his 14-year-old daughter wrote for him as a school project and which she gave to him for Christmas. He discussed the meaning of the poem to him. He talked about his decision to make his children a priority, about the times he spends with them, and about his children seeking his physical and emotional support. He also spoke of the moment his daughter was born and when she looked at him for the first time. He remembered a strong feeling of love and refused to let her go until he had to take her to the nursery a few hours later. Some have called the impact a newborn has on a father *engrossment*, "a sense of absorption, pre-occupation, and interest in the infant" that releases the potential for involvement (Greenberg & Morris, 1974, p. 521). Yet at the same time, my client's stories and memories link his positive experiences as a father to his feelings about the lack of his own father's support, presence, and involvement in his life. My client represents the positive impact fathering has on men and their children.

Of the 108 million men in the United States, over half (65 million) are fathers. The majority of men under age 55 have children in their homes (U.S. Census Bureau, 2006). Historically, psychologists and behavioral scientists focused their studies on mothers' significant roles of parenting while ignoring fathers' contributions (Cabrera, Tamis-LeMonda, Bradley, Hofferth, & Lamb, 2000; Coley, 2001; Kay, 2006; Lamb, 1975). Thus, fathers were invisible in the child development literature (Coley, 2001) because they were perceived to have secondary and marginal parenting roles. However, over the past several decades, many psychologists who study child development and family relations have shifted their perspectives on father-child relations.

One of the purposes of this chapter is to suggest a strength-based approach for working with fathers. For this approach, we conceptualize a five-stage counseling model by first addressing the historical context and rationale for using a strength-based approach. Further, father involvement and positive experiences of being a father are examined to assist mental health providers in creating effective interventions. Finally, a clinical vignette illustrating the application of this strength-based approach is provided. Due to the scant literature of strength-based approaches and clinical interventions with fathers, we draw conclusions from the parallel literature on counseling men.

## POSITIVE FATHER INVOLVEMENT

Fathers' current roles are not limited to being providers and disciplinarians. The responsibilities for a father have expanded to include an expectation of involvement with his children, nurturance of both spouse and children, provider of moral and ethical guidelines, and educator and role model (Barrows, 2004; Coley, 2001; Jain, Belsky, & Crnic, 1996; Marsiglio, Day, & Lamb, 2000). Many fathers are spending more time with their children, assuming an ever-increasing set of child-care tasks, and filling new paternal roles, such as primary caregiver as a stay-at-home father (Cabrera et al., 2000; Coleman & Garfield, 2004; Riley & Glass, 2002; Rochlen, McKelley, Suizzo, & Scaringi, 2008). The shift from seeing fathers as uninvolved and peripheral to the more recent perspective of viewing fathers as significant and involved has had personal and clinical implications for men. From the distant and absent provider, to the involved father, and to the more recent co-parent father (E. H. Pleck & Pleck, 1997), fathers have increased expectations to be involved and to perform as positive role models for their children. As a result, fathers find themselves in blurred and often contradictory roles as they try to meet expectations without much training. For example, due to men's socialization, many fathers may lack parenting skills, have limited role models, and may experience role expectations that excuse and even encourage noninvolvement (J. H. Pleck, 1997; Quinn, 1999). The current authors believe that the lack of training and experience with nurturing often results in a father's perceived lack of self-efficacy and competency. Importantly, fathers' belief in their ability to parent and their partners' confidence in their parenting skills significantly impacts father involvement (e.g., Bouchard, Lee, Asgary, & Pelletier, 2007; Fagan & Barnett, 2003).

A father's salience to family life and to his growing child's development is widely acknowledged (e.g., Blankenhorn, 1995; Lamb, 2004; E. H. Pleck & Pleck, 1997). High father-involvement is associated with significant childhood social, emotional, and cognitive outcomes. Over 20 years ago, Lamb (1986) was clear in his summary of father involvement: "Children seem better off when their relationship with their father is close and warm" (p. 12). Lamb's observation still holds true today. More contemporary research examines the complexity of the positive impact of father involvement on child development. Children with involved fathers are more confident, are better able to deal with frustration, have higher grade point averages, and are more likely to mature into compassionate adults (U.S. Department of Health and Human Services, 2006). Conversely, children with absent fathers can have problems in many areas: poor school achievement, early childbearing, difficulty with psychological adjustment, aggression, and risk-taking behavior (Cabrera et al., 2000; Pope & Englar-Carlson, 2001). The positive impact that fathers can have is true for resident biological fathers, stepfathers, nonresident fathers, and father-figures.

Fathers often provide their children the freedom to explore and promote active, physical play (Collins & Russell, 1991). In a father's play, both father and child often become enthralled in the intensity of the experience. Active, physical play can teach children self-control, social cues about managing emotions, and recognition of others' emotional cues. Children gain an understanding of limits by learning that kicking, biting, and other forms of physical violence are not acceptable. During physical activities, fathers can positively influence the emotional lives of children by validating feelings and recognizing and praising accomplishments (Gottman, 1998). Fathers' strengths can be seen in the ability to draw out infants' and children's emotional expression across a wide range of intensity that helps a child learn to tolerate an array of people and situations and to regulate his/her emotions (Cassidy, Parke, Butkovsky, & Braungart, 1992). Bowlby (1982) posited that fathers also engage in mentorship and encourage children in the face of challenges. Fathers can serve as sensitive, supportive, and gently challenging companions for children in their attempts to move beyond the family to explore the world (Grossman et al., 2002; Marsiglio et al., 2000).

## *Father Involvement as a Key Factor to Positive Fathering*

Current definitions of father involvement expand the notion of face-to-face engagement to include some of the managerial functions of parenting (Parke, 2000). Father involvement has been defined as having three components: *engagement, accessibility,* and *responsibility* (Lamb, Pleck, Charnov, & Levine, 1987). Engagement refers to the father's direct contact, caregiving, and shared interactions with his child. Accessibility refers to the father's potential availability and presence, regardless of the actual interactions between father and child. Finally, responsibility refers to the role of ensuring that a child is taken care of and arranging for resources to be made available to the child. Responsibility can mean financial resources, but also refers to a father's participation in tasks such as doctors' visits, selecting child care and babysitting, arranging after-school care, and taking care of sick children. Some evidence suggests that responsibility may be the most important component of father involvement (Lamb, 2000). Yet for many fathers, financial child support remains the most important form of parental responsibility (Christiansen & Palkovitz, 2001). Fathers continue to be the main financial providers in families. Even in dual-income families, fathers still tend to have heightened importance as providers due to economic and wage discrepancies.

It is important to make the distinction between quantitative and qualitative experiences of father involvement (Lamb, 2000; Lamb, Pleck, Charnov, & Levine, 1985, 1987). The quality of father-child involvement is more important than the actual amount (Lamb, 1997; Palkovitz, 1997). For fathers to be effective, just being around is not enough; children experience more benefit when the father-child relationship is supportive (Amato & Rejac, 1994). Positive fathers are involved and available to their children. Responsive fathering (e.g., warmth, attention, sensitivity) and participation during specific activities with children are important elements of positive father involvement (Doherty, Kouneski, & Erickson, 1998).

It is apparent that father involvement significantly affects children's overall well-being. Yet, positive father involvement includes nontraditional male roles that some men may be unfamiliar or uncomfortable with because most fathers have been socialized within the context of their role as breadwinner. We suggest that a strength-based approach is an effective way to address the diverse needs of fathers in counseling. Strength-based perspectives are part of the emerging field of positive psychology (Smith, 2006), which is the "scientific study of ordinary human strengths and virtues... [Positive psychology] asks how can psychologists explain the fact that, despite all the difficulties, the majority of people manage to live lives of dignity and purpose" (Sheldon & King, 2001, p. 216). Although positive psychology has been applied to many domains within the field of psychology, the application of positive psychology to working with men has been limited (Kiselica, Englar-Carlson, Horne, & Fisher, 2008; Kiselica, Stevens, & Englar-Carlson, 2006). Strength-based counseling draws on principles from counseling psychology, multicultural counseling, social work, prevention, solution-focused, and narrative therapy movements (Smith, 2006). Although three recent books included material on strength-based work with fathers that moves beyond deficit perspectives (Brotherson & White, 2006; Fagan & Hawkins, 2001; Hawkins & Dollahite, 1996), to the knowledge of these authors, the application of positive psychology has not been specifically applied to fathering.

We believe that utilizing aspects of positive psychology, such as strengths, capacity to love and nurture, courage, and future-mindedness (e.g., modeling and educating; Seligman & Csikszentmihalyi, 2000) can help practitioners understand, assess, and treat fathers. When mental health providers see fathers from a deficit model, such as experiencing a father as uninvolved with his children, opportunities for empathy and effective interventions are reduced. The mental health provider may have failed to recognize that the apparently uninvolved father may be spending long hours at work because of a strong belief that he must provide financially. Positive psychology can be used to help practitioners develop empathy toward fathers, establish rapport, and effectively utilize fathers' strengths in their interventions.

We do not contend that all fathers or fathering aspects are positive. We recognize that many fathers endorse traditional masculine gender roles that hold views of women's roles as caregivers who are responsible for the children, where fathers' roles involve providing financially and disciplining children. Further, a significant number of fathers are absent and do not pay child support. However, with men who wish to look at their fathering experiences, either directly or more often indirectly through current issues, we believe that positive psychology and utilization of fathers' strengths can allow them to broaden traditional gender roles. In this context, a strength-based approach provides a balance to a deficit model by including the strengths and positive qualities of fathers. This lens provides mental health providers ways to conceptualize fathers that may lead to increased empathy and more effective interventions.

## *What Brings Fathers to Counseling?*

It is important to examine fathers' reasons for seeking help. For many men, including fathers, seeking counseling is difficult (Addis & Mahalik, 2003; Fagan & Hawkins, 2001; Good, Dell, & Mintz, 1989; Kiselica, 2008; Shappiro, 2001). Historically, men seek therapy for a limited number of reasons: (1) for themselves as a last resort, (2) with their wives for marriage counseling, or (3) with their families for family therapy (Brooks, 1998; Chamow, 1978). Fathers typically begin individual counseling for issues *not* related to fatherhood, such as work problems, relationship issues, alcohol/substance abuse, and a host of other external reasons. Fatherhood may be viewed as background noise in an already stressful life. Some fathers come to counseling after complaints from their spouses/partners about their lack of involvement with the family.

Some literature describes men as not seeking help at all, or, when they do, they are perceived as difficult clients who come to counseling reluctantly, are uncomfortable being in therapy, and avoid disclosure and expression of feelings (Mahalik, Good, & Englar-Carlson, 2003). Research on noncustodial fathers gives a similar description of clients who are difficult to engage, yet in need of help (Lehr & MacMillan, 2001). Gender role norms for men reinforce that seeking help from a primary care physician is more acceptable than from a mental health professional (Hudson, Campbell-Grossman, Fleck, Elek, & Shipman, 2003). Further, fathers encounter obstacles for seeking help that are not related to gender role socialization. For example, Kiselica (2008) identifies harmful stereotypes and lack of understanding of teen fathers, policies and procedures devaluing the roles of fathers, underfunded and understaffed programs geared for fathers, female-oriented programs, and simply being too overwhelmed to seek help as some of the reasons teen fathers do not get the professional help they need. The reluctance to seek help, coupled with multilayered stressors, can leave fathers with limited options. It is important for mental health providers to deliver positive, aware, and sensitive services to fathers based on their specific needs. Effective mental health services act to broaden fathers' options of whom they can turn to for help.

Fathers can be treated in different modalities, such as family, couple, individual, and group therapy. Mental health providers and educators can make these services available and attractive to fathers with effective interventions that can help retain fathers who seek help (Fagan & Hawkins, 2001). Most men and fathers who receive counseling report satisfaction and have successful outcomes (Fagan & Hawkins). Shappiro (2001) makes the seemingly obvious, yet critical, observation that "fathers are men" (p. 403), thus indicating that any consideration of working with fathers exists within the larger context of counseling men.

Gender role socialization can shape men's identities and behaviors and how fathers are perceived by others. Few men indicate they have had satisfactory models of fatherhood (Daly, 1993), and for most men, caring for siblings was not a major responsibility. Society largely views involved parenting as mandated for mothers, yet optional for fathers. As fathers' images change and they become more positive and involved, interventions need to shift to reflect this change. The application of strength-based counseling with fathers can be an effective approach for successful therapeutic outcomes. By addressing fathers' strengths rather than focusing on deficits and negative perceptions of selves, spouses, partners, or society, mental health providers can increase fathers' self-efficacy and involvement.

## *Positive Fathering*

We believe an important question to consider is, What are the aspects of positive fathering? The answer seems particularly relevant as traditional core features of mothering (sustenance and nurturance) are easier to define, yet still we are not sure what "good fathering" means—though we seem to have an idea of what "bad fathering" means (Marks & Palkovitz, 2004). Vann (2007) described the key to being a "good father" lies in the ability to provide for children's emotional and physical needs and model a respectful relationship with their mother. Vann includes in his definition of a good father the following (p. 267):

> [A good father]... makes a commitment to a married or long-term relationship with the mother of his children or, if they are divorced or separated, a commitment to a positive co-parenting relationship; exhibits good communication and relationship skills; maintains contact with his children's school teachers...; refrains from negative behaviors such as substance abuse, domestic violence, criminal behavior, etc.; engages in positive age appropriate activities with his children on a consistent basis; and, works with the children's mother to ensure adequate household income and budgeting.

Vann's definition includes many characteristics that fit the expanded roles expected from today's fathers. Some of these roles, such as relationship skills and engagement with teachers, are not typically focused on in traditional male socialization. These roles are likely to be foreign to many fathers who were raised to be financial providers. Despite this lack of training, both adolescents and fathers generally rated fathers as successful parents who demonstrated specific strengths in listening, being honest in their expression of feelings, fair disciplinarians, and providing children freedom to be alone (Strom, Beckert, Strom, Strom, & Griswold, 2002). Further, many fathers report a desire to be more involved with the caregiving of children and perceive current social expectations to do so (Henwood & Proctor, 2003).

## POSITIVE IMPACT ON FATHERS

Although most of the research on fathers has looked at the effects of fathers on their children, fathering is a reciprocal process where men gain positive meaning from interactions with their children. Traditionally, work roles have been viewed as central to men's psychological health, as the workplace was understood as the setting where men established identities and developed self-worth. Recently, however, some research has challenged these notions and looked at the importance of the paternal role. Most research finds fatherhood experiences to be positive in a man's life (Palkovitz, 2002). Fatherhood has a transforming effect on men and encourages them to reevaluate their priorities and become more caring human beings who are concerned about future generations (Knoester & Eggebeen, 2006). The positive impact of children on fathers is validated by correlations that are often found for fathers living with their children. Once fathers step away from coresidence, the power of fatherhood dissipates (Eggebeen & Knoester, 2001). Some research suggests that fatherhood may lead men to question what is important in life and helps fathers clarify values and set priorities (Palkovitz, 2002; Parke, 1995; Snarey, 1993).

Fatherhood may act in similar ways to marriage by reducing health-risk behaviors (e.g., smoking, alcohol use, dangerous activities) because fatherhood may serve as a signal to men that they have someone to live for, thus encouraging more healthy and responsible behaviors (Eggebeen & Knoester, 2001). Additionally, over time, fathers have less psychological distress because emotional involvement with children acts as a buffer against work-related stress (Barnett, Marshall, & Pleck, 1992). Positive effects of fathering include children as a source of happiness and increased physical activity, providing fathers with a sense of accomplishment, well-being, and contentment. Additionally, fatherhood leads to more intergenerational, extended family, and other external social interactions. The presence of children in a man's life often encourages men to become more involved in community and service-oriented organizations, to establish more frequent contacts with extended kin, and to get more involved in faith-based community activities. These associations are most pronounced for resident fathers (Eggebeen & Knoester, 2001; Knoester & Eggebeen, 2006). Fathers often find their social lives change to less time with friends and associates and more time in social relationships that directly or indirectly include their children. As fathers age, they grow into roles as community leaders and mentors and become more concerned with the next generation. Fatherhood seems to advance a man's ability to understand himself as an adult, including developing empathy and care for others (Palkovitz, 2002).

Although most fathers initially experience a decline in marital satisfaction and increased stress when a baby is born, there is some evidence indicating that over time fatherhood increases marital stability (Cowan & Cowen, 1992). Competent fatherhood has been associated with marital satisfaction in midlife (Heath & Heath, 1991; Snarey, 1993). Fathers often experience a greater commitment to the work force (Kaufman & Uhlenberg, 2000; Knoester & Eggebeen, 2006) out of a need to provide (Snarey, 1993), yet moderate a desire to overcommit to their jobs (Coltrane, 1995). Thus, it appears that involved fathers tend to have happier relationships and more successful careers. It also suggests that positive fathering helps men connect with the adaptive, positive parts of themselves.

## APPLYING A STRENGTH-BASED APPROACH TO WORKING WITH FATHERS

We believe that helping fathers feel comfortable with roles not traditionally associated with men, yet critical for involved fathers, is congruent with the goals of strength-based counseling. Drawing from Smith's (2006) strength-based counseling model, we formulated a five-stage strength-based model for working with fathers: rapport and therapeutic alliance, assessment, identification of strengths, interventions, and resiliency and termination. Although an exhaustive description of this model is beyond the scope of this chapter, our goal is to introduce the model and illustrate its components as they apply to working with fathers.

### *Rapport and Therapeutic Alliance With Fathers*

Therapeutic alliance starts with the first contact with a client, lasts throughout the counseling process, and is the essence of any therapeutic relationship. However, certain factors can contribute to the development of therapeutic relationships with fathers. First, it is important to utilize some of the existing knowledge pertaining to engaging men in therapy. Many fathers do not hear—nor do they feel—that they are important in the lives of their children (Parke & Brott, 2003) and may even wonder if they matter. Social and relational support for fathers is essential if they are to become nurturing and involved with their children and to remain so. Individual counseling can be an important source of that support. Perhaps already feeling defensive being in therapy, the client must feel that his needs, desires, and style are acceptable to the therapist (Shappiro, 2001). The counselor can provide empathy and listen to the struggling father. To create a safe, therapeutic alliance, it is important for mental health providers to acknowledge the process of asking for help and to reinforce that men seeking counseling are showing courage and strength (Rabinowitz & Cochran, 2002). Based on empirical research on teenage fathers, Kiselica (2003) identified tactics to establish rapport with boys and men, such as displaying magazines appealing to men and fathers (e.g., sports, men's health), using flexible time scheduling, displaying humor and appropriate self-disclosure, engaging in collaborative work and goal setting, and using the client's language. Shappiro (2001) noted that the most important factor in successful relationships and interventions with fathers is making counseling male-friendly. Good, Gilbert, and Scher (1990) advocate using Gender Aware Therapy when working with clients. They highlight the importance of including gender as an essential aspect of counseling and allowing clients to explore and develop their own gender-related experiences. Although often hidden, fathers' own gender socialization and the experience of male gender roles on being a father are important to investigate in the beginning of and throughout the therapeutic relationship.

Finally, it is important for therapists to explore their own knowledge and perceptions of men and fathers. The notion that mental health providers lack training in working with men and fathers and may hold unfavorable views of these populations is not new. Liu (2005) calls for the inclusion of men and patriarchal issues in the multicultural competencies guidelines for psychologists. Although most mental health providers (Marriage and family therapists, social workers, psychologists) are trained to work with individuals, couples, and families, there is a lack of training for these professionals in men's and fathers' issues. Robertson and Fitzgerald (1990) suggested that experienced therapists were more pathologizing of male clients who held nontraditional roles (e.g., men who chose not to engage in the provider role) and treated them differently in therapy. Common assumptions about men include that men do not listen well, are not emotional, are competitive, are risk taking, are entitled and privileged, need control, and fear vulnerability (Kiselica, Stevens, & Englar-Carlson, 2006). Shappiro (2001) asserts that therapy typically uses traits more congruent with mothers' traditional roles than fathers' roles, suggesting that therapy can be awkward for fathers. This discomfort in therapy is compounded by therapists who have gaps in their knowledge of fathers. Thus, it is important for mental health providers to gain knowledge about fathers and be aware of the range of strengths to establish rapport and be empathic when working with fathers.

## Assessing Fathers Presenting Problems in the Context of Positive Father Involvement

Fathers who come to therapy should be provided with a thorough clinical intake as part of the first assessment session. However, a typical intake may lack some important information that is specific to fathers and to fathers' strengths. We would like to highlight in this section some assessment suggestions when working with fathers from a strength-based approach. These recommendations are not all-encompassing, but serve as initial considerations that take into account issues related to fathers' male socialization and strengths. Thus, we will not focus on some of the categories that are typically assessed with fathers, such as age, socioeconomic status, career, presenting problems, and medical and psychological history. Instead, we will focus on assessing fathers' roles in the context of positive fathering, specifically positive father involvement.

Jimerson, Sharkey, Nyborg, and Furlong (2004) suggest that strength-based assessment empowers people with hope, optimism, and motivation for change. We suggest starting the assessment with an honest appraisal of how the male client is a good father. One way to assess the positive contributions that a father makes to his children and family is through the idea of generative fathering. Hawkins and Dollahite

(1996) and their associates have devoted considerable attention to the ways that fathers care for the next generation. *Generative fathering* is "a non-deficit perspective of fathering rooted in the proposed ethical obligation for fathers to meet the needs of the next generation" (Dollahite & Hawkins, 1998, p. 110). This idea builds on Erikson's concept of generativity in life-span development theory and also incorporates a contextual emphasis, suggesting that good fathering is generative work. Generative fathering describes fathers who respond readily and consistently to a child's developmental needs over time. Fathering becomes a way for men to provide and protect their children, but also a means to contribute to the development of a new generation. Being a "good father" becomes an important aspect of identity for many men and also a way of contributing to social welfare. Assessing the strength of a client's desire to give to the next generation can be very useful in designing appropriate interventions to increase father involvement.

The assessment may result in the discovery of some important masculine strengths that a father holds, such as male ways of caring, male self-reliance, and the worker-provider tradition. It is also important to gain insight into a man's motivation for fathering: Where and how did you learn to be a father? What was your relationship like with your father? What impact do you believe your relationship with your father has on your current parenting? Who were your male or fatherlike role models? What are your hopes and dreams for your children? What traditions handed down to you by your father do you want to continue with your children? Which of his traditions do you want to discontinue or change? This specific knowledge can help deepen therapeutic conceptualization and interventions.

For some fathers, particularly among those who have been socialized to be detached emotionally from their children, male socialization and the changing role expectations of fathers are difficult and painful (Silverstein, Auerbach, & Levant, 2002) and may interfere with their generative fathering ability and motivation to be an involved father. This difficulty reveals the conflict some fathers face as they find the new expectation of fatherhood freeing and fulfilling, yet the reality of meeting these expectations (e.g., more emotionally available, provider of nurturance, boundaries between work and family) can be challenging. Therefore, it is important to also explore masculine gender-role conflicts associated with fatherhood (Silverstein et al.). Fathers may shy away from positive involvement, accepting societal messages that they cannot be as competent as are mothers (e.g., mothers are better at nurturing and calming babies down, making dinners, helping children to complete homework). Positive masculinity focuses on expanding fathers' roles to include a more nurturing, accessible, responsible, and engaged attachment and connection with children. Mental health providers can assess and help normalize the stress that fathers experience with gender role strain and assist fathers in redefining their ideas of masculinity and fatherhood to include such roles (Silverstein et al.).

O'Neil and Luján, in Chapter 3 in this book, developed an assessment paradigm that looks at fathers' gender role conflict (GRC). This new paradigm helps assess fathers' adherence to traditional roles that may impede attempts to be an involved father. O'Neil and Luján suggest asking fathers what beliefs and values they hold that conflict with positive fathering. By identifying strict gender roles, mental health providers can help fathers explore the origin and function of these roles and collaborate with fathers to develop acceptable alternatives. This GRC assessment is congruent with strength-based counseling because it involves fathers' understanding of their perceived obstacles to being involved and positive fathers. Other aspects of positive fathering that can be assessed include emotional intelligence, self-efficacy, and character strength (Jimerson et al., 2004). Finding solutions based on fathers' strengths (Smith, 2006) is a natural outgrowth of the assessment.

## *From Deficits to Strengths: Evaluating Fathers' Strengths*

Strength-based counseling does not focus only on clients' positive aspects while ignoring problems or inventing strengths. Strength-based counseling helps mental health providers identify strengths so that clients can recognize and build on them (Smith, 2006). Hays (1996, p. 192) suggests asking, "What are the [client's] strengths related to...age or generational identity, experience with disability, religion, ethnicity...which the psychologist, the client, or the client's family might be overlooking?" We believe that this question can apply well to the often unnoticed strengths of fathers. Identifying strengths can help increase father involvement, fathering self-efficacy and perceived competency, level of support from spouse, parenting skills, and nurturance.

Further, therapists' perceptions can impact the therapeutic relationship and interventions. Tremblay and L'Heureux (2005) notes that many men experience shame about feeling inadequate. Thus, it is important for therapists to emphasize personal strengths and counter feelings of shame when working with men (Tremblay & L'Heureux, 2005). The implications for fathers are obvious. Many fathers see themselves as lacking parenting skills (J. H. Pleck, 1997) or positive paternal role models, which may result in shame and low confidence and may reduce fathers' involvement. Exploring fathers' perceptions and actual parenting skills and the feelings associated with these elements is important.

Mental health providers can utilize strengths typically associated with masculinity, such as problem-solving skills, hard work, and logic as essential variables for learning and applying parenting skills. Levant (1995) notes some positive attributes associated with masculinity, including man's sacrificing his needs for the benefit of his family, ability to tolerate pain, demonstrating love in actions rather than words, commitment, and risk taking in the face of danger. Kiselica et al. (2006) adds to Levant's lists of positive attributes by noting that men's socialization tends to foster being protective of and loyal to friends and family, ability to withstand pressure, and taking on the provider role. Many of these characteristics are qualities fathers bring to a family relationship. Recognizing these qualities as strengths provides an opportunity for the therapist to shift fathers', their partners', and their children's perceptions and appreciation of fathers. Utilizing fathers' strengths and assessing the costs and benefits associated with these qualities will be further discussed and illustrated in the intervention section.

An additional factor to consider when evaluating fathers' strengths is the range of perspectives of positive fathering based on different contexts and populations. Fatherhood itself has been described as a socially constructed role that mirrors the definition and ideas of a particular culture and society. Due to pluralistic realities in contemporary society, a degree of uncertainty remains about the definition of the "ideal" father (Furrow, 1998). The importance of the family and the nature of the fathering role are likely to vary across racial and ethnic groups. Smith (2006) asserts that cultures influence how one views and determines what is perceived as a strength as opposed to a weakness. This includes how society, different populations within society, and individuals perceive different populations of fathers. We recommend that mental health providers working with diverse populations of fathers become aware of and knowledgeable about specific cultural nuances, gender role expectations, current definitions of positive fathering, and fathers' strengths. For example, while working with gay fathers, what are the therapist's assumptions about the client's potential strengths or growth edges as a father? Or, in certain parts of the country, teaching your son how to box and going out drinking with him when he comes of age are seen as an essential bonding experience by some. Others may view this as inappropriate.

### *Interventions Toward Building Strengths and Positive Change*

Drawing from the strength-based literature, we suggest interventions that allow clients to understand their capacity to be positive fathers. The interventions suggested are not exhaustive, but represent an attempt to identify strength-based interventions that could be applied to increase father involvement, parenting skills, self-efficacy, support from spouse and family, and own satisfaction with fathering. The goal is for fathers to access and recognize their internal and sometimes hidden efficacy around nurturing, empathy, patience, being in-the-moment, and being process oriented. These characteristics are essential for positive parenting and involvement. Our belief is that fathers can lead their family with strength as they gain the sense of self-efficacy necessary to be an involved father (Vann, 2007).

Smith (2006) notes the importance of allowing clients to narrate their lives, identifying strengths in clients' stories, and helping clients recognize times in their lives when they had control over their present-ing problems. Mental health providers can ask fathers questions to help them identify their strengths: What do you do well as a father? What do others in your family look to you for? What special characteristics do you have or tasks do you do that can be applied to your role as a father? Whom (friend, sibling, grandparent, etc.) or what (pet) did you nurture and take care of when you were growing up? What kinds of activities do you like or excel in that you can do with your children or family? What do you do well at work that you can apply to fathering? These sample questions can help fathers in individual counseling and fathers and their partners in couples or family therapy identify strengths and skills that may have not been previously recognized or acknowledged.

For example, the first author worked with a father who is a police officer and who wanted to better his relationship with his children. Instead of focusing on what the father perceived as his fathering defi-cits, I asked him what strengths he saw in himself that allowed him to become a successful, high-ranking officer. The client responded with strengths related to listening to and caring for the policemen under him, always being on time, preparing for tasks, being honest, being sensi-tive, and being a problem solver. However, he did not utilize the same strengths with his family due to traditional gender roles and perceived expectations. He realized that he was fearful that being vulnerable and expressing feelings to his wife would result in his wife leaving him. Through our work, he was able to generalize his professional strengths to his relationship with his family, allowing him be vulnerable and com-municate his fears to his wife and become more emotionally expressive, nurturing, and involved with his children.

Using strengths to work with fathers is a bidirectional process. A different client, who views himself as an involved and nurturing father, presented with difficulties in his career. By identifying his strengths as a parent, we were able to increase his efficacy and productivity in his professional life.

It is important to link the identified strengths to the father's perceived meaning of fatherhood and involvement with children. For many men, the meaning and practice of fatherhood are related to experiences with their own fathers and parents. J. H. Pleck (1997) noted that when a man views his own father's parenting as positive, he is more likely to model his father's level of involvement. Men whose fathers were involved in raising them tend to be more involved, take more responsibility, show more warmth, and closely monitor their children's behavior and activity (Hofferth, 1999; Parke, 1995). Further, previous caregiving and child-care experiences seem to prepare fathers to be more involved (Gerson, 1993; J. H. Pleck, 1997). Fathers with more gender-equitable attitudes and experiences in their own childhood tend to be more active, respon-sible, and warm (Hofferth, 1998).

However, many fathers were not socialized nor did they receive guid-ance about the qualities essential for positive fathering. In many ways, society's message is that fathers do not possess the necessary skills and experiences to be effective parents. Thus, it is important for mental health providers to dispel the belief that fathers cannot be nurturing or effective parents by helping fathers connect with previous nurturing and caregiving experiences that were positive. Mental health providers' facilitation of such memories and experiences is congruent with the goals of a strength-based model where fathers' strengths guide change. The third author of this chapter often asks fathers to recall times in their life when they remember themselves as nurturing. Some of the common memories that fathers recall include being camp counselors, handling demands of younger siblings, taking care of their pets, being part of sport teams, and so forth. Congruent with a strength-based approach, the goal is for fathers to find exceptions to perceived deficits and weakness ("I don't know how to be nurturing or empathic"). These exceptions provide experiences and activities to foster efficacy and excitement about the desired positive aspects of fathering. For fathers who have difficulty recalling any nurturing memories, the use of guided imagery or working with pictures of their father when they were growing up can help to elicit memories.

Depending on the context, the activities or tasks performed by fathers who are committed to their families can be viewed negatively or positively. Stevens's cost-and-benefit interventions illustrate clinical work with men by reframing perceived deficits (e.g., men don't feel, men don't communicate well, men are aggressive, men just want sex) to men's strengths (providers, protectors, loyal, problem solvers, strong, etc.). We would like to apply the cost/benefit analysis to interventions to help fathers (and their families) identify and capitalize on fathers' strengths to become effective parents. Stevens asserts the importance of acknowledging fathers' strengths by recognizing the benefits of fathers' approaches to life. He developed a list of strengths with their respective benefits, such as, a responsible father can be relied on by his family; a physical and strong father can provide security to the family; a practical and rational father can be time efficient and accomplished in problem solving. However, some of the strengths and approaches to life may cost fathers in significant ways. For example, a father who is practical, rational, and emotionally inexpressive may demonstrate difficulty with being nurturing and connecting with his children. Being driven to succeed may result in a father's limited accessibility to his family. Operating from a problem-solving mode can create emotional disconnection from his family and decrease opportunities for empathic connections with family members. By helping fathers identify and assess the costs and benefits of their approach to fatherhood, mental health providers can assist fathers to prioritize and determine which aspects of their lives are congruent with positive father involvement. Fathers are empowered to make educated and active decisions about their fathering, based on the costs and benefits of their perceived strengths.

We also feel it is valuable to highlight the importance of educating fathers about effective ways to support the mother/partner by working with both the father and his partner. A conflict between mother and father tends to result in children suffering. A father can better support mother and family dynamics by taking on more of the child-related household tasks, thus easing the mother's workload (J. H. Pleck, 1997). Sharing tasks requires flexible gender roles, which will lead to increased father involvement and positive fathering.

Finally, many fathers may not be aware of what it means to be an involved father or what the positive aspects of fathering are. Thus, it is important to educate fathers about positive fathering; the aspects of involvement; and the positive impact on children, partners, and selves. Levine and Pitt (1996) noted that a father's comfort and willingness to parent increases with education and training. (A comprehensive review of educational interventions for fathers is beyond the scope of this chapter. Interested readers may see Fagan & Hawkins, 2001.)

## Support to Promote Resiliency and Termination

Partner, family, and systemic support are critical to fostering responsible and involved fathering. For many men, the leap from provider to involved father is immense and is less likely to be accomplished without the support from family, community, and workplace (Lupton & Barclay, 1997). Support and positive feedback from wives specifically has been seen as critical to fathers' involvement (Hawkins & Fagan, 2004; Parke, 1996). Thus, an important aspect of positive interventions with fathers should include increased communication and support from wives, partners, and/or mothers of the children. We suggest allowing appropriate time to reflect on the strengths fathers identified and internalized during counseling and how these can best be supported in the future.

Further, positive psychology on the macro level calls for the development of systemic and institutional climates that foster strengths such as responsibility, resiliency, and caring in men (Hawkins & Fagan, 2001; Seligman & Csikszentmihalyi, 2000). Schools, workplace environments, public policy, and governmental programs (e.g., programs promoting strong marriages, National Fatherhood Initiative) can serve as key components to promote responsible and positive fathering. Mental health providers can help fathers recognize institutional resources to promote positive fathering. For example, High Dosage Head Start programs for fathers have been linked with increased father involvement and high math scores for children (Fagan & Iglesias, 1999). Fathering empowerment programs increase fathers' beliefs in their ability to teach their children (Fagan & Stevenson, 2002). Thus, we contend that multilevel support for fathers (personal, familial, institutional, and societal) will increase fathers' perceived self-efficacy and competency. In turn, this support will empower fathers' resiliency and the ability to maintain involvement with children and family.

Finally, most men (and women, too) are not typically socialized to manage transitions and endings of relationships in an emotionally healthy manner. It is important to help fathers learn to be empathic, nurturing, and communicative during transitions within significant relationships (separation or divorce, children moving out, children ending their own significant relationships, etc.). We contend these skills are important to be learned in counseling as elements of positive fathering. The father can then use these skills during his own transitions and model compassion, respect, and integrity for his children. Appropriately terminating counseling can demonstrate an emotionally healthy way of transitioning or ending a relationship.

The proposed model offers a way to help fathers recognize and utilize their strengths to increase positive fathering and father involvement. However, the stages in the model are fluid and not discrete. We see the stages as connected, and the different tasks of specific stages can be used throughout counseling. The following case example will illustrate the application of a strength-based approach.

## CASE EXAMPLE

Greg (pseudonym) is a 51-year-old male, born in Illinois, and the oldest son of Greek immigrant parents. Greg is college educated, runs his own investment company, and has been making low-to-middle six figures for the past 10 years. Greg married when he was 21 and divorced with no children 3 years later. Greg remarried at age 39 and separated 7 months ago. He and his wife have a 9-year-old daughter. When his wife moved out, they made arrangements for their daughter to share time between their two homes. Greg's parents had divorced when Greg was 8 years old. His father died when Greg was 21, and his mother lives in another state.

Greg has a history of alcohol abuse, which began in college. Since the birth of his daughter, he has abstained from alcohol. Greg has some health issues, such as hypertension and diabetes. Upon the recommendation of his wife's therapist, they were referred to a male counselor for couples' therapy. This was the first time Greg had been in counseling. Greg's wife complained that he was too controlling in the relationship and did not show her enough affection. Greg believed he was generous and accommodating to his wife's needs and wanted her to understand the pressures of his business. He wanted the marriage to work and did not want his daughter to be from a divorced family. After 2 months of couples' therapy, Greg's wife, Anna, made it clear she wanted a divorce. Greg continued to see his counselor after the separation.

## EARLY ASSESSMENT

Greg presented himself in a friendly and engaging manner. His success in the business world was a huge accomplishment, which he wore proudly. His life was measured in the many responsibilities at work and at home. In most of his waking hours he was in the "doing" mode and taking care of multiple business and family tasks. Greg became accustomed to achieving his goals and getting what he wanted. Through hard work, persistence, and intelligence, he had built his dream life: a beautiful wife, adoring daughter, luxurious home, and successful business. Greg was sober for almost a decade, doing so on sheer willpower and a strong desire to be sober for his daughter.

It was the fear of emotional distance from his daughter that motivated Greg to continue therapy. He was very attached to his daughter. He wanted her to have a happy childhood and indulged her with attention and material goods. Like most fathers, Greg had dreams for her. His dreams at first glance appeared to be "businesslike": Go to the best school and build a career. Greg was deeply concerned about the impact of the separation and divorce on his daughter's well-being. Not only was he in emotional crisis trying to cope with the separation, but the fear of losing his daughter also opened up some deep wounds from his childhood. He acknowledged that he did not want his daughter to experience the type of abandonment and humiliation he felt growing up. Because of a "nasty" divorce and an early death, his father was not part of his life. Greg resented his father and felt that if his father had been around more, he would not have been teased and taunted as a child.

Greg had the financial resources and emerging desire to be an involved father. Greg's high stress level and minimal social support made him vulnerable to an alcohol relapse. He was spending much more time alone and missed being with his daughter on a daily basis. Greg was very much like what David and Brannon (1976) label the "sturdy oak," a man with a bravado of toughness, confidence and self-reliance; and, like an oak tree, boys and men must stand tall, be ever-present, and provide protection to those in need. Although Greg was a deeply caring and empathic man, he had a difficult time being vulnerable and asking for help.

## TREATMENT SUMMARY

Greg had numerous interrelated issues explored during the course of treatment. Many had relevance to his role as a father, and others pertained to the separation and divorce. Two themes emerged in terms of treatment issues relating to his role as a father and his relationship with his daughter. The first therapeutic theme centered on his health and remaining sober. The second theme dealt with staying connected to his daughter.

Greg's desire to be an integral part of his daughter's life was not congruent with how he physically took care of himself. Knowing that his own father died when Greg was a young man raised a type of uncomfortable dissonance for him. Greg was diagnosed with high blood pressure and blood sugar problems more than 7 years ago. While he worried about his health, he had an extremely difficult time changing his habits. Greg was quite open to discussing a lifelong pattern of soothing through food. What appeared to have the most impact in treatment by creating new patterns was Greg's willingness to share his dreams about being with his daughter as they both grew older. Sessions slowed down as Greg described his feelings and ideas about his daughter's future college graduation, her wedding, and his becoming a grandfather. Tears rolled down his face as he experienced what he described as the joy of sharing and the fear of not being at these future celebrations. Greg also became aware of the anger that he felt toward his father for not taking better care of himself and dying at an early age. His pain and anger toward his father opened up awareness that he did not want his own daughter to feel the same type of pain and anger. His increased empathy for his daughter and wanting to be a "good" father by protecting her from future pain had a tremendous impact on his motivation and ability to change some lifelong habits.

Like many men with a "sturdy oak" disposition, Greg felt isolated and lacked genuine social support. He described his therapist as his friend, and being in therapy as a place he could let down his defenses. Much of the world, except for his therapist, did not know the intense pressure and pain Greg experienced on a day-to-day basis. He was embarrassed to cry in session, but could not help himself. Greg wanted to stay sober. He started to open up more about his fear of drinking. He was first and foremost afraid that if he relapsed, then he would be in jeopardy of losing his daughter. Greg said his ex-wife would try to stop him from being with his daughter if he started drinking again. He began to share more of his personal struggles with some selected friends. His connection with others and willingness to share his vulnerability soothed him in similar ways to drinking. While he did not want to be a "weeping willow," he also did not want to be confined to being only a "sturdy oak." Greg found it both surprising and reinforcing when other men he opened up to shared similar tales of fear and anxiety. His sense of shame and isolation was reduced significantly.

Greg's other challenge and opportunity was what he described as the pressures of being a single parent. The custody agreement included his daughter being half-time with Greg and half-time with her mother. We utilized his confidence and creative problem-solving skills he used at work as strengths that were capitalized on and generalized to being an involved father. His confidence to make things happen in business translated into his personal life. Greg made some huge business rearrangements to make time for being a single father and to stay involved with his daughter. He let go of business opportunities that obligated him to travel out of town. Greg let his business associates know of his plans to change some of his work patterns to accommodate his new parenting role. Greg would also ask questions in session about raising a daughter. His concern for her and anxiety about doing the "wrong thing" as a parent showed a vulnerable and courageous side. He shared stories of his daughter's successes and struggles with the gleam of an engaged and proud parent. His time with his daughter became sacred time.

Over time, Greg's parenting approach and reflection became much more process-oriented rather than business-oriented. He became less concerned about what he considered "make or break" decisions that would influence his daughter's future and focused more on the connection of everyday interactions. Greg worked through some of the rejection he felt when his daughter was upset about leaving her mother and having an extended stay with him. The opportunities of the crisis became apparent and served as a chance to reevaluate his priorities and gain a type of self-efficacy he had never experienced. He came to trust that over time the day-to-day interactions would serve as the glue to their relationship for now and the future. Greg was open to understanding better the developmental needs of children his daughter's age. Gradually, Greg became more trusting of his abilities as a single father.

## CONCLUSION

To make the strength-based approach used in the case example more transparent, we would like to highlight some essential elements. First, the language and orientation used by the counselor and the author of the case example reflect seeing fathers through a positive, rather than a deficit, lens. Like many fathers, Greg initially sought help at his wife's request for a crisis in their marriage. By viewing Greg's continued therapy after the marital separation as courageous, the counselor helped to build rapport. He describes Greg's crisis as an opportunity for positive change.

The importance of assessing fathers' gender socialization and gender role conflict is reflected by the counselor's identification of Greg's *doing* rather than *being*. Greg measured success by accomplishments at work and providing for his family, while neglecting his health and emotionally isolating. Rules of masculinity, such as the sturdy oak, were also assessed as part of the impact that gender socialization had on Greg's fathering. Aspects of O'Neil and Luján's GRC assessment were applied, specifically the father wound. Finally, it is clear that at the onset of therapy, Greg's involvement as a father included only the responsibility of providing financially. This assessment of Greg's involvement facilitates the counselor's work on integrating into Greg's definition of fathering the roles of accessibility and engagement.

The therapist's success in increasing Greg's involvement was assisted by using positive interventions to generalize his strengths. Greg's obvious strengths were identified, including being responsible, a creative problem solver, a hard worker, and others. Instead of focusing on Greg's deficits as a father, the therapist focused on positive imagery and dreams of future positive interactions and involvement in his daughter's life. This linkage was a turning point in changing his eating and exercise habits. Thus, through the use of cost and benefit analyses, Greg realigned his priorities and changed his schedule to achieve his goals. Finally, viewing Greg's questions about parenting as courageous and showing vulnerability were imperative in reducing his shame and facilitating change. Greg's questions were used as opportunities for education. The therapist also focused on helping Greg get support from friends and others to reinforce his changes and build resiliency (staying involved, maintaining sobriety, and remaining healthy). By being mindful of most fathers' significant strengths and positive qualities, the impact of a strength-based approach to counseling fathers can create alternatives for men to be involved, present fathers.

## REFERENCES

Addis, M. E., & Mahalik, J. R. (2003). Men, masculinity, and the contexts of help-seeking. *American Psychologist, 58*, 5–14.

Amato, P. R., & Rejac, S. J. (1994). Contact with non-resident parents, interpersonal conflict, and children's behavior. *Journal of Family Issues, 15*, 191–207.

Barnett, R. C., Marshall, N. L., & Pleck, J. H. (1992). Men's multiple roles and their relationship to men's psychological distress. *Journal of Marriage and the Family, 54*, 358–367.

Barrows, P. (2004). Fathers and families: Locating the ghost in the nursery. *Infant Mental Health Journal, 25*(5), 408–423.

Blankenhorn, D. (1995). *Fatherless America: Confronting our most urgent social problem.* New York: Basic Books.

Bouchard, G., Lee, C., Asgary, V., & Pelletier, L. (2007). Fathers' motivation for involvement with their children: A self-determination theory perspective. *Fathering, 5*(1), 25–41.

Bowlby, J. (1982). *Attachment and loss: Vol. 1 Attachment* (rev. ed.). New York: Basic Books.

Brooks, G. R. (1998). *A new psychotherapy for traditional men.* San Francisco: Jossey-Bass.

Brotherson, S. E., & White, J. M. (Eds.). (2006). *Why fathers count: The importance of fathers and their involvement with children.* Harriman, TN: Men's Studies.

Cabrera, N. J., Tamis-LeMonda, C. S., Bradley, R. H., Hofferth, S., & Lamb, M. E. (2000). Fatherhood in the twenty-first century. *Child Development, 71*(1), 127–136.

Cassidy, J., Parke, R., Butkovsky, L., & Braungart, J. (1992). Family-peer connections: The roles of emotional expressiveness within the family and children's understanding of emotions. *Child Development, 63*(3), 603–618.

Chamow, L. (1978). Some thoughts on the difficulty men have initiating individual psychotherapy. *Family Therapy, 5*(1), 67–71.

Christiansen, S. L., & Palkovitz, R. (2001). Why the "good provider" still matters. *Journal of Family Issues, 22,* 84–106.

Coleman, W. L., & Garfield, C. (2004). Fathers and pediatricians: Enhancing men's roles in the care and development of their children. *Pediatrics, 113*(5), 1406–1411.

Coley, R. L. (2001). (In)visible men: Emerging research on low-income, unmarried, and minority fathers. *American Psychologist, 56*(2), 743–753.

Collins, W., & Russell, G. (1991). Mother-child and father-child relationships in middle childhood and adolescence: A developmental analysis. *Developmental Review, 11*(2), 99–136.

Coltrane, S. (1995). The future of fatherhood: Social, demographic, and economic influences on men's family involvements. In W. Marsiglio (Ed.), *Fatherhood: Contemporary theory, research, and social policy* (pp. 255–274). Thousand Oaks, CA: Sage.

Cowan, C. P., & Cowan, P. A. (1992). *When partners become parents.* New York: Basic Books.

Daly, K. (1993). Reshaping fatherhood: Finding the models. *Journal of Family Issues, 14*(4), 510–530.

David, D. S., & Brannon, R. (1976). *The forty-nine percent majority: The male sex role.* New York: Random House.

Doherty, W., Kouneski, E., & Erickson, M. (1998). Responsible fathering: An overview and conceptual framework. *Journal of Marriage & the Family, 60*(2), 277–292.

Dollahite, D. C., & Hawkins, A. J. (1998). A conceptual ethic of generative fathering. *The Journal of Men's Studies, 7,* 109–132.

Eggebeen, D. J., & Knoester, C. (2001). Does fatherhood matter for men? *Journal of Marriage and Family, 63,* 381–393.

Fagan, J., & Barnett, M. (2003). The relationship between maternal gatekeeping, paternal competence, mothers' attitudes about the father role, and father involvement. *Journal of Family Issues, 24*(8), 1020–1043.

Fagan, J., & Hawkins, A. J. (Eds.). (2001). *Clinical and educational interventions with fathers.* Binghamton, NY: Haworth.

Fagan, J., & Iglesias, A. (1999). Father involvement program effects on fathers, father figures, and their Head Start children: A quasi-experimental study. *Early Childhood Research Quarterly, 14*(2), 243–269.

Fagan, J., & Stevenson, H. C. (2002). An experimental study of an empowerment-based intervention for African American Head Start fathers. *Family Relations, 51*(3), 191–198.

Furrow, J. (1998). The ideal father: Religious narratives and the role of fatherhood. *The Journal of Men's Studies, 7,* 17–32.

Gerson, K. (1993). *No man's land: Men's changing commitment to family and work.* New York: Basic Books.

Good, G. E., Dell, D. M., & Mintz, L. B. (1989). Male role and gender role conflict: Relations to help seeking in men. *Journal of Counseling Psychology, 36*(3), 295–300.

Good, G. E., Gilbert, L. A., Scher, M. (1990). Gender aware therapy: A synthesis of feminist therapy and knowledge about gender. *Journal of Counseling & Development, 68*(4), 376–380.

Gottman, J. M. (1998). Toward a process model of men in marriages and families. In A. Booth & A. C. Crouter (Eds.), *Men in families: When do they get involved? What difference does it make* (pp. 149–192). Mahwah, NJ: Erlbaum.

Greenberg, M., & Morris, N. (1974). Engrossment: The newborn's impact on the father. *American Journal of Orthopsychiatry, 44,* 520–531.

Grossman, K., Grossman, K. E., Fremmer-Bombik, E., Kindler, H., Scheuerer-Englisch, H., & Zimmerman P. (2002). The uniqueness of the child-father attachment relationship: Fathers' sensitive and challenging play as a pivotal variable in a 16-year longitudinal study. *Social Development, 11*(3), 301–337.

Hays, P. (1996). Culturally responsive assessment with diverse older clients. *Professional Psychology: Research and Practice, 27*(2), 188–193.

Hawkins, A. J, & Dollahite, D. C. (Eds.). (1996). *Generative fathering: Beyond deficit perspectives.* Thousand Oaks, CA: Sage.

Hawkins, A. J., & Fagan, J. (2001). Clinical and educational interventions with fathers: A synthesis. In J. Fagan, & A. J. Hawkins (Eds.), *Clinical and educational interventions with fathers* (pp. 285–293). Binghamton, NY: Haworth.

Heath, D. H., & Heath, H. E. (1991). *Fulfilling lives: Paths to maturity and success.* San Francisco: Jossey-Bass.

Henwood, K. L., & Procter, J. (2003). The "good father": Reading men's accounts of paternal involvement during the transition to first time fatherhood. *British Journal of Social Psychology, 42,* 337–355.

Hofferth, S. (1998). *Health environments, healthy children: Children in families.* Ann Arbor, MI: Institute for Social Research, University of Michigan.

Hofferth, S. (1999, April). *Race/ethnic differences in father involvement with young children: A conceptual framework and empirical test in two-parent families.* Paper presented at the Urban Seminar on Fatherhood, Harvard University, Cambridge, MA.

Hudson, D. B., Campbell-Grossman, C., Fleck, M. O., Elek, S. M., & Shipman, A. (2003). Effects of the new fathers network on first-time fathers' parenting self-efficacy and parenting satisfaction during the transition to parenthood. *Issues in Comprehensive Pediatric Nursing, 26,* 217–229.

Jain, A., Belsky, J., & Crnic, K. (1996). Beyond fathering behaviors: Types of dads. *Journal of Family Psychology, 10*(4), 431–442.

Jimerson, S. R., Sharkey, J. D., Nyborg, V., & Furlong, M. J. (2004). Strength-based assessment and school psychology: A summary and synthesis. *The California School Psychologist, 9*, 9–19.

Kaufman, G., & Uhlenberg, P. (2000). The influence of parenthood on the work effort of married men and women. *Social Forces, 78*(3), 931–947.

Kay, T. (2006). Where's dad? Fatherhood in leisure studies. *Leisure Studies, 25*(2), 133–152.

Kiselica, M. S. (2003). Transforming psychotherapy in order to succeed with adolescent boys: Male-friendly practices. *Journal of Clinical Psychology, 59*(11), 1225–1236.

Kiselica, M. S. (2008). *When boys become parents: Adolescent fatherhood in America.* New Brunswick, NJ: Rutgers University Press.

Kiselica, M. S., Englar-Carlson, M., Horne, A. M., & Fisher, M. (2008). A positive psychology perspective on helping boys. In M. S. Kiselica, M. Englar-Carlson, & A. M. Horne (Eds.), *Counseling troubled boys: A practitioner's guidebook* (pp. 31–48). New York: Routledge.

Kiselica, M. S., Stevens, M., & Englar-Carlson, M. (2006, August). Promoting strengths and addressing dysfunction during clinical work with men. In M. S. Kiselica (Chair), *Toward a positive psychology of boys, men, and masculinity.* Symposium presented at the Annual Convention of the American Psychological Association, New Orleans, LA.

Knoester, C., & Eggebeen, D. J. (2006). The effects of the transition to parenthood and subsequent children on men's well-being and social participation. *Journal of Family Issues, 27*, 1532–1560.

Lamb, M. E. (1975). Fathers: Forgotten contributors to child development. *Human Development, 18*, 245–266.

Lamb, M. E. (1986). The changing role of fathers. In M. E. Lamb (Ed.), *The father's role: Applied perspectives* (pp. 3–27). New York: John Wiley.

Lamb, M. E. (Ed.). (1997). *The role of the father in child development* (3rd ed.). New York: John Wiley.

Lamb, M. E. (2000). The history of research on father involvement: An overview. *Marriage & Family Review, 29*, 23–42.

Lamb, M. E. (Ed.). (2004). *The father's role in child development* (4th ed.). New York: John Wiley.

Lamb, M. E., Pleck, J. H., Charnov, E. L., & Levine, J. A. (1985). Paternal behavior in humans. *American Psychologist, 25*, 883–894.

Lamb, M. E., Pleck, J. H., Charnov, E. L., & Levine, J. A. (1987). A biosocial perspective on paternal behavior and involvement. In J. B. Lancaster, J. Altman, A. Rossi, & L. R. Sherrod (Eds.), Parenting across the lifespan: Biosocial perspectives. New York: Academic.

Lehr, R., & MacMillan, P. (2001). The psychological and emotional impact of divorce: The noncustodial fathers' perspective. *Families in Society, 82*(4), 373–382.

Levant, R. F. (1995). Toward the reconstruction of masculinity. In R. F. Levant & W. S. Pollack (Eds.), *A new psychology of men* (pp. 68–89). New York: Basic Books.

Levant, R. F. (1998). Men's changing roles. *The Family Psychologist, 6*(2), 4–6.

Levine, J. A., & Pitt, E. W. (1995). *New expectations: Community strategies for responsible fatherhood.* New York: Families and Work Institute.

Liu, W. M. (2005). The study of men and masculinity as an important multicultural competency consideration. *Journal of Clinical Psychology, 61,* 685–697.

Lupton, D., & Barclay, L. (1997) *Constructing fatherhood: Discourses and experiences.* Thousand Oaks, CA: Sage.

Mahalik, J. R., Good, G. E., & Englar-Carlson, M. (2003). Masculinity scripts, presenting concerns, and help seeking: Implications for practice and training. *Professional Psychology: Research and Practice, 34,* 123–131.

Marsigilo, W., Day, R. D., & Lamb, M. E. (2000). Exploring fatherhood diversity: Implications for conceptualizing father involvement. *Marriage and Family Review, 29*(4), 269–293.

Marks, L., & Palkovitz, R. (2004). American fatherhood types: The good, the bad, and the uninterested. *Fathering, 3,* 113–129.

Palkovitz, R. (1997). Reconstructing involvement: Expanding conceptualizations of men's caring in contemporary families. In A. J. Hawkins & D. C. Dollahite (Eds.), *Generative fathering: Beyond deficit perspectives.* Thousand Oaks, CA: Sage.

Palkovitz, R. (2002). *Involved fathering and men's adult development: Provisional balances.* Mahwah, NJ: Lawrence Erlbaum.

Parke, R. D. (1995). Fathers and families. In M. Borenstein (Ed.), *Handbook of parenting: Status and social conditions of parenting* (pp. 27–63). Mahwah, NJ: Lawrence Erlbaum.

Parke, R. D. (2000). Father involvement: A developmental psychological perspective. *Marriage and Family Review, 29,* 43–58.

Parke, R., & Brott, A. (2003). Yes, fathers really matter! In M. Coleman & L. Ganong (Eds.), *Points & counterpoints: Controversial relationship and family issues in the 21st century (an anthology)* (pp. 182–186). Los Angeles: Roxbury.

Pleck, E. H., & Pleck, J. H. (1997). Fatherhood ideals in the United States: Historical dimensions. In M. E. Lamb, *The role of the father in child development* (3rd ed., pp 33–48). New York: John Wiley.

Pleck, J. H. (1997). Paternal involvement: Levels, sources, and consequences. In M. E. Lamb (Ed.), *The role of the father in child development* (3rd ed., pp. 61–103). New York: John Wiley.

Pope, M., & Englar-Carlson, M. (2001). Fathers and sons: The relationship between violence and masculinity. *The Family Journal: Counseling and Therapy for Couples and Families, 9*(4), 367–374.

Quinn, P. (1999). Supporting and encouraging father involvement in families of children who have a disability. *Child and Adolescent Social Work Journal, 16*(6), 439–454.

Rabinowitz, F. E., & Cochran, S. V. (2002). Recommendations for clinicians concerning psychotherapy with men. *Clinician's Research Digest, 20*(26), 1–2.

Riley, L., & Glass, J. L. (2002). You can't always get what you want: Infant care preferences and use among employed mothers. *Journal of Marriage and Family, 64*(1), 2–15.

Robertson, J., & Fitzgerald, L. F. (1990). The (mis)treatment of men: Effects of client gender role and life-style on diagnosis and attribution of pathology. *Journal of Counseling Psychology, 37*(1), 3–9.

Rochlen, A. B., McKelley, R. A., Suizzo, M, & Scaringi, V. (2008). Predictors of relationship satisfaction, psychological well-being, and life satisfaction among stay-at-home fathers. *Psychology of Men & Masculinity, 9*(1), 17–28.

Seligman, M. E. P., & Csikszentmihalyi, M. (2000). Positive psychology: An introduction. *American Psychologist, 55*(1), 5–14.

Shappiro, J. L. (2001). Therapeutic interventions with fathers. In G. R Brooks & G. E. (Eds.), *The new handbook of psychotherapy and counseling with men: A comprehensive guide to settings, problems, and treatment approaches* (pp. 403–423). San Francisco, CA: Jossey Bass.

Sheldon, K. M., & King, L. (2001). Why positive psychology is necessary. *American Psychology, 56*(3), 216–217.

Silverstein, L. B., Auerbach, C. F., & Levant, R. F. (2002). Contemporary fathers reconstructing masculinity: Clinical implications of gender role strain. *Professional Psychology: Research and Practice, 33*(4), 361–369.

Smith, E. J. (2006). The strength-based counseling model: A paradigm shift in psychology. *Counseling Psychologist, 34*(1), 13–79.

Snarey, J. (1993). *How fathers care for the next generation: A four-decade study.* Cambridge, MA: Harvard University.

Strom, R. D., Beckert, T. E., Strom, S. K., Strom, P. S., & Griswold, D. (2002). Evaluating the success of Caucasian fathers in guiding adolescents. *Adolescence, 37*(145), 131–149.

Tremblay, G., & L'Heureux, P. (2005). Psychosocial intervention with men. *International Journal of Men's Health, 4*(1), 55–71.

U.S. Census Bureau. (2006). Facts for features: Father's Day, June 18. Retrieved March 15, 2007, from http://www.census.gov/Press-Release/www/releases/archives/facts_for_features_special_editions/006794.html

U.S. Department of Health and Human Services. (2006). Promoting responsible fatherhood. Retrieved December 17, 2006, from http://fatherhood.hhs.gov/

Vann, N. (2007). Reflections on the development of fatherhood work. *Applied Developmental Science, 11*(4), 266–268.

# 3

# An Assessment Paradigm for Fathers and Men in Therapy Using Gender Role Conflict Theory

JAMES M. O'NEIL AND MELISSA L. LUJÁN

Over the last four decades, the patriarchal system was weakened by more robust definitions of fathering. Narrow definitions of fathering came under scrutiny, and inaccurate stereotypes were exposed. The stereotype that only women can effectively nurture children has been challenged and debunked. This sexist stereotype devalues men and deprives children of fathers' significant contributions to their human development. Redefining fathering to include the emotional, psychological, and spiritual development of children is one of the most significant outcomes of the feminist and men's movements. The redefinition of fathering holds promise for more functional families and more satisfying family roles for men. New definitions of fathering can also have gender role implications when working with men during therapy.

Being a father, having a father, or losing a father shapes a man's gender role identity. Therefore, fathering can be a critical variable in understanding men in therapy. In this chapter, fathering is discussed as a diagnostic category to assess men's psychological problems using the gender role conflict (GRC) theory. One of the challenges of doing therapy with men is explaining how psychological problems can be

related to sexist gender roles. Few paradigms, if any, exist that conceptualize fathering as a diagnostic category for men in therapy. Fathering
assessment paradigms that assess men's covert masculinity problems are
presented in this chapter. The paradigms imply that fathering can be a
major assessment area for men in therapy.

What is lacking in the psychological literature are paradigms that
assess fathers and their sons in therapy. During a literature review, few
sources were found addressing how to assess fathers and their sons in
therapy. Manuscripts have been published on different types of fathers
and their problems (Kiselica, 1995; Moreland & Schwebel, 1979; Shapiro, 2001; Silverstein, Auerback, & Levant, 2002; Yamamota & Tagami,
2004). Shapiro (2001) discussed how to help men with the transition
to fatherhood and resolve later fatherhood concerns. Silverstein et al.
(2002) discussed discrepancy strain as an issue with fathers and provided some clinical strategies for intervention. Other authors have
focused on teenage fathers (Kiselica, 1995), Japanese fathers (Yamamoto & Tagami, 2004), and psychoeducational programs for fathers
(Moreland & Schwebel, 1979). These previous publications have established fathering as an important concept for therapists, but how fathering could relate to the psychotherapeutic process has gone unexplored.

We first provide an overview of GRC theory and how it is relevant
to fathering. Overt and covert contexts to assess men's fathering problems are discussed. Using these contexts, we then present a GRC assessment paradigm on fathering that clinicians can use when working with
men in therapy. Masculinity ideology, the father wound, and the GRC
model are discussed as important theoretical perspectives when using
the fathering assessment paradigms. Research relevant to GRC, fathering, and the assessment paradigm is briefly reviewed. At the end of the
chapter, a more elaborate diagnostic paradigm is presented when assessing fathers in therapy. A brief clinical vignette is presented demonstrating how the assessment paradigms might be used.

## DEFINING THE RELEVANCE OF GRC TO FATHERING

The construct of GRC has evolved over the last 25 years with numerous
theoretical statements, empirical studies, and operational definitions
(O'Neil, 1981, 2006, 2008; O'Neil, Helms, Gable, David, & Wrightsman, 1986; O'Neil & Egan, 1993; O'Neil & Fishman, 1992; O'Neil,
Fishman, Kinsella-Shaw, 1987; O'Neil, Good, & Holmes, 1995; O'Neil
& Nadeau, 1999). GRC is defined as a psychological state in which
socialized gender roles have negative consequences for the person or
others. GRC occurs when rigid, sexist, or restrictive gender roles result
in restriction, devaluation, or violation of others or self (O'Neil, 2008;
O'Neil et al., 1995). GRC limits one's human potential or restricts
another person's potential. Four psychological domains and three personal experiences further define GRC and represent the complexity of

GRC in people's lives. These domains and personal experiences of GRC are also relevant to assessing men and fathers in therapy.

The psychological domains of GRC define how socialized gender roles are learned in sexist and patriarchal societies. The four domains of GRC include *cognitive*, how we think about gender roles; *affective*, how we feel about gender roles; *behavioral*, how we act, and how we respond to and interact with others and ourselves because of gender roles; and *unconscious*, how gender role dynamics beyond our awareness affect our behavior and produce conflicts (O'Neil et al., 1986; O'Neil et al., 1995). How these GRC domains relate to fathering has gone unexplained. Men may experience GRC in terms of how they think or feel about their fathering roles, have conflicting thoughts and emotions about their own fathers, or behave in dysfunctional ways with their own children. With unconscious GRC, a man would be unaware of the emotional and psychological issues related to his own father or limitations to his own fathering.

The personal experiences of GRC constitute the negative consequences of conforming to, deviating from, or violating the gender role norms of masculinity ideology, resulting in devaluations, restrictions, and violations. Gender role devaluations are negative critiques of self or others when conforming to, deviating from, or violating stereotypic gender role norms of masculinity ideology. Devaluations result in lessening of personal status, stature, or positive regard. Gender role restrictions occur when confining others or oneself to stereotypic norms of masculinity ideology. Restrictions result in controlling people's behavior, limiting one's personal potential, and decreasing human freedom. Gender role violations result from harming oneself, harming others, or being harmed by others because of sexism and restrictive gender role norms. To be violated is to be victimized and abused, which causes psychological and physical pain. According to GRC theory and the empirical research, gender role restrictions, devaluations, and violations have a direct negative impact on men's interpersonal, career, family, and health lives (O'Neil, 1981, 2008; O'Neil et al., 1995; O'Neil & Nadeau, 1999). How men's personal experiences of GRC affect fathering has not been fully conceptualized and, therefore, conceptual analyses are needed.

The overall premise is that fathers' GRC negatively affects their capacity to parent effectively. A man can devalue himself for his inept fathering or restrict his parenting because of masculine stereotypes. Furthermore, when sons or daughters feel devalued, restricted, or violated by their father, they can experience negative emotions and thoughts that affect their overall functioning. A typical fathering conflict may occur when sons deviate from traditional masculinity ideology. Boys who show feminine qualities or fail to meet fathers' expected masculine norms of success can be devalued and restricted by fathers who enforce masculinity ideology and restrictive stereotypes. Father/daughter dynamics can also be affected if the daughter deviates from expected feminine norms and values. Girls who are tomboys or who are not feminine may be devalued by fathers who endorse strict enforcement of femininity ideology. For GRC to be a useful construct with assessing fathers, both overt and covert contexts of fathering problems need to be conceptualized.

## Overt and Covert Contexts of Fathering Problems and GRC

For an assessment paradigm to be established, specific contexts for fathers' problems need to be described. Both overt and covert contexts can explain how fathering, GRC, and the therapeutic process may interact. The overt and covert fathering contexts have clinical importance for therapists when assessing men in therapy.

Overt contexts of fathering are defined as easily identified fathering problems that are obvious to the man or his therapist. Overt fathering problems are very concrete, visible, and usually do not require endless probing or unconscious uncovering. The most obvious fathering problems are actual conflicts that fathers have with their sons and daughters that negatively impact family life. These kinds of problems can be generated from a host of issues that are part of adolescence and family life, such as showing respect, adhering to family norms, obedience, authority and autonomy issues, peer selection, dating, curfews, and many others. Persistent and unresolved problems between fathers and their children can be a painful part of family life from the early years through adulthood. Overt fathering problems also relate to spousal conflicts with child rearing, dual career dilemmas (O'Neil et al., 1987), and sharing family power (Silverstein et al., 2002).

First-time fathers may also have unique problems. Men who parent for the first time may have insecurities about their lack of experience or fears of assuming fathering roles. Fathers may have inadequate knowledge of how to father or have difficulty transitioning into these new roles. Furthermore, Shapiro (2001) suggests that fathers may have problems during childbirth with performance anxieties and worries. Additionally, those entering fatherhood at later stages in their lives or at a young age may pose special problems for men. Fathering likely produces increased pressure to fulfill the provider role and meet additional financial costs. Men may fear losing freedom because of fathering or worry about balancing both work and parenting responsibilities. All of these overt contexts are important to consider when doing therapy with men who are fathers.

The covert contexts of men's fathering are less obvious, more complex, and many times unconscious to the client. The covert contexts of men's fathering problems may include unconscious gender role conflicts that limit a man from solving the overt fathering problems discussed above. This means that gender roles can be primary ways to assess men's problems with fathering and overall psychological functioning. Three covert fathering contexts are masculinity ideology; the father wound, defined as unfinished business with one's own father; and men's patterns of GRC. These three covert contexts are discussed as dynamic forces that shape men's fathering problems and psychological functioning.

## *Overt and Covert Fathering Contextual Model*

The covert contexts of fathering provide a rationale for clinicians to assess a father's problems and psychological functioning. The model shown in Figure 3.1 depicts the overt and covert fathering contexts related to GRC and ineffective parenting. Arrows A1 and B1 imply that restrictive masculinity ideology, unfinished problems with one's father, and the father wound are related to higher GRC. Furthermore, the model implies that higher GRC relates to inconsistent, inept, ineffective, dysfunctional, and dissatisfying fathering. Research and theory exist to support the relationship of masculinity ideology with GRC, as shown by arrow A1 (O'Neil, 2008; Pleck, 1995; Pleck, Sonenstein, & Ku, 1993). No empirical research has documented that clients' unfinished business with their fathers or the father wound relate to GRC, as is implied with arrow B1. There is some research indicating that higher GRC may relate to ineffective fathering for men in general (Alexander, 1999; DeFranc & Mahalik, 2002; McMahon, Winkel, & Luthar, 2002; O'Neil, 2008) as depicted in Figure 3.1, but no research has been completed with fathers who are clients. The concepts in Figure 3.1 are operationally defined and discussed in subsequent sections.

### Masculinity Ideology and Fathering

Restrictive and stereotypic masculinity ideology is the first covert context to understand fathers in therapy. Masculinity ideology refers to "...beliefs about the importance of men adhering to culturally defined standards for male behavior" (Pleck, 1995, p. 19). Fathers who adhere

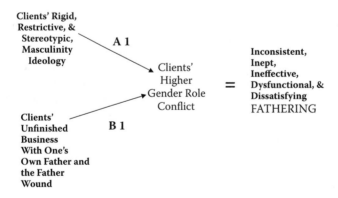

**Figure 3.1**   Overt and covert fathering contexts related to gender role conflict and ineffective fathering.

to strict norms of masculinity may have a limited behavioral repertoire with their children. Masculinity ideologies are primary values and standards that define, restrict, and negatively affect boys' and men's lives (Levant et al., 1992; Mahalik et al., 2003; Pleck, 1995; Pleck et al., 1993; Thompson & Pleck, 1995). Men's cultural beliefs about their roles as fathers can produce negative consequences for their children. For example, a father's masculinity ideology may include the following beliefs: (a) emotions are feminine and should be avoided, (b) power and control are essential to be masculine, (c) toughness is an essential male quality and vulnerability should be avoided, (d) competition and winning are ways to demonstrate masculinity, and (e) the heterosexual orientation is the only way to be a real man or woman. These cultural beliefs can contribute to problems in effective fathering and overall interpersonal functioning.

Many men are unaware that they endorse a masculinity ideology that dictates their attitudes and behaviors in fathering and other interpersonal relationships. Restrictive masculinity ideology may produce rigid views of fathering, distorted gender role schemas (Mahalik, 2001; O'Neil & Nadeau, 1999), and patterns of GRC. These distorted schemas and patterns can restrict sons' and daughters' gender role ideologies and identities and reinforce sexist attitudes and behaviors in both fathers and their children.

### Unfinished Business With Fathers: The Father Wound

The second fathering context in Figure 3.1 relates to a man's past relationship with his own father. "Unfinished business" with fathers is defined as unresolved tensions, problems, and conflicts that negatively affect a man's personal and interpersonal functioning. Almost everyone has unfinished business with their father. The critical question is whether these issues affect a man's fathering and overall psychological health. Unfinished business with fathers spans a continuum from minor conflicts with only limited negative effects to more serious problems like the father wound. We define the father wound as a child's internalization of a father's emotional/psychological problems and pain. Sons and daughters can experience their father's pain as they observe him throughout childhood. The father wound can be conscious or unconscious. In adulthood, the same pain may be present and passed on to his children. Sons or daughters make their fathers' pain their own, and in this way the father wound becomes intergenerational. The wound can affect the development of the personality, overall psychological functioning, and the ability to father effectively.

For example, the first author counseled a client named Nick, a 35-year-old White father who was emotionally, socially, and interpersonally insecure. Nick expressed intense anger, anxiety, and depression, but could not identify the source of his symptoms. He disclosed chronic unhappiness, aloneness, and despair. After a careful examination of

Nick's family history, it was apparent that he had a father wound and unfinished business with his father. Nick at first denied having unresolved problems with his father. After many months of probing, it was apparent that he lacked respect for his father, felt sorry for him, and was angry at him for years of negativity and neglect. Nick reported that his father had continuously devalued people and found fault with anyone he encountered. His father's wounds included self-hate, low self-esteem, inability to trust others, and grief about not being able to function effectively both in work and in close relationships. His father expressed these negative emotions daily, and Nick absorbed his father's pain throughout childhood and adolescence. Therefore, Nick's father's wounds became his own. He expressed both his father's pain and his own through anger, anxiety, and depression. Examples such as this make the father wound an important domain for therapists to assess. This is particularly salient because the father wound can be transmitted intergenerationally and be complexly related to masculinity issues and GRC.

## GRC Model

GRC is hypothesized to contribute to dysfunctional fathering. Therefore, Figure 3.2 shows the GRC model as the second paradigm to assess fathers in therapy (O'Neil, 2008, 1981; O'Neil et al., 1995). A brief overview of the concepts in Figure 3.2 is given here (for more detail about the theory, see O'Neil, 2008; O'Neil et al., 1995; O'Neil & Nadeau, 1999). In the center of Figure 3.2, men's gender role socialization and the masculinity ideology and norms are shown as conceptually related to men's fear of femininity. Men's conscious and unconscious fears of femininity have existed in the literature for many years (Blazina, 2003; Boehm, 1930; Freud, 1937; Hays, 1964; Horney, 1967; Jung, 1953, 1954; Lederer, 1968; Norton, 1997). How the fear of femininity relates to dysfunctional fathering has gone unexplored by theorists and researchers. Men's fears of femininity are theoretically linked to the four patterns of GRC. Figure 3.2 shows these four patterns of GRC including: success/power/competition (SPC); restrictive emotionality (RE); restrictive affectionate behavior between men (RABBM); and conflict between work and family relations (CBWFR). The four patterns of GRC are operationally defined below.

RE is defined as having restrictions and fears about expressing one's feelings as well as restrictions in finding words to express basic emotions. RE may also include restricting other people's emotions. RABBM represents restrictions in expressing one's feelings and thoughts with other men and difficulty touching other men. This pattern implies limited emotional disclosure and affection toward others. The third factor, SPC, describes strong desires for success pursued through competition and power. CBWFR reflects restrictions in balancing work, school, and family relations resulting in health problems, overwork, stress, and a lack of leisure and relaxation.

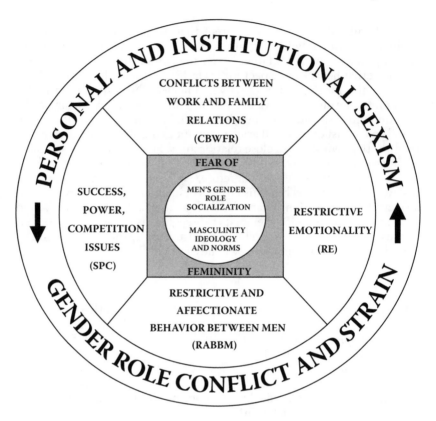

**Figure 3.2** Gender role conflict model: Patterns of men's gender role conflict. *Source:* Modified from O'Neil, Good, and Holmes (1995). Reprinted by permission: Basic Books, a member of Perseus Book Group.

Finally, on the outside of Figure 3.2, personal and institutional sexism and GRC and strain are shown as an overarching reality that shapes men's lives. This part of the model implies that sexist structures in society and men's gender role socialization are directly related to men's GRC. The model in Figure 3.2 is a primary way to summarize the theoretical premises of men's GRC and has relevance to assessing fathers in therapy.

The critical clinical question is how do masculinity ideology, the fear of femininity, and the patterns of GRC relate to ineffective fathering? Overall, to be a fully effective father, men may need to transcend sexist and restrictive masculinity ideologies and norms. This means that functional fathers have confronted their fears of femininity and GRC. They have worked through inevitable dilemmas related to restrictive gender roles. To effectively father, men need to have a flexible and expansive view of gender roles and resolve patterns of GRC depicted in Figure 3.2. For example, fathers who are unable to label, express, or experience deep emotions and empathize with their sons and daughters (i.e., RE) are likely to have significant limitations in positive fathering. Children are often emotionally expressive, and fathers who possess RE may be unable to process their feelings. Fathers who have unresolved GRC with SPC may be limited in dealing with the inevitable power and control issues with sons and daughters throughout the different life stages. Fathers with unresolved GRC with homophobia or restricted definitions of affection, intimacy, and sexuality may be ineffective in helping their children with homophobia in their schools, sexual identity issues, and constructive sex education.

## Empirical Research on Gender Role Conflict and Fathering

What empirical evidence supports assessing men's GRC in the context of fathering and family life? Some research exists supporting the development of an assessment paradigm that links GRC with both overt and covert contexts of fathering. Research does show that GRC significantly relates to emotional problems that may interfere with fathering, such as depression, anxiety, marital dissatisfaction, substance abuse, homophobia, and violence toward others (O'Neil, 2008). Furthermore, men's GRC has been theoretically and empirically related to attitudes and behaviors that negatively impact others (J. A. Hayes & Mahalik, 2000; O'Neil, 1981, 2008; O'Neil & Egan, 1993; Pleck, 1995). Other studies indicate that RE has been significantly associated with problems with sociability and intimacy (Sharpe, Heppner, & Dixon, 1995), a lack of interpersonal competence/closeness, and less intimate self-disclosure (Bruch, Berko, & Haase, 1998). Although these studies lack a specific fathering context, the results do have implications for understanding dynamics between fathers and their children.

Only three studies have directly assessed whether GRC relates to fathering issues (Alexander, 1999; DeFranc & Mahalik, 2002; McMahon et al., 2000). In one of the only studies that assessed father-son GRC, men who perceived their fathers and themselves to have less GRC reported closer attachments to and less psychological separation from both parents (DeFranc & Mahalik, 2002). McMahon et al. (2000) found that drug-dependent men's RE was significantly associated with a restricted definition of fathering. Alexander (1999) found that RE significantly related to parenting dissatisfaction and a lack of parenting self-efficacy. Additionally, he found that, when men's RE increased, parenting self-efficacy and fathering satisfaction decreased. Other studies have found nonsignificant or mixed results when studying the relationship of GRC to father-son mutuality (Marrocco, 2001), sex offenders' father-son relationships (Gullickson, 1993; Todryk, 1999), and attachment to parents (Covell, 1998; Swenson, 1998).

Healthy fathering presumes that sons and daughters have bonded with their fathers and are securely attached to them. Researchers have argued that GRC relates to problems with attachment, separation, individualization, disidentification, and conflictual independence. What is interesting is that theorists have more closely associated boys' attachment problems with mothers rather than with fathers. Attachment to parents and GRC has been investigated in ten studies (O'Neil, 2008). All the patterns of men's GRC have significantly correlated with attachment to both mothers and fathers. Six studies used either canonical correlations or structural equation modeling documenting the relationship of GRC to attachment (O'Neil, 2008). Overall, these initial studies suggest that GRC is related to complex interpersonal dynamics that affects attachment and separation from parents. These results have implications for understanding how fathering and GRC moderate and mediate each other.

## *Summary of GRC Theory and Research Relevant to Fathering*

From the previous theory and research, we conclude the following: Socialized, sexist, and restrictive gender roles internalized as masculinity ideology can produce GRC that negatively affects men's potential for fathering. Men's unfinished business and internalized wounds of their fathers can produce GRC and other psychological problems that can negatively affect fathering. Restrictive and sexist cognitions and emotions about masculinity and fears of femininity can produce gender role schemas that can negatively affect fathering. Fears of femininity and homophobia can negatively affect fathering in terms of emotional and affectionate expression. The patterns of men's GRC (SPC, RE, RABBM, CBWFR) limit men's capacity to father. Fathers can restrict, devalue, and violate their children because of sexist and restrictive gender roles, which can affect boys' and girls' capacity to attach to parents and therefore to be fathered. Fathers' GRC and both sons' and daughters' GRC dynamically interact over the lifespan. Research in three studies indicates that GRC is related to restrictions in fathering. Additional research indicates that GRC is related to men's problems in interpersonal relationships, intimacy, emotional expression, and self-disclosure. Attachment problems are related to men's GRC, but how these bonding patterns relate to fathering is unknown. Overall, there is enough theory and research for clinicians to begin to make diagnostic assessments of men's fathering issues during therapy. Based on the previous theory and research, an initial diagnostic schema to assess fathers' GRC is presented below.

## DIAGNOSTIC SCHEMA TO ASSESS FATHERS DURING THERAPY

Figure 3.3 depicts a diagnostic schema to assess fathers during therapy and includes eight domains that can be used to assess fathers in the covert or overt gender role contexts discussed earlier. The diagnostic schema's goal is to provide domains that therapists can use when developing treatment plans with fathers. The eight domains are described in the following sections.

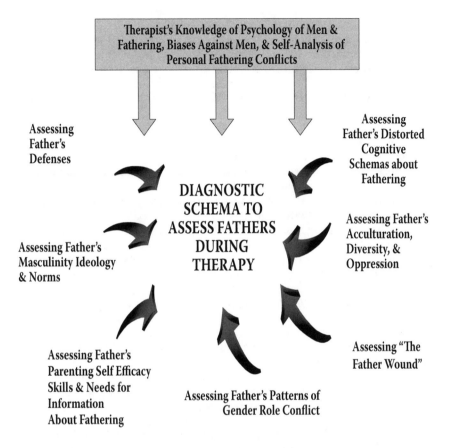

**Figure 3.3** Diagnostic schema to assess fathers during therapy.

### Therapist's Knowledge of the Psychology of Men and Fathering, Bias Against Men, and Self-Analysis of Personal Fathering Conflicts

This self-assessment area has three dimensions. Therapists need to assess their knowledge about fathering and the psychology of men. Therapists can assess the knowledge they have on fathering and the psychological consequences of restrictive gender roles. No standard curriculum currently exists on what therapists should know when doing therapy with men in the context of GRC. Until such a curriculum exists, therapists should consult with the current authorities on therapy with men (Brooks & Good, 2001; Englar-Carlson & Stevens, 2006; Pollack & Levant, 1998; Rabinowitz & Cochran, 2002). Furthermore, therapists should also consult the literature on fathering and its relevance to helping men (Kiselica, 1995; Lamb, 2004; Osherson, 1987; Shapiro, 2001).

Another critical domain for therapists to assess is biases toward fathers and men. Therapists' biases against men have been documented (Robertson & Fitzgerald, 1990), but few studies have assessed prejudice against fathers. Two studies have shown that therapists' GRC significantly relates to having less liking for nontraditional and homosexual men (M. M. Hayes, 1985; Wisch & Mahalik, 1999). Current stereotyping and having biases against men are probably as frequent as they were with women in the 1970s (Brodsky & Holroyd, 1975). Therefore, therapists need to evaluate continuously the degree that their stereotypic biases may affect their assessment of fathers.

The third issue is therapists' awareness of unfinished business or father wounds they might have with their own fathers. This is a critical countertransference issue when using fathering as a diagnostic category. Therapists can assess whether they have unresolved conflicts with their own fathers that may interfere with the therapy processes. Without this awareness, therapists may not recognize a client's problems with fathering and avoid discussing it. Expressed more precisely, countertransference may impede the therapeutic process.

## Assessing Father's Masculinity Ideology and Norms

Assessing masculinity ideology and norms with fathers includes probing values and standards that define, restrict, and negatively affect a man's life. There are numerous questions that can be asked about masculinity ideology during therapy. The critical question is what internalized masculine values does the client have that restrict his approaches to fathering? More specifically, how much do rigid, sexist, or stereotypic values impede positive fathering? Were these masculine values learned from the client's own father? Therapeutic questions about a client's masculinity ideology can be an important part of therapy with men. Many fathers may not know any alternative male values to replace restrictive and sexist ones. The therapist can help the client discern new values that are not sexist or restrictive. This therapeutic process involves discussing the healthy aspects of men's gender roles and patterns of positive masculinity with fathers (O'Neil & Luján, in press; Luján & O'Neil, 2008). This means identifying men's strengths, such as responsibility, courage, altruism, resiliency, service, protection of others, social justice, perseverance, generativity, and nonviolent problem solving. This kind of activity moves away from what is wrong with men and fathers, and toward identifying the qualities that empower men to improve their fathering, their families, and their lives.

## Assessing Father's Defenses

Discussion of a man's fathering and his past experiences as a son are issues that may activate psychological defenses. To our knowledge, no studies have correlated men's defensiveness and problems with fathering. Defensiveness is important to assess because many theorists have conceptualized men's socialization experiences as a defensive process (Boehm, 1930; Jung, 1953; O'Neil & Nadeau, 1999). Defensiveness may serve various functions for fathers that therapists can actively assess. For example, defensiveness can mediate difficult and powerful emotions, help men cope with fears about appearing feminine or being emasculated, and help men protect against perceived losses of power and control. These defensive functions could be important vantage points to understand fathers in therapy. Additionally, therapists can point out that defensiveness can produce restrictions in thought and behavior, emotional and cognitive distortions, overreactions, cognitive blind spots, and increased potential for restriction and devaluation of others (O'Neil & Nadeau, 1999). The client can consider how these defensive postures affect his parenting or other parts of his life.

Therapists can directly explore a client's defensiveness about his father or fathering competence. One quick way to assess whether there is defensiveness related to a client's fathering is to ask some pointed questions. For example, the client could be asked, "How does your relationship with your father affect (a) your current problems as a man, and (b) your effectiveness as a father with your own children?" Verbal and nonverbal responses to these questions could determine how to proceed with the therapeutic process. Wherever there are strong defenses, there are also usually deep emotions. The assessment of defensiveness about fathering can also be a strategy to uncover repressed or difficult emotions about one's own father or fathering.

### Assessing Father's Distorted Cognitive Schemas About Fathering

Distorted cognitive schemas about fathering are inaccurate, narrow, and sexist views of gender roles as they impact fathering. Distorted cognitive schemas develop when men experience pressure, fear, or anxiety about meeting or deviating from stereotypic notions of masculinity. Many men have internalized a definition of fathering that is based on rigid and patriarchal values. The traditional definition of fathering exclusively focuses on provider roles, discipline, protection, and enforcement of a moral code. Traditional definitions of fathering have excluded important emotional, psychological, and educational processes. Therefore, traditional fathering may not include active involvement with such important male issues as emotional development, introspection, spiritual and sexual education, self-confidence, fears of failure, problem solving, and decision making. Some fathers may define these issues as feminine, women's work, and not part of traditional masculinity ideology.

What can therapists do with distorted cognitive schemas about fathering? Mahalik (1999, 2001) has identified four steps in helping men with their distorted cognitions, including (a) assessing the specific areas of men's cognitive distortion; (b) educating men about how cognitions, feelings, and behaviors are interrelated; (c) exploring the illogical nature and accuracy of the cognitive distortions; and (d) modifying the biased distortions with more rationality. These steps provide a useful framework for working with distorted cognitive schemas, GRC, and fathering issues. Exploring and resolving fathers' distortions about the meaning of masculinity and fathering can enhance the therapeutic alliance and set the stage for emotional release and effective problem solving.

## Assessing Father's Acculturation, Diversity, and Oppression

There is diversity with fathering values and attitudes based on race, class, age, ethnicity, religion, sexual orientation, and acculturation experience. Therapists and clients can explore how ethnic, racial, and acculturation variables affect fathering attitudes and values. Different races, classes, and ethnicities approach fathering in unique ways that need to be understood. For those fathers who have acculturated to American society, there may be contradictions in fathering values between this society and their society of origin. The therapist may need to help the man understand his parenting in the context of his racial, ethnic, and cultural identity (Wester, 2008). Therapists can help fathers reconcile conflicting values about fathering in terms of their cultural and bicultural identities. Therapists also need to consider how diversity variables can promote positive parenting and how they can produce barriers. Most importantly, these diversity issues need to be understood in the context of the overall societal demands on men that can be oppressive and sexist.

Personal oppression from sexism, racism, classism, ethnocentrism, heterosexism, or any other discrimination needs to be assessed in the context of any man's fathering role. An oppressed man is usually angry, humiliated, emasculated, and vulnerable. For example, a father who cannot provide for his family (a basic masculine mandate in our society) because of racism is likely to feel angry, vulnerable, worthless, shamed, embarrassed, desperate, and inadequate as a man. When a man experiences these emotions, effective fathering may become irrelevant or less important. Survival and how to avoid further discrimination and humiliation may become the main priority. Some men will compensate for the oppression by becoming hypermasculine or aggressive. Oppression, discrimination, and poverty are not conducive to effective fathering and are serious barriers to many men's desires to be positive fathers. Therapists need to have multicultural, acculturative, and diverse perspectives on fathering when working with a wide array of men.

## Assessing the Father Wound

Assessment of the father wound during the therapy process is complex. Many times assessing the family of origin can help the therapist explore whether the client has internalized a father wound. Sometimes, simple exercises or homework assignments can uncover the wounds. For example, having a client draw a picture of his overall relationship with his father in the past or present can bring wounds into clear focus. Another activity could be writing a brief essay on the quality of the relationship with his father as a young boy. Having the client bring in a picture of his father can help focus the discussion of the father-son relationship. Many times, the path to healing is through increased compassion for the father's wound as he experienced it.

### Assessing Father's Patterns of Gender Role Conflict

Therapists can assess the four empirically derived patterns of GRC (SPC, RE, RABBM, CBWFR) in the context of men's fathering roles and functions (see Figure 3.2). The assessment of men's patterns of GRC as part of the therapy process has support from the research. All four GRC patterns have significantly correlated with depression, anxiety, stress, low self-esteem, shame, intimacy problems, marital dissatisfaction, homophobia, attachment problems, and abuses of women (O'Neil, 2008). The GRC patterns and these problems can impede effective fathering. For example, fathers need to be able to process their own emotions and the feelings of their children since family life can be emotionally charged. Constructive use of power and control is critical in successful parenting as sons and daughters test limits and challenge authority. Restriction of affectionate behavior can produce distance between fathers and their children. The CBWFR is a critical problem to be resolved because stress and fatigue do not contribute to effective fathering.

Direct questioning of clients about the degree to which they experience the patterns of gender role conflict is one way to assess fathers. Additionally, the gender role conflict scale (GRCS) and the gender role conflict checklist (O'Neil, 1988) can be used as diagnostic tools both in therapy (O'Neil, 2006; Robertson, 2006) and workshops for men (O'Neil, 1996, 2001; O'Neil & Roberts Carroll, 1988). The direct assessment of GRC can help clients develop a gender role vocabulary that can help them understand their psychological problems. Identifying GRC patterns can also stimulate discussion and emotional disclosure about the personal experience of fathering. One of the primary roles for the therapist is to listen to the client's story about being a man, interpret the story from a gender role perspective, and provide support for making healthy changes.

### Assessing Self-Efficacy in Fathering and Needs for Information About Fathering

In our literature search we found information about parenting self-efficacy but no specific theory or measures on fathering self-efficacy. Fathering self-efficacy is defined as the father's belief in his ability to effectively fulfill parental roles, functions, and responsibilities. As with attitudes about problem solving (Heppner, Witty, & Dixon, 2004), we hypothesize that a father's belief in his ability to father effectively is one of the most critical variables in actually developing positive fathering. From our perspective, fathering self-efficacy is more likely to occur if fathers have useful information on fathering roles, functions, and processes. Many fathers will have insufficient information about how to father, and this lack of information can produce insecurities about parenting or unrealistic norms about positive fathering. Therapists can be a source of information on the positive effects that fathers can have on their children. Books and articles can be given to fathers to help them develop a personal framework for parenting and how to create enjoyable fathering.

Many fathers can obtain needed information and fathering skills in psychoeducational group programs. These psychoeducational interventions can be developed by mental health professionals using the content in Figures 3.1–3.3. Changing strongly socialized attitudes about fatherhood may require potent interventions over extended periods of time. Furthermore, how to attract men to these fathering programs may require creative advertising. Research indicates that titles and formats can activate negative attitudes about help seeking (Blazina & Marks, 2001; Robertson & Fitzgerald, 1992; Rochlen, McKelley, & Pituch, 2006). Fathering programs should be described in positive terms that communicate men's strengths and vitality.

## APPLICATION OF THE ASSESSMENT PARADIGM TO THERAPY

### *Overall Assessment and Background*

The client mentioned earlier in the chapter, Nick, is a good example of using the assessment paradigm in therapy. As was stated, Nick had a father wound. His presenting problems were chronic depression, anxiety, and angry outbursts at his son. Nick had no idea why he experienced these problems. He also wondered why he felt distance and ambivalence about his own son.

The first step was to complete a family history on Nick's relationship with his own parents. Nick reported that his father was distant, neglectful, and emotionally harsh. Nick's father was a second-generation Irish American who had developed a masculinity ideology that included restrictive emotionality and a strong need for total control in all situations. Nick's father also had high needs for success and power, but he had failed to move beyond his entry-level sales job. Therefore, he felt small, insignificant, and powerless.

There was distance between Nick and the therapist in the initial therapy sessions. It was the same distance he experienced with his father, his son, and most relationships with other men. The therapist acknowledged Nick's courage in seeking help and facing his problems. His pain was quite evident. He had flat affect and expressed his embarrassment for being in therapy. The interpersonal distance toward the therapist slowly diminished as Nick began to feel safe and accepted. The assessment paradigm in Figure 3.3 helped determine Nick's overall psychological and interpersonal state in the following assessment domains.

## Assessing Masculinity Ideology and Norms

The therapist hypothesized that Nick might have restrictive masculinity ideology that related to his psychological problems. Nick's masculinity ideology and norms were assessed. The therapist asked questions about how Nick saw his male role in the context of family, work, and society. The therapist also asked these same questions about Nick's father. The conclusion was like father, like son. Both father and son held rigid views of masculinity that limited their behavioral repertoire and impacted their interpersonal functioning in their father-son relationships.

## Assessing Father's Defenses

Nick's defenses were assessed by asking him what part he personally played in his interpersonal problems. He had a highly developed defensive structure that included both denial and projection. He denied that any of his problems were his own and blamed others for his pain and failures. When challenged on his position, he evidenced nonverbal cues of discomfort and annoyance. The therapist recognized this defensiveness and realized that these defenses were likely to operate during the entire therapy process.

## Assessing Father's Distorted Cognitive Schema About Fathering

The therapist also assessed Nick's cognitive distortions about masculinity and fathering roles. Nick had numerous distortions about what "positive fathering" means. Just as with his own father, he believed that restricting emotions and stern discipline were the building blocks for effective parenting. Even though he had internalized his father distortions, he was angry about feeling neglected and disconfirmed by his father. Consequently, Nick did not have a positive fathering context to relate to his own son.

## Assessing Father's Acculturation, Diversity, and Oppression

Nick had limited awareness of how his Irish American ethnicity related to his overall functioning as a man. There was no awareness of how his Irish ancestors had passed down masculine values and norms that were primarily sexist and interpersonally restrictive. The acculturation domain was assessed through taking a family history and having Nick create a family tree. Through these activities, Nick was able to see how his ethnic values were operating.

## The Father Wound

As mentioned earlier, the father wound was quite evident in Nick's psychological dynamics. Nick had observed his father's wounds throughout childhood, but was unaware of why his father was so cold, detached, and unable to connect to him personally or socially. The father wound was defined for Nick. He was given a homework assignment to uncover any information about his father's childhood and adolescence that may have contributed to his father's wounds becoming his own.

## Assessing Father's Patterns of Gender Role Conflict

Nick's patterns of GRC were assessed using the gender role conflict scale. All four of the patterns of GRC were highly rated. High scores were found with RE, SPC, RABBM, CBWFR. Explaining these scores to Nick included discussions about the cost of restrictive gender roles. Furthermore, the therapist presented information about how conceptions of masculinity can be a hazard to men's mental health and functioning in fathering roles.

## Assessing Self-Efficacy in Fathering and Needs for Information About Fathering

Nick's fathering self-efficacy was simply assessed by asking him what he knew about fathering skills. From his response, it was very apparent that Nick had few skills and limited information about fathering. The therapist provided a list of fathering skills in the following areas: listening, communication skills, discipline, problem solving, dealing with emotions, and child safety. The next step was to have Nick read about fathering skills as the initial area to address in changing his fathering approach. The therapist also mentioned that research has shown that active fathering decreases the frequency of behavior problems, enhances cognitive development, and decreases delinquency (Sarkadi, Kristiansson, Oberklaid, & Bremberg, 2008). The goal of exposing Nick to information on fathering was to enhance Nick's self-efficacy in fathering.

Using these insights, the therapist was able to create a treatment plan for Nick that allowed him to work with his father wound, GRC, and his other psychological problems.

# FINAL THOUGHTS

The three assessment paradigms represent our initial ideas on how to use fathering as a focal point during men's therapy. Further elaboration on the theoretical linkages between fathering and GRC are needed. Research correlating fathering issues with GRC would help document these theoretical links. Furthermore, research that focuses on important concepts such as the father wound and father's self-efficacy could help therapists develop better treatment plans for fathers. Case studies of clients who have fathering problems or who have worked through fathering issues are critically needed. Documented interventions by therapists who have helped fathers could make fathering a more credible diagnostic area. Moreover, therapists can create paradigms of positive parenting that fathers can use in becoming more effective fathers. These positive dimensions of fathering can help men see fathering not as masculine or feminine, but as one of the most rewarding and challenging human roles in adult life.

## REFERENCES

Alexander, P. E. (1999). The relationship between masculinity ideology and gender role conflict to parenting and marital issues. (Doctoral dissertation, University of Missouri-Columbia). *Dissertation Abstracts International, 59*, 3678.

Blazina, C. (2003). *The cultural myth of masculinity.* Westport, CT: Praeger.

Blazina, C., & Marks, I. (2001). College men's affective reactions to individual therapy, psychoeducation workshops, and men's support group brochures: The influence of gender role conflict and power dynamics upon help seeking attitudes. *Psychotherapy, 38*, 297–305.

Boehm, F. (1930). The femininity-complex in men. *International Journal of Psychoanalysis, 11*, 444–469.

Brodsky, A., & Holroyd, J. (1975). Report of the task force on sex bias and sex-role stereotyping in psychotherapeutic practice. *American Psychologist, 30*, 1169–1175.

Brooks, G. R., & Good, G. E. (Eds.) (2001). *The new handbook of psychotherapy and counseling with men: A comprehensive guide to settings, problems, and treatment approaches.* San Francisco: Jossey-Bass.

Bruch, M. A., Berko, E. H., & Haase, R. F. (1998). Shyness, masculine ideology, physical attractiveness, and emotional inexpressiveness: Testing a mediational model of men's interpersonal competence. *Journal of Counseling Psychology, 45*, 84–97.

Covell, A. (1998). Characteristics of college males who are likely to sexually harass women: A test of a mediated model. (Doctoral dissertation, University of Southern California, 1998). *Dissertation Abstracts International, 60*, 2400.

DeFranc, W., & Mahalik, J.R. (2002). Masculine gender role conflict and stress in relation to parental attachment and separation. *Psychology of Men and Masculinity, 3*, 51–60.

Englar-Carlson, M., & Stevens, M.A. (Eds.) (2006). *In the room with men: A casebook of therapeutic change.* Washington, DC: APA Books.

Freud, S. (1937). Analysis terminable and interminable. In D. Rieff (Ed.), *Freud: Therapy and techniques* (pp. 233–271). New York: Macmillan.

Gullickson, G. E. (1993). Gender role conflict in sex offenders. (Doctoral dissertation, University of Iowa, 1993). *Dissertation Abstracts International, 55,* 2008.

Hayes, J. A., & Mahalik, J. R. (2000). Gender role conflict and psychological distress in male counseling center clients. *Psychology of Men and Masculinity, 2,* 116–125.

Hayes, M. M. (1985). Counselor sex-role values and effects on attitudes toward, and treatment of non-traditional male clients. (Doctoral dissertation, Ohio State University, 1985). *Dissertation Abstracts International, 45,* 3072.

Hays, H. R. (1964). *The dangerous sex: The myth of feminine evil.* New York: Pocket Books.

Heppner, P. P., Witty, T. E., & Dixon, W. A. (2004). Problem-solving appraisal and human adjustment: A review of 20 years of research using the Problem Solving Inventory. *The Counseling Psychologist, 32,* 344–428.

Horney, K. (1967). *Feminine psychology.* New York: Norton.

Jung, K. (1953). *Animus and anima.* Collected Works, vol. 7. New York: Pantheon.

Jung, K. (1954). *Concerning archetypes, with special reference to the anima concept.* Collected Works, vol. 9, Part I. New York: Pantheon.

Kiselica, M.S. (1995). *Multicultural counseling with teenage fathers.* Thousand Oaks, CA: Sage.

Lamb, M. E. (2004). *The role of the father in child development* (4th ed). Hoboken, NJ: John Wiley & Sons.

Lederer, W. (1968). *The fear of women.* NY: Harcourt, Brace, Jovanovich.

Levant, R. F., Hirsch, L., Celentano, E., Cozza, T., Hill, S., MacRachorn, M., et al. (1992). The male role: An investigation of contemporary norms. *Journal of Mental Health Counseling, 14,* 325–337.

Luján, M. L., & O'Neil, J. M. (2008, August). Investigating parameters of healthy masculinity using the Positive Masculinity Checklist. Paper to be presented at the American Psychological Association, Boston, MA.

Mahalik, J. R. (1999). Incorporating a gender role strain perspective in assessing and treating men's cognitive distortions. *Professional Psychology: Research and Practice, 30,* 333–340.

Mahalik, J. R. (2001). Cognitive therapy for men. In G. R. Brooks & G. E. Good (Eds.), *The new handbook of psychotherapy and counseling with men: A comprehensive guide to settings, problems, and treatment approaches, Vol. 2* (pp. 544–564). San Francisco: Jossey-Bass.

Mahalik, J. R., Locke, B. D., Ludlow, L. H., Diemer, M. A., Scott, R. P., Gottfried, M., et al. (2003). Development of the Conformity to Masculine Norms Inventory. *Psychology of Men and Masculinity, 4,* 3–25.

Marrocco, F. A. (2001). Gender role conflict in young males as a function of paternal/filial mutual identification and personal warmth and empathy. (Doctoral dissertation, Long Island University, 2001). *Dissertation Abstracts International, 52,* 4226.

McMahon, T. J., Winkel, J. D., & Luthar, S. S. (2000, August). Gender role conflict, drug dependence, and fatherhood: A comparative analysis. In J. M. O'Neil & G. E. Good (Chairs), *Gender role conflict in the year 2000: Innovative directions.* Symposium conducted at the American Psychological Association, Washington, DC.

Moreland, J., & Schwebel, A. I. (1979). A gender role transcendent perspective on fathering. *The Counseling Psychologist, 9,* 45–53.

Norton, J. (1997). Deconstructing the fear of femininity. *Feminism & Psychology, 7*, 441–447.

O'Neil, J. M. (1981). Male sex-role conflict, sexism, and masculinity: Implications for men, women, and the counseling psychologist. *The Counseling Psychologist, 9*, 61–80.

O'Neil, J. M. (1988). The gender role conflict checklist. Storrs, CT: Department of Educational Psychology, University of Connecticut.

O'Neil, J. M. (1996). The gender role journey workshop: Exploring sexism and gender role conflict in a coeducational setting. In M. A. Andronico (Ed.), *Men in groups: Insights, interventions, psychoeducational work* (pp. 193–213). Washington, DC: APA Books.

O'Neil, J. M. (2001). Promoting men's growth and development: Teaching the new psychology of men using psychoeducational philosophy and interventions. In G. Brooks & G. E. Good (Eds.), *The new handbook of psychotherapy and counseling with men: A comprehensive guide to settings, problems, and treatment approaches* (pp. 639–663), vol. 2. San Francisco: Jossey-Bass.

O'Neil, J. M. (2006). Helping Jack heal his emotional wounds: The gender role conflict diagnostic schema. In M. Englar-Carlson & M. Stevens (Eds.), *In the therapy room with men: A casebook about psychotherapeutic process and change with male clients* (pp. 259–284). Washington, DC: American Psychological Association.

O'Neil, J. M. (2008). Summarizing twenty-five years of research on men's gender-role conflict using the gender role conflict scale: New research paradigms and clinical implications. *The Counseling Psychologist, 36*, 358–445.

O'Neil, J. M., & Egan, J. (1993). Abuses of power against women: Sexism, gender role conflict, and psychological violence. In E. Cook (Ed.), *Women, relationships, and power: Implications for counseling* (pp. 49–78). Alexandria, VA: ACA Press.

O'Neil, J. M., & Fishman, D. (1992). Adult men's career transitions and gender role themes. In D. Lea & Z. Leibowitz (Eds.), *Adult career development: Concepts, issues, and practices*. Alexandria, VA: American Association for Counseling and Development Press.

O'Neil, J. M., Fishman, D. M., & Kinsella-Shaw, M. (1987). Dual-career couples' career transitions and normative dilemmas: A preliminary assessment model. *The Counseling Psychologist, 15*(1), 50–96.

O'Neil, J. M., Good, G. E., & Holmes, S. (1995). Fifteen years of theory and research on men's gender role conflict: New paradigms for empirical research. In R. Levant & W. Pollack (Eds.), *The new psychology of men* (pp. 164–206). New York: Basic Books.

O'Neil, J. M., Helms, B., Gable, R., David, L., & Wrightsman, L. (1986). Gender role conflict scale (GRCS): College men's fears of femininity. *Sex Roles, 14*, 335–350.

O'Neil, J. M. & Luján, M. L. (in press). Preventing boy's problems in schools through psychoeducational programming: A call to action. *Psychology in the Schools*.

O'Neil, J. M., & Nadeau, R. A. (1999). Men's gender-role conflict, defense mechanism, and self-protective defensive strategies: Explaining men's violence against women from a gender-role socialization perspective. In M. Harway & J. M. O'Neil (Eds.), *What causes men's violence against women?* (pp. 89–116). Thousand Oaks, CA: Sage Publications.

O'Neil, J. M., & Roberts Carroll, M. (1988). A gender role workshop focused on sexism, gender role conflict, and the gender role journey. *Journal of Counseling and Development, 67,* 193–197.

Osherson, S. (1987). Finding our fathers: The unfinished business in manhood. New York: Fawcett.

Pleck, J. H. (1995). The gender role strain paradigm: An update. In R. F. Levant & W. S. Pollack (Eds.), *A new psychology of men* (pp. 11–32). New York: Basic Books.

Pleck, J. H., Sonenstein, F. L., & Ku, L. C. (1993). Masculinity ideology and its correlates. In S. Oskamp & M. Costanzo (Eds.), Gender issues in social psychology (pp. 85–110). Newbury Park, CA: Sage Publications.

Pollack, W. S., & Levant, R. F. (1998). *New psychotherapies for men.* New York: Wiley.

Rabinowitz, F. E., & Cochran, S. V. (2002). *Deepening psychotherapy with men.* Washington, DC: American Psychological Association.

Robertson, J. M. (2006). Finding Joshua's soul: Working with religious men. In M. Englar-Carlson & M. A. Stevens (Eds.), *In the room with men: A casebook of therapeutic change.* Washington, DC: APA Books

Robertson, J. M., & Fitzgerald, L. F. (1990). The (Mis)treatment of men: Effects of client gender role and life-style on diagnosis and attribution of pathology. *Journal of Counseling Psychology, 37,* 3–9.

Robertson, J. M., & Fitzgerald, L. F. (1992). Overcoming the masculine mystique: Preferences for alternative forms of assistance among men who avoid counseling. *Journal of Counseling Psychology, 39,* 240–246.

Rochlen, A. B., McKelley, R. A., & Pituch, K. A. (2006). A preliminary examination of the "Real Men. Real Depression" campaign. *Psychology of Men and Masculinity, 7,* 1–13.

Sarkadi, A., Kristiansson, R., Oberklaid, F., & Bremberg, S. (2008). Fathers' involvement and children's developmental outcomes: A systematic review of longitudinal studies. *Acta Paediatrica, 97,* 153–158.

Shapiro, J. L. (2001). Therapeutic interventions with fathers. In G. R. Brooks & G. E. Good (Eds.), *The new handbook of psychotherapy and counseling with men: vol. 1. A comprehensive guide to settings, problems, and treatment approaches* (pp. 403–423). San Francisco: Jossey-Bass.

Sharpe, M. J., Heppner, P. P., & Dixon, W. A. (1995). Gender role conflict, instrumentality, expressiveness, and well-being in adult men. *Sex Roles, 33,* 1–18.

Silverstein, L. B., Auerbach, C. F., & Levant, R. F. (2002). Contemporary fathers reconstructing masculinity: Clinical implications of gender role strain. *Professional Psychology and Practice, 33,* 361–369.

Swenson, B. H. (1998). Men and self-disclosure about personal topics: The impact of gender role conflict, self-esteem, and early relationship with father. (Doctoral dissertation, The Fielding Institute, 1998). *Dissertation Abstracts International, 59,* 4543.

Thompson, E. H., & Pleck, J. H. (1995). Masculinity ideologies: A review of research instrumentation on men and masculinities. In R. Levant & W. Pollack (Eds.), *A new psychology of men* (pp. 129–163). New York: Basic Books.

Todryk, L. W. (1999). Gender role conflict in sex offenders revisited: A follow-up study. (Doctoral dissertation, Alder School of Professional Psychology, 1999). *Dissertation Abstracts International, 60,* 4256.

Wester, S. R. (2008). Male gender role conflict and multiculturalism: Implications for counseling psychology. *The Counseling Psychologist, 36,* 294–324.

Wisch, A., & Mahalik, J. R. (1999). Male therapists' clinical bias: Influence of client gender roles and therapist gender role conflict. *Journal of Counseling Psychology, 46,* 51–60.

Yamamoto, J. & Tagami, F. (2004). The relationship between the support for a father's "incomprehensibility" of his son and the change of the father-son relationship. *Japanese Journal of Counseling Science, 37,* 319–327.

# *Counseling Fathers Across Ethnic Groups*

# Mexican American Fatherhood

## Culture, Machismo, and Spirituality

JOSEPH M. CERVANTES

Fatherhood has become an increasingly important dialogue in lifespan development (Bozett & Hanson, 1991; Parke, 2000; Shapiro, Diamond, & Greenberg, 1996). As reported by Marsiglio, Amato, Day, and Lamb (2000), the scholarship on fatherhood over the last 15 years has highlighted a major field of study that has included critical discourse about methodological inquiry, national surveys and fathering measures, father involvement in childhood outcomes, father-child relationships, and the inclusion of nonresident fathers. However, little attention has been paid to the study of culturally diverse fathers and the differential impact on the life cycle of ethnic minority families (Hunter & Davis, 1992; Rogers & White, 1993). Consequently, the study of fathers through the '90s decade has focused its understanding of culturally diverse men on extrapolation from married and middle-class populations, limiting the empirical knowledge base of those individuals and families who do not fit into this framework (Coley, 2001).

Perceptions of ethnic minority parenting, particularly fatherhood, have been defined primarily by a view that low-income and minority fathers do not fit the traditional married, residential, and financially supportive images that have historically characterized normative lifespan frameworks. Therefore, these perceptions have been cast in negative, nonaffirming images regarding the relationship to a family's well-being (Coley, 2001). Garcia Coll et al. (1996) have commented on the need to situate parenting within a larger contextual perspective that incorporates the effects of racism, cultural factors, and the wider social environments of schools and neighborhoods. As such, ethnic minority fatherhood has not been addressed or centered within its appropriate developmental pathway, which adds to inappropriate assumptions that have influenced counseling practice (Muir, Schwartz, & Szapocznik, 2004).

This chapter will focus exclusively on Mexican American father-hood and the various dimensions of this cultural group whose roles and responsibilities have major significance to communities across the United States (Hayes-Bautista, 2004). Practitioners cannot afford to have the stereotyped images of Latinos continue to influence clinical beliefs that are often made about this cultural group. As reported by Chavez (2001), some of these primary images that have flooded the media have included Latinos described primarily as undocumented immigrants, gangbangers, and welfare mothers. These visual stimuli have served to define inappropriately the population demographics of this group, as well as to bias attitudes and respective sentiments to define Mexican American fathers. By association, these attitudes have direct impact on clinical practice and related proposed interventions.

Mexican American fathers have not been given the level of scholar-ship and subsequent understanding of clinical practice that is deserved, in part due to the lack of interest with this cultural reference group and the related stereotypes (Baca Zinn, 1982; Mirande, 1997; Torres, Sol-berg, & Carlstrom, 2002). Coley (2001) indicated that ethnic minority fathers have been viewed as invisible men due to their unique life cir-cumstances and the understanding of a developmental framework that has been based on a radically different normative standard. As such, stereotypes specific to Mexican American males have been influenced primarily by assumptions and attitudes describing this group as sex-ist, manipulative, and subject to a negative interpretation of masculine attributes, such as machismo (Cervantes, 2006; Torres et al., 2002).

This chapter will outline several different areas relative to Mexican American fatherhood to assist the counseling professional in develop-ing a deeper awareness of this population and will propose culturally competent clinical interventions. I will discuss this conceptual dia-logue within the following major headings: population and immigra-tion dynamics, Mexican American fatherhood and culture, case studies related to the diversity of Mexican American fathers, role of spirituality, and counseling issues and intervention. Brief case studies will be used to illustrate particular areas of discussion. In addition, a more extended case will be presented at the conclusion to provide an example of how this author works with this population.

## POPULATION AND IMMIGRATION DEMOGRAPHICS

According to the U.S. Census Bureau (2007), Latinos constitute about 14.2% or 40.5 million of the U.S. population, and Mexicans constitute the largest Latino subgroup, at nearly 26 million. Of this group, approximately 31% of Mexicans living in the United States are immigrants, and another 9% are immigrants who have become naturalized citizens of the United States. Martin (2003) reported that approximately a million legal immigrants become legal permanent residents each year in the initial step toward U.S. citizenship.

The relevance of these data is the observation that, when examining Mexican American fatherhood, the issue of immigration status plays a significant role in many important psychological factors: parenting, therapeutic expectations reflecting differences in cultural values and traditions, employment and residential stability, physical availability to family, and legal status (Chavez, 2001; Falicov, 1998; Mayo, 1997; McLoyd, Cauce, Takeuchi, & Wilson, 2000; Portes & Rumbaut, 2001). Although Latinos are a diverse group, this population, inclusive of Mexican and Mexican Americans, is typically unified by the Spanish language and the Catholic religion (Falicov, 1998, 1999; Matovina & Riebe-Estrada, 2002; Zambrana, 1995).

### Relevant Immigration Dynamics

Any discussion of Mexican Americans, including fatherhood, needs to consider the issue of immigration (Taylor & Behnke, 2005). Contextual factors can play a significant role in assessment and intervention. However, this literature base is vast and will not be discussed in this writing. Refer to the following authors for more specific understanding of immigration: Hays-Bautista, 2004; Portes & Rumbaut, 1996; Suarez-Orozco & Suarez-Orozco, 2001. This chapter will address only the post–World War II Latino, often referred to as the Latino baby boom generation (1950–1964), who grew up heavily influenced by mainstream American culture. This identified generation of Latinas and Latinos is primarily of Mexican American background.

The rise in immigration from Mexico significantly increased through the 1990s, which resulted in several implications for Mexican American families. Newly arrived immigrants, unlike earlier generations spanning 20 years, did not have the benefit of the knowledge and experience resulting from the civil rights movements. As a result, limited exposure to social justice dialogue made these newer arrivals less aware of their rights and, by association, their connection with the brotherhood of well-established Mexican American communities. As Latino-owned businesses in strip malls and companies headed by Latino CEOs have increased, the influence in many Spanish-speaking communities has become more obvious. The influx of Latinos over the past decade has allowed this cultural group to define its own identity.

The history of the second-generation immigrant has supported a continued theme of Latino influence throughout the United States (Portes & Rumbaut, 2001). As the current backlash of Mexicans who are undocumented has resulted in factory raids, the building of fences and walls across border towns, and the levying of financial sanctions on employers who hire undocumented individuals, Latinos continue to significantly influence the nation (National Council of La Raza, 2007). This history has also added to a diverse understanding of how the ethnic label "Mexican American" has come to be categorized (Cervantes, 2004; Griswold del Castillo, 1984). It is within this backdrop that Mexican American fathers have become a relevant population demographic, one that is salient to counseling practice and that mandates the requirement for subsequent clinical competency (American Psychological Association, 2003).

## MEXICAN AMERICAN FATHERHOOD AND CULTURE

A critical dialogue about men was not initiated until Bill Moyers's PBS special on Robert Bly, "A Gathering of Men," aired in 1990. This national opportunity to discuss the challenges of being male in society brought attention to the truth about masculinity, the need for initiation rituals in passing from boyhood to manhood, and a new vision for an understanding of manhood (Bly, 1990; Bly, Hillman, & Meade, 1992). These early writings began to ask fundamental questions: How are men and women different from each other? How do these differences affect emotional and physical well-being? and How does a social construction of masculinity impact the lives of men and their pathways as partners and fathers (Brooks, 2001)? There are other questions that were not asked: How does cultural diversity contribute to the shaping of men and, by association, the development of fatherhood? More directly, what does this cultural shaping look like for Mexican American fathers?

The absence of writing concerning Latino fathers, specifically Mexican American fathers, has been due primarily to an earlier emphasis on White middle- and upper-class families, stereotypes of ethnic minority males, and the bias toward viewing women as primary gatekeepers and protectors of family life (Coley, 2001; Torres et al., 2002; Zambrana, 1995). The limited descriptions of Mexican American fathers have not been complimentary and invite images that are negative and stereotypical. Writing by Diaz-Guerrero over 50 years ago (1955) described Mexican males as authoritarian, aloof, reserved or restrictive in emotion, and prone to aggressiveness—characteristics described as *core* characteristics of both Mexican and Mexican American men. By association, these characteristics have been attributed to fatherhood without any validity to this conceptual linkage. Other examples have included Oscar Lewis's (1960, 1961) ethnographic studies in rural and urban Mexico that portrayed the father as dominant, authoritarian, and maker of all major decisions in the household. In addition, relations with children were described as distant, with severe physical punishment used to maintain respect of children and spouse. These reference labels have carried over toward perceptions of Mexican American fathers and the assumed relationships with their children (Mirande, 1988).

Contrasting and distinct views of fatherhood in more recent years have described Mexican and Mexican American fatherhood in a more positive light, reflecting characteristics such as being supportive, protective, engaged in parenting functions, and fully involved in the life span of families (Cervantes & Sweatt, 2004; Griswold del Castillo, 1984; Meir & Ribera, 1993; Powell, 1995; Sanchez, 1993; Santiago-Rivera, Arredondo, & Gallardo-Cooper, 2002). Despite the stereotypic and biased overtone that was set by early writers (Diaz-Guerrero 1955; Lewis 1960, 1961; Paz 1961), a relevant question to consider is, How should Mexican American fatherhood be understood in the 21st century?

A helpful discussion about fatherhood was presented by Cabrera, Tamis-LeMonda, Bradley, Hofferth, and Lamb (2000), who commented on four primary social trends that have impacted children's lives: women's increased labor force participation, involvement of fathers in intact families, cultural diversity in the United States, and absence of nonresidential fathers in the lives of children. As such, the changing American family has been impacted by the development of more single-parent families and biological father absence. In addition, immigration and acculturation have had related impact on indexes of behavior and psychological stability with Latina and Latino families. Some of the conclusions reached by Cabrera, Tamis-LeMonda, Bradley, Hofferth, and Lamb (2000) are that mothers will continue to be an essential focus in the parenting, mothers will more likely experience full-time employment outside the home, and adolescents may be reared with unpredictable expectations of their future lives.

It is significant to note that these conclusions are based on a broad overview of societal forces that affect families as a whole. Specific to Mexican American families, fathers in this cultural group are still in the process of shaking off old stereotypes, managing the label of being macho as young adult males (Mirande, 1997), and navigating the related arenas of ethnic labeling and the acculturative process (Velasquez & Burton, 2004). The question of how Mexican American fatherhood is impacted by these four social trends in the new millennia is unclear. However, it is important to recognize the qualitatively distinct social and cultural forces, especially regarding the issue of fathering for Mexican American males (McLoyd et. al., 2000).

Dilworth-Anderson and Burton (1996) and Stack and Burton (1993) observed that traditional family developmental theories are limited in their view on lifespan issues specific to many ethnic and cultural communities. As such, these authors underscore that, for many families, their lives are impacted by social-structural forces such as racism, unemployment, and poverty. A further critique is provided by Falicov

(1998), who comments on the role of the migration experience as being a major experiential pathway for Mexican and Mexican American families. Interestingly, this major life episode has not played a role in the development of lifespan theories. Our understanding of Mexican American fatherhood has been defined by misunderstanding, stereotypes, and developmental theories that are disapproving, judgmental, and unrelated to the everyday life experience of this cultural group (Casas, Turner, & Ruiz de Esparza, 2001; Mayo, 1997; Mirande, 1988; Ramirez & Arce, 1981).

Newer observations of Mexican American fatherhood in the 21st century have been offered by several authors who comment on the importance of not making broad generalizations of Latinos about their roles, responsibilities, and involvement in the family. For example, Torres et al. (2002) debunk the myth of machismo and encourage this attribute to be placed within a perspective that integrates historical backdrop, acculturation status, socioeconomic status, and family functioning. A similar observation made by Cervantes (2006) addressed this issue through a case study highlighting a more holistic view of machismo as related to Mexican American men.

Parra-Cardona, Wampler, and Sharp (2006) report on the significant diversity that is noted with Mexican American fathers and their subsequent involvement in teaching the value of harmony in relationships outside the home. In addition, Parke and Buriel (1998) comment on the distinct cultural traditions evident with Cuban, Puerto Rican, and Mexican American men relative to their specific roles as fathers and the shaping that they do to provide unique strength in their protective nature with families. A consistent theme with these writers is that there is limited information on this cultural reference group and that the relevant parameters to understanding Mexican American fatherhood have not been well understood. Implied in their comments is the acknowledgment of the wide diversity of fatherhood development with Mexican American men and the inaccuracies in making broad generalizations. These assumptions then reflect on how psychological care becomes defined. Refer to writing by Cervantes and Sweatt (2004) for a review of best practices guidelines with Mexican American families that have direct implication for understanding fatherhood.

Some critical dimensions toward framing Mexican American fatherhood that can assist practitioners toward more accurate assessments in the counseling process include the following: ethnic identification, culturally relevant perceptions of fatherhood, perceptions of masculinity, and machismo and role identity.

## Ethnic Identification

Latino male identity and fatherhood have not historically been linked in the literature. However, clinical experience finds a meaningful connection between the quality of the relationship, attachment, parenting, and values of being a father. For example, early writing by Valdez, Barron, and Ponce (1987) reported on the diversity that exists in the self-identification process with Mexican Americans who have used a variety of ethnic labels to identify themselves, including Spanish American, Hispanic, Latino, Chicano, and Tex-Mex. While their study is not specific to fatherhood, these authors indicate that the reference point of masculinity is defined by the cultural self-identification process that impacts the level of acculturation. As such, the demeanor and style that Mexican American fathers hold may be influenced by their ethnic identification.

The importance of ethnic labeling is relevant as assumptions are often made by practitioners based on subjective beliefs about what it means to identify as Mexican American. Casas and Pytluk (1995) provided a comprehensive review of ethnic identity formation specifically with Mexican Americans that examined several models relative to understanding ethnic identity with this group. A related commentary is made from a feminist perspective by Ramirez and Arce (1981), who discussed the significant diversity of acculturation trajectories that were evident with Mexican American families. This observation was updated by Pasch et al. (2006), who commented on the relevance of questioning stereotypes and not cataloging Latina/Latino groups into single identities due to the diversity of contexts related to nationality, migration history within group variability, and acculturation. Interested readers can consult Knight, Bernal, Cota, Garza, and Ocampo (1993), Bernal, Knight, Garza, Ocampo, and Cota (1990), and Phinney (1990) for an expanded discussion of ethnic identity. As such, understanding Mexican American fathers should permit sensitivity to the diverse ways in which this cultural label is understood and, subsequently, how roles and parenting as fathers are self-appointed and incorporated.

## Culturally Relevant Perceptions of Fatherhood

The task of fatherhood is generally grounded in learning to provide nurturance, integrating effective problem-solving skills, managing stress, and balancing displays of affection and disagreement in the parenting role (Cabrera et al., 2000). In addition, the characteristics of families that shape parental involvement with children tend to involve a combination of factors such as gender, age, father, mother, co-parent factors, and life events such as employment, birth of children, health crises, and so forth (Coley & Hernandez, 2006; Wood & Repetti, 2004). For Mexican American fathers, this shaping is influenced by primary cultural values such as family (*familismo*), respect for others and the elderly (*respeto*), and the need to dictate the appropriate child-rearing practices that are important for youth to learn (*ser buen educado*). Halgunseth, Ispa, and Rudy (2006) comment on these cultural values and motivational roots that impact parenting practices, role of parental control, and responsiveness to others as some of the primary cultural characteristics.

Falicov (1998) provides similar observations about how Mexican and Mexican American families shape particular cultural values and beliefs through family socialization and parental control.

The understanding of how Mexican American fathers are influenced by culture and family socialization is an important clinical consideration in the assessment process for psychological treatment of this population. This point has been underscored by Eggebeen and Knoester (2001), who note that fathers differ significantly from nonfathers as they become involved in having children. It is important not to make assumptions about the presence of certain cultural values with Mexican American fathers, but rather ask and assess what is relevant so that a meaningful framework with the client can be adjusted. An additional observation made by Hernandez (2002) is on the issues of poverty, social class, and immigration as shaping the role of fatherhood for Mexican American teen fathers. Failure to address this contextual background will result in important dimensions being missed that would highlight areas such as emotional coping, life challenges and resilience, and impact of low socioeconomic status with the Mexican American client (Liu, Soleck, Hopps, Dunston, & Pickett, 2004).

## *Perceptions of Masculinity*

There is a salient connection between the incorporation of a masculine attitude and fatherhood (Frago & Kashubeck, 2000; Parra-Cardona, Wampler, & Sharp, 2006). This observation is directly applicable to Mexican American males where masculine styles and Latino male identity are recognized to be diverse (Torres et al., 2002). Thompson and Pleck (1995) comment on the "masculinity ideology" that acknowledges the traditional, socially constructive nature of masculinity. These authors assert the impact that distinct racial, ethnic, or religious groups as well as social class have on manhood development. A similar analogy is found with Latino masculinity that also varies across interethnic cultural groups and is impacted by cultural reference, gender role expectations, and sociopolitical reality. As such, Mexican American men integrate some form of masculinity into their roles as fathers based on acculturation level, degree of perception regarding an alliance with the Mexican male ideology, education, and social class (Coltrane, Parke, & Adams, 2004; Zamarripa, Wampold, & Gregory, 2003). The negative side of Mexican American men who incorporate a style of masculine identity associated with Mexican culture is that they are likely to experience levels of stress and depression (Fragoso & Kashubeck, 2000) and develop rigid gender roles that underscore patriarchy and dominance (Casas, Wagenheim, Banchero, & Mendoza-Romero, 1994).

Practitioners working with Mexican American fathers should inquire about how perceptions, cultural beliefs, and parenting style impact male gender self-reference and prior cultural learning relative to ethnic identification.

## Machismo and Role Identity

The term *macho* or *machismo*, which is typically related to Mexican and Mexican American males, has been based on cultural myths, stereotypes, and media, and refers to a stylized set of actions in respect to hypersexual and aggressive behaviors and a propensity to define relational roles in a permanent partnership (Casas et al., 2001; Falicov, 1998; Quintero & Estrada, 1998; Rodriguez, 1996). The characteristic of machismo continues to have significant understanding relative to how it is defined for Mexican American males and subsequently for this population of fathers. The study by Abreu, Goodyear, Campos, and Newcomb (2000) provides a useful reminder of the difficulty in overidentifying with a more traditional Mexican male role identity. The identification of the more traditional Mexican male role underscores a machismo set of behavior traits that are rigid, authoritarian, and restricted in emotion, much as described by Diaz-Guerrero (1955). In brief, the development of a macho attitude at this level can be disrespectful to one's personhood, destructive in family relationships, and dangerous to one's health. Awareness of this for practitioners may be useful relative to how to work with those fathers who may display more of these characteristics, yet be unaware of the impact it may have on their families and relationships.

## CASE STUDIES RELATED TO THE DIVERSITY OF MEXICAN AMERICAN FATHERHOOD

A consistent theme of fatherhood with this ethnic and cultural population has been the issue of diversity. This diversity is based not only on the construction of maleness within social class, culture, race, ethnicity, and age (Kimmel & Messher, 1992), but also in the incorporation of distinct cultural values that shape fatherhood for this ethnic group. How Latino males describe themselves as men is a useful backdrop to understand fatherhood (Fragoso & Kashubeck, 2000). In addition, the construct of *machismo* is an important reference point to help orient the practitioner to ethnic identification, cultural expectations, and the subsequent role incorporated by the client (Arciniega, Anderson, Tovar-Blank, & Tracey, 2008). Gilmore (1990) reaffirmed in his cross-cultural study of masculinity that *concepts of manhood are universal, and as a result of the characterization of* machismo *for Mexican American males, this personality attribute is not specific to that cultural reference group.* Consequently, there is a critical interaction between self-descriptions of manhood, machismo, and fatherhood that are important dimensions to consider when working with Mexican American fathers. Despite the negative stereotypes the machismo attribute has had with Mexican American men (Casas at al., 2001; Diaz-Guerrero, 1955; Mirande, 1997; Torres et al., 2002), Latino males continue to view being macho as a relevant dimension toward a self-definition of manhood (Quintero & Estrada, 1998). Obviously, the link to fatherhood is immediately present.

Three case studies are presented with brief commentary after each to provide an experiential reference point to these issues raised in this section as related to fatherhood.

Elio Juanes is a 28-year-old male of Mexican American background who grew up in a low-income community. He is experiencing significant difficulty with the peer group he has selected as his primary social support network. This peer group has been labeled as a "tagger club"* whose actions have resulted in destruction of property. As a result, Elio spent a year in Juvenile Hall when he was 17 years old. Since then, he has not graduated from high school and has been involved in low-income jobs making minimum wage. He is having difficulty managing a more stable existence for himself and his live-in girlfriend, Janey. His view of being a man was formed early on by a father who abandoned him, his younger brothers, and mother when Elio was 11 years of age. Consequently, the consistent message he received from his mother was that, as the oldest, he was now designated as the protector of the family and needed to look out for everyone, including her. As such, Elio feels that his role in his emerging family is one where being a man means that you protect your family yet are watchful of those elements that can cause threat to the family. As a result, he has taken a position that his manhood means the need to be aggressive and physical to protect those you love.

The case of Elio suggests that this individual's life has been influenced by low socioeconomic status and expectations from his family about how to perform as a young adult male. Family modeling has instructed him to be watchful and aggressive in his role as a family member and subsequent parent. The probability that he would develop a relationship with a partner that may include aggressiveness and potential violence is heightened, given a protector mythology that is framed by this individual's social and family history.

Mark Gonzalez is a 21-year-old Mexican American young adult who has just graduated from a local university with a degree in engineering. He has been given the opportunity to tour Europe for a month as a graduation present from his parents. He indicated that, as a result of his graduation success, he has been able to consider an elite university to enter graduate study in chemical engineering, following in the footsteps of his father. His immediate plans are to "sow wild oats with female friends" and experience life to the fullest. His view of manhood was influenced by a father who strongly encouraged him to pursue his education, as well as by an uncle and a male mentor teacher who taught him to go after what he can but also take responsibility for his actions. This individual's view of manhood is one that he still wants to explore as he believes there is "too much of a kid inside me" before maturing into a role that may characterize the rest of his life.

---

* A tagger club is a loosely connected peer reference group which will characteristically vandalize public property with spray painting various images and personal identification to express group sentiment.

In contrast to the first case, Mark has a male mentor who has taught him about responsibility, yet has also made room for some permissiveness that has influenced his socialization. This individual's incorporation of the macho/protective role will likely take a different avenue regarding his image of parenting and fatherhood as he readies himself for that developmental stage. These two cases suggest that an affirmation of masculinity will dictate a certain pattern into fatherhood depending on the contextual background of the individual.

Antonio Gamboa, a 50-year-old Mexican American male, describes how as a child he was molested by an older brother and made fun of for his sensitivity and artistic ability. Although in the United States since he was 17 years of age, Antonio has never achieved permanent legal residence. Although there was significant respect for their mother, a single parent who worked 12-hour days in a lemon-packing plant, she essentially was never home to manage the discipline of her children. He learned that women were play objects. As a teenager, Antonio impregnated two of his girlfriends, one of whom he married. By his mid-20s, Antonio had served 6 months in jail for a domestic violence charge, had continued to verbally abuse his wife and young daughters, and was never home to play any significant role as a father and caretaker.

By his late 40s, Antonio found himself to be more self-reflective, yet unsophisticated emotionally as to how to handle this awareness. He commented on how his absent father would likely have raised him, although this dialogue brought tears and resentment over a perception of imagined, lost family opportunities. Antonio was able to observe how unsteady and nonloving his life had become and how he had contributed to a now detached relationship among himself and his daughters. Even his son, a 29-year-old Latino male, had been disengaged from his father because his son viewed him as "too Mexican and a man that I would never want to be like."

Antonio's case reflects the modeling of a destructive machismo attribute and an incorporated image of being a Latino male that has haunted him throughout his young adulthood, marriage, and now as an astute observer of his own adult behavior (Welland & Ribner, 2008). This individual's background is reflected in a history of abuse; the absence of a parent at home to model appropriate caregiving behavior; and a model of a negative, masculine role that was aggressive, manipulative, and sexually promiscuous. The available case material does not address the question of his immigration status or what impact this might have on his own personal and family development as a father. However, this would be an area of inquiry for the practitioner relative to uncovering why citizenship never became important for him and how this status may have impacted his own self-identification, ethnic affiliation, and political loyalty.

Each of these three cases provides an illustration of the relationship between masculinity, acculturation and social status, and ethnic identity. Challenges in fatherhood observed for these individuals suggest that Elio Juanes would define his role in a more autocratic style, Mark Gonzalez would likely be more informed in his parenting, while Antonio

Gamboa has had a history of internalized conflict and self-destructive patterns of behavior that have already had a significant negative effect on his family. The interplay of machismo with other relevant contextual dimensions in each case has distinct outcomes that are important for the practitioner to understand. Evaluating the incorporation of the male gender role can provide meaningful clinical information toward an understanding of how fatherhood can be evaluated and a subsequent, culturally appropriate treatment plan developed.

## ROLE OF SPIRITUALITY

An area that has not been well explored and has proven of limited education to clinical practitioners has been the topic of spirituality (Richards & Bergin, 2000). The backdrop of spirituality for Mexican American fathers is a meaningful one as it relates to a history of religious and spiritual influence dating back centuries. This dimension for Mexican American fathers may be important in helping clients make salient connections to their socialization history with family and showing how this linkage is relevant to the role of being a father.

Religion and spirituality have been significant themes of human functioning within the indigenous communities of Mexico for several centuries (Carrasco, 1990) and a major aspect with Mexican American families as this dimension is viewed to regulate behaviors, attitudes, and relationships (Cervantes & Ramirez, 1992; Carrillo & Tello, 1998; Falicov, 1999). As Carrasco (1990) notes, the map of Mesoamerican traditions was organized by and around ceremonial centers modeled on a vision of the structure of the universe. This structure told how the world was made and how supernatural forces organized the cosmos (Leon-Portilla, 1962).

Matovina and Riebe-Estrada (2002) provided a meaningful subtext to the role of a Mesoamerican belief system in the lives of Mexican American families, who typically have been socialized by a Catholic theological perspective. Their writing is consistent with other authors including Carrillo and Tello (1998), Ramirez (1998), and Rodriguez (1994), who describe Mesoamerican belief systems as ancient rituals and beliefs that honor the sacredness of life and the various energies and ancestors in prayer. These beliefs are expressed in rituals like Day of the Dead ceremonies, honoring the Blessed Virgin, pilgrimages to sacred and ancient shrines, and a communal understanding of the presence of spiritual beings. These communal teachings underscore the religious and spiritual experiences of Mexican Americans (Matovina & Riebe-Estrada, 2002; McNeill & Cervantes, 2008), which emphasize a mixture of mestizo and indigenous beliefs that predate the conquest (Josephy, 1991; Ortiz de Montellano, 1990). These rituals, traditions, and belief systems have survived to the present among Mexican American populations.

How does this ancestral and spiritual heritage impact the role of fatherhood with Mexican American men in the present? Falicov (1999) discussed themes of folk health and illness, disorders of the supernatural, spiritual and magical healing, and indigenous healers referred to as *curanderos* and *yierberos*, commonly known as herbalists. She acknowledged a widespread influence of religion and spirituality with Latina/Latino families, as do Anzaldua (1987) and Quinonez (1998), although their reference point is often communicated through storytelling, cultural mythology, and poetry. The critical discourse and poetry of these authors reflect a historical belief in Mesoamerican cosmology. It is the current writer's belief that the images and historical ancestry of Mesoamerica are linked directly to fatherhood for Mexican American men.

The phrase *la cultura cura* refers to the spiritual element that is coupled with the socialization process of Mexican American families. The healing dimensions of culture and an intuitive awareness of the sacredness of life are often the backdrop to this socialization process. This element emphasizes indigenous ways that introduce ideas of balance, harmony, reflective feedback for the individual, and the relevance of family integration (Carillo & Tello, 1998). Ramirez (1983, 1998) underscores the mestizo world view of life as a psychospiritual imperative where there are lessons to learn that are directed by a higher source. Examples of this heritage left by Mesoamerican traditions for those of Mexican and Mexican American background are noted in beliefs in spirits and ancestors and their influence on behavior, patronage, and images of the Blessed Virgin. These images are often coupled with elaborate altars in many Mexican American homes (Rodriguez, 1994) and can include the public display of various religious images on T-shirts, cars, and calendars, which also serve as a reminder to belief systems that predate a nation's conversion to Catholicism.

Cervantes (2003) coined the term *mestizo spirituality* to reflect this systematic attention to a belief system, tradition, and cosmovision emphasizing wholeness, harmony, balance in one's relationships, and the learning of life's lessons. Lastly, this perspective emphasized a belief in a theistic cosmology that is always present, protects, influences, and engages all life. Tello (1998) highlighted this spiritual reference point for Mexican American men and the trauma resulting from the fractured psyche and disassembled indigenous beliefs that resulted from the Conquest of Mexico. The effects of the conquest have been described as intergeneration posttraumatic stress disorder by Duran and Duran (1995) among indigenous and First Nation people in the United States. In reference to fatherhood, Tello (1998) discussed the healing tree philosophy, which he described as symbolically emphasizing a positive centering base of principles that promoted emotional, family, and community well-being. These principles are described as follows:

Acknowledgement of ancestral wisdom that is necessary for growth and healing

Development of vision that reflects one's true self as it impacts the wellness of one's family and community

Development of interdependence among families and communities

Belief in a circular learning process in which pride in one's ethnic cultural background and respect for the belief systems of others is fundamental

Living life with a sense of spirit that promotes newness and well-being in one's relationship with self and others

Examples of writings that have demonstrated cultural awareness of these psychospiritual principles are noted in recent studies. Parke and Buriel (1998) comment on the distinctive cultural traditions that shape father relationships and the impact that those teachings have on family and community. Niska (2001) reports on the use of family stories with Mexican American parents who used this format as a way to learn new strategies to assist with socialization and resolution of family issues, and to stabilize well-being. Parke et al. (2004) commented on how Mexican American men teach the value of maintaining harmony and balance in their subsequent roles as fathers. This commentary on spirituality with Mexican American men is a useful way to conceptualize a more integrated meaning of machismo as the caretaking, protective, and ancestral wisdom aspects are emphasized (Cervantes, 2006; Falicov, 1999; Tello, 1998; Welland & Ribner, 2008). The recovery of a spiritual base can be a relevant therapeutic task for practitioners with this client population (Cervantes & Parham, 2005; McCabe, 2007).

Both Montoya (1992) and Carrillo and Tello (1998) make direct reference to the Mexican American male as having a wounded male spirit that needs healing. Their commentary is fueled by observations of this Latino cultural group being impacted by cultural transition, nonresolution about ethnic identity, and the meaning of spirituality in their lives. From these authors' points of view, the Mexican American male cannot be a complete father until he has integrated a more culturally unified reference point of his spiritual well-being. As such, a Mexican American man cannot be fully complete in his manhood nor as a parent unless he is able to recognize the truth of his word, the sense of responsibility, and the rejection of any abuse. In addition, to take time to reflect and pray, be sensitive and understanding, speak with support and clarity to others, and model honesty and love are understood to be fundamental aspects of being a Mexican American male and a father (Cervantes, 2006; Carrillo & Tello, 1998).

A salient observation in this writing is that Mexican American fatherhood is a more holistic integration of self that includes spirituality as the subtext to functioning and involvement with children and family. This reclaiming of life lessons from the Mexican American's historical past may be a relevant principle in professional consultation with this group of fathers. It is being suggested that learning about and hearing the life histories of Mexican American fathers is an important intervention that will assist in the professional relationship, therapeutic attachment, and the setting aside of stereotypes that will facilitate meaningful psychological outcomes. Consequently, a salient theme in the therapeutic relationship is the topic of *familia,* which continues to be a primary organizing base and underscores the role of fatherhood with Mexican American males (Cervantes & Sweat, 2004; Santiago-Rivera et al., 2002). As such, the phrase *la cultura cura* underscores the integration and healing process that is a socialized aspect of Mexican American families and characterizes a relevant aspect of fatherhood.

## CASE ILLUSTRATION

The following case provides an extended discussion of a characteristic counseling process that I conduct with Latino fathers. I saw this individual for 9 months, resulting in a mutual termination following self-exploration, increased learning about his role in the family, and satisfaction with how his life had changed.

David Jimenez is a 35-year-old Mexican American father who was raised through young adulthood by his parents. He is the oldest son of four siblings, the rest of whom are females. He reported that his father was an alcoholic, and about the time that David was 5, his father entered an Alcoholics Anonymous program and was reformed. He indicated that he has been married for 10 years and has three children, all under age 8.

A brief history of David reveals that his entry into counseling was the result of a DUI over a year ago. He was found swerving on the road, stopped by the highway patrol, and subsequently ticketed. Although he was required to attend only 10 visits of counseling, David has been seen for over 30 outpatient visits through the 9-month period of professional involvement. Following graduation from high school, he joined the Marine Corps and served 4 years of active duty during which he was trained as a medical corpsman. Following discharge he received further training as a medical technician and has been working at a local hospital ever since.

Additional history found that he had struggled in his marriage, feeling that he was not good enough as a life partner and sometimes reporting that his parenting was "bordering on abuse." He felt guilty that he was not the caretaker that he learned to be from his mother. Alternatively, early memories of his father were of a "push and shove incident" between his parents that culminated in his father attending AA. Consequently, David indicated that although he was no longer drinking, his father struggled with family intimacy and was never able to tell David how proud he was of David's accomplishments, particularly the honorable discharge from the military.

David indicated that only in the last several years has he identified as being Latino, specifically, American of Mexican descent. He vividly recalled "unkind teasing" through elementary school regarding his last name, the accents of his parents, and the fact that he was dark skinned. As a result, David felt that his ethnic identification was not to consider himself as Mexican American, but rather to identify with many of his White classmates and take on values that were consistent with this peer group. During high school, the values of independence and lack of regard for family clashed with his parents' expectations and resulted in significant conflict until David left for the Marine Corps.

David reported that following discharge from the military, he wandered for a year without work trying to assess what he would do with his life. This wandering resulted in his completing additional training as a medical technician and dating a young woman in his community, which resulted in marriage. He reported the marriage to be stable, although he felt that his ability to be empathic and sensitive to her needs was a struggle for him. Not until he began counseling did he begin to realize that perhaps the role modeling he received from his father may have been a significant aspect of this difficulty in the marriage. This issue, along with the fact that he had received a DUI and had to attend counseling for a period of time, were the primary reasons for initiating counseling.

## COMMENTARY

David's initial entry into counseling found him to be reluctant, suspicious of what to expect, and unclear about my role as the psychotherapist. I quickly became aware of his cautiousness to self-disclose. He knew he was there for a required number of visits, and it seemed that he was only willing to comply to meet the requirements set by the court. After some rapport building with inquiry about his family, his young children, and his personal history, the remainder of the first and the follow-up counseling visits found him demonstrating considerably less defensiveness.

A significant theme that became a foundation for our therapeutic interaction was his responsibility to his family, both immediate and extended. When David would speak about related early-developmental history, he would lapse into some Spanish language phrases, sometimes mimicking one or both of his parents about what they might say to him about his growing up and the need to be a "responsible man." When language switching would occur, I would respond in kind, thus affirming my tracking of his language and also modeling a personal awareness of Latino values and beliefs. It was within this dialogue that I elected to ask about his Latino affiliation which he described as being "Hispanic or sometimes Mexican American, depending on how I feel about myself." Closer inquiry about this ethnic affiliation found him to have some confusion about those values that he believed originated from his Mexican background and those that seemed to clash with the rearing of his children and the issue of connecting with his wife. The therapeutic agenda was being set as he discussed the stories of alcohol abuse related by his mother about his father and how that impacted their relationship. A similar theme was now being replayed in David's relationship with his wife. This parallel process also contributed to his confusion over how to be an effective parent.

The first several sessions with David were primarily oriented toward fostering trust in this professional experience and establishing a level of intimacy that could be helpful toward his personal recovery. While he initially indicated that he would only remain for the required 10 visits, after the third session he became invested in continuing the sessions for his self-learning. This was David's first experience in counseling, and so the expectations of this professional interaction, advantages of confidentiality, and simply having the opportunity to be self-reflective in a trusting environment were a significant impetus to his therapeutic commitment. There was immediate identification with me, as a Latino male professional, which has proven to be a helpful and salient connection with many Latino clients regarding an assumed ability to be culturally sensitive. Following the trust-building stage, David began to utilize the next several visits to replay memories from his early past. The snapshot pictures that he had of his father when he was still drinking were the imaginal seeds that fueled the therapeutic dialogue.

A characteristic theme that occurs in my experience with Latino male clients, particularly if they are fathers, is the issue of protection of family and the safety of children. This preoccupation was also evident with David and interwoven with the lack of intimacy that he felt with his wife. Interestingly, the vocabulary of machismo never was raised throughout the entire counseling period. However, the common descriptors of this cultural attribute were found in how he incorporated and reported on his sense of manhood and ethnic identity. These observations were seen in the protection dialogue that was evident with his family as well as in the need to be resilient and strong in adversity, a characteristic he learned from his parents while growing up as well as during his time in the military. Blended into this counseling relationship were the issues of *familia* and intimacy, the two primary concerns that underlined his personal insecurities. The topic of *familia* was often discussed relative to not only his immediate but also his extended family. I have found it important to help examine with the client what "family" means for him, as this theme is a frequently diverse, cultural rubric that can have several different explanations depending on the life experience, socialization process, and any related experiences of postimmigration history. This case found David to be a third-generation Latino, which means that his great-grandparents were the initial immigrants.

The theme of intimacy dominated a central focus of counseling with David. This theme was reflected in how he learned to relate to his father, the kinds of relationships that he shared with intimate friends, and the level of emotional connection that he felt with his wife. While there was some uncovering work related to understanding the dynamics of past history, the primary orientation as a transpersonal practitioner was to initiate an opening to his psychological experience of early fatherhood with his own father to replace anger and resentment with peace (Epstein, 2007).

David's memories of his father slowly spilled out as the handle on a faucet turned to a slow trickle. This faucet quickly gained momentum, and an emotional deluge was released, allowing him to confront the lack of touch and loving attention and the minimal opportunities for intimate play with his father. David would become emotional at times and feel angry at himself for feeling deprived of what could have been. This therapeutic dialogue was framed within deep, ambivalent feelings about being angry at his father, yet recognizing what his father was able to provide for him as a stable, financially responsible parent.

The theme of ethnic identity and feelings of manhood were significant in David's decision to enter the military. He felt that he needed to prove to his father that he could be brave enough to withstand military life, be true to his self-definition of Mexican background, and externalize an appearance of the man he was becoming. This discussion eclipsed into several counseling visits regarding his views of manhood and what he wanted to convey to his children as a father. Within this context, David was able to rewrite his family script, redefine his role as family protector, and integrate a more loving and nurturing involvement as a father.

The dialogue about manhood merged into issues related to emotional intimacy with his wife. He made the needed connection about the lack of touch and affectionate embrace that he did not learn from his father and only minimally from his mother. David admitted to some objectification of his wife relevant to being a sexual image for him while at the same time having guilt over mentally placing her in that position. As a result, this guilt allowed him to open to new learning beyond what he saw modeled by his parents toward more authenticity with his wife. This movement in counseling shifted toward a dialogue of intimacy relative to what he had learned from his mother and, more importantly, what his wife could teach him.

As this case evolved toward termination, feelings of authentic regard for his wife became more prominent, as did a comfortableness in expressing his masculine identity. David came to describe himself as being a man who had intimate feelings for his wife, which did not compromise his ability to be loving and caring, yet also feeling more secure in his manhood and emotionally connected in his fatherhood role.

## COUNSELING ISSUES AND INTERVENTION

Scholarship that eventually fuels counseling theory and practice in the area of fatherhood for Mexican American men has been seriously absent. Despite the lack of interest in this cultural group and the stereotypes that have potentially molded the practice arena relative to intervention with Mexican American fathers, the understanding of Latina/Latino families has come a long way since the literature review by Ramirez and Arce (1981).

This chapter has attempted to introduce the unique cultural perspective that is inclusive of diverse family patterns, a deeper appreciation of contextual background, and the academic stereotypes that have coexisted in the literature about Mexican Americans through the 1960s and 1970s (Diaz-Guerrero, 1955; Paz, 1961; Lewis, 1960, 1961). These stereotypical perceptions have included parental absence, nonparticipation in treatment, punitive role modeling toward family, and stereotypical personality characteristics. Each of these descriptions could lead the practicing clinician to develop a disregard and biased assessment of Mexican American fathers.

The following recommendations may assist the counseling professional in increasing cultural competency and developing a relevant practice with Mexican American fathers that can minimize bias and provide more accurate assessments.

Immigration for Mexican American families continues to be a predominant theme in the lives of this cultural group. In assessing Spanish-speaking families, the issue of immigration may be a significant aspect in the counseling process, particularly if there are immediate family members still residing in Mexico and if the designated caretakers (e.g., parents) work two or more jobs to financially stabilize a family. The safety and permanency for children is unstable if legal residing status is not resolved (Bacallao & Smokowski, 2007). Each of these areas could impact the role of fatherhood for Mexican American males relative to security concerns, stability of family, and consistency of parenting messages.

Consideration of family variability due to acculturation that impacts bilingual ability and adherence to specific cultural values is an important aspect in the understanding of this population. Velasquez, Arrellano, and McNeill (2004) underscore the importance of recognizing diversity within Mexican American families. Therefore, practitioners should not make assumptions about the presence of certain cultural values, but inquire about those particular themes that have been integrated into a Mexican American father's socialization history. This will allow the assessment and therapeutic process to be tailored to that particular individual.

Socioeconomic status is an important factor in working with families (Liu, 2002; Liu et al., 2004). It would be important for the practitioner to pay attention to the effects of poverty on fatherhood and family functioning. Eamon and Mulder (2005) comment on how poverty and a lower level of neighborhood quality can contribute to the development of antisocial behavior and subsequent nonparticipation in the broader community. Mexican American fathers residing in compromised neighborhoods may view their life situations as hopeless, leading to minimizing their potential contributions. This, in turn, may cause feelings of hopelessness for counselors (Kuther & Wallace, 2003). Viewing Mexican American fathers as having cultural assets will invite a more meaningful relationship between therapist and client.

Help-seeking behaviors for Mexican American fathers have been influenced by experiences of poverty, racism and discrimination, and cultural oppression (Gonzalez, 2000). Nonparticipatory involvement in counseling and/or the perception of not being entitled to belong or participate as a member in the community have been relevant dimensions toward mental health utilization. Valdes et al. (1987) comment on the issue of entitlement and how this understanding of counseling may be important to consider with this population. Actively encouraging participation for Mexican American fathers by allowing them to share experiences of fatherhood and commenting on the unique sociocultural background they bring to counseling may enhance feelings of entitlement and the embracing of an effective treatment process.

Cultural attributes, particularly machismo, should be understood within a cultural context (Gilmore, 1990). A relevant way to address the incorporation of this assumed personality attribute is to inquire about how Mexican American fathers have learned to protect family members and what elements are important in this protective stance. This approach may allow fathers in this cultural group to feel more open to express themselves and inclined to disclose more specific ways they cope with issues related to cultural oppression, prejudice, and related unfair treatment as part of their incorporated ethnic identity.

It is recommended that during the assessment process and in counseling with Mexican American men cultural referencing be addressed. Understanding what his Mexican American ethnic identity means for a particular father could provide meaningful information about his unique beliefs as well as expectations about the counseling process.

It would be important to ask Mexican American fathers what it has been like to be a father and to have children. This inquiry may assist in disclosing meaningful clinical information that will likely shape treatment goals. In addition, this inquiry will also assist the practitioner in evaluating critically the cultural framework that is consistent with the client's belief system and socialization experience toward fostering personal development in the roles of fatherhood and protector of one's family (Coltrane et al., 2004; Wisman, 2005).

The issue of spirituality has been described as a relevant backdrop for Mexican American families when treating fathers. The key to addressing this issue will depend on the nature of the referral, the specific concerns presented by the Mexican American client, and the therapist's level of comfort with this dimension of human functioning. Mexican American fathers, as a function of their indigenous history, are often oriented to the role of organizing truth in one's heart and building a foundation of authentic reality for oneself and family as an important aspect to spiritual being (Duran & Duran, 1995). Further, Carrillo and Tello (1998) note that this theme is an important, self-reflective, and meaningful affirmation of how one functions in the world (Anzaldua, 1987; Cervantes & Parham, 2005; Matovina & Riebe-Estrada, 2002; Montoya, 1992; Velasquez et al., 2004). As such, the stage is set for this culturally salient dialogue with Mexican American fathers.

In treating Mexican American fathers, it will be important for the practitioner to evaluate stereotypes of perceptions of this cultural group and prejudice that may exist with the themes of Latino and masculinity. Acknowledging one's own cultural beliefs and stereotypes about manhood and how they impact effective and therapeutic psychological care is a relevant developmental principle for clinical and counseling practice (Englar-Carlson & Stevens, 2006).

## POSTSCRIPT

Mexican American fathers have generations of history to disclose relative to their personal life stories, relationships to family, and involvement as protectors of their respective families and communities. Each of the case vignettes and the more extended case illustration have intended to provide a meaningful voice to this fatherhood population in order to enhance awareness, education, and clinical competency. It is hoped that the writing and cases cited offer meaningful avenues for dialogue with Mexican American fathers and those practitioners who are treating them toward more effective psychological care and mutual understanding.

## REFERENCES

Abreu, J. M., Goodyear, A. C., Campos, A., & Newcomb, M. D. (2000). Ethnic belonging and traditional masculinity ideology among African American, European American, and Latinos. *Psychology of Men & Masculinity, 1,* 75–86.

American Psychology Association (2003). Guidelines on multicultural education, training, research, practice, and organizational change for psychologists. *American Psychologist, 58,* 377–402.

Anzaldua, G. (1987). *Borderlands/La Frontera: The New Mestiza.* San Francisco: Spinsters/Aunt Lute.

Arciniega, G. M., Anderson, T. C., Tovar-Blank, Z. G., & Tracey, T. J. G. (2008). Toward a fuller conception of machismo: Development of a traditional machismo and Caballerismo Scale. *Journal of Counseling Psychology, 55,* 19–33.

Baca Zinn, M. (1982). Chicano men and masculinity. *Journal of Ethnic Studies, 10,* 29–44.

Bacallao, M. L., & Smokowski, P. R. (2007). The costs of getting ahead: Mexican family system changes after immigration. *Family Relations, 56,* 52–66.

Bernal, M., Knight, G., Garza, C., Ocampo, K., & Cota., M. (1990). The development of ethnic identity in Mexican-American children. *Hispanic Journal of Behavioral Sciences, 12,* 3–34.

Bly, R. (1990). *Iron John: A book about men.* Menlo Park, CA: Addison-Wesley.

Bly, R., Hillman, J., & Meade, M. (Eds.). (1992). *The rag and bone shop of the heart: Poems for men.* New York: Harper Collins.

Bozett, F. W., & Hanson, S. M. H. (1991). *Fatherhood and families in cultural context.* New York: Springer.

Brooks, G. R. (2001). Masculinity and men's mental health. *Revision, 25,* 24–37.

Cabrera, N. J., Tamis-LeMonda, C. S., Bradley, R. H., Hofferth, S., & Lamb, M. E. (2000). Fatherhood in the twenty-first century. *Child Development, 71,* 127–136.

Carrasco, D. (1990). *Religions of Mesoamerica.* New York: Harper & Row.

Carrillo, R., & Tello, J. (Eds.). (1998). *Family violence and men of color: Healing the wounded male spirit.* New York: Springer.

Casas, J. M., Wagenheim, B. R., Banchero, R., & Mendoza-Romero, J. (1994). Hispanic masculinity: Myth or psychological schema meriting clinical consideration. *Hispanic Journal of Behavioral Sciences, 16*, 315–327.

Casas, J. M., Turner, J. A., & Ruiz de Esparza C. A. (2001). Machismo reunited in a time of crisis. In G. R. Brooks & G. E. Good (Eds.), *The new handbook of psychotherapy and counseling with men* (pp. 754–779). San Francisco: Jossey-Bass.

Casas, J. M., & Pytluk, S. D. (1995). Hispanic identity development: Implications for research and practice. In J. G. Ponterotto, J. M. Casas, L. A. Suzuki, & C. M. Alexander (Eds.), *Handbook of multicultural counseling* (pp. 155–180) Thousand Oaks, CA: Sage.

Cervantes, J. M. (2003). Mestizo spirituality: A counseling model for Chicano and Native/indigenous peoples. Unpublished manuscript.

Cervantes, J. M. (2004). Mexican Americans: A prospective analysis and clinical update. In C. Negy (Ed.), *Cross-cultural psychotherapy: Toward a critical understanding of diverse clients* (pp. 85–107). Reno, NV: Bent.

Cervantes, J. M. (2006). A new understanding of the macho male image: Exploration of the Mexican American man. In M. Englar-Carlson & M. A. Stevens (Eds.), *In the room with men: A casebook of therapeutic change* (pp. 197–224). Washington, DC: American Psychological Association.

Cervantes, J. M., & Parham, T. A. (2005). Toward a meaningful spirituality for people of color. *Cultural Diversity and Ethnic Minority Psychology, 11,* 69–81.

Cervantes, J. M., & Ramirez, O. (1992). Spirituality and family dynamics in psychotherapy with Latino children. In L. A. Vargas & J. D. Koss-Chionino (Eds.), *Working with culture: Psychotherapeutic interventions with ethnic minority children and adolescents* (pp.103–128). San Francisco: Jossey Bass.

Cervantes, J. M., & Sweatt, L. I. (2004). Family therapy with Chicana/o. In R. J. Velasquez, L. M. Arellano & B. W. McNeil (Eds.), *The Handbook of Chicana/o psychology and mental health* (pp. 285–322). Mahwah, NJ: Lawrence Erlbaum.

Chavez, L. R. (2001) *Covering immigration: Popular images and the politics of the nation.* Berkeley: University of California.

Coley, L. R. (2001). (In)visible men: Emerging research on low-income, unmarried, and minority fathers. *American Psychologist, 56,* 743–753.

Coley, L. R., & Hernandez, C. D. (2006). Predictors of paternal involvement for resident and nonresident low-income fathers. *Developmental Psychology, 42,* 1041–1056.

Coltrane, S., Parke, R. D., & Adams, M. (2004). Complexity of father involvement in low-income Mexican-American families. *Family Relations, 53,* 179–189.

Diaz-Guerrero, R. (1955). Neurosis and the Mexican family structure. *American Journal of Psychiatry, 112,* 411–471.

Dilworth-Anderson, P., & Burton, L. M. (1996). Rethinking family development: Critical conceptual issues in the study of diverse groups. *Journal of Social and Personal Relationships, 13,* 325–334.

Duran, E., & Duran, B. (1995). *Native American: Postcolonial Psychology:* Albany State University of New York Press.

Eamon M. K., & Mulder, C. (2005). Predicting antisocial behavior among Latino young adolescents: An ecological system analysis. *American Journal of Orthopsychiatry, 75,* 117–127.

Eggebeen, D. J., & Knoester, C. (2001). Does fatherhood matter for men? *Journal of Marriage and Family, 63*, 381–393.

Englar-Carlson, M., & Stevens, M. A. (Eds.) (2006). *In the room with men: A casebook of therapeutic change.* Washington, D.C.: American Psychological Association.

Epstein, M. (2007). *Psychotherapy without the self: A Buddhist perspective.* New Haven, CT: Yale University Press.

Fragoso, J. M., & Kashubeck, S. (2000). Machismo, gender role conflict, and mental health in Mexican American men. *Psychology of Men & Masculinity, 1*, 87–97

Falicov, C. J. (1998). *Latino families in therapy: A guide to multicultural practice.* New York: Guilford Press.

Falicov, C. J. (1999). Religion and spiritual folk traditions in immigrant families: Therapeutic resources with Latinos. In F. Walsh (Ed.), *Spiritual Resources in Family Therapy* (pp. 104–120). New York: Guilford Press.

Garcia Coll, C. T., Lamberty, G., Jenkins, R., McAdou, H. P., Crnic, K., Wasik, B. H., & Vasquez Garcia, H. (1996). An integrative model for the study of developmental competencies in minority children. *Child Development, 67*, 1891–1914.

Gilmore, D. D. (1990), *Manhood in the making: Cultural concepts of masculinity.* New Haven, CT: Yale University Press.

Gonzalez, M. G. (2000). *Mexicanos: A history of Mexicans in the U.S.* Bloomington, IN: Indiana University.

Griswold del Castillo, R. (1984). *La Familia: Chicano families in the urban southeast 1848 to the present.* Notre Dame: University of Notre Dame Press.

Halgunseth, L. C., Ispa, J. M., & Rudy, D. (2006). Parental control in Latino families: An intergraded review of the literature. *Child Development, 27*, 1282–1297.

Hayes-Bautista, D. E. (2004). *La nueva California-Latinos in the Golden State.* Berkeley: University of California Press.

Hernandez, R. (2002). Fatherwork in the Crossfire: Chicano Teen Fathers Struggling to "Take Care of Business." *Julian Samora Research Institute,* Working Paper # 58.

Hunter, A., & Davis, J. (1992). Constructing gender: An exploration of Afro-American men's conceptualization of manhood. *Gender and Society, 6*, 464–479.

Josephy, A. M. (Ed.) (1991). *America in 1492: The world of the Indian people before the arrival of Columbus.* New York: Vintage Books.

Kimmel, M. S., & Messher, M. A. (1992). *Men's lives.* New York: Macmillan

Knight, G. P., Bernal, M. E., Cota, M. K., Garza, C. A., & Ocampo, K. A. (1993). Family socialization and Mexican American identity and behavior. In M. E. Bernal & G. P. Knight (Eds.), *Ethnic identity: Formation and transmission among Hispanics and other minorities* (pp. 105–129). Albany: State University of New York Press.

Kuther, T. L., & Wallace, S. A. (2003). Community violence and sociomoral development: An African American cultural perspective. *American Journal of Orthopsychiatry, 73*, 177–189.

Leon-Portilla, M. (1962). *The broken spears: The Aztec account of the Conquest of Mexico.* Boston: Beacon Press.

Lewis, O. (1960). *Tepoztlan.* New York: Rinehart & Winston.

Lewis, O. (1961). *The Children of Sanchez.* New York: Random House.

Liu, W. M. (2002). The social class-related experience of men: Integrating theory and practice. *Professional Psychology: Research and Practice, 33,* 355–360.

Liu, W. M., Soleck, G., Hopps, J., Dunston, K., & Pickett, T. Jr. (2004). A new framework to understand social class in counseling: The social class worldview model and modern classism theory. *Journal of Multicultural Counseling and Development, 32,* 95–122.

Marsiglio, W., Amato, P., Day, R. D., & Lamb, M. E. (2000). Scholarship on fatherhood in the 1990's and beyond. *Journal of Marriage and the Family, 62,* 1173–1191.

Martin, S. (2003). The politics of U.S. immigration reform. *The Political Quarterly,* 132–149.

Matovina, T., & Riebe-Estrada, G. (Eds.) (2002). *Horizons of the sacred: Mexican traditions in U.S. Catholicism.* Ithaca, NY: Chusma Publications

Mayo, Y. (1997). Machismo, fatherhood, and the Latino family: Understanding the concept. *Journal of Multicultural Social Work, 5,* 49–61.

McCabe, G. H. (2007). The healing path: A culture and community-derived indigenous therapy model. *Psychotherapy: Theory, Research, Practice, Training, 44,* 148–160.

McLoyd, C. M, Cauce, M. A., Takeuchi, D, & Wilson, L. (2000). Marital process and parental socialization in families of color: A decade review of research. *Journal of Marriage and Family, 62,* 1070–1093.

McNeill, B., & Cervantes, J. M. (Eds.) (2008). *Latina/o healing practices: Mestizo and indigenous perspectives.* New York: Praeger Press.

Meir, M. S., & Ribera, F. (1993). *Mexican Americans/American Mexicans: From Conquistadores to Chicanos.* New York: Hill & Wang.

Mirande, A. (1997). *Hombres y machos: Masculinity and Latino culture.* Boulder, CO: Westview.

Mirande, A. (1988). Chicano fathers: Traditional perceptions and current realities. In P. Bronstein & C. P. Cowan (Eds.), *Fatherhood today: Men's changing role in the family* (pp. 93–106). New York: John Wiley.

Montoya, J. (1992). *In formation: 20 years of Joda.* San Francisco: Chusma Publications.

Muir, A. J., Schwartz, J. S., & Szapocznik, J. (2004). A program of research with Hispanic and African American families: Three decades of intervention development and testing influenced by the changing cultural context of Miami. *Journal of Marital and Family Therapy, 30,* 285–303.

National Council of La Raza (2007). *Paying the price: The impact of immigration raids on America's children.* Washington, D.C.: National Council of La Raza.

Niska J. K. (2001). Therapeutic use of parental stories to enhance Mexican American family socialization: Family transition to the community school system. *Public Health Nursing, 18,* 149–156.

Ortiz de Montellano, B. R. (1990). *Aztec medicine, health, and nutrition.* New Brunswick: Rutgers University Press.

Parke, R. D. (2000). Father involvement: A developmental psychological perspective. *Marriage and Family Review 29,* 43–58

Parke, R. D., & Buriel, R. (1998). Socialization in the family: Ecological and other perspectives. In W. Damon (Ed.), *Handbook of child psychology* (pp. 463–552). New York: Wiley.

Parke, R. D., Coltrane, S., Borthwick-Duffy, S., Powers, J., Adams, M., & Fabricius, W. (2004). Assessing father involvement in Mexican-American families. In R. D. Day & M. E. Lamb (Eds.), *Conceptualizing and measuring father involvement* (pp. 17–38). Mahwah, NJ: Lawrence Erlbaum.

Parra-Cardona, R. J., Wampler, S. R., & Sharp, A. E. (2006). "Wanting to be a good father": Experiences of adolescent fathers of Mexican descent in a teen fathers program. *Journal of Marital and Family Therapy, 32,* 215–231.

Pasch, A. L., Deardorff, J., Tschann, M. J., Flores, E., Penilla, C., & Pantoja, P. (2006). Acculturation, parent-adolescent conflict, and adolescent adjustment in Mexican American families. *Family Process, 45,* 75–86.

Paz, O. (1961). *The labyrinth of solitude.* New York: Grove Press.

Phinney, J. (1990). Ethnic identity in adolescents and adults: Review of the research. *Psychological Bulletin, 108,* 499–514.

Portes, A., & Rumbaut, R. (1996). *Immigrant American: A portrait.* Berkeley: University of California Press.

Portes, A., & Rumbaut, R. G. (2001). *Legacies: The story of the immigrant second generation.* Berkeley: University of California Press.

Powell, D. R. (1995). Including Latino fathers in parent education and support programs. In R. E. Zambrano (Ed.). *Understanding Latino families: Scholarship, policy, and practice* (pp. 85–106). Thousand Oaks, CA: Sage Publications.

Quinonez, N. H. (1998). *The smoking mirror.* Albuquerque, NM: West End Press.

Quintero, G. A., & Estrada, A. L. (1998). Cultural models of masculinity and drug use: "Machismo" heroin and street survival on the U.S.-Mexican border. *Contemporary Drug Problems, 25,* 147–168.

Ramirez, M. (1983). *Psychology of the Americas: Mestizo perspectives in personality and mental health.* Elmsford, NY: Pergamon Press.

Ramirez, M. (1998). *Multicultural/multiracial psychology: Mestizo perspectives in personality and mental health.* Northvale, NJ: Jason Aronson.

Ramirez, O., & Arce, C. H. (1981). The contemporary Chicano family: An empirically based review. In A. Barron (Ed.), *Explorations in Chicano psychology* (pp. 3–28). New York: Praeger.

Richards, P. S., & Bergin, A. E. (Eds.) (2000). *Handbook of psychotherapy and religious diversity.* Washington, DC: American Psychological Association.

Rodriguez, J. (1994). *Our Lady of Guadalupe: Faith and empowerment among Mexican-American women.* Austin, TX: University of Texas Press.

Rodriguez, L. (1996). On Macho. In R. Gonzalez (Ed.), *Muy Macho: Latino men confront their manhood* (pp. 187–201). New York: Anchor Books.

Rogers, R. H., & White, J. M. (1993). Family development theory. In Boss, P. G., Doherty, W. J., LaRossa, R., Schuman, W. R., Steinmetz, S. K. (Eds.), *Source Book of Family Theories and Methods* (pp. 225–254). New York: Plenum Press.

Sanchez, G. J. (1993). *Becoming Mexican American: Ethnicity, culture, and identity in Chicano Los Angeles, 1900–1945.* New York: Oxford Press.

Santiago-Rivera, A. L., Arredondo, P., & Gallardo-Cooper, M. (2002). *Counseling Latinos and la familia: A practical guide.* Thousand Oaks, CA: Sage Publications.

Shapiro, J. L., Diamond, M. J., & Greenberg, M. (Eds.) (1996). *Becoming a father: Contemporary social, development, and clinical perspectives.* New York: Springer Publishing Company.

Stack, C. B., & Burton, L. M. (1993). 'Kingscripts.' *Journal of Comparative Family Studies, 24,* 157–170.

Suarez-Orozco, C., & Suarez-Orozco, M. M. (2001). *Children of immigration.* Cambridge: Harvard University Press.

Taylor, B. A., & Behnke, A. (2005). Fathering across the border: Latino fathers in Mexico and the U.S. *Fathering: A Journal of Theory, Research, & Practice about Men, 2,* 99–120.

Tello, J. (1998). El hombre noble buscando balance: The noble man searching for balance. In R. Carrillo & J. Tello (Eds.) *Family Violence and Men of Color: Healing the Wounded Male Spirit* (pp. 31–52). New York: Springer Publishing Company.

Thompson, E.H., & Pleck, J.H. (1995). Masculinity ideologies: A review of research instrumentation on men and masculinities. In R.F. Levant & W. S. Pollack (Eds.), *A new psychology of men* (pp. 129–163). New York: Basic Books.

Torres, J. B., Solberg, V. S. H., & Carlstrom, A. H. (2002). The myth of sameness among Latino men and their machismo. *American Journal of Orthopsychiatry, 72,* 163–181.

United States Census Bureau. (2007). *The American Community-Hispanics: 2004.* Washington, D.C.: U.S. Department of Commerce.

Valdes, L., Barron, A., & Ponce, F. Q. (1987). Counseling Hispanic men. In M. Scher, M. Stevens, G. Good, & G. A. Eichenfield. (Eds.), *Handbook of counseling & psychotherapy with men* (pp. 203–217). Newburg Park: Sage Publications.

Velasquez, R. J., Arellano, L. M., & McNeil, B. W. (Eds.) (2004). *The handbook of Chicana/o psychology and mental health.* Mahwah, NJ: Lawrence Erlbaum Associates, Inc.

Velasquez, R. J., & Burton, M. P. (2004). Psychotherapy of Chicano men. In R. J. Velasquez, L. M. Arrellano, & B. W. McNeill (Eds.), *The handbook of Chicana/o psychology and mental health* (pp. 177–192). Mahwah, NJ: Lawrence Erlbaum Associates, Inc.

Welland, C., & Ribner, N. (2008). *Healing from violence: Latino men's journey to a new masculinity.* New York: Springer Publishing Company.

Wisman, A. (2005). Integrating culturally based approaches with existing interventions for Hispanic/Latino families coping with schizophrenia. *Psychotherapy: Theory, Research, Practice, Training, 42,* 178–197.

Wood, J. J., & Repetti, R. L. (2004). What gets dad involved? A longitudinal study of change in parental child caregiving involvement. *Journal of Family Psychology, 18,* 237–249.

Zamarripa, M. X., Wampold, B. E., & Gregory, E. (2003). Male gender role conflict, depression, and anxiety: Clarification and generalizability to women. *Journal of Counseling Psychology, 50,* 333–338.

Zambrana, R. E. (Ed.) (1995). *Understanding Latino families: Scholarship, policy, and practice.* Thousand Oaks, CA: Sage.

# 5

# *Working With Asian American Fathers*

ATSUKO SETO, KENT W. BECKER,
AND NIRUPMA NARANG

BEING A FATHER

My first feeling of joy
The excitement of being a father
A natural instinct to bond

Guide my children to succeed
Help and support them to reach their potential
Teach them to be kind, generous, and respectful

Wishing for us to always be close
An unbreakable bond
To be passed down to future generations

PRADEEP NARANG
*October 2007*

Pradeep is an Asian Indian American and a father of two adolescents. His 20-year-old daughter is an aspiring journalism student who hopes to empower women through her writing. His 14-year-old son is a freshman in high school, talented in computer technology, and loves to play football and tennis. As a father, Pradeep hopes his children will be grounded in Indian cultural values while also embracing their bicultural identity and exploring their own interests. Oftentimes, Asian American fathers are portrayed as "distant fathers" who are less involved in the lives of their children. However, these fathers deeply love their children and desire to have a close father-child relationship. Pradeep's poem illustrates his strong yearning to guide his children to become compassionate human beings while also fostering unbreakable multigenerational family bonds. His voice is a testimony to how Asian American fathers genuinely care about their families.

Although literature pertaining to fathering has grown substantially over the past two decades, research is sparse when compared with mothering (Ang, 2006). Studies investigating parenting among Asian Americans often consist solely of mothers or include a small number of fathers (S. Y. Kim & Wong, 2002). Therefore, extant practice and research on Asian American fathers shows substantial limitations (McLoyd, Cauce, Takeuchi, & Wilson, 2000), supporting the need for increased attention to this population as well as counseling strategies that are culturally sensitive.

This chapter is divided into two major parts. The first section covers elements pertinent to the identity of Asian American fathers. Understanding Asian Americans from sociocultural and historical perspectives is crucial in clinical work (Kinoshita & Hsu, 2007). Therefore, this section briefly explores masculinity and ethnic identities of Asian American fathers, the impact of immigration and acculturation, and fathering and father-child relationships within Asian cultures. The second portion of the chapter offers helpful recommendations professionals can incorporate when working with this population.

Asian Americans have been one of the fastest growing ethnic populations in the United States (Dinh & Nguyen, 2006; Hall & Eap, 2007) and are expected to reach 22 million by 2025, making up 6.5% of the total U.S. population (Chen, Sullivan, Lu, & Shibusawa, 2003). Comprised of over 40 subgroups (Kinoshita & Hsu, 2007) and 20 nationalities (Schoen, 2005), Asian Americans are heterogeneous in that they represent diverse cultural, ethnic, linguistic, religious, and immigration backgrounds (Dinh & Nguyen, 2006; Kinoshita & Hsu, 2007). Consequently, generalization of study findings and literature across the Asian American population raises the concern of overlooking the within-group diversity represented by each Asian ethnic group. The primary purpose of this chapter, therefore, is not to generalize the experiences of Asian American fathers, but rather to share our perspectives on this diverse population and invite others to do the same. We believe that increased dialogue will help create stronger advocacy work for this population. Research that acknowledges the diversity among fathers of Asian heritage and counseling approaches respectful of their familial and cultural contexts will help address this gap in the literature.

# UNDERSTANDING ASIAN AMERICAN FATHERS

## *Asian American Identity*

While Asian Americans are praised as a *model minority*, the group is also perceived as invisible. Sun and Starosta (2006) conducted a qualitative study investigating the perceived invisibility among Asian American professionals. Although some study participants reported their visibility as an individual, all agreed that Asian Americans as a group are invisible (Sun & Starosta, 2006). The authors further stated that the experience of mistreatment and feeling invisible occurred for study participants who have limited language proficiency as well as those who are U.S.-born and speak fluent English. Asian Americans have been labeled as "perpetual foreigners or aliens" (W. M. Liu & Chang, 2007, p. 198) and continue to remain in a minority status in the United States despite the rapid population increase. "To this day, Asian Americans are still singled out for racism and experience marginalization" (W. M. Liu, 2002, p. 108). For Asian American fathers, this social invisibility could undermine a father's role as a leader in the family, which in turn reinforces a negative self-image. Furthermore, a man's embracing his Asian ethnic identity as well as all the cultural heritages that make up who he is becomes a complex task.

According to a qualitative study involving Asian Indian fathers in the United States (Inman, Howard, Beaumont, & Walker, 2007), the ethnic identity of these fathers was maintained through strong family ties; participation in cultural, religious, and organizational activities; and the practice of traditional cultural values. Some fathers stated that their cultural and religious practices were essential to self-discipline. Conversely, the discontinuation of guidance from one's own parents and the Asian Indian community, and a lack of interest toward Asian Indian culture in the mainstream society were identified as barriers for maintaining a healthy ethnic identity. The Asian Indian fathers' bicultural identity was defined by their Asian identity being the primary focus at home and their American identity being prominent at work (Inman et al., 2007).

This study's findings raise several interesting points. First, maintaining one's ethnic identity is left to an individual or family rather than being supported by a larger system such as mainstream society. Second, individuals are capable of interacting with Asian and American cultures, but these elements are often kept separate rather than integrated. While separation of two cultures may be practical, it requires individuals to shift their attitudes and behaviors to function in a particular cultural context. Oftentimes, fathers adapt to the mainstream culture as they work outside the family while maintaining Asian cultural values at home. The question "Is there a way Asian American fathers can feel truly accepted by and connected to more than one culture without altering their behaviors and attitudes?" deserves consideration.

It is critical to help Asian American fathers develop and maintain a strong sense of self-worth as well as fostering an optimal ethnic identity that transcends both Asian and mainstream American cultures. Cheryan and Tsai (2007) proposed that the identities of Asian, American, and Asian American are essential in understanding Asian American ethnic identity. This perspective is based on the notion that one's ethnic identity can be broadly defined by "the attachment one feels to one's cultural *heritages,* including those not based specifically on one's country of origin" (Cheryan & Tsai, p. 125). Identities of both Asian and American are considered imperative to U.S.-born as well as foreign-born individuals, although the degree to which one embraces these identities varies (Cheryan & Tsai). In addition to understanding Asian and American identities as individual entities, supporting Asian American fathers to establish and maintain a sense of belonging to both Asian and American cultures promotes the integration of two identities rather than a severance. Acceptance in both cultures reduces the feeling of alienation and helps maintain self-worth. Moreover, a sense of connection to both identities is not only essential for a father to foster his own identity, but also can impact how he supports the identity development of his children.

### *Asian American Masculinity*

Masculinity of Asian American fathers may be understood within a context of relationships. D. Sue (2005) explained that for Asian American men, "...maleness is not defined individually but as a function of how the individual relates to others" (p. 366). Unlike the Western emphasis of individualism, Asian American men operate from a perspective of "collective self" in which individuals are "...constantly searching for ways to assimilate self into a social context without losing the prominence of family in all decisions" (Ino, 2005, p. 260). It is possible that the masculinity of an Asian American father is closely associated with how the needs of the family are being met through his loyalty as a son, brother, husband, and father to his family and his dedication to fulfill these roles. Furthermore, males in traditional Asian families are raised to follow their predecessors by maintaining cultural values and passing them on to future generations (D. Sue, 2005). Deviating from this expectation could negatively reflect upon their masculinity.

Because norms and expectations set forth by mainstream society differ from traditional values and masculinity as defined in Asian cultures, Asian American men often struggle to establish their masculinity within these dual contexts (W. M. Liu & Chang, 2007; D. Sue, 2005). A similar perspective is shared by Chua and Fujino (1999), who suggested that Asian American men experience a double standard of being a male and a minority in the mainstream society. Therefore, redefining their masculinity is a challenge. The development of Asian American masculinity is an intricate process shaped by various factors including traditional Asian cultural values, norms of mainstream society, and the experience of being a minority (D. Sue, 2005). While more literature discussing the masculinity of Asian American men is available today, there have been a limited number of studies conducted to examine the development of masculinity of Asian American men (Chua & Fujino). A lack of resources and social support to promote optimal Asian American masculinity makes it difficult for fathers to have strong self-confidence. Consequently, a father may feel less competent about being the head of the family or a strong role model for his children.

## Impact of Immigration on Family Relationships

Individuals of Asian heritage have immigrated to the United States throughout different time periods. Immigrants arrived in the United States during the mid-1800s and early 1900s, during World War II, the Korean War, and around the time of the Immigration Act of 1965 (B. S. Kim, 2007). Immigration continues to influence Asian American populations in today's society. In 1998, foreign-born individuals represented over 60% of the Asian and Pacific Islander population (Riche, 2000). According to a review of the U.S. Census, close to 90% of children with Asian heritage have foreign-born parents (S. Y. Kim, Gonzales, Srroh, & Wang, 2006). As a result of immigration, various aspects of one's life, including "physical, psychological, financial, spiritual, social, language, and family adjustment" (Mui & Kang, 2006, p. 244), occur within the process of acculturation. Consequently, acculturation becomes a process that requires resiliency and adaptation among individuals as well as the ongoing integration of "old and new" within a multigenerational family.

Asian American men tend to take longer to acculturate into mainstream society than their female counterparts (D. Sue, 1996). This raises concern for the psychological well-being of these fathers and their families. For example, gender roles within a family are often altered, especially when women seek jobs for financial reasons (Dinh & Nguyen, 2006). The concept of women working outside a family may conflict with the traditional values and religious beliefs with which these fathers strongly identify. For instance, Hindu, one of the primary religions for Asian Indians, has its emphasis on a subordinate role of women (Seegobin, 1999). Confucianism in Chinese culture also dictates a submissive role of women in a male-dominant family hierarchy (Chung & Chou, 1999; E. Lee, 1997). It is possible that some fathers become adamant in their traditional roles in an attempt to maintain the lifestyle that the family had in their homeland. Furthermore, immigration could result in lowering the social and economic status of Asian American men (D. Sue, 2005) as they face numerous challenges such as limited language proficiency and career opportunities, lack of cultural understanding, and the experience of being a minority. In their study, Takeuchi and his colleagues (2007) found that mental illnesses, including anxiety, depression, and psychiatric disorders, were more prevalent in Asian American males who self-reported low English proficiency. Consequently, stress resulting from immigration and acculturation could significantly affect psychological health (Chen et al., 2003), increase the risk of domestic violence (I. J. Kim, Lau, & Chang, 2007), and create multigenerational conflicts (McLoyd et al., 2000).

In addition, fathers may face a greater struggle to fulfill their responsibility as the financial provider. With the exception of Japanese families, Asian American families have an average household that is larger than European American families (McLoyd et al., 2000). Extended family members are more likely to be included in a household, particularly among Filipino and Vietnamese American families (S. M. Lee, 1998). A large household may be explained by the emphasis on strong family ties in Asian cultures as well as the necessity for survival. A father's strong commitment to his family contributes to the welfare of each family member and ensures multigenerational family prosperity. However, caring for a large family can be challenging and at times overwhelming in a society where Asian cultural norms are considered unique rather than standard.

## Fathering and Father-Child Relationships: Challenges

Interdependence among family members is a central theme in Asian American families (Yee, DeBaryshe, Yuen, Kim, & McCubbin, 2007). These families are more likely than European American families to live with their aging parents. This practice is in accordance with the value of *filial piety*, in which adult children assume the responsibility to care for their aging parents (Yu, 1999). The practice of filial piety also extends to the responsibility to carry on family traditions (J. M. Kim, 2003). The roles of "strict father, kind mother" (Yu, 1999, p. 21) are ascribed to parents, and patriarchal hierarchy governs family functioning, placing the father as the most powerful authority figure (S. Y. Kim & Wong, 2002).

A male-dominant hierarchy is the norm within many Asian cultures (Dinh & Nguyen, 2006), and the position of a father serves to maintain clear leadership in the family as well as to teach children to be obedient and respectful, attributes considered essential for appropriate child development (S. Y. Kim & Wong, 2002). Consequently, a traditional family hierarchy positions the father to remain distant from his children due to his financial responsibility as well as to gain the respect of his children. However, the traditional family hierarchy may be threatened when a cultural clash between a father and his children occur. This intergenerational conflict may arise when differences are not openly discussed and understood; therefore, a father's ability to work through the differences with his children will determine whether the relationships will suffer or grow. Because success of one's child reflects a father's paternal ability, fathers with traditional values are likely to remain strict with their children rather than being open to negotiations (D. Sue, 2005). Fathers with traditional values may perceive their sternness as appropriate and desirable. On the other hand, children who are more aligned with Western cultural norms may find this fathering approach restrictive and controlling. It is also a challenge for a father to communicate to his Western-oriented children how his love is evident in traditional roles. For example, a traditional father may not tell his children, "I love you," or hug them to express his affection, because these forms of expression are not congruent with Asian cultural orientation. If children equate a father's love to emotional and physical expressions, the lack of affectionate behaviors may be perceived as rejecting.

Dinh and Nguyen (2006) found that a significant acculturative gap between fathers and their college-aged children was associated with increased parent-child conflicts and decreased relationship satisfaction. The findings suggest that perceived acculturative gaps between fathers and children affect the quality of interactions, which in turn may amplify the level of stress in father-child relationships. Maladjustment such as domestic violence and alcohol abuse may occur when Asian American men with strong roots in Asian heritage have to adapt to changes in traditional values (D. Sue, 2005). Prevalence of domestic violence is also explained as an attempt to maintain the traditional masculinity and family hierarchy (W. M. Liu, 2002). Therefore, it is crucial to support fathers in effectively communicating with their children, whose cultural orientations may be different from their own.

## Fathering and Father-Child Relationships: Strengths

Strong father-child relationships contribute to optimal child development. R. X. Liu (2005) examined the impact of parent-child relationships on the psychological health of adolescents and found that Asian American male adolescents with close bonds to their fathers reported lower risk levels of suicidal ideation. Another study investigating fathers' involvement with first, second, and third generations of immigrant youth indicated the importance of fathers' roles in reducing the risk of substance use and delinquent behaviors (Bronte-Tinkew, Moore, Capps, & Zaff, 2006).

Traditional functions of a father, often framed in negative terms (strict, distant, authoritarian, etc.), also have positive meanings in the father-child relationship. A qualitative study including Asian fathers and their children revealed that children respected and appreciated their fathers who sacrificed their needs to provide financial stability for the family (Shwalb et al., 2004). Although these children wanted to spend more time with their fathers, they also felt loved by their fathers. A father's love for his family was reflected in his ability to provide financial security that offered better educational opportunities, which in turn led to the success of his children. Fathers believed they set positive examples for their children by demonstrating important moral principles, such as a strong work ethic, self-discipline, and a good personal disposition. These fathers also demonstrated a willingness to alter their fathering styles. For example, some fathers reported that living in the United States made them express their affections to their children more openly and spend more time with their children. Most importantly, these fathers felt that integrating positive fathering characteristics from both Asian and American cultures contributed to a sense of fulfillment as a man and a father (Shwalb et al., 2004).

## COUNSELING ASIAN AMERICAN FATHERS

### *Potential Barriers*

In the past few decades, there has been an increased number of mental health services established that are consistent with Asian cultural values and practices (Chen et al., 2003). However, the frequency of service utilization varies significantly from one area in the United States to another (Leong, Chang, & Lee, 2007). In addition, it may be difficult to find culturally sensitive services unless individuals live within a highly populated Asian American community. Furthermore, extant research examining the utilization of mental health services has focused on specific subgroups (e.g., college-aged populations) within the Asian American population (Leong et al., 2007; Hall & Eap, 2007), making generalizations difficult. Similar challenges are observed in the research pertaining to psychometrics (Kinoshita & Hsu, 2007; Hall & Eap, 2007), as many of the existing assessment instruments are not culturally sensitive to Asian Americans (Kinoshita & Hsu, 2007). A consensus among scholars suggests that continued enhancement of culturally aligned mental health services including assessment and interventions is essential to the well-being of Asian Americans.

Consumer concerns including the fear of *losing face* (Hall & Eap, 2007; Park, 2006), the concept of *shame* (D. W. Sue & Sue, 2003), and the stigma attached to mental illness (Ino, 2005) often become barriers for seeking counseling services. Stereotypes associated with the model minority portray Asian Americans as a successful and well-adjusted group and overlook the issues faced by individuals and their need for mental health services (Inman & Yeh, 2007). In addition to these cultural barriers, mental health providers need to be sensitive to a client's experience in counseling, because client dissatisfaction with mental health services has been noted in the literature. According to the review of existing literature by Leong, Chang, and Lee (2007), Asian American clients reported less satisfaction with their treatment than did white clients. Differences in communication styles and discrepancies between counselors and clients about the expectations toward counseling may contribute to client discontent. While more resources are available to help professionals understand Asian cultural values as a way of explaining a client's perception of and attitude toward counseling, little is known about gender-sensitive approaches to counseling

Asian Americans. Studies investigating variables associated with positive counseling relationships and outcomes among Asian American men will afford professionals the knowledge to develop counseling strategies that consider the family, gender roles, cultural values, and masculinity of the client.

For mental health services to be more relevant to Asian American fathers, agencies and professionals are encouraged to provide information in multiple languages, staff professionals of Asian background, and develop outreach efforts with ethnic communities. Offering traditional counseling services that are tailored to the needs of Asian American fathers is also imperative. For example, D. Sue (1996) recommended the use of gender-specific groups to promote the optimal development of self-identity among Asian American men. A men's group may be useful to fathers in exploring the dimensions of their identity, including masculinity, ethnic and racial identities, gender roles, and family roles as interrelated with their role of father. Counseling groups that are exclusive to Asian American men or fathers are not only therapeutic but also promote the concept of community ties for the clients. In addition to traditional counseling services and allowing fathers to address their concerns, social bonding events that are less stigmatized and correspond with cultural traditions can be an ideal setting for education and support building. For example, effective parenting can be explored at a movie night where fathers view and discuss films pertaining to Asian American families. Potluck meals representing their ethnic foods provide a forum for fathers to share their cultural heritage.

## Counseling Interventions

Literature specific to counseling Asian American fathers is sparse. However, the following recommendations are general to Asian American clients and provide a framework for counselors to establish rapport with fathers seeking counseling. Each recommendation highlights the importance of recognizing, honoring, and fostering the therapeutic relationship when working with Asian American fathers.

*Seek a respectful counselor-client match.* To maximize counseling outcomes, offering clients the opportunity to request a counselor of specific cultural background may be helpful (Ino, 2005). Although the ethnic match of the counselor and client does not guarantee successful counseling outcomes, the importance of an ethnic and cultural match and its positive impact on clients has been noted in several studies (Hall & Eap, 2007). Therefore, asking a father's preference of counselor background could ease his initial anxiety toward counseling and foster the therapeutic alliance. Furthermore, having bilingual and bicultural professionals is considered essential in supporting foreign-born individuals (Zane, Hatanaka, Park, & Akutsu, 1994). Counselors also need to assess the impact of prejudice and discrimination on a client's life and understand how such experiences are manifested within the counseling relationship (Kinoshita & Hsu, 2007). The counselor's age, gender (Itai & McRae, 1994), and credentials (Seegobin, 1999) may influence the client's perception of the counselor. A cultural assumption may exist in that one's wisdom and expertise are related with age, life experience, and education (Ino, 2005).

Due to a cultural emphasis placed on respect for elders and patriarchal family structure, Asian American fathers may prefer older male counselors to other counselors. Parental experience of the counselor may also be important for fathers who struggle with parenting issues and seek counseling for advice. A counselor-client match is subjective and varies from one individual to another; therefore, the counselor needs to be comfortable with responding to questions that the client has about the counselor or counseling itself. In addition to credentials and professional experience, counselors need to collaborate with fathers throughout the counseling process. For example, a counselor may ask a father a question such as, "What fathering practices exist in your culture that are important for me to know about?" Doing so invites the client to actively participate in the session and demonstrates respect for his experience, perspective, and expertise.

An example of counselor-client match can be seen in the case of Mr. Yang, an immigrant from China and a father of three young children. He requested a counselor who speaks Mandarin because talking in his native language helped him be himself rather than having to "rethink" in English. It was important for Mr. Yang to have this option when seeking counseling services. When a young female bilingual counselor was assigned to work with Mr. Yang, he remained apprehensive. However, his attitude shifted gradually as the counselor self-disclosed her experience in counseling children and their parents as well as having been a substitute teacher in the past. Having a counselor with the ability to speak his native language and the knowledge of parent-child relationships was the "match" Mr. Yang needed.

*Explore the significance of immigration.* As discussed in the previous section, immigrant families are faced with a myriad of stressors in the process of acculturation. Not only can access to resources be limited, but also individual and familial identity (who they are as individuals and as a family) may need to be refined or redefined to make necessary adjustments. Varying degrees of loss are often associated with immigration as individuals leave familiar cultural and social environments. One's self-worth may be diminished as the experience of prejudice and discrimination amplifies feelings of isolation, inadequacy, fear, anger, and humiliation. Contrary to this negative impact, it is empowering to individuals to reflect on how they prevailed over hardships associated with immigration and acculturation. This introspection highlights a person's optimism and ability to excel despite adversity, strengths that may be overshadowed by the ongoing struggles of adjusting to a new culture.

Takeshi is an immigrant from Japan who has lived in America for over 10 years. As the counselor created a genogram of Takeshi's family, his stories began to unfold. He first came to the United States as an international student. After graduating from college, Takeshi found a computer company that would petition for him to obtain his work visa. This was "a dream come true" for Takeshi. During these years, he had visited his parents in Japan only twice due to financial limitations and immigration concerns. The genogram revealed that Takeshi is an only child with aging parents in Japan. Since he became a lawful permanent resident, he has been able to visit his parents more frequently; however, the feeling of guilt for not caring for his parents has intensified. In counseling, Takeshi expressed his frustration about how immigration regulations had created constraints in his life and caused sadness for his parents. Guilt and shame consumed him with the thought of failing his parents by becoming a "disloyal" son. The session took a positive turn when the counselor asked if Takeshi believed that his parents are proud of his accomplishments. Takeshi said he always felt their love and pride. He continued on, telling about a phone conversation with his mother who said that the physical distance never got in the way of feeling close to him. He spoke about his deep gratitude for his parents and his renewed commitment to carry on their legacy.

*Maintain client dignity.* A strong rapport with Asian American men that is based on genuine caring and respect is essential and helps clients maintain their dignity (Ino, 2005; Park, 2006). The concept of *saving face* is particularly important for Asian American fathers whose definition of self is understood within a context of relationships. The stigma attached to mental illnesses is prevalent in Asian communities as well as perceiving a psychological illness as a sign of weakness or unfortunate fate (Ino, 2005). Therefore, some Asian American fathers may hold a belief that they are too weak to handle stress or have failed their families by receiving outside help. In seeking help, a father may think of himself as an inadequate provider and feel guilty for bringing shame to his family. For an Asian American father who is often portrayed as a strong leader in the family, acknowledging one's psychological distress could contradict with his self-image of how he "should" be as a father. Therefore, counselors need to communicate their respect to the father as well as to his family members regardless of their physical presence in a session. Counselors are encouraged to acknowledge that a client's caring attitude toward his family is reflected in his willingness to seek professional help, and session outcomes will not only benefit him but could also nurture relationships within his family. By framing counseling as a healthy coping mechanism, counselors promote a nonpathological view of a father's help-seeking behavior and assist him in addressing his concerns.

The story of Mr. Rao illustrates the significance of maintaining client dignity to build rapport with the client. Mr. Rao was a divorced father of two children. Feeling depressed, he sought service at a university counseling center. Mr. Rao stated that coming to the university was easier than going to a local counseling agency. "It is less obvious this way." In session, rather than normalizing his fear, the counselor focused on Mr. Rao's courage to face the stressors in his life. The counselor also affirmed Mr. Rao's help-seeking behavior by stating that parents want to role model healthy coping skills to their children, and his decision to seek counseling may be an example of such skills.

*Recognize emotions with cultural sensitivity.* In providing culturally respectful services, counselors must be mindful of recognizing how their value systems influence their perceptions of and approaches to treating clients. When counselors lack the understanding of a client's cultural orientation, they run a risk of imposing their own view on the client and overlooking the potency of the client's value system. For example, emotional expressiveness and personal disclosure may be perceived as a sign of weakness by Asian American men (D. Sue, 1996). To avoid pathologizing a father's tendency to control his emotions, it is helpful for a counselor to understand his behavior within a cultural context. For Asian Americans, confining one's emotions may be an attempt to refrain from exposing him and others to shame (W. M. Liu & Iwamoto, 2006). Within Asian families, fathers attend to financial needs of the family and physical needs of children, whereas mothers are responsible for facilitating father-child interactions as well as providing their children with emotional support (D. W. Sue & Sue, 2008). Consequently, Asian American fathers may have their emotions suppressed, not because they are reluctant to express their emotions, but because they act within the cultural norms. In Japanese culture in particular, a man's ability to contain his emotions is considered part of his empathic responses (Hieshima & Schneider, 1994). Therefore, a father's lack of emotional expressiveness may be understood as his attempt to be strong for others who are in emotional pain.

While these cultural assumptions explain emotional constraint among Asian American men, counselors also need to be sensitive to the pressure some men may experience to conform to this cultural expectation. Psychological distress has been reported among Asian American men who experienced gender role conflict in relation to the cultural practice of emotional restriction (W. M. Liu & Iwamoto, 2006). W. M. Liu and Iwamoto further stated that these men were more likely to hold Asian cultural values. To gain comfort in identifying and expressing feelings in a congruent and authentic manner, Asian American fathers will benefit from examining the cultural norms and their own expectations about the expression of emotions as well as recognizing the positive influence of emotional awareness on the development of their children. Counselors can also avoid overgeneralization by having an awareness of how emotions are more openly displayed in some Asian cultures than in others. For example, Filipino Americans tend to be more emotionally expressive compared with other Asian groups (Sustento-Seneriches, 1997).

Mr. Nakano's counseling experience speaks to the importance of understanding emotional expression among many Asian American fathers. Mr. Nakano attended an initial family session with his wife and 11-year-old son, who suffered from high levels of anxiety. Mrs. Nakano began crying while talking about her son being teased at school, which in turn also brought tears to their son's eyes. Several times during the session, a counselor kept referring to Mr. Nakano and asking him to talk about his feelings. While Mr. Nakano appeared to be perplexed, his wife assured the counselor that he was sad and very much concerned about his son. The counselor gently confronted Mr. Nakano for "bottling up his emotions." Only the mother and the son returned for the next session.

*Identify strengths within the context of relationships.* Utilizing a client's personal strengths to create change is essential in counseling. However, when a counselor encourages an Asian American father to identify his strengths, the father may perceive the discussion as "bragging" about one's achievements. This type of expression could conflict with the cultural norm of humbleness. A more culturally consistent approach would be to identify his strengths within pertinent interpersonal relationships. For example, his compassion and dependability are reflected in his relationships with his aging parents; his resiliency is reflected in his ability to raise a child in a bicultural society; and his love for his family is demonstrated in his commitment to provide financial support.

It may also be important for a father to articulate how certain people and relationships helped develop personal characteristics that are essential to fathering. For example, the father may say his grandfather showed him the importance of patience and the selfless act of providing for his family. A father's desire to acknowledge others' support in developing his positive personal qualities or achieving his accomplishments may be more aligned with his cultural practice rather than recognizing them as his own successes. A counselor can compliment a father on having insight into the strengths of other family members and their positive influence on him. Many Asian Americans also rely on their spiritual and religious beliefs to cope with life struggles (Inman & Yeh, 2007). Fathers with strong religious and spiritual beliefs may attribute personal strengths to their strong faith. Therefore, engaging in dialogue about how his faith helps him overcome struggles may be helpful.

Mr. Hizon is a well-established businessman. Several years ago, he started a small restaurant that has grown into a successful catering service. In a counseling session, Mr. Hizon attributed his success to his parents, who showed him the meaning of hard work, honesty, and strong family ties. When the counselor wondered if Mr. Hizon has difficulty taking ownership of his achievement, Mr. Hizon replied by saying, "I tend to think that my accomplishments are the results of my hard work and support of others who guided me along the way. We rely on each other to succeed." The counselor genuinely asked Mr. Hizon about how he is perceived by others. "My friends tease me by telling me that I thank people too much, but they also tell me that my generosity is a rare quality," said Mr. Hizon with smile on his face. The counselor invited Mr. Hizon to further explore what his friends and family appreciate about him as well as what he values in these people and relationships.

*Assist with masculinity conflicts.* As mentioned previously, Asian American men experience a double standard for being a male minority. They have been perceived as an invisible group (D. Sue, 2005) while also being portrayed as a model minority for their strong work ethic and achievements. It is as though Asian American men face a second-class syndrome in which they constantly have to overcome societal barriers. Experiencing contradicting messages that society projects on Asian American men makes it difficult for them to develop optimal gender and ethnic identities. This struggle to gain self-worth affects men's ability to fulfill their role of fathering and guide their children to value their cultural backgrounds that make up who they are. Therefore, assisting a father in fostering a positive sense of self will not only be beneficial to his personal growth, but could also be a contributing factor in the development of his children.

Park (2006) addressed the importance of helping Asian American men explore and understand how their masculinity shapes other aspects of their lives. He explained that acknowledging one's discomfort is a crucial step in gaining comfort with one's own identity as an Asian American man. Park's concept can be generalized to help reframe struggles that fathers experience in their journey of being men and fathers: Discomfort is not a sign of weakness but a process of reaching a higher level of authenticity. Asian American fathers not only experience societal barriers firsthand, but also witness their children facing the issues of prejudice and discrimination. To be a caring and strong father, he must understand the complexity of his own Asian American identity, be patient with his own growth, and identify with his children's experience as he offers encouragement.

Jonathan, a new father, talked about his disappointment with a recent incident where his son came home from school crying because he was teased for his physical appearance. "My son should be stronger. He should not be ashamed of who he is," Jonathan said with frustration in his voice. The counselor asked Jonathan to explore what he would like his son to know about being a Korean American in a small community. This exploration led Jonathan to realize that although he treasured the family closeness and strong work ethic that were passed down from generation to generation, he somewhat felt constrained by his Korean ethnic background. In a subsequent counseling session, Jonathan discussed his insecurity of not acting like a "real man" in the eyes of his Korean parents and his American colleagues. He explored his increased self-doubt in his ability to guide his son to cope with the pressure of "living up to the expectations." As Jonathan expressed this challenge, it was critical for his counselor to reframe his struggle as part of the journey of being a man and becoming a father.

*Understand the relationship between cultural orientation and the parent-child relationship.* Although a clash of cultural values is not the foundation of all parent-child conflicts, it does strain the relationship when a parent is unable to openly discuss these differences with his child. Resolving a cross-generational conflict may require an accurate assessment of the degree to which a family maintains an ethnic culture, adopts a mainstream culture, or integrates both cultures. E. Lee's (1989) classifications of Chinese American families, *traditional, transitional, bicultural, and Americanized family,* describe families based on the birthplace of parents and children, familiarity of Western and Chinese cultures, and English language acquisition. Lee's conceptual framework can be applied to families of other Asian groups and helps counselors recognize differences in levels of cultural adaptations within a family as well as potential risks of intergenerational conflicts associated with cultural clash. Family roles may be influenced by how "traditional" or "Americanized" a family experiences themselves. Less acculturated fathers tended to be the least involved with their children, whereas highly acculturated fathers were more actively engaged in parenting (Jain & Belsky, 1997). E. Lee (1989) explained that a patriarchal family hierarchy is likely to shift into a more egalitarian relationship when families are bicultural. Lee's terms may be used as a conceptual framework to help understand how Asian and American cultures in a family influence the parent-child relationship.

Parent-child conflicts could be presented to a family as their struggle to incorporate diverse cultural values practiced by different generations into their daily lives (J. M. Kim, 2003). In session, a counselor can reframe a father's disagreements with his child as their challenge to work out differences presented in two cultures. For example, an Asian culture emphasizes family connectedness and social harmony, whereas the mainstream culture places value on autonomy. Therefore, finding a balance between these polarized value systems is a difficult task for many families. As a father better understands his child's struggle in navigating through a bicultural environment where differing values are practiced, his commitment to overcome cultural barriers for his child may increase. Reframing, when used effectively, can help an Asian American family view their problems in a more accepting way that allows positive changes to occur (J. M. Kim, 2003).

The case of Jonathan presented in the previous section may also illustrate this point. Jonathan's feeling of insecurity can be further explored by examining the degree to which Asian and American cultures are incorporated into his family's functioning as well as how he has attempted to resolve differences between these two cultures to embrace his bicultural identity. In addition, discussing how these two cultures are complementary may help Jonathan become more culturally integrated. As Jonathan better understands his own ethnic identity development, he is encouraged to identify with his son's struggles as a bicultural individual. A counselor can reframe a parent-child conflict as differences in Asian and American cultures and ask Jonathan to think about how he and his son can work together to handle such a cultural clash.

*Work from a systems perspective.* Working from a systems orientation is helpful in a variety of ways, and literature pertaining to family therapy for Asian and Asian American families is available to help assist counselors (e.g., J. M. Kim, 2003; Ng, 1999). A counselor may greet a father first to acknowledge the family hierarchy (J. M. Kim, 2003) or ask the father to describe the decision-making process and role responsibilities in the family, a vital step in the assessment of family structure (Janey, 2003). While these suggestions are helpful in establishing rapport with a father, a common challenge professionals face is a lack of involvement from Asian American fathers in therapy. The image of being a distant father combined with the cultural practice of a patriarchal family structure has normalized the absence of fathers in therapy sessions. Including fathers in family therapy may raise anxiety among family members who operate within the norm of an absent father. Some families may also exempt a father from participation in therapy out of respect for his role as the financial provider whose time is preoccupied by his work responsibilities. Family therapy, when used effectively, can contribute to both personal growth and relationship improvement by helping the family experience healthier ways of relating. For example, an Asian American father who wants to guide his child's success may tend to be overly critical and judgmental and fail to recognize that his approach is counterproductive. The father's lack of awareness may be due to a cultural norm of being a strict father. Counseling could provide an opportunity for a father to see the circumstances through his child's eyes and become a more supportive parent who sets clear expectations for his child while also offering encouragement and understanding.

A systems orientation can also be applied when working with individual clients, allowing a father to examine his concerns within relational contexts. Maintaining harmony within the family and in social interactions is essential to Asian American men (Ino, 2005). Therefore, counseling sessions can be used to explore how a father hopes to create harmony within his nuclear family, family of origin, extended family, ethnic community, and mainstream society. A father can explore how different aspects of his identity (being a minority, man, father, son, husband, etc.) are interrelated and hinder or nurture particular relationships. An emphasis placed on circularity within a systems perspective may also encourage him to understand how his transformation may bring about positive changes in various aspects of his life.

Our final case example speaks to the power of having fathers present in family therapy. Mary and her parents attended family therapy after she was found self-mutilating. In sessions, Mary talked about needing to escape from her feeling of guilt for not being a "perfect" daughter to her parents, who financially sacrificed themselves to send their daughter to a prestigious university. The more her parents gave Mary their guidance to improve her grades, the worse she felt about herself. Both parents were deeply saddened by how far they had pushed their daughter. "We only wanted the best for our daughter," the father quietly said to the therapist. When the therapist asked the father to share his thoughts with his daughter, he stated, "I don't know if I ever said this to you, but I want you to know that I love you." His words melted the tension in the room and the family started to cry. The counselor complimented the daughter's courage to speak up and the father's strength to listen to her voice.

## CONCLUSIONS

Faces of Asian American fathers are ever diverse. These fathers differ in their country of origin, understanding of Asian and American cultures, value orientation, language acquisition, and socioeconomic status. Asian American fathers may feel caught between Western and Eastern cultures as they try to establish social status in the mainstream society while also embracing their ethnic roots as people of Asian heritage. As stated earlier, fathers feel more "whole" when they successfully incorporate fathering practices from both Asian and American cultures into their own parenting style. Asian American fathers in the United States are exposed to a myriad of fathering characteristics that may expand their views of fatherhood. Living in a bicultural/multicultural context helps these fathers broaden their perspectives, but it also makes it difficult for them to solidify their identity. Part of the counseling process, therefore, may be to encourage a father to work through his own anxiety about trying new skills to find his own fathering style. Promoting multiple perspectives rather than endorsing a "one size fits all" image of a father is critical when counseling Asian American fathers.

## REFERENCES

Ang, R. P. (2006). Fathers do matter: Evidence from an Asian school-based aggressive sample. *The American Journal of Family Therapy, 34,* 79–93.

Bronte-Tinkew, J., Moore, K. A., Capps, R. C., & Zaff, J. (2006). The influence of father involvement on youth risk behaviors among adolescents: A comparison of native-born and immigrant families. *Social Science Research, 35,* 181–209.

Chen, S., Sullivan, N. Y., Lu, Y. E., & Shibusawa, T. (2003). Asian Americans and mental health services: A study of utilization patterns in the 1990s. *Journal of Ethnic & Cultural Diversity in Social Work, 12*(2), 19–42.

Cheryan, S., & Tsai, J. L. (2007). Ethnic identity. In F. T. L. Leong, A. G. Inman, A. Ebreo, L. H. Yang, L. Konoshita, & M. Fu (Eds.), *Handbook of Asian American psychology* (2nd ed., pp. 125–139). Thousand Oaks, CA: Sage.

Chua, P., & Fujino, D. C. (1999). Negotiating new Asian-American masculinities: Attitudes and gender expectations [Electronic version]. *Journal of Men's Studies, 7,* 391–413.

Chung, Y. B., & Chou, D. S. (1999). American-born and oversea-born Chinese Americans: Counseling implications. In K. S. Ng (Ed.), *Counseling Asian families from a systems perspective* (pp. 146–158). Alexandria, VA: American Counseling Association.

Dinh, K. T., & Nguyen, H. H. (2006). The effects of acculturative variables on Asian American parent-child relationships [Electronic version]. *Journal of Social and Personal Relationships, 23,* 407–426.

Hall, G. C. N., & Eap, S. (2007). Empirically supported therapies for Asian Americans. In F. T. L. Leong, A. G. Inman, A. Ebreo, L. H. Yang, L. Konoshita, & M. Fu (Eds.), *Handbook of Asian American psychology* (2nd ed., pp. 449–467). Thousand Oaks, CA: Sage.

Hieshima, J. A., & Schneider, B. (1994). Intergenerational effects on the cultural and cognitive socialization of third- and fourth-generation Japanese Americans. *Journal of Applied Developmental Psychology, 15,* 319–327.

Inman, A. G., Howard, E. E., Beaumont, R. L., & Walker, J. A. (2007). Cultural transmission: Influence of contextual factors in Asian Indian immigrant parents' experiences. *Journal of Counseling Psychology, 54*(1), 93–100.

Inman, A. G., & Yeh, C. J. (2007). Asian American stress and coping. In F. T. L. Leong, A. G. Inman, A. Ebreo, L. H. Yang, L. Konoshita, & M. Fu (Eds.), *Handbook of Asian American psychology* (2nd ed., pp. 323–339). Thousand Oaks, CA: Sage.

Ino, S. M. (2005). Clinical work with Asian men. In M. D. Glicken (Ed.), *Working with troubled men: A contemporary practitioner's guide* (pp. 260–272). Mahwah, NJ: Lawrence Erlbaum.

Itai, G., & McRae, C. (1994). Counseling older Japanese American clients: An overview and observations. *Journal of Counseling and Development, 72,* 373–377.

Jain, A., & Belsky, J. (1997). Fathering and acculturation: Immigrant Indian families with young children. *Journal of Marriage & Family, 59,* 873–883.

Janey, B. A. (2003, March). *Masculinity ideology and gender role conflict across cultures: Implications for counseling African, Asian, and Hispanic/Latino men.* Paper presented at the American Counseling Association Conference, Anaheim, CA.

Kim, B. S. (2007). Acculturation and enculturation. In F. T. L. Leong, A. G. Inman, A. Ebreo, L. H. Yang, L. Konoshita, & M. Fu (Eds.), *Handbook of Asian American psychology* (2nd ed., pp. 141–158). Thousand Oaks, CA: Sage.

Kim, J. M. (2003). Structural family therapy and its implications for the Asian American family. *The Family Journal: Counseling and Theory for Couples and Families, 11,* 388–391.

Kim, I. J., Lau, A. S., & Chang, D. F. (2007). Family violence among Asian Americans. In F. T. L. Leong, A. G. Inman, A. Ebreo, L. H. Yang, L. Konoshita, & M. Fu (Eds.), *Handbook of Asian American psychology* (2nd ed., pp. 363–378). Thousand Oaks, CA: Sage.

Kim, S. Y., Gonzales, N. A., Srroh, K., & Wang, J. J. L. (2006). Parent-child cultural marginalization and depressive symptoms in Asian American family members. *Journal of Community Psychology, 34,* 167–182.

Kim, S. Y., & Wong, V. Y. (2002). Assessing Asian and Asian American parenting: A review of the literature. In K. Kurasaki, S. Okazaki, & S. Sue (Eds.), *Asian American mental health: Assessment methods and theories* (pp. 185–203). Netherlands: Kluwer Academic.

Kinoshita, L. M., & Hsu, J. (2007). Assessment of Asian Americans: Fundamental issues and clinical applications. In F. T. L. Leong, A. G. Inman, A. Ebreo, L. H. Yang, L. Kinoshita, & M. Fu (Eds.), *Handbook of Asian American psychology* (2nd ed., pp. 409–428). Thousand Oaks, CA: Sage.

Lee, E. (1989). Assessment and treatment of Chinese-American immigrant families. *Journal of Psychotherapy and the Family, 6*, 99–122.

Lee, E. (1997). Chinese American families. In E. Lee (Ed.), *Working with Asian Americans: A guide for clinicians* (pp. 46–78). New York: The Guilford Press.

Lee, S. M. (1998, June). Asian Americans: Diversity and growing. *Population Bulletin, 53*(2). Retrieved September 4, 2007, from the Population Reference Bureau Web site: http://www.prb.org/

Leong, F. T. L., Chang, D. F., & Lee, S. H. (2007). Counseling and psychotherapy with Asian Americans: Process and outcomes. In F. T. L. Leong, A. G. Inman, A. Ebreo, L. H. Yang, L. Konoshita, & M. Fu (Eds.), *Handbook of Asian American psychology* (2nd ed., pp. 429–447). Thousand Oaks, CA: Sage.

Liu, R. X. (2005). Parent-youth closeness and youth's suicidal ideation: The moderating effects of gender, stages of adolescence, and race or ethnicity [Electronic version]. *Youth & Society, 37*, 145–175.

Liu, W. M. (2002). Exploring the lives of Asian American men: Racial identity, male role norms, gender role conflict, and prejudicial attitudes. *Psychology of Men and Masculinity, 3*, 107–118.

Liu, W. M., & Chang, T. (2007). Asian American masculinities. In F. T. L. Leong, A. G. Inman, A. Ebreo, L. H. Yang, L. Konoshita, & M. Fu (Eds.), *Handbook of Asian American psychology* (2nd ed., pp. 197–211). Thousand Oaks, CA: Sage.

Liu, W. M., & Iwamoto, D. K. (2006). Asian American men's gender role conflict: The role of Asian values, self-esteem, and psychological distress. *Psychology of Men & Masculinity, 7*, 153–164.

McLoyd, V. C., Cauce, A. M., Takeuchi, D., & Wilson, L. (2000). Marital processes and parental socialization in families of color: A decade review of research. *Journal of Marriage & Family, 62*, 1070–1093.

Mui, A. C., & Kang, S. Y. (2006). Acculturation stress and depression among Asian immigrant elders. *Social Work, 51*, 243–255.

Ng, K. S. (Ed.). (1999). *Counseling Asian families from a systems perspective.* Alexandria, VA: American Counseling Association.

Park, S. (2006). Facing fear without losing face: Working with Asian American men. In M. Englar-Carlson & M. A. Stevens (Eds.), *In the room with men: A casebook of therapeutic change* (pp. 151–173). Washington, DC: American Psychological Association.

Riche, M. F. (2000, June). America's diversity and growth: Signposts for the 21st century. *Population Bulletin, 55*(2). Retrieved September 7, 2007, from the Population Reference Bureau Web site: http://www.prb.org/

Schoen, A. A. (2005). Culturally sensitive counseling for Asian Americans/ Pacific Islanders. *Journal of Instructional Psychology, 32*, 253–258.

Seegobin, W. (1999). Important considerations in counseling Asian Indians. In K. S. Ng (Ed.), *Counseling Asian families from a systems perspective* (pp. 83–94). Alexandria, VA: American Counseling Association.

Shwalb, D., Bubb, R., Daveline, A., Humpherys, C., Evans, K., Erickson, M., et al. (2004). Coming to America: Asian fathers cross cultures. *Marriage and Families*. Retrieved September 21, 2007, from http://marriageand-families.byu.edu/issues/2004/spring/comingtoamerica.aspx

Sue, D. (1996). Asian men in groups. In M. P. Andronico (Ed.), *Men in groups: Insights interventions psychoeducational work* (pp. 69–80). Washington, DC: American Psychological Association.

Sue, D. (2005). Asian American masculinity and therapy: The concept of masculinity in Asian American males. In G. R. Brooks & G. E. Good (Eds.), *The new handbook of psychotherapy and counseling with men: A comprehensive guide to settings, problems, and treatment approaches* (Rev. ed., pp. 357–368). San Francisco: Jossey-Bass.

Sue, D. W., & Sue, D. (2003). *Counseling the culturally diverse: Theory and practice* (4th ed.). New York: John Wiley & Sons.

Sue, D. W., & Sue, D. (2008). *Counseling the culturally diverse: Theory and practice* (5th ed.). New York: John Wiley & Sons.

Sun, W., & Starosta, W. J. (2006). Perceptions of minority invisibility among Asian American professionals. *The Howard Journal of Communications, 17*, 119–142.

Sustento-Seneriches, J. (1997). Filipino American families. In E. Lee. (Ed.), *Working with Asian Americans: A guide for clinicians* (pp. 101–124). New York: The Guilford Press.

Takeuchi, D. T., Zane, N., Hong, S., Gong, F., Gee, G. C., Walton, E., et al. (2007). Immigration-related factors and mental disorders among Asian Americans [Electronic version]. *American Journal of Public Health, 97*, 84–90.

Yee, B. W. K., DeBaryshe, B. D., Yuen, S., Kim, S. Y., & McCubbin, H. I. (2007). Asian American and Pacific Islander families: Resiliency and life-span socialization in a cultural context. In F. T. L. Leong, A. G. Inman, A. Ebreo, L. H. Yang, L. Konoshita, & M. Fu (Eds.), *Handbook of Asian American psychology* (2nd ed., pp. 69–86). Thousand Oaks, CA: Sage.

Yu, M. M. (1999). Multimodel assessment of Asian families. In K. S. Ng (Ed.), *Counseling Asian Families from systems perspective* (pp. 15–26). Alexandria, VA: American Counseling Association.

Zane, N., Hatanaka, H., Park, S. S., & Akutsu, P. (1994). Ethnic-specific mental health services: Evaluation of the parallel approach for Asian-American clients. *Journal of Community Psychology, 27*, 68–81.

# 6

# *Another Side of Invisibility*
## *Present and Responsible*
## *Black Fathers*

ANDERSON J. FRANKLIN

Some Black men are engaged with their families as spouse and father. They are often overlooked, invisible to the public, and ignored in our theory, research, and practice (Connor & White, 2006). In this chapter, I will discuss how this circumstance of public invisibility involves particular challenges for Black men and delineates the struggle faced by these Black fathers who are the exception rather than the rule. I will also present some of the implications for working with these present fathers in counseling and therapeutic settings. Fundamental to working with present Black fathers is an understanding that many subscribe to conventional notions of both masculinity and fatherhood, while male roles in the contemporary men's movement make new transitions away from old models. The adherence to traditional male gender roles creates a unique role strain, one mixed with race, gender, and psychohistorical contexts central to understanding the world of Black men and the position of present Black fathers in it.

## STATUS OF BLACK MEN AND FATHERS

Black fathers engaged and present in the lives of their children must contend with overwhelming public misconceptions about Black men as determined by media portrayals and public discourse (Franklin, 1999; Franklin & Boyd-Franklin, 2000). The present Black father is embedded in census data and other social indicators, such as child care, education, and health of children (McLoyd, Hill, & Dodge, 2005). Likewise, they are embedded in communities of African descent if attention is paid to their presence and various family contributions.

There are 36 million people who identify as being Black in the United States, or 13% of the general non-institutionalized population. Of the 8.8 million Black families, 48% were married couple families, 43% were maintained by a woman with no spouse present, and 9% were maintained by Black men with no spouse present. When considering the marital status of Black men specifically, 45% never married, 39% were married, 4.1% had separated, 2.7% were widowed, and 8.3% had divorced (McKinnon, 2003). Within each of these statistical categories are responsible Black fathers. I know this from years of clinical and professional experiences working with fathers as much as I do from my social network and personal experiences of friends and family. We must conclude in interpreting these statistics that within the 48% married couple African American families there are men who are fathers and heads of household. Of the 9% of Black families maintained by a Black man with spouse not present, a number of the fathers, if not the majority, are responsible men. Likewise within the widowed, divorced, and separated categories, there are Black fathers. Moreover, of the 45% never married, there are responsible custodial and noncustodial Black fathers. Therefore, some disaggregating of these statistics to further identify Black fathers in the home with their children is warranted.

The mental health profession is often preoccupied with the larger statistical cohort of problematic fathers and ignores the smaller cohort of present, responsible Black fathers because of their socially acceptable and nonproblematic profile. It is analogous to the focus on the deficit model. For example, educators' greater focus on the learning-disabled versus gifted child, or the disruptive versus nondisruptive child, is understandable given the magnitude of one set of concerns over the other.

Present Black fathers are a group about whom little is known except what is inferred from their conformity to the desired social norm of fathers in the home. Little research and clinical data exist on the challenges faced by these Black men, who in good faith try to be the engaged and responsible father, spouse, copartner, and/or head of household. We know less about how Black fathers manage their paternal role across different socioeconomic levels, such as lower- to upper-income fathers. Poverty and low income do not preclude committed, responsible, and present Black fathers any more than Black middle-upper-income fathers guarantee present, responsible fathering. Further, a father's physical presence in the family does not mean the man, ethnicity not-withstanding, is an available, committed, responsible parent to his children (Habrowski, Maton, & Grief, 1998; McLoyd et al., 2005; Staples & Johnson, 2005; Johnson, 1998). Parenthood/fathering is a complex, multidimensional role in the family system.

## FACTORS IN MARRIAGE AND FATHERHOOD

Lack of employment is a major risk to Black fathers' being present and responsible in the home and with their children (McLoyd & Enchautegui-de-Jesús, 2005). Not being able to be a provider or feeling that one's status as a provider is tenuous places Black men at risk. Bowman (1992) found that quality of life for Black men, as well as self-esteem, was boosted by the degree of support provided by family, despite unemployment or instability of the provider role. Therefore, there are Black fathers who, in spite of fewer employment opportunities and successes, are present and responsible in the family. Black fathers' fulfilling of commitments and responsibilities in nonconventional male provider roles reflects adaptability of roles, which is seen as a strength of Black families. Hill (1977, 1999) and Boyd-Franklin (2003) noted that Black families had a number of strengths, including strong kinship bonds, strong work orientation, adaptability of family roles, high achievement orientation, and strong religious orientation. Clearly the capacity of the Black father to adapt to other supportive family roles when not employed is important.

Billingsley's (1992) study of the Black family in *Climbing Jacob's Ladder* sees the importance of role sharing and adaptability to non-conventional masculinity roles as frequent within even middle-class Black families. This can be overlooked by counselors and therapists who assume that Black men in middle-class families endorse more White male role family values in their conventional masculinity ideology. It could also be mistaken as conforming to the new emerging male role ideology and not viewed as a legacy within the Black family. Black men have been seen by a cohort of Black children sharing household responsibilities (Connor & White, 2006; White & Cones, 1999). The trend of role adaptability is likewise reflected in the capacity of the Black female spouse to perceive the value of her male partner's nonconventional provider contributions to the family. Many Black fathers have fiscal parity or, not uncommonly, make less than the female partner wage-earner in stable employment circumstances as well as transient unemployment times. There are engaged, stay-at-home Black fathers, often due to difficulties finding satisfactory and dignifying employment. Many in the Black community viewed the feminist movement as paradoxical to the historic role played by Black women, who worked and raised their children for generations, given the difficulties Black men had with steady employment (Hooks, 1981; McLoyd & Enchautegui-de-Jesús, 2005; McLoyd et al., 2005).

# DEALING WITH THE MYTH OF FATHER PRESENCE

One of the psychological stressors for Black present fathers is dealing with the myth of their presence in the home, much less that they are responsible and committed to the family. For those fathers who are unemployed, unintentional stay-at-home Black fathers, their being home is more suspect and demeaned by the notions of Black male malingering talked about in community controversy and public discourse. The labeling of "indolent" is particularly stinging for those fathers who are unemployed or refuse to dignify underemployment but want to and look for work. Fathers in treatment and in a variety of other consultation contexts have discussed their frustrations and even anger that their presence does not dispel notions of disengaged and inept fathers. More upsetting is when such notions are held by other Black people, including at times their own family and friends.

The overwhelming public assumptions about the Black family without a man in the house have credence by the number of Black female heads of households (McKinnon, 2003). The absent Black father is as much a looming social reality as it is a statistic. This presents a major challenge for men in the home who are bothered by the implications of applying this statistic to their situation. The dominance of this profile of Black fathers makes the present father to either ignore this portrayal, insulate himself from the implications, or challenge it directly when confronted by misconceptions of him as a father. The clinical work with Black men in response to the absent Black father image spans the emotional spectrum. For some Black fathers, the negative images and lack of expectations of being a good father discourage and even promote abandonment of the role.

## *Invisibility Syndrome as a Risk to Stable Father Presence*

Many present Black fathers believe that their parental contributions are truly invisible and underappreciated, and they face an uphill climb to offset public beliefs. Consistent with the theory and clinical assumptions of the invisibility syndrome (Franklin, 1999; Franklin, 2004; Franklin, 2007), repeated assaults on the self by slights and race/gender stereotypes put the man's psychological well-being at risk. An inability to have emotional resilience that protects self-esteem, self-concept, and self-efficacy from race/gender misassumptions can lead to debilitating outcomes. Assuming an "unexpected male role," such as being a present Black father, has the gender role stress from contradicting the prevalent notions that Black fathers are absent in the lives of their children and the family. No matter how positive the contributions, a present Black father who continually has to prove he is a valued, responsible father can lead to "burnout" and/or compromised contributions to the family system by negative attributions that undermine integrity and self-respect.

These negative risks are evident in the case of Jim and Ann and include challenges to self-esteem, self-efficacy, and capacity for marital partnership and parental competency.

## CASE OF JIM AND ANN: STRESS FROM THE UNEXPECTED BLACK FATHER PRESENCE

Jim and Ann were in parental consultation sessions in support of their son's therapy for problems in school. This meeting was one of only three sessions with both parents and a Black male counselor, given Jim's initial reluctance to attend counseling, believing this intervention could best be handled by his wife, Ann. It was Jim's perspective that it was a mother's duty to follow up on these specific parental responsibilities, a perspective that fits his traditional gender role beliefs. Moreover, like many men, he was skeptical of counseling as an effective tool for solving his son's problems. According to the "brotherhood code" of Black men, which is greatly focused upon protecting and providing for the family, he had to demonstrate the ability to take care of his own personal family business (Franklin, 2004; White & Cones, 1999). These problems with his son were private family matters. Generally, Black families do not like to disclose their intimate problems to strangers or, as Jim often referenced in counseling sessions, "we don't air our dirty linen in public" (Boyd-Franklin, 2003). Part of the success in getting Jim to come in for the consultation sessions was due to Ann's deliberately finding a Black male counselor. She did this believing it would make Jim more willing to come to the sessions since he would be talking to a man and, more so, a Black professional man. In addition, Jim would also be motivated by a desire to help his son. A child's school performance or behavior is a primary motivation for many fathers to come to counseling sessions. Ann was also gambling on an assumption that a Black professional, particularly a male, would understand Black family matters and the concerns of Black fathers. Furthermore, she felt that any ongoing individual counseling with her son would be better served by a Black male counselor, another male role model familiar with the family challenges of raising an African American son (Boyd-Franklin & Bry, 2000; Boyd-Franklin, Franklin, & Toussaint, 2000). Ann also knew that if Jim, who was sensitive to slights of Black males, did not connect to the early counseling sessions, he would devalue its worth and urge abandoning this intervention.

Sanchez-Hucles (2000), in *The First Session With African Americans*, discusses the importance of making a connection in the initial meeting and understanding what transpires dynamically between counselor and client. Often African Americans enter counseling with a healthy suspicion about the process. Men see counseling as a reflection of an inability to solve their own problems. Therefore, they can enter the counseling process guarded and armed with protective devices that come across as resistance. They can take the form of defensiveness to protect their image or stoicism in the form of recognizing life is tough but they need no help to minimize the problem. One means of lessening resistance is by the counselor's being genuine and not coming across as judgmental. Ann's determination to meet these conditions for counseling contributed to the achievement of therapeutic goals for the school year with their son.

With their combined incomes, Jim as a local delivery truck driver and Ann as a school secretary, they were a working middle-class family. They had been married for 12 years with a son, Ade, age 10, and a daughter, Nia, age 7. Their son had been in counseling for disruptive clowning behavior in class as well as academic performance below both teachers' and parents' expectations and knowledge of his abilities. Jim and Ann were concerned about staying on top of Ade's school performance, homework preparations, and behavior in school. Both were concerned with how Ade's behavior reflected upon him as a young Black boy and upon the family. The racial identity of Ade as a young Black man and the importance that both sets of grandparents attached to a family legacy of high morals and personal achievement were a source of tension between Jim and Ann. They had some different points of view about how to fulfill their families' expectations. The process of honoring family-of-origin values created another category of couple's issues for them to resolve, given their occasionally different views on how best to achieve this mutual aspiration.

During one bedroom conversation, Ann engaged Jim about her pet peeve that he should attend more teacher-parent conferences. Lamb, Pleck, Charnov, and Levine (1987) include attending children's school activities as fulfilling the responsibility component of an involved father. Participating in Ade's school conferences has always been problematic, given Jim's starting-before-dawn work schedule and needing to retire early at night. Attending teacher-parent conferences disrupted his sleep and his next day's work performance. However, although bothered by the consequence to him, his belief in its importance, independent of Ann's provocative stance on the issue, resulted in his occasionally attending evening teacher-parent meetings.

Upon arrival at the school for a teacher-parent conference, Jim was confronted by the (Black) security guard about his presence, which annoyed Jim. His wandering through the hallways looking for his son's classroom resulted in several other interactions by staff questioning his presence. By the time he reached the meeting he was irritated by his reception. In the meeting with the teacher, Jim perceived the teacher as having an instructional tone that essentially scripted a message that he could take to Ann, which seemed to imply that he could not properly represent their conversation. Jim experienced this as an affront to his intelligence, a disrespect of his role as father, and dismissal of him as a person of value. To add insult to injury, the teacher ended their session with punctuating remarks that Jim should make certain "Ade's mother" (not even his wife) get in touch with her if she has any questions. Jim interpreted that to mean she genuinely thought he was only a messenger, disinterested in his son's issues, not equally the responsible parent as Ann, much less a competent bearer of information.

When he got home, Ann asked Jim if he had gone to the meeting and gotten all of the teacher's concerns about Ade. This fully angered him. First, he thought Ann was questioning his commitment to attend the meeting, and secondly, that he wished to be allowed the privilege of representing his visit on his own terms. Ann's inquisition and tone, combined with Jim's anger and outbursts, triggered by both his experiences at the school and Ann's attitude, became the filter through which his school visit was discussed. Seemingly caught in a self-fulfilling family drama, significant pieces of his school visit were lost in the couple's bickering. Jim felt that the teacher's inference of Ann's parental superiority was dismissive of him. Consequently, Ann's concern about Jim's parental ability to handle a meeting with the teacher was confirmed by the couple's bickering. Jim came across to Ann as incapable of managing school visits. Jim and Ann accepted this marital communication challenge as something on which they must continue to work. A sign of resilience in their enduring marriage was their willingness to do so. Nevertheless, for several parent consultations about their son, Jim talked about the stress he felt when people treated him as a "Black male stereotype" before getting to know him. This view extended to his wife, whose questioning manner made Jim feel that she shared in the beliefs of others about Black fathers' competency.

Jim's concerns reflected the views of other responsible fathers with whom I have worked. Resolving these concerns in an appropriate and dignified manner that protects self-esteem and maintains self-efficacy is an emotional challenge and test of resilience. The essential psychological consequences are identity stress and conflict embodied by some of the following male and paternal aspirations: (a) trying to be a different Black father/male role model than the norm in the eyes of your children and spouse, (b) fighting your own demons about fatherhood while learning on the job, and (c) embracing conventional provider/protector notions in a time of contemporary restructuring of masculinity ideology (Bowman, 1992).

## Trying to Be a Different Black Father

One of the initial challenges for Jim and Ann when they decided to marry was the history of their former relationships. Each had his/her own notions of marriage and family. Jim's ideas constituted unique personal pressure. He did not want the negative characterizations of Black fathers to be a part of how his wife and children experienced him as husband and father. He made a vow prior to his marriage that he would be a different man in the family than the public notions of the Black father. He knew that both he and Ann had had the typical experiences of love in their young adult relationships with its fulfillments and disappointments. Both were very aware of the popular beliefs and facts about the difficulty in Black male and female relationships. The preponderance of single mothers and female heads of households and lack of available Black male partners were common knowledge in the Black community and for them too. All of these factors strengthened their commitment to each other and have helped their marriage to endure. The desire to defy the decline in African American marriages (Tucker & Mitchell-Kernan, 1995) was paramount to their union. Jim was going to be the "good Black father." He knew it was hard to avoid the social conversations about the Black male/female relationship challenges, given its portrayal in the Black magazines and media and other general public sources. He internalized a vow that had personal criteria of the good father. His development of an internal standard to which he assessed his daily accomplishments was influenced by what others believed about Black men. Whenever he experienced encounters contradictory to his views of a good father, like at the school, it worried him. He rejected notions of his unworthiness with indignation, angered that his good-father-self was not apparent. Confronting the stereotype requires extra personal psychic energy to protect the self-image as a good father. It contributes to identity stress and role strain by the necessity for Jim to engage and reject imposed negative stereotypes.

These couple counseling sessions for Jim and Ann were interspersed throughout a year of working with their son individually as well as in family sessions. This was an important arrangement for the treatment intervention. Connecting with Jim and reinforcing his parental roles, understanding of his son's issues, as well as how to manage both his son's behavior and his response as a father, was accomplished within a family therapy model. Many of the complexities of gender roles within the Black community, the impact of racism upon the family system, socialization of identity in raising children, and particularly the scope of psychosocial risks for Black males, make couple therapy important in achieving the partnership necessary for successful parenting (Boyd-Franklin & Franklin, 1998).

## *Fighting Your Own Demons About*
## *Fatherhood While Learning on the Job*

A part of the challenge to being the present and responsible father for Black men is addressing their own childhood experiences with their fathers (Toldson & Toldson, 2006). Given the absence of many Black fathers in the family, a considerable number of men have no role models about fathering (Caldwell & Reese, 2006). There are those who have fathers present but inaccessible in many essential ways. These are fathers who come home but do not engage in their children's interests. These present but inaccessible fathers can be unresponsive to the emotional needs of their children and physically isolate themselves in a favorite respite hideaway in the house or demand compliance to a self-serving household decorum of children who are "seen but not heard."

However, a number of responsible, engaged Black fathers have had the experience of being raised in a family or "village" of positive Black male role models in the form of grandfathers, uncles, cousins, or other males. These are responsive and engaging Black male figures who have taken particular interest in them. Some responsible Black fathers give credit to their athletic coaches for molding their father behavior and for guiding values from their mentorship. For some others, there are fathers more than adequate and even fathers of excellence, who create a high standard of behaviors to emulate (Connor & White, 2006; Parham, 2006). With the public assumptions of Black fathers' absence as background for comparison, fatherhood for Black men comes with many demons about competency. Learning on the job is a common practice, but not a reliable confidence builder. Confidence comes with time and experience. Learning about being a father while fathering cannot be overemphasized. This inadequacy of knowledge threatens efficacy. It is complicated by personal aspirations about fatherhood while simultaneously coping with in-the-moment self-evaluation of fathering competence.

Being the present and responsible Black father involves confronting one's own demons about fatherhood. One of those demons is reconciling personal notions regarding the "good-enough" father with public presumptions about Black fathers. This task on the surface appears no different from the task of many fathers, irrespective of race and ethnicity, but Black fathers have the history of Black men in the United States that contributes to their paternal identity as well as general restructuring of family in contemporary society.

Depending upon prior exposure to babies, children, and adolescents and introspection about one's own life journey, most men have little experience at this kind and level of caretaking projected upon the new, emerging father role. Moreover, it has been inconsistent with masculinity ideology and traditional male role behavior (Majors & Billson, 1993; Pleck, 1995; Watts & Jagers, 1997). Jim knew he was somewhat different in this regard. He did have some experience with caretaking as a youth. As the oldest child he helped his parents with his brothers and sisters by being put into caretaking roles, nontraditional for male socialization. In this respect, another unacknowledged role of some Black men is the older male sibling caretaker or male "parentified child," a category often presumed to be filled by girls. These early sibling caretaker experiences also contribute to notions of how to be the "good-enough" present and responsible Black father for men.

Hrabrowski, Maton, and Grief (1998), in their discussion of father-son relationships growing out of interviews with Black fathers who raised high-achieving college men, provide a guide and some insight into the "good Black father." Six strategies of successful parenting emerged from their study:

1. Child-focused love—encouraging their sons, praising their efforts and accomplishments, and recognizing failures while promoting resilience
2. Strong limit-setting and discipline—setting clear rules and limits with a focus upon work, respect, and telling the truth
3. High expectations—holding high expectations and helping to direct priorities, such as homework first, while advocating for advanced placements, appropriate schooling, and gifted programs. "Don't let down the family" was an important value conveyed.
4. Open, consistent, and strong communication—talking openly with their sons about the realities of life; being consistent in what values are conveyed and principles of discipline; being available to talk
5. Positive racial identification and positive male identification—teaching their sons about what it means to be Black and male in the United States; helping their sons to not let the race and gender issues be a deterrent to their success, but to understand the challenges that

they may face from it; taking pride in African American history and the accomplishments of many in numerous areas

6. Drawing upon community resources—particularly emphasizing the importance of the Black church in the community and extended family, both blood and fictive kin, as resources continually at the root of success of Black people; teaching the value of "it takes a village to raise the child"

A fundamental message fathers shared with their sons was: "Yes, there is bias in society. But don't let it hold you back."

## Being a Father in Times of Contemporary Restructuring of Masculinity Ideology

The conventional notions about a father being the provider-protector of the family as his primary role are under contemporary challenge with the feminist and male movements (Smiler, 2004, 2006). Reconciling this debate is an individual process as much as it is a group process. Moreover, the individual male's proclivity to both traditional or contemporary male ideology and behavior is frequently central to Black couples' relationships. The precarious employment status of many Black males causes Black women to assess the capacity of prospective partners to fulfill the provider role. Likewise, the realities of employment opportunities make many Black males think of how this legacy of instability (e.g., last hired/first fired) will impact them as well as the duration of the relationship. In particular, there is consideration of self-esteem, self-concept, and self-efficacy. Competency in roles is an issue in Black male-female relationship dynamics (Tucker & Mitchell-Kernan, 1995). Although interchangeability of roles has been a practice for generations within Black families (Billingsley, 1992; Staples & Johnson, 2005), women in support of men who have difficulty and instability in the job market with much less upward mobility must be careful of how stay-at-home roles for the man are understood in the relationship. These circumstances can be humiliating to the man, particularly if the traditional provider role model is internalized as central to his masculine identity.

Another stress experienced by the present, responsible Black father is the change and ambiguity of male roles in the family during contemporary times. Fathers are being asked to be more responsive, nurturing, and engaged in the lives of their children (Jain, Belsky, & Crnic, 1996; Marsiglio, Day, & Lamb, 2000). Interchangeability of roles and partnering are becoming the parental model. On the other hand, while the public debates new behaviors for men in marriage and in fathering, many Black fathers continue to embrace traditional male values about being a father and spouse. Among some within the Black community, there is a belief that African values toward family should be the model

(Akbar, 1991; Nobles, 1985). This calls for more emulating of African values, traditions, and practices that bind the family. Nobles (1985), who is a strong proponent of this ideology in his work at The Institute for the Advanced Studies of Black Family Life and Culture, expresses this core belief. On this point, Mbiti (1970) observed that, for Africans, the individual owed his very existence to all the members (living, dead, and yet to be born) of the family, tribe, or clan. Mbiti further notes that the individual did not and could not exist alone. The individual was an integral part of the collective unit, that is, the family. In recognition of this kind of awareness, others (Mbiti, 1970; Nobles, 1976) have noted that the traditional African view of "self" is contingent upon the actual existence of others (Nobles, 1985, p. 55).

A further example of instilling African values within the family and community is the African American holiday celebration of Kwanzaa, which begins each year on December 26 and is observed every day for 7 days. Conceived by Maulana Karenga (1989), a professor of Black studies at California State University at Long Beach, Kwanzaa urges African Americans to follow the seven principles (Karenga, 1989). Based on Pan-African values stressing the centrality of Afrocentric family, community, and culture, the seven principles utilize Swahili at its roots to provide a value orientation guide for the family: unity (umoja), self-determination (kujichagulia), collective work and responsibility (ujima), cooperative economics (ujamaa), purpose (nia), creativity (kuuba), and faith (imani).

Given the decline in marriage and family within the African American community, serious debate and alternative proposals abound as to how to resolve this social circumstance. A context for understanding how Black fathers originate their conceptions and standards on fathering should result from such proposals.

With the restructuring of women's role in the family and workplace along with the push of feminism for decades, men have found their traditional roles under assault and pressured for change (Staples & Johnson, 2005). For Black men, this presents unique challenges to masculinity ideology rooted in the Black experience but also a part of generic assumptions about masculinity. It is context molded by historic realities of Black male development for generations from slavery, through segregation by Jim Crow laws and liberation by the civil rights movement of the 1960s and 1970s, to contemporary assimilation perspectives emboldened by a growing Black middle class. Part of the challenge to contemporary Black male development is determining what connection fathers have to that legacy.

Black male history inevitably frames assumptions and expectations for the present responsible Black father as he pursues his own means to parenting. One area where this is exemplified is the struggle to maintain a stable family over generations of racism and discrimination (Staples & Johnson, 2005). Contemporary Black responsible fathers continue in the tradition of Black men who provide for their families under such circumstances. Though some generational differences exist, some of the old realities of decades past of Black men's struggle with education, employment, and ability to provide for their families feel very much a part of the present for some Black fathers. The contemporary disparities and familiar outcomes in these essential areas lead many to believe they are fundamentally still due to racism (Franklin, 2007). Black men and the Black community must evolve another perspective than conventional beliefs about racism as determining reasons for Black men in the home. Black men's aspirations to fulfill traditional notions of masculinity are still very much a work in progress, given social barriers. Therefore, as Black men acquire stature and stability from attained goals evolved from traditional masculinity ideology, it is now transforming into devalued old roles. This shifting social construction is partially why adherents to African psychology such as Nobles (1985) and Akbar (1991) would view aspects of masculinity ideology connected to African male values of self as family and community as essential to another model of the responsible father. Present, responsible Black fathers therefore are often fulfilling expectations of hard-earned traditional male role entitlements only to be encouraged to transform to another model for which they have had little consultation, much less that are reflective of their psychosocial realities.

## MENTAL HEALTH AND COUNSELING ISSUES

The challenge to counselors working with Black men who are responsibly present in the homes or in the lives of their children is to first acknowledge the normality of this behavior for these men. It is not allowing the legitimacy of present, responsible Black fathers to be repudiated by public assumptions about Black men. Counselors therefore must be aware of their own beliefs upon initial contact with Black male clients and most certainly when working with responsible fathers.

### *First Contact and Initial Counseling Sessions*

First contact and beginning sessions have numerous risks for connecting with clients. It is a highly impressionistic experience, as it is a professionally engaged process. This is especially salient for Black male clients whose assessment of empathic connections is primary in social encounters (Franklin, 1999; Stevenson, Winn, Walker-Barnes, & Coard, 2005). It links to perceived counselor knowledge and sensitivity to realities of race and gender. When we unpack some of what Jim was feeling by his marital strife and from the school visit, his initial session purposefully probed for the counselor's understanding about Black couple relations distinct from Black fatherhood. However, these probes were not just for the generic understanding of male roles but rather with particular intent (often through innuendo) on discovering how aware the counselor was of sensitivities evoked by Black couples' relationship issues. Therefore, counselors need to be informed about Black couples as well as Black male issues. For example, when the session led to discussing the purpose of the meeting, Jim often dotted his comments with references to Black couples' issues with verbal footnotes, such as "Well, you know how we are." Our credibility as counselors to clients is often contingent upon their belief in our understanding of them (Sue & Zane, 1987). Therefore, one interpretation would lead us to respond from our knowledge about couples; another would lead us to connect how fathering is contextualized by those couple issues. However, Jim with his phrase "how *we* are" was also soliciting our depth of insight into the Black experience. Our insight at this first contact may need to be no more than to express recognition that there are special circumstances for Black men and women raising a Black child. Conveying this message of empathic understanding is embodied by the genuineness of what knowledge the counselor has about its substance. Counselors do not have to be all-knowing as much as persons of integrity.

Because bonding is the goal of initial sessions, impressing with knowledge and insights into the Black experience or struggles of the Black father must be tempered and balanced. Therefore, another counselor risk in these first sessions is being too impressive and insightful with knowledge. Overly impressing our clients with our awareness conveys more artificiality than authenticity. It can also get ahead of the therapeutic process, outpacing clients' readiness for disclosure and therefore comfort with the counseling context.

## Understanding Black Fathers' Parental Concerns

If we explore some of Jim's concerns about his son, Ade, we learn more about his view of being the responsible parent. His concerns about his son were tied to his role as father but almost equally to how his wife perceived him as a husband and father. Her perceptions of him reflected some of the public attitudes. His self-concept integrated both husband and father role identities and created the lens through which he filtered counselor-client dynamics. It was rooted in race as much as it was in a gender perspective. Moreover, it is easy for the counselor to fix upon one perspective at the expense of the other.

Therefore, when Jim voiced his worries, they were laced with mixed motives. When Jim and Ann were asked about their concerns, they easily listed them, although originating from different perspectives. At first impression one can interpret them to be no different from parents in general. They were concerned about their son's academic success and performance, the need to stay on top of his school work, teachers' perceptions of their son's school behavior, grade tracking and preparation, as well as school safety. For the counselor, critical and empathic listening in working with Black men is disentangling the race and gender perspectives as presented in the therapeutic process. It can be easier for the counselor to embrace the universalistic gender perspective for personal comfort if discussing race, racism, and ethnic issues is uncomfortable. For example, both perspectives are embedded in the concern about his son's academic success and performance. The gender perspective can be linked conventionally to the desire that his son get a good education so he can be the best provider. Education is related to marketability for workplace opportunities, which elevates attractiveness in future relationships. The race perspective can be linked to lingering indicators of an achievement gap for Blacks and in particular a more critical discrepancy for Black males.

For Jim, his concern is wrapped in the knowledge that his son must achieve with help from monitoring parents but is still captive to the daunting factors behind the gap in achievement of Black males. This persistent reality of the achievement gap for Blacks puts his son at risk in unclear ways, except for reliance upon racism hypotheses. Nevertheless, it creates a quandary for him as a father and husband, as well as a man. What do they do beyond the typical parental monitoring that insures their son will not become emblematic of the achievement gap? For within conventional notions of masculinity, fulfillment of the protector role will presume some ability by Jim as father to insulate his son from these risks to his education and therefore future opportunities. To fail is an affront to Jim's identity. He has failed, therefore, both as a man and as a Black man, unable to find a way to rise above the inequities well known in the community. So Jim's motives and behavior in counseling place self-respect at risk.

## Personal Inner Conflicts Embedded in Black Fatherhood

Respect is a motive for being the good-enough father for present, responsible Black fathers. Therefore, inner conflicts that can compromise being a good father and defying the odds are a threat. Self-respect and respect from others is sacred in the Black male experience (Franklin, 2004). It is dramatically explicit in youth culture by the many rules that revolve around peer relationships and identity. The consequences of disrespect are legendary by the many acts of Black male on male violence. But the sacredness of respect is immersed in the Black male culture across many practices and styles adopted by men as motivation for positive recognition. It is embodied in dress, use of language, courtship, rules of friendship, honoring beliefs, and generativity in defying the odds (Franklin, 2004).

Jim saw his own insecurities as threatening his mission to be the good, present, responsible father. For example, his agreement to attend the parent-teacher conference, prodding by his wife notwithstanding, filled him with misgivings. Ann's beliefs that Jim would not adequately get the job done properly had some merit. Jim knew how uncomfortable the school environment made him feel, given the ghosts from his own school history as a child. He felt inadequate in articulating some of his concerns about education, in part because of self-consciousness about his literacy and also from constraining his anger when he perceived both he and his son were being disrespected by assumptions of school personnel. Moreover, he did not want his frequent indignation about Black male treatment to compromise the family image and status in the school, something his wife emphasized as of value. On the other hand, he had to maintain his self-integrity.

The multitude of inner personal conflicts can be a challenge to becoming the good, present father that many engaged Black males feel is so important to their identity. Acknowledging inner conflicts and then struggling to find ways to resolve their impact challenge Black male beliefs about competency. The perceived insensitivity to Black male issues by the profession only raises questions about the efficacy of counseling to remedy conflicts. Although inner conflicts for Black males include the scope of personal vulnerabilities known to counselors and mental health providers, for Jim as a striving, responsible, and engaged Black father, the challenges covered his concerns about his personal identity issues. His identities included being a parent, good marital partner, sibling, son, and friend in the Black "brotherhood," as well as his continually evolving identity as a man and person of African descent. The evolving of Jim as an emerging competent Black father must be viewed within his resilience across his lifespan. He has been a generative man and father finding ways to succeed, mindful of his strengths and weaknesses. It is important not to perceive his inner conflicts as pathologic but rather as precursors to resilient behavior that can be built upon.

For example, Franklin (2004) discusses angry indignation as one common reaction to slights by Black men that is frequently experienced by others as uncalled-for aggressive posturing rather than a justified response. This interpretation of intent as threatening obscures the legitimacy and curative purpose of this behavior. Choosing how to manage anger can lead to complex internal conflicts based on the difficulties of appraising when acts are worthy of indignation to determining one's response to them.

More broadly it can be viewed within the framework of Shanchez-Hucles' (2000) discussion of protective mechanisms employed by African Americans in response to persons' perceived to threaten the psychic safety of the person. Therefore, the community axiom "Don't get mad, but get even," which prescribes a resolution that says "you have to be twice as good to get as much," is an indigenous protective message used by many Black parents to teach their children how to cope with, interpret, and act upon perceived injustices. In some families this manifests as motivating children to study hard and become greater than people's expectations. Consequently, Jim's indignation about his treatment by the teacher was further fueled by his perception of his wife's complicit and condescending attitude. His anger could be seen in clinical treatment through the lens of pathologic notions of Black male anger. However, consistent with the lessons of resilience implied in these axioms, a positive frame of interpretations was utilized by the counselor to convert and channel Jim's legitimate indignation into getting more involved in his son's school life as well as preparing him for the realities of being Black and male in society. It is what some Black clinicians might consider as using a patient's "healthy cultural paranoia" toward positive outcomes (Boyd-Franklin, 2003; Grier & Cobbs, 1992). This intervention was not out of the realm of possibilities for Jim, because he had heard and lived by these axioms on racism preached by his parents. They were consistent with his values of protecting his family and being a good father. Therefore, Jim's being indignant and expressing it becomes a healthy, survivor response even if he does not always gain complete satisfaction with the outcomes.

## EFFECTIVE COUNSELING INTERVENTIONS WITH BLACK MEN: SOME FINAL OBSERVATIONS

These sensibilities of Jim mirror the complexities of understanding and working with Black fathers. There are some fundamental considerations in making counseling interventions effective with Black fathers. They include but are not limited to the following: (1) understanding the psycho-history of the Black experience, (2) knowing one's own beliefs and attitudes toward Black men (i.e., countertransference issues), (3) reaching out and being genuine in engaging Black fathers, and (4) keeping an open mind to adjust the suitability of models of intervention for Black fathers.

### *Understanding the Psychohistory*

Counselors working with Black fathers should know about the history of Blacks in America as well as the psychosocial impact of racism and structural inequalities on Black fathers. It is equally important to comprehend the consequences to mental and physical health as a function of the life conditions and circumstances determined by various African American communities. Included in this is knowing and appreciating the ethnic and social class diversity within the African American population that presents its own specialized challenges in working with Black fathers.

### *Knowing One's Own Attitudes*

It is particularly important for counselors to know their own attitude toward Black fathers. Assumptions about Black men abound in the form of numerous stereotypes. This can quickly be revealed in any survey of the public about how they perceive Black men. Franklin (2004) discusses opening training workshops with mental health professionals working with Black men utilizing this approach to get participants in touch with their perceptions. Preconceived attitudes can influence the counselor-client relationship. The powerful dynamic of a therapist's own thoughts and feelings in treatment is central to the analytic concept of transference and countertransference.

## Reaching Out and Being Genuine

It is important for counselors to consider approaches that reach out to Black men and fathers toward engaging them in the counseling process. Fathers in general do not seek out counseling, and Black fathers are no exception. Moreover, with the scarcity of Black counselors, much less Black male counselors, the motivation to seek counseling is further limited. Going out to families in their homes is a useful model for reaching out to Black men in the community (Boyd-Franklin & Bry, 2000). Therefore, finding ways to teach Black fathers about the purposes and ways in which counseling can be useful for men who father is essential to helping them engage in the process. Additionally, conveying the importance of confidentiality will reassure men and fathers that their personal business and vulnerabilities are safe within this therapeutic process. Most of all, the ethics of counseling and best practices should be conveyed with genuineness and honesty in the interpersonal communications.

## Adjusting the Suitability of Interventions

Related to reaching out and genuineness in the counseling process is adjusting the suitability of interventions. As in the case of Jim and Ann, several therapeutic modalities were employed to maximize being effective with them: couples and family therapy as well as individual counseling sessions when appropriate. No one approach was as sacred as was adaptability to the circumstances of the needs of the clients in the counseling process. This was particularly necessary to engage Jim, given his initial resistance and singular focus upon helping his son. Initially, Jim was more intent on understanding his son's problems than on understanding how his behavior, and his wife's behavior, might contribute to them.

In conclusion, understanding the issues and challenges for present and responsible Black fathers requires, first, acknowledgment of their existence in spite of perhaps their exception. Moreover, for Black fathers their experience in fulfilling this role is immersed within the larger challenges of being Black and male in the United States. Counselors need to be mindful of the legacy and history of Black men while allowing for individual differences in the interpretation and meaning of that history with any given person. Fundamentally, Black fathers are diverse in their orientation to being male and of African descent. On the other hand, there are shared values and meanings about being Black and male that are embodied by the conventional wisdom of Black males in their experience of a "brotherhood" (Boyd & Allen, 1995; Franklin, 2004). It is important for counselors to be able to work with these both within- and between-group similarities and differences.

# REFERENCES

Akbar, N. (1991). *Visions for black men*. Nashville, TN: Winston-Derek Publishers.

Billingsley, A. (1992). *Climbing Jacob's ladder: The enduring legacy of African-American families*. New York: Simon & Schuster.

Bowman, P. J. (1992). Coping with provider role strain: Adaptive cultural resources among black husband-fathers. In A.K.H. Burlew, W. C. Banks, H. P. McAdoo, & D. A. Azibo (Eds.), *African American psychology: Theory research and practice* (pp. 135). Newbury Park, CA: Sage.

Boyd H., Allen R. L. (Ed.). (1995). *Brotherman: The odyssey of black men in America*. New York: Ballantine Books.

Boyd-Franklin, N. (2003). *Black families in therapy: Understanding the African American experience* (2nd ed.). New York: Guilford Press.

Boyd-Franklin, N., & Bry, B. H. (2000). *Reaching out in family therapy: Home-based, school, and community interventions*. New York: Guilford Press.

Boyd-Franklin, N., Franklin, A. J., & Toussaint, P. (2000). *Boys into men: Raising our African American teenage sons*. New York: Dutton/Penguin Books.

Boyd-Franklin, N., & Franklin, A. J. (1998). African American couples in therapy. In M. McGoldrick (Ed.), *Re-visioning family therapy: Race, culture, and gender in clinical practice* (pp. 268–281). New York: Guilford Press.

Caldwell, L. D., & Reese, L. (2006). The fatherless father: On becoming dad. In M. E. Connor, & J. L. White (Eds.), *Black fathers: An invisible presence in America* (pp. 169–187). Mahwah, NJ: Lawrence Erlbaum Associates Publishers.

Connor, M. E. (2006). My dad, my main man. In M. E. Connor, & J. L. White (Eds.), *Black fathers: An invisible presence in America* (pp. 73–86). Mahwah, NJ: Lawrence Erlbaum Associates Publishers.

Connor, M. E., & White, J. L. (Eds.). (2006). *Black fathers: An invisible presence in America*. Mahwah, NJ: Lawrence Erlbaum Associates Publishers.

Franklin, A. J. (1999). Invisibility syndrome and racial identity development in psychotherapy and counseling African American men. *Counseling Psychologist, 27*(6), 761–793.

Franklin, A. J. (2004). *From brotherhood to manhood: How black men rescue their relationships and dreams from the invisibility syndrome*. New York: John Wiley & Sons.

Franklin, A. J. (2007). Gender, race, and invisibility in psychotherapy with African American men. In J. C. Muran (Ed.), *Dialogues on difference: Studies of diversity in the therapeutic relationship* (pp. 117–131). Washington, DC: American Psychological Association.

Franklin, A. J., & Boyd-Franklin, N. (2000). Invisibility syndrome: A clinical model of the effects of racism on African-American males. *American Journal of Orthopsychiatry, 70*(1), 33–41.

Grier, W. H., & Cobbs, P. M. (1992). Black rage. New York: Basic Books.

Habrowski, F., Maton, K., & Grief, G. (1998). *Overcoming the odds: Raising academically successful African American males*. New York: Oxford University Press.

Hill, R. (1977). *The strengths of black families*. New York: Emerson-Hall.

Hill, R. (1999). *The strengths of black families: Twenty-five years later*. Lanham, MD: University Press of America.

Hooks, B. (1981). *Black women and feminism*. Boston: South End Press.

Jain, A., Belsky, J., & Crnic, K. (1996). Beyond fathering behaviors: Types of dads. *Journal of Family Psychology, 10*(4), 431–442.

Johnson, E. H. (1998). *Brothers on the mend: Understanding and healing anger for African American men and women.* New York: Pocket Books.

Karenga, M. (1989). *The African American holiday of KWANZAA: A celebration of family, community, & culture.* Los Angeles: University of Sankore Press.

Lamb, M. E., Pleck, J. H., Charnov, E. L., & Levine, J. A. (1987). A biosocial perspective on paternal behavior and involvement. In J. B. Lancaster, J. Altmann, A. S. Rossi, & L. R. Sherrod (Eds.), *Parenting across the life span: Biosocial dimensions* (pp. 111–142). Hawthorne, NY: Aldine Publishing Co.

Majors, R., & Billson, J. M. (1993). *Cool pose: The dilemmas of black manhood in America.* New York, NY: Touchstone Books/Simon & Schuster.

Marsiglio, W., Day, R. D., & Lamb, M. (2000). Exploring fatherhood diversity: Implications for conceptualizing father involvement. *Marriage and Family Review, 29*(4), 269.

Mbiti, J. S. (1970). *African religions & philosophy.* Oxford; Portsmouth, NH: Heinemann.

McKinnon, J. (2003). The black population in the United States: March 2002. Washington, DC: U.S. Census Bureau, Current Population Reports, Series P20-541.

McLoyd, V. C., & Enchautegui-de-Jesús, N. (2005). Work and African American family life. In V. C. McLoyd, N. E. Hill, & K. A. Dodge (Eds.), *African American family life: Ecological and cultural diversity* (pp. 135–165). New York: Guilford Press.

McLoyd, V. C., Hill, N. E., & Dodge, K. A. (Eds.). (2005). *African American family life: Ecological and cultural diversity.* Duke Series in Child Development and Public Policy. New York: Guilford Press.

Nobles, W. W. (1976). Toward a reflective analysis of black families: The absence of a grounding (or how do you know what you know?). Invitational Symposium, Atlanta University School of Social Work, Atlanta, GA.

Nobles, W. W. (1985). *Africanity and the black family: The development of a theoretical model.* Oakland, CA: Black Family Institute Publication.

Parham, T. A. (2006). David Leroy Hopkins: The face of conscious manhood. In M. E. Connor, & J. L. White (Eds.), *Black fathers: An invisible presence in America* (pp. 113–123). Mahwah, NJ: Lawrence Erlbaum Associates Publishers.

Pleck, J. H. (1995). The gender role strain paradigm: An update. In R. F. Levant, & W. S. Pollack (Eds.), *A new psychology of men* (pp. 11–32). New York: Basic Books.

Sanchez-Hucles, J. (2000). *The first session with African Americans: A step by step guide.* San Francisco: Jossey-Bass.

Smiler, A. P. (2004). Thirty years after the discovery of gender: Psychological concepts and measures of masculinity. *Sex Roles, 50*(1–2), 15–26.

Smiler, A. P. (2006). Living the image: A quantitative approach to delineating masculinities. *Sex Roles, 55*(9–10), 621–632.

Staples, R., & Johnson, L. B. (2005). *Black families at the crossroads: Challenges and prospects.* San Francisco: Jossey-Bass.

Stevenson, H. C., Winn, D., Walker-Barnes, C., & Coard, S. I. (2005). Style matters: Toward a culturally relevant framework for interventions with African American families. In V. C. McLoyd, N. E. Hill, & K. A. Dodge (Eds.), *African American family life: Ecological and cultural diversity* (pp. 311–334). New York: Guilford Press.

Sue, S., & Zane, N. (1987). The role of culture and cultural techniques in psychotherapy: A critique and reformulation. *American Psychologist, 42*(1), 37–45.

Toldson, I. A., & Toldson, I. L. (2006). A father's call: Father-son relationship survival of critical life transitions. In M. E. Connor, & J. L. White (Eds.), *Black fathers: An invisible presence in America* (pp. 147–168). Mahwah, NJ: Lawrence Erlbaum Associates Publishers.

Tucker, M. B., & Mitchell-Kernan, C. (Eds.). (1995). *The decline in marriage among African Americans: Causes, consequences, and policy implications.* New York: Russell Sage Foundation.

Watts, R. J., & Jagers, R. J. (Eds.). (1997). *Manhood development in urban African-American communities.* New York: The Haworth Press.

White, J. L., & Cones, J. H. (1999). *Black man emerging: Facing the past and seizing a future in America.* New York, London: Routledge.

# 7

# *Counseling Caucasian Fathers*

## *Affirming Cultural Strengths While Addressing White Male Privilege*

JESSE OWEN AND JON GLASS

Working with fathers offers unique opportunities and challenges for therapists to navigate. Cultural influences, economic pressures, and family structures can strongly influence how fathers feel about themselves and their involvement with their families. Caucasian fathers are not immune to these pressures. Counselors can benefit from broadening their conceptualizations and intervention approaches to help Caucasian fathers cope with the unique challenges they face as majority men.

The therapeutic literature discussing the dynamics of treating men has been steadily growing (Fagan & Hawkins, 2001; Good, Thomson, & Brathwaite, 2005; Mahalik, Talmadge, Locke, & Scott, 2005; Ogrodniczuk, 2006), which aids our understanding of how to work with a subset of men—fathers. Many of these theorists have encouraged therapists to consider how fathers' gender roles, such as primacy of work, self-reliance, and need for emotion control (see Mahalik, Good, & Englar-Carlson, 2003) can influence the process of therapy (Owen, Stratton, & Rodolfa, 2008). Further, the majority of the fatherhood research, sampling primarily Caucasian fathers, has produced cogent findings about (a) the positive impact of father involvement on children, (b) the multidimensional nature of father involvement (e.g., engagement, accessibility, and responsibility), and (c) the father's role in the family system (Lamb, 1997, 2004; Lamb, Pleck, Charnov, & Levine, 1987; Orbuch, Thornton, & Cancio, 2000; Popenoe & Whitehead, 2003). Collectively, these findings provide a foundation for understanding Caucasian fathers and will be expanded upon here as we further delineate cross-cultural influences that can impact Caucasian fathers.

At present, the theoretical and empirical literature has not fully vetted the specific dynamics for counseling Caucasian fathers. As such, we present a trans-theoretical model that blends cultural strengths, White male privilege, and identity (e.g., fatherhood, masculinity) with a systemic therapeutic approach. A systemic approach recognizes that fathers fulfill various roles (e.g., father, husband, co-worker, friend) that exist within their respective subsystems (e.g., home, children's school, work), and may be sources of support and/or stress. Accordingly, conceptualizing fathers' lives and presenting issues through these systems allows for an understanding of elements that are amenable to change as well as highlighting systems that are positive sources of support. This approach focuses on creating awareness of how they as fathers interact within their systems, what they can change to improve their interactions, and how they can cope with aspects they cannot change. This chapter is not intended to be prescriptive or a complete guide, but instead is designed to illuminate salient aspects of the treatment of Caucasian fathers. Specifically, we will start our discussion by examining the cultural values and gender roles that can shape Caucasian fathers. Second, we provide an overview of the cultural landscape, the demography, that defines Caucasian fathers. Next, we analyze the consequences of having privilege in America. Lastly, we provide a case study of a Caucasian father in counseling and offer a conceptualization based on a systemic model that includes fatherhood identity and societal factors.

## WHITE AMERICA: FATHERS' VALUES
## AND MASCULINE GENDER ROLES

Research has indicated that culture is an important source of variability in psychological experience in humans generally (not just minority groups) and that ignoring cultural variables in any population of study can impede our understanding of psychological phenomena (APA, 2002; Sue, Bucceri, Lin, Nadal, & Torino, 2007). Thus, therapists should acknowledge the differences among cultures, expand their understanding of the universal role of culture in human functioning to increase cultural competence, and ultimately initiate conversations with their clients to explore the unique meaning of clients' cultural heritage. These cultural conversations are important because failure to recognize or attend to the cultural heritage of Caucasian clients has been related to poorer therapy outcomes (Owen, Imel, et al., 2009).

As we consider the topic of Caucasian fathers, we should be careful not to assume that all Caucasian fathers share the same value systems. In fact, there is likely more diversity within Caucasian fathers, based on factors such as nationality, religion, social economic status, immigration status, relationship status, than there is between ethnic groups. For instance, the label of Caucasian includes over 50 nationalities (e.g., Italian, Irish, Greek, Russian), with some of the larger (numerically speaking) being from German and English ancestry (Roberts, 2004). While all of these groups share the experience of being immigrants to the United States, their journeys have been varied. Moreover, common descriptions of Caucasians in the United States have not disentangled religion from culture values (see Kiselica, 1995).

While the unique meaning of a client's cultural heritage will supersede any global description of White culture, we feel that it might be useful for therapists to be aware of some common aspects of Caucasian fathers to orient their work. These common descriptions are also consistent with some definitions of the value systems that embody Caucasian individuals (e.g., values that are associated with Caucasians who have been in the United States for generations; Kiselica, 1995). We recognize that this approach is not all-encompassing and recommend to readers other volumes (e.g., *Ethnicity & Family Therapy*; McGoldrick, Giordano, & Garcia-Preto, 2005) for full and separate discussions of the many ethnicities that comprise Caucasians.

## Caucasian Value System

Many Caucasian fathers have internalized the cultural value of individualism, which in turn can shape their interactions with the family. For instance, the primary family roles for many Caucasian fathers are to (a) be strong (at times the dominant figure in the family), (b) provide financial support, and (c) protect the family. Further, some have redefined fathers' role in the family as being more engaged—teaching, disciplining, and providing love and affection (Summers et al., 1999). Strength is found in fathers' self-reliance, personal determinism, self-control, and success (McGoldrick & Rohrbaugh, 1987). Accordingly, many White fathers place importance on practical solutions, psychological tough-mindedness (e.g., fortitude, limited emotional expression), and logic. Given their perceived position of power in the family, Caucasian fathers balance reliance on the family for support with their internally driven coping styles (e.g., denial, humor). Family connections through activities are also important for many Caucasian fathers (e.g., sporting events, tasks around the home, family dinners). The family unit is typically defined by the nuclear family (Kiselica, 1995); however, for many Caucasian fathers (e.g., Jewish, Italian, Greek), the importance of extended family is also paramount (McGoldrick et al., 2005).

Caucasian fathers' orientation to child development also reflects the quest for individuation and separation, with some exceptions for various groups. The values of self-sufficiency, achievement, efficiency, loyalty, and pride are some of the cornerstones of development. Many of these values can be witnessed in verbal and nonverbal interactions, such as viewing time as sacred (e.g., being on time, valuing others' time), speaking clearly, maintaining eye contact, and keeping promises (Kiselica, 1995).

Work and education is another key value shared by many Caucasian fathers. While the current trends suggest that many Caucasian men want their partners to work (Popenoe & Whitehead, 2003), it does not negate that Caucasian fathers view work as a source of self-fulfillment and pride. Personal accomplishments at work can be internally motivating and can contribute to Caucasian fathers' sense of contribution to the family. On the other hand, long hours at work and a dominant role in the family can produce distance with family members. This orientation to work also reflects the internal schema that personal effort can overcome external barriers. Accordingly, many Caucasian fathers rely on working as a metaphor for problems they face in other areas of their lives (McGoldrick et al., 2005). For instance, Caucasian fathers may believe that hard work and determination can overcome family disputes.

Given the importance of work and education, Caucasian fathers from lower socioeconomic statuses may face unique challenges. They may experience distress from not being able to provide for their families or not fulfilling their perceived gender role that is linked with work (Liu, 2002; Mahalik et al., 2003; O'Neil, Good, & Holmes, 1995). These negative attributions may lead to feeling depressed or ashamed of their actions (e.g., "I can't provide for my kids," "I am a failure"). Many individuals of lower socioeconomic status encounter varied mental health and relational difficulties (e.g., substance use, domestic violence, gender mistrust, low family/community support; Stanley, Young, & Pearson, 2005). On the other hand, Caucasian fathers from higher socioeconomic status may feel stress from trying to balance the demands of work and family (Cooper, 2000). For instance, both feelings of guilt and the need for achievement may indicate that fathers have internalized societal messages about what it means to be a Caucasian father (e.g., the breadwinner), but these messages may conflict with personal values, such as commitment to family. Many of the cultural values also complement typical masculine gender roles in the United States.

## MASCULINE GENDER NORMS

In one of the most comprehensive normative models of masculinity, Mahalik and colleagues (2003) proposed 11 masculine norms based primarily on Caucasian men: (a) drive to win and be successful, (b) desire for emotional control or to not express emotions, (c) engaging in risk-taking behaviors, (d) acceptance of physical violence if necessary,

(e) beliefs that men should have more power than women, (f) being comfortable with asserting oneself or controlling a situation, (g) desire for multiple sexual partners, (h) tendency to be self-reliant, (i) not approving of homosexuality, (j) desire to be seen as important, and (k) a primary focus on the importance of work. Over time, individuals learn or internalize gender norms based on cultural and societal messages, and ultimately these norms contribute to the formation of individuals' schema or self-concept. In turn, Caucasian fathers model to their children what it means to be a man through their interactions with their children and other family members.

The degree to which individuals are flexible in their expression of gender norms, and subsequently meet the demands of the environment, will likely lead to better psychological health (Mahalik et al., 2003; Pleck, 1995). For instance, a man who does not easily emote may experience negative reactions from a partner who expects him to be more emotionally expressive. However, this characteristic may benefit a man who works in a high-stress environment that requires a calm, logical responding style. In other words, conforming to masculine norms might be adaptive in some situations, while maladaptive in others (Mahalik et al., 2003; O'Neil, 2008; Pleck, 1995).

Given the cultural values and gender norms of independence and self-reliance, it is not surprising that many Caucasian fathers do not seek help and/or view therapy as a means of last resort (McGoldrick et al., 2005). Many of the traditional therapeutic norms, such as being emotionally expressive, reliant on the therapist for help, and self-disclosing, can be in opposition to the internalized messages that many Caucasian fathers embody. Clinical suggestions have also highlighted that the traditional modes of therapy (e.g., high reliance on verbal emotional expression) may need to be adapted for some traditionally masculine clients (Heesacker & Prichard, 1992; Robertson, Lin, Woodford, Danos, & Hurst, 2001; Robertson & Fitzgerald, 1992; Wester, Vogel, Pressly, & Heesacker, 2002). For instance, therapeutic approaches can promote flexibility in coping styles by (a) fostering awareness and acceptance about the relationship between gender norms and current behaviors, (b) challenging negative thoughts about expressing emotions and seeking social support, and (c) encouraging new modes of expression that may be uncomfortable (Levant, 1998; Mahalik, 1999; Mahalik et al., 2003; Ogrodniczuk, 2006; Robertson & Freeman, 1995; Wong & Rochlen, 2005). These therapeutic interventions may serve to supplement more traditional ways of relating with others and coping with problems. In support of these suggestions, Owen, Wong, and Rodolfa (2009) found that clients who conformed more conformity to masculine norms were more likely to report that emotionally expressive and/or experiential interventions were most helpful in their process of change (as compared with cognitive interventions or psychoeducation).

However, therapists may also want to consider alternative therapeutic interventions in which the approach or modality of therapy may more closely match Caucasian fathers based on their cultural and gender norms. For instance, in a series of analogue studies, nonclinical masculine men favored less traditional approaches to therapy (e.g., workshops, seminars, online counseling; Robertson & Fitzgerald, 1992; Rochlen, Land, & Wong, 2004) or simply less emotion-focused therapy (Wisch, Mahalik, Hayes, & Nutt, 1995). Moreover, masculine individuals are more likely to express their feelings in written formats versus verbal (Robertson et al., 2001). These approaches may appeal to Caucasian fathers in particular because they are more educational in nature, allowing men to feel some level of control over the therapy process where they do not feel forced to disclose uncomfortable emotions.

## WHITE AMERICA: THE DEMOGRAPHY OF CAUCASIAN FATHERS

In considering the landscape of Caucasian fathers, beyond cultural values and gender norms, there is wisdom to be gained by looking at the larger societal context. In this section, we briefly highlight some consistent themes in the literature about Caucasian men's sociocultural attitudes about family, financial/education influences on the family, and perception of commitment. In doing so, our goal is to contextualize Caucasian fathers' cultural values and gender norms within the broader environmental influences with the hope that counselors will consider these factors in their conceptualizations and implementation of therapeutic services.

Recent U.S. census data (2007) suggests that nearly 80% of men are White, non-Hispanic. Current estimates show that approximately 90% of these men will marry in their lifetimes (Connidis, 2001). Despite these figures, Caucasian individuals express less of a desire to want to marry (as compared to racial/ethnic minorities; Karney, 2003), which may reflect values of independence and autonomy. Additionally, this attitude may be reflective of an increase of alternatives to marriage, such as cohabitation. Cohabitation is 1,200% more common today than in the 1960s; however, it is also associated with an increased risk of divorce if partners do marry (Popenoe & Whitehead, 2005). Currently, this level of risk is associated with the importance of making clear decisions about the long-term commitment with their partner prior to living together (Stanley, Rhoades, & Markman, 2006). Unfortunately, many people are unaware of this risk and, in fact, Caucasian men view cohabitation as a safe and equally beneficial relationship to marriage.

The fragility of these cohabitation relationships is also highlighted by findings that suggest that nearly 75% of children in cohabitating unions are likely to see their parents' relationship end (Bumpass & Lu, 2000), as compared with current estimates that project that nearly 40% to 50% of couples marrying today will end in divorce (Raley & Bumpass, 2003). There are many fathers who are involved with their children after a divorce or separation; however, fathers who do not marry their children's mothers have been shown to be less consistent and have more negative interactions with their children (Hofferth & Anderson, 2003). Thus, the level of commitment and relationship decisions can have a large impact on Caucasian fathers' ability to be involved with their families.

Lastly, in the sociocultural discussion of Caucasian men's values of self-reliance and autonomy, there is considerable conjecture about men's "commitment phobia." However, there is little evidence to suggest that men differ from women in their levels of commitment in marriage (Stanley & Markman, 1992; Stanley, Markman, & Whitton, 2002). Some of the differences that are witnessed between men and women, on average, involve the meaning of being married and having children (Stanley, 2002). For instance, Caucasian men's perception of having a child is typically categorized as a major step in responsibility, not only personally as they mold the next generation, but also in terms of the financial stability they believe they must ensure for their child (Stanley, 2002). In fact, there is a positive correlation between family income and father's engagement (Bronte-Tinkew, Carrano, & Guzman, 2006). Thus, it appears that a primary obligation for many Caucasian fathers is first to provide for the family and then attend to other roles.

## CAUCASIAN FATHERS: WHITE MALE PRIVILEGE

Mental health providers are increasingly aware of cross-cultural factors, such as racial identity and gender, that may influence the therapy process. In discussions of culture, White identity has been described as "colorblind" with "cultureless attitudes" and includes notable societal privileges (Devos & Banaji, 2005; Helms, 1995; Perry, 2001). At more pronounced levels of White identity, there is an increased awareness both of their personal heritages and of the societal privileges (beyond economic) that influence their lives (Helms, 1995). An understanding that there is a range of awareness—from cultureless to culturally aware—highlights the diversity about what it means to be Caucasian.

One aspect of White identity, privilege, bridges aspects of identity and societal influence (McIntosh, 1998). White male privilege describes the unearned benefits of being male and Caucasian. Much of privilege is assumed and subsequently not generally recognized (McIntosh, 2003). Privilege, while presumably a benefit, may also result in difficulties in fatherhood. For instance, privilege for some Caucasian fathers might lead them to advantages in their work (e.g., advanced compensation) but disadvantages of reduced involvement with their children (e.g., limited time off after the birth of a child). Privilege also may produce dissonance or guilt for some fathers as they reflect on the societal benefits. Dissonance might also be related to how fathers manage these seemingly competing facets of privilege (e.g., increased finances versus time with family).

In this process, Caucasian fathers can feel pressure to be silenced in sacrifice (Cooper, 2000) as they continue to work at the cost of disengagement from their families. That is, some fathers may feel that they "should" sacrifice their family time in favor of work and may do so feeling that they cannot voice displeasure (i.e., silent sacrifice). This sense of silent sacrifice may be exacerbated by an avoidance of relational conflicts with partners (Markman, Stanley, & Blumberg, 2001). Furthermore, Caucasian fathers' gender roles might increase their sense of obligation (Pleck, 1993)—interpreted as "that is what men are supposed to do." Over time, Caucasian fathers could feel constrained in their roles, particularly if their accomplishments and investments are not recognized. Simply, White male privilege might reinforce their masculine norms and be perpetuated by assuming unquestioning positions in their roles at work and home.

Therapists can play a key role in helping Caucasian fathers explore how White male privilege impacts their work and family roles. In the initial sessions with Caucasian fathers, therapists should initiate discussion about assumed roles or "unspoken norms" both in the family and at work that influence their sense of autonomy and well-being. This period of discovery can elicit existential insights and questions about what it means to be a Caucasian father in today's society. Through this process, these men may experience guilt, disillusionment, ambivalence, and helplessness about how privilege has impacted their lives. The goal is not to make Caucasian fathers feel guilty for the existence of privilege, but rather it is to help them understand what role privilege has on their overall well-being and to empower them to recognize the impact of privilege on their relationships with others. For instance, fathers who assume the provider role might do so under privilege of higher income potential (as compared with women), thus assuming it is best for their families for them to work. However, this might produce distress for the father who does not want to continue working in a job that distances him from the family. Therefore, therapists will also need to encourage Caucasian fathers who experience such conflict to voice their feelings and not succumb to sacrifice by silence. Caucasian fathers should also recognize that, when voicing their feelings to their partners, they are coming from a privileged position, which may be off-putting to others who do not have privilege (e.g., women, racial/ethnic minorities). It may also be difficult for partners to understand how privilege can be burdensome for some Caucasian fathers, as the partners may only see the benefits. Thus, fathers and their partners may benefit from understanding how every choice comes at benefit and cost, even choices based on privilege.

## CASE STUDY

To help illustrate these elements of cultural strengths and white male privilege, we will explore a case study. Afterward, a conceptualization and specific intervention strategies are offered.

Paul, a 38-year-old Caucasian small-business manager has been married for the past 10 years to Meghan, a teacher's assistant. They have two children, ages 9 and 7. Paul described himself as a "middle-class guy with blue-collar values" and went on to explain that this means "men work hard and take care of their families." He stated that he believes his parents were "traditional parents" and "I was not really raised to talk much about my feelings…" He continued, "My family did not discuss issues very openly, and my parents talked about grown-up issues away from the kids." Paul stated that his mother "pretty much raised us," suggesting that she took care of their daily needs. He described his father as a quiet man who worked insatiably to build a family business. Ten years ago, Paul inherited the family business after his father suffered a heart attack.

Paul came to therapy after a referral from his physician, who diagnosed an ulcer. Paul stated he would like to work on his anger and noted that lately he is more irritable. Paul explained that his stress is due to his work obligations and money problems at home. The primary conflict for Paul and Meghan revolved around money, more specifically, sizable credit card debt. "She takes the boys out to eat all the time and they have a great time. I'm stuck at work, footing the bill." Further, he stated that he feels like he is stuck in his provider role out of concern about what cutting back at work would mean for his children's welfare now and in the future.

Upon assessment, it was clear that Paul's fatherhood identity was marked by high devotion to his work as a way to provide for the family; however, the cost was disengagement from his family. He stated, "I love my family and would do anything for my kids…that is what a father is supposed to do." It was evident in his tone that Paul was very proud of his role, and his hard work demonstrated his strong commitment to his children and his wife. However, he felt unappreciated and did not have a voice in the family. When the therapist asked if he had ever considered divorce, he replied "Divorce just isn't an option. It's not something I believe in, and I would never leave my kids." Simply, he views his familial relationships as strained, with work becoming more of an obligation.

Further, he stated that he does not see himself as a "strong father" anymore. When questioned about the meaning of being a "strong father," Paul responded, "I don't feel respected…my kids don't listen to me…and I feel like things are getting out of control." He described himself as "defeated on the money issue" and powerless to communicate effectively with Meghan. Paul stated that he cannot win arguments with his wife and typically avoids conversations about money. He also remarked that Meghan has discussed how unhappy and abandoned she feels in the marriage.

## Conceptualizing Paul: Fatherhood Identity, Privilege, and Family Commitment

This case illustrates how Paul's functioning is greatly influenced by his fatherhood identity, family commitment, and systemic factors related to privilege. Based on this understanding, we start our conceptualization through a trans-theoretical model that consists of two major poles: Family Commitment and Fatherhood Identity (see Figure 7.1). As seen in the figure, family commitment is anchored by dedication

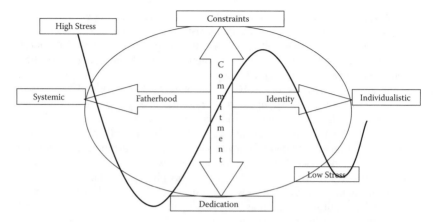

**Figure 7.1**   Theoretical model of father identity, stress, and commitment

and constraint attributions. Fatherhood identity is anchored by systemic and individualistic perspectives. The curved line reflects the theoretical assumption that
stress is more likely when fathers perceive their time spent in activities as obligations (i.e., constraint attributions) and these obligations are directly affecting others
(i.e., the family or systemic perspective).

The first dimension, fathers' commitment attributions, describes potential motivating factors related to their actions, investments, and connections to their family
systems (Hall & Fincham, 2005; Stanley & Markman, 1992). The nature of dedication is best understood as an intrinsic desire/enjoyment to be with one's partner or
family. It encompasses *"we-ness"* or couple/family identity (e.g., "we are a team"),
having a long-term vision of the family, making the family a priority, and making
sacrifices for one's partner/family for the good of the family (also see Stanley &
Markman, 1992). On the other hand, constraint attributions (e.g., financial constraints, concern for partner/child welfare, social pressures) refer to fathers' beliefs
that their actions are out of obligation to or concern for the family, which is likely
to produce stress. For some Caucasian fathers, their levels of dedication and constraints may be influenced by White male privilege. For instance, Paul's role as the
primary provider was further reinforced when he was handed his father's business,
a form of privilege.

We contend that how fathers feel about their actions (e.g. obligation versus
pride) when engaged with family, work, and so forth, are essential considerations
in treatment. Paul, for example, believed that his role is to work hard for the family, and he generally feels prideful about his ability to provide. However, this work
ethic comes at a cost of time spent with his family. Paul's dedication decreased
as he felt left out from family activities and disrespected by his children. Subsequently, his attributions about work have shifted from pride to obligation and
feeling that he needs to work out of concern for the children's welfare. Constraint
attributions may appear to have a negative valence, but it likely motivates couples
and families to stay together even in difficult times. Indeed, constraints alone are
not sufficient to maintain a healthy relationship or functional family system and

historically have been far less associated with relationship quality than dedication (Adams & Jones, 1997; Johnson, Caughlin, & Huston, 1999; Stanley & Markman, 1992). For example, in the vignette we will see that Paul feels committed to his family because it is a duty rather than a fulfilling emotional relationship. In a sense, this constraint is helpful in keeping the family connected. However, it also creates feelings of resentment in Paul. The therapist will capitalize on these feelings, using them as a tool to lead the client to a deeper exploration of his role as a father.

The second dimension, fatherhood identity, includes the level of involvement defined by engagement, responsibility, and accessibility (Lamb, 2004) to the family as shaped through intergenerational learning, societal messages, and current relationships (Kerr & Bowen, 1988; Stanley, Blumberg, & Markman, 1999). For Caucasian fathers in the United States, the individualistic messages about achievement and self-fulfillment may be more pronounced than in collective cultures. Additionally, we assert that this polarity is not static and best thought of as the degree to which Caucasian fathers' involvement promotes the family (systemic) or the self (individualistic).

Lamb (2000) described engagement as how much time the father spends doing something with the child, such as playing or feeding. Fathers' responsibility is defined by how much time fathers spend in monitoring or attending to children's welfare (Lamb, 2000), including providing financial means for them. For Paul, he has the privilege of managing the family business, which has heightened his role as the provider in the family. This role is currently creating dissonance because Paul is limited in his engagement with his family. Lastly, accessibility refers to how available fathers are to the family. A father would be considered accessible if he were near the child or close enough that the child could make physical contact if so desired, for example, reading in a room while the child watches TV in another room (Lamb). Paul's high level of responsibility comes at the expense of his accessibility and engagement with his family, leaving him feeling conflicted regarding his role within his family.

Father involvement may benefit both the family and the father's sense of self. Systemic fatherhood identity is marked by spending time with and near the family (e.g., engaged and accessible) and having intentions to promote the welfare of the family. In contrast, individualistic fatherhood identity is characterized by self-propagating activities where family is typically a secondary consideration to personal accomplishments. Paul's fatherhood identity is best described as a desire to spend time with his family and a clear dedication to their welfare. To help illustrate how this conceptualization can inform interventions, we will examine each polarity separately.

## Intervening With a Focus on Fatherhood Identity

There are many approaches to promote fatherhood identity. We will focus primarily on ways therapists can empower Caucasian fathers by (a) developing better insight about their fatherhood identity, (b) gaining an appreciation of how their fatherhood identity impacts others as well as related societal privileges, and (c) adapting new strategies for change. Ultimately, it is important to capitalize on the strengths of fathers to restore their relationships within the family and honor their personal identities. We will use our case study of Paul to illuminate potential therapist-client interactions.

To foster insight about fatherhood roles and identity, therapists can start by examining clients' role models (likely their own fathers). One approach is to contrast their best and worst memories about their interactions with their fathers (and mothers) during childhood (Benjamin, Rothweiler, & Critchfield, 2006). For instance, these questions can examine how connected (e.g., connected—emancipated) and loved (e.g., loved—rejected) the client felt in childhood and connect these experiences to their current sense of self.

In the second session with Paul, his therapist (John) explored his experiences about feeling connected with his father:

| | |
|---|---|
| *Therapist:* | "Paul, could you describe some experiences with your father when you felt really connected to him?" |
| *Paul:* | "I remember when my father took me to work with him throughout my teens. He was great at work and he made me feel like I was a key player in the business…I remember him saying how proud he was of me for being so interested in work." |
| *Therapist:* | "Sounds like you and your father really bonded around work?' |
| *Paul:* | "Yeah, you know…now that I think of it, most of my fond memories of my dad are when we were at work." |
| *Therapist:* | "What meaning do you take from that?" |
| *Paul:* | "Well, hmm, it makes me wonder why we did not have more fun times at home." |

In this excerpt, we see that by examining Paul's memories of his father he is able to reflect on how he and his father connected as well as develop new awareness about what roles he did not play in Paul's life. These questions can easily be adapted to ask a client about their worst memories with their father. Later on in that session, the therapist inquires about how loved he felt by his father:

| | |
|---|---|
| *Therapist:* | "When you and your father were connected, how did he convey that he loved you?" |
| *Paul:* | "I just knew he did…we did stuff together, he came to my football games in high school. I could tell he was proud of me." |
| *Therapist:* | "It sounds like your father was there for you during times that were important to you." |
| *Paul:* | "Yeah, even though he worked a lot, he made an effort to show up for my games. He was able to make his own schedule because he owned the business." |
| *Therapist:* | "Did he tell you that he was proud of you for your personal accomplishment?" |
| *Paul:* | "Hmm, not really. I just knew he was." |
| *Therapist:* | "Were there times when you wanted him to say it?" |
| *Paul:* | "Yeah, I can remember my mom saying that he was proud of me, but I never heard him say it…and at times, when he was tired or working late, I really thought I had to prove myself to him." |

In this passage, we see that Paul's relationship with his father can be described by positive, loving feelings that were primarily unspoken and demonstrated by being engaged and accessible to Paul (e.g., going to games). Paul's father's level of involvement is a good example of how White male privilege can be both helpful and harmful. On the one hand, his father was able to provide for the family by owning his own business, which also allowed him time to attend Paul's games. On the other hand, Paul's father worked long hours. Further, Paul at times felt distant from his father and felt that he had to prove himself to gain approval from his father. To connect these memories to Paul's current role as a father, a therapist can bridge the past to the present with a focus on ideal fatherhood identity:

*Therapist:* "How do you think you are like your father?"
*Paul:* "I see a lot in common...I picked up his work ethic...and (looking down)... I also feel distant from my kids...you know, I have missed a lot of their life due to my work."
*Therapist:* "That sounds difficult, to realize that you missed parts of your children's lives."

----later that session---

*Therapist:* "What positive aspects of your father do you want to carry forward?"
*Paul:* "I like that I am dedicated to work. It gives a sense of purpose for me... you know, it also makes me feel good to provide for my family..."
*Therapist:* "Anything that you would like not to carry forward?"
*Paul:* "I think that I am too much like my father when it comes to giving to my kids and my wife. If I am being honest, I can't remember the last time I told them I was proud of them."
*Therapist:* "That sounds important to you."
*Paul:* "It really is..."
*Therapist:* "What other ideal qualities would you like to embody as a father?"
*Paul:* "I really want to be there for my kids. I want them to know me...I feel like I never really knew my dad..."

In this passage, we see the therapist connecting Paul's past relationship with his father to his current role as a father. There appears to be an intergenerational transmission of privilege associated with the family business that provides some definition of Paul's fatherhood identity. It also highlights some individualistic identity that is gained through work, a common masculine norm (Mahalik et al., 2003; O'Neil et al., 1995). The therapist also encourages Paul to reflect on other ideal qualities of being a father, which can foster insight into potential future roles as a father that may not be directly tied to his own father (National Fatherhood Initiative, 2003).

Beyond promoting personal insight about fathers' identity, it is also important to recognize that this identity exists in a social and family context. Therefore, therapists can explore how fathers can be more effective in their communication about their fatherhood identity with their family. In this next passage, we see how the therapist explores how Paul communicates his role in the family to his family in session four:

*Therapist:* "How do you communicate your needs in the family?"

*Paul:* "Well, I think that they know that work is important to me and for them."

*Therapist:* "It also sounds like you have a need to be engaged with your family?"

*Paul:* "Yes I do, but you know I feel that is secondary to my work. I've got a lot of responsibility for the business; the work isn't going to get done unless I'm there."

*Therapist:* "So, you don't think that you can have both family and work?"

*Paul:* "I think I can have both, but it seems like they, my family... they don't involve me...you know they don't ask me to do things."

*Therapist:* "Is it hard for you to say that you want to be involved?"

*Paul:* "I shouldn't have to ask for that."

*Therapist:* "Is it that you shouldn't have to ask for that or that you feel uncomfortable asking?"

*Paul:* "I think it's a bit of both."

*Therapist:* "I see. What comes up for you when you think about asking to be involved?

*Paul:* "I feel weak...I mean, it doesn't seem very manly to say, 'Please include me, I'm lonely.' And you know, it reminds me of how I felt when I was trying to prove myself to my father."

*Therapist:* "You mean seeking approval from your father?"

*Paul:* "Yes...."

As seen here, for Paul to ask to be engaged with his family relates to his feelings of being weak. Also, the therapist is able to access Paul's need for approval. Instead of verbalizing his needs, Paul stays quiet—albeit distressed. Like many men, he is reluctant to expose his emotions because he sees them as weak. As such, therapeutic interventions focusing on how to approach the conversation as well as processing internal scripts that are barriers for him may be fruitful for him to get his needs met. Paul also identifies strongly with his work role; he sees it as an important position. His need to feel important is being met through work, and the therapist will need to address how that influences his role in the family.

When Paul engages in new conversations with his family and ultimately becomes more involved in the family, new roles may need to be negotiated. Given societal messages that Paul has internalized, such as men should work to provide for the family, some dissonance may evolve as new roles emerge. For instance, as Paul and his family adjust to the new roles, changes may also occur in Paul's orientation to work (see Silverstein, Auerbach, & Levant, 2002). This process might reinstate his sense of competence as a father and give him a better appreciation of his role in the family.

## *Interventions Focused on Family Commitment*

Marital and family commitment highlights another central dynamic in the treatment of Caucasian fathers. In our model, we suggest that therapists (a) examine fathers' perceptions of constraints and dedication attributions, (b) develop new strategies that reduce or buffer constraint attributions (e.g., obligation or concern) and foster actions that will lead to higher levels of dedication, and (c) uncover deeper feelings that drive attributions about commitment. Markman and colleagues (2001) describe feelings, such as lack of recognition or lack of acceptance by the family/partners, as hidden issues that might drive arguments about salient family issues (e.g., how to mange money) and might decrease dedication. Excerpts from our case study, session two, provide an example of some clinical interventions for working with family commitment. It should be noted that while we discuss fatherhood identity and family commitment separately, they often occur simultaneously.

| | |
|---|---|
| *Therapist:* | "How do you feel about your role in the family?" |
| *Paul:* | "Well, I feel that I work for the family." |
| *Therapist:* | "Do you feel that you and Meghan are a team?" |
| *Paul:* | "Not right now. I used to feel that way with her…. but it seems like Meghan and the kids are moving on without me and I am working to support them." |
| *Therapist:* | "Do you find it rewarding that you are supporting them?" |
| *Paul:* | "Not really. I feel like I am giving up part of my life so they can have their life." |
| *Therapist:* | "Do you feel that you can voice this concern with your family?" |
| *Paul:* | "No, I feel that if I did that they would look at me weird…you know I am doing what a man is supposed to do. My father did this for me growing up…" |
| *Therapist:* | "It sounds like it is an obligation for you to work for your family." |
| *Paul:* | "It seems like that right now. I used to enjoy working for the family… when we did more together." |
| *Therapist:* | "What keeps you going along this path?" |
| *Paul:* | "I do it for my kids. It's their future…I'm not going to leave them hanging." |

In this excerpt, we see Paul's commitment is marked by a lack of *we*-ness (i.e., no team) with Meghan and the family. His distant relationship with Meghan appears to be also influencing his sense of connection with his children, a common spillover effect in families (Christensen & Heavey, 1990; Fauchier & Margolin, 2004). Additionally, Paul appears to be working out of obligation and concern for his children's future (e.g., high levels of constraint). In this next passage, we will see how Paul has reflected on his feelings about commitment in the family and the approaches the therapist implements to promote change:

--- Start of session 7 ---

| | |
|---|---|
| *Paul:* | "Doc, last week I started to think that I need to do more for myself. You know, if Meghan and the kids are going out to have fun, then I should too." |
| *Therapist:* | "It sounds like you want to have more balance and fun in your life." |

| | |
|---|---|
| *Paul:* | "You bet. I need to think of me. It's really up to me to take charge here..." |
| *Therapist:* | "How do you see this approach getting you closer to your goal of wanting to be closer to your family, you know, a team....and feeling less obligated to the family?" |
| *Paul:* | "I am not sure. I feel that I cannot change them, but I can change me." |
| *Therapist:* | "What is getting you to believe that you cannot change your interactions with the family?" |
| *Paul:* | "They just seem happy to do their own thing, without me." |
| *Therapist:* | "We talked before about you communicating with Meghan about your role in the family. Have you taken some steps toward that goal?" |
| *Paul:* | "Not really. I feel somewhat...I guess you call it silenced...in my talks with Meghan. She just says that I need to work for the family and she is right on that point. It was basically my choice to take over the family business..." |
| *Therapist:* | "Good. It sounds like you have started the conversation. What gets in the way of you expressing how you feel about being involved in family activities?" |
| *Paul:* | "Umm...you know, we talked about how I want to be accepted. I don't feel that she wants my role to change in the family...What can I say to Meghan about that?" |
| *Therapist:* | "So you worry if Meghan will accept you if your role in the family changed?" |
| *Paul:* | "Yes, I don't like to admit it, but that is part of it...The other part is I don't know how to bring up the topic." |
| *Therapist:* | "Well, let's talk about this. There seems to be two sides of this. First, there appears to be some fear whether she will accept you or not. Second, it sounds like it might be helpful to talk about how to approach the topic." |
| *Paul:* | "Yeah, that's it in a nutshell." |
| *Therapist:* | "By not talking about your feelings of acceptance with Meghan, then I suspect that things might stay static for you." |
| *Paul:* | "So, I can't get around that conversation..." (said smiling) |
| *Therapist:* | "It seems like you know that will be helpful for you." |
| *Paul:* | "Yeah, I just know those conversations are tough for me." |
| *Therapist:* | "Well, let's spend some time looking at how you can approach the conversation and what it means for you to do so." |

In this passage, we see that by Paul's reflecting on his hidden issue of acceptance, he initially moved further away from dedication to the family. His reluctance to approach the topic was rooted, in part, by his fear of not being accepted. The therapist highlighted the issue and encouraged him to face this issue more directly to promote more communication and dedication with Meghan and ultimately with his family. Paul recognizes that it is up to him to make changes, and the therapist channels this self-reliance to motivate Paul to have difficult conversations with Meghan. In the next session, Paul reflected that the conversation went well and that Meghan was open to him. He also reported that he was able to have a voice and expand his role (e.g., more engagement) in the family. A month later he reported that things were returning to a better balance, that work seemed less like an obligation to the family as he was able to be engaged with the family.

## SUMMARY

This case study demonstrated one useful way in which incorporating family commitment, fatherhood identity, and salient cross-cultural aspects (e.g., privilege) related to Caucasian fathers can be helpful. The therapist in this case was able to increase awareness of the client's fatherhood identity by exploring his past and ideal values. Further, the therapist motivated the client to reflect on his commitment in the family and identified ways to enhance his level of engagement and dedication with the family.

In this chapter, we set out to discuss some salient cross-cultural issues related to therapy with Caucasian fathers. By examining aspects of White male privilege, cultural strengths, fatherhood identity, and family commitment, we hope that this chapter continues the dialogue about working with Caucasian fathers. The focus on multicultural theory and multicultural competence, in particular, have increased awareness of the importance of gender, ethnicity, and culture in all human interaction (including White). However, there is a paucity of theoretical research for understanding White fathers and, more specifically, the process and outcome of counseling with White fathers. Accordingly, we look forward to new research examining the therapy process with Caucasian fathers.

## REFERENCES

Adams, J. M., & Jones, W. H. (1997). The conceptualization of marital commitment: An integrative analysis. *Journal of Personality and Social Psychology, 72*(5), 1177–1196.

American Psychological Association. (2002). Guidelines on multicultural education, training, research, practice, and organizational change for psychologists. APA Council of Representatives.

Benjamin, L. S., Rothweiler, J. C., & Critchfield, K. L. (2006). The use of the structural analysis of social behavior (SASB) as an assessment tool. *Annual Review of Clinical Psychology, 2*, 83–109.

Bronte-Tinkew, J., Carrano, J., & Guzman, L. (2006). Resident fathers' perceptions of their roles and links to involvement with infants. *Fathering, 4*(3), 254–285.

Bumpass, L., & Lu, H. (2000). Trends in cohabitation and implications for children's family contexts in the United States. *Population Studies, 54*(1), 29–41.

Christensen, A., & Heavey, C. L. (1990). Gender and social structure in the demand/withdraw pattern of marital conflict. *Journal of Personality and Social Psychology, 59*, 73–81.

Connidis, I. A. (2001). *Family ties and aging.* Thousand Oaks, CA: Sage.

Cooper, M. (2000). Being the "go-to guy": Fatherhood, masculinity, and the organization of work in Silicon Valley. *Qualitative Sociology, 23*(4), 379–405.

Devos, T., & Banaji, M. R. (2005). American = White? *Journal of Personality and Social Psychology, 88*(3), 447–466.

Fagan, J., & Hawkins, A. J. (Eds.). (2001). *Clinical and educational interventions with fathers.* Binghamton, NY: Haworth Press.

Fauchier, A., & Margolin, G. (2004). Affection and conflict in marital and parent-child relationships. *Journal of Marital and Family Therapy, 30*(2), 197–211.

Good, G. E, Thomson, D. A., & Brathwaite, A. D. (2005). Men and therapy: Critical concepts, theoretical framework, and research recommendations. *Journal of Clinical Psychology, 61*(6), 699–711.

Hall, J. H., & Fincham, F. D. (2005). Relationship dissolution following infidelity: The roles of attributions and forgiveness. *Journal of Social and Clinical Psychology, 25,* 508–522.

Heesacker, M., & Prichard, S. (1992). In a different voice, revisited: Men, women, and emotion. *Journal of Mental Health Counseling, 14*(3), 274–290.

Helms, J. E. (1995). An update of Helm's White and people of color racial identity models. In J. G. Ponterotto, M. J. Casas, L. A. Suzuki, & C. M. Alexander (Eds.), *Handbook of Multicultural Counseling* (pp. 181–198). Thousand Oaks, CA: Sage.

Hofferth, S. L., & Anderson, K. G. (2003). Are all dads equal? Biology versus marriage as a basis for paternal investment. *Journal of Marriage and Family, 65,* 213–232.

Johnson, M. P., Caughlin, J. P., & Huston, T. L. (1999). Tripartite nature of marital commitment: Personal, moral, and structural reasons to stay married. *Journal of Marriage and the Family, 61,* 160–177.

Karney, B. R. (2003). Florida Baseline Survey. Unpublished Document.

Kerr, M., & Bowen, M. (1988). *Family Evaluation.* New York: Norton.

Kiselica, M. S. (1995). *Multicultural counseling with teenage fathers: A practical guide.* Thousand Oaks, CA: Sage.

Liu, W. M. (2002). The social-class related experiences of men: Integrating theory and practice. *Professional Psychology: Research and Practice, 33*(4), 355–360.

Lamb, M. E. (1997). *The role of the father in child development* (3rd ed.). New York: John Wiley & Sons Inc.

Lamb, M. E. (2000). The history of research on father involvement: An overview. In H. E. Peters, G. W. Peterson, S. K. Steinmetz, & R. D. Day (Eds.), *Fatherhood: Research, Intervention, and Policies* (pp. 23–58). New York: Haworth Press.

Lamb, M. E. (2004). *The role of the father in child development* (4th ed). Hoboken, NJ: John Wiley & Sons Inc.

Lamb, M., Pleck, J. H., Charnov, E. L., & Levine, J. A. (1987). A biosocial perspective on paternal behavior and involvement. In J. B. Lancaster, J. Altman, A. Rossi, & L. R. Sherrod (Eds.), *Parenting across the lifespan: Biosocial perspectives.* New York: Academic.

Levant, R. F. (1998). Desperately seeking language: Understanding, assessing, and treating normative male alexithymia. In W. S. Pollack & R. F. Levant (Eds.), *New psychotherapy for men* (pp. 35–56). Hoboken, NJ: John Wiley & Sons Inc.

Mahalik, J. R. (1999). Incorporating a gender role strain perspective in assessing and treating men's cognitive distortions. *Professional Psychology: Research and Practice, 30*(4), 333–340.

Mahalik, J. R., Good, G. E., & Englar-Carlson, M. (2003). Masculinity scripts, presenting concerns and help-seeking: Implications for practice and training. *Professional Psychology: Theory, Research and Practice, 34*, 123–131.

Mahalik, J. R., Talmadge, W. T., Locke, B. D., & Scott, R. P. J. (2005). Using the conformity to masculine norms inventory to work with men in a clinical setting. *Journal of Clinical Psychology, 61*, 661–674.

Markman, H. J., Stanley, S., & Blumberg, S. (2001). *Fighting for your marriage: New and revised edition.* San Francisco, CA: Josey-Bass.

McGoldrick, M., Giordano, J., & Garcia-Preto, N. (2005). *Ethnicity and family therapy* (3rd ed.). New York: Guilford Press.

McGoldrick, M., & Rohrbaugh, M. (1987). Researching ethnic family stereotypes. *Family Process, 26*(1), 89–99.

McIntosh, P. (1998). White privilege: Unpacking the invisible knapsack. In M. McGoldrick (Ed.), *Re-envisioning family therapy: Race, culture, and gender in clinical practice* (pp. 147–152). New York: Guilford Press.

McIntosh, P. (2003). White privilege: Unpacking the invisible knapsack. In S. Plous, (Ed), *Understanding prejudice and discrimination* (pp. 191–196). New York: McGraw-Hill.

Ogrodniczuk, J. S. (2006). Men, women, and their outcome in psychotherapy. *Psychotherapy Research, 16*, 453–462.

O'Neil, J. M. (2008). Summarizing 25 years of research on men's gender role conflict using the Gender Role Conflict Scale: New research paradigms and clinical implications. *Counseling Psychologist, 36*(3), 358–445.

O'Neil, J. M., Good, G. E., & Holmes, S. (1995). Fifteen years of theory and research on men's gender role conflict: New paradigms for empirical research. In R. F. Levant & W. S. Pollack (Eds.), *A new psychology of men* (164–206). New York: Basic.

Orbuch, T. L., Thornton, A., & Cancio, J. (2000). The impact of marital quality, divorce, and remarriage on the relationships between parents and their children. *Marriage & Family Review, 29*(4), 221–246.

Owen, J., Imel, Z., Tao, K., Smith, A., Wampold, B., & Rodolfa, E. (2009). Cultural ruptures in short-term therapy: A multilevel analysis. Manuscript revise and resubmit.

Owen, J., & Rodolfa, E. (2009). Clients' perceptions of helpful therapeutic processes: Conformity to masculine norms and common factors. Manuscript under review.

Owen, J. J., Stratton, J. S., & Rodolfa, E. (2008). Initial evidence for the relationship between the conformity to male norms inventory, therapy effectiveness, and working alliance. Manuscript revise and resubmit.

Perry, P. (2001). White means never having to say you're ethnic: White youth and the construction of "cultureless" identity. *Journal of Contemporary Ethnography, 30*(1), 56–91.

Pleck, J. H. (1993). Are family supportive employer policies relevant to men? In J. C. Hood (Ed.), *Men, work, and family. Research on men and masculinities series* (Vol. 4, pp. 217–237). Thousand Oaks, CA: Sage.

Pleck, J. (1995). The gender role strain paradigm: An update. In R. F. Levant & W. S. Pollack (Eds.), *A new psychology of men* (pp. 11–32). New York: Basic.

Popenoe, D., & Whitehead, B. D. (2003). State of our Unions: Annual report. *Piscataway, NJ: National Marriage Project.*

Popenoe, D., & Whitehead, B. D. (2005). State of our Unions: Annual report. *Piscataway, NJ: National Marriage Project.*

Raley, R. K., & Bumpass, L. (2003). The topography of the divorce plateau: Levels and trends in union stability in the United States after 1980. *Demographic Research, 8,* 245–260.

Roberts, S. (2004). *Who we are: The changing face of America in the twenty-first century.* New York: Times Books.

Robertson, J. M., & Fitzgerald, L. F. (1992). Overcoming the masculine mystique: Preferences for alternative forms of assistance among men who avoid counseling. *Journal of Counseling Psychology, 39*(2), 240–246.

Robertson, J. M., & Freeman, R. (1995). Men and emotions: Developing masculine-congruent views of affective expressiveness. *Journal of College Student Development, 36*(6), 606–607.

Robertson, J. M., Lin, C. W., Woodford, J., Danos, K. K., & Hurst, M. A. (2001). The (un)emotional male: Physiological, verbal, and written correlates of expressiveness. *Journal of Men's Studies, 9*(3), 393–412.

Rochlen, A. B., Land, L. N., & Wong, Y. J. (2004). Male restrictive emotionality and evaluations of online versus face-to-face counseling. *Psychology of Men & Masculinity, 5*(2), 190–200.

Silverstein, L. B., Auerbach, C. F., & Levant, R. F. (2002). Contemporary fathers reconstructing masculinity: Clinical implications of gender role strain. *Professional Psychology: Research and Practice, 33*(4), 361–369.

Stanley, S. M. (2002). *What is it with men and commitment, anyway?* Keynote address to the 6th Annual Smart Marriages Conference. Washington, D.C.

Stanley, S. M., Blumberg, S. L., & Markman, H. J. (1999). Helping couples fight for their marriages: The PREP approach. In R. Berger & M. Hannah (Eds.), *Handbook of preventative approaches in couple therapy* (pp. 279–303). New York: Brunner/Mazel.

Stanley, S. M., & Markman, H. J. (1992). Assessing commitment in personal relationships. *Journal of Marriage and the Family, 54,* 595–608.

Stanley, S. M., Markman, H. J., & Whitton, S. W. (2002). Communication, conflict and commitment: Insights on the foundations of relationship success from a national survey. *Family Process, 41*(4), 659–675.

Stanley, S. M., Rhoades, G. K., & Markman, H. J. (2006). Sliding vs. deciding: Inertia and the premarital cohabitation effect. *Family Relations, 55,* 499–509.

Stanley, S. M., Young, G., & Pearson, M. (2005). Love, poverty, and marriage. Presentation at Smart Marriages Conference. Denver, CO.

Sue, D. W., Bucceri, J., Lin, A. I., Nadal, K. L., & Torino, G. C. (2007). Racial microaggressions and the Asian American experience. *Cultural Diversity and Ethnic Minority Psychology, 13*(1), 72–81.

Summers, J. A, Raikes, H., Butler, J., Spicer, P., Pan, B., Shaw, S., et al. (1999). Low-income fathers' and mothers' perception of the father role: A qualitative study in four early Head Start communities. *Infant Mental Health Journal, 20*(3), 291–304.

U.S. Census. (2007). ACS Demographic and Housing Estimates: 2007. In *American Community Survey.* Retrieved October 2, 2008, from http:// factfinder.census.gov/servlet/ADPTable?_bm=y&-geo_id=01000US&-qr_name=ACS_2007_1YR_G00_DP5&-ds_name=&-_lang=en&-redoLog=false&-format=

Wester, S. R., Vogel, D. L., Pressly, P. K., & Heesacker, M. (2002). Sex differences in emotion: A critical review of the literature and implications for counseling psychology. *Counseling Psychologist, 30*(4), 630–652.
Wisch, A. F., Mahalik, J. R., Hayes, J. A., & Nutt, E. A. (1995). The impact of gender role conflict and counseling technique on psychological help seeking in men. *Sex Roles, 33*(1), 77–89.
Wong, Y. J., & Rochlen, A. B. (2005). Demystifying men's emotional behavior: New directions and implications for counseling and research. *Psychology of Men & Masculinity, 6*(1), 62–72.

# *Counseling Specific Populations of Fathers*

# 8

# Challenges and Clinical Issues in Counseling Religiously Affiliated Fathers

## JOHN M. ROBERTSON

The dilemma can be perplexing: how to help a man who maintains that his clearly ineffective fathering practices are rooted in his religious values? It is a "dilemma" in the classic sense of the word; it forces a choice between two unfavorable alternatives. On the one hand, if a clinician strongly recommends that a father change behavior that is based on deeply held religious views, then two risks follow. One is the loss of professional credibility ("If you don't respect my faith, how can I respect your parenting advice?"). The other is the possible precipitation of a religious crisis during which the fathering behavior may worsen. On the other hand, if the clinician ignores the religious motivation driving unsuccessful fathering practices, then alternative risks emerge. The father may feel offended that the importance of his worldview is overlooked. The counselor will miss opportunities to discuss fathering in the context of values and beliefs that the father will find motivating, and the overall likelihood of enduring change is reduced. This dilemma is not merely academic; children's welfare is involved.

The relevance of this dilemma is revealed in provocative news stories, as this sample illustrates:

Parents use religious reasons to avoid vaccinating their children (LeBlanc, 2007).

Parents demand that a book showing same-sex parents be removed from the school to protect their child's "spiritual safety" (Simon, 2005).

Parents cite religious values as an explanation for corporal punishment of their children (Armacost, 2001; Goolsby, 2006).

Nearly two-thirds of American adults believe that children should learn religious views of creation in their public schools (Goodstein, 2005).

Divorced parents fight over which religious teachings to present to their children (Grossman, 2007).

Clinicians cannot avoid the problems inherent in this dilemma. The numbers are too large. Data reported in the following section make two overwhelmingly important points: the population of the United States is *heavily* religious, and the religious views and values of U.S. adults are *highly* diverse.

## CHALLENGES IN WORKING WITH RELIGIOUSLY AFFILIATED FATHERS

Three issues make working with religiously affiliated fathers especially challenging. The overwhelming majority of American men have a religious preference, and religious beliefs are diverse and detailed. Research indicates that religious affiliation can be associated with measurable benefits for men, and a man's religious views can strongly influence his thoughts about masculinity and proper fathering behavior. This section addresses each of these three factors.

### *Most U.S. Men Have a Religious Preference*

*More than four of every five American men identify with a religious group.* In 2004, The General Social Survey (Davis & Smith, 2004) reported that a large majority of American adults (85%) have a specific religious preference, while only 14.4% say their preference is "None." The American Religious Identification Survey found very similar numbers: 81% of U.S. adults identify with a particular religious group, and 14.1% identify with no religious group (Kosmin, Mayer, & Keysar, 2001).

The *diversity* of religious affiliation in the U.S. is an equally important factor to consider. The annually released Yearbook of American and Canadian Churches (Lindner, 2006) lists 217 different church bodies in the United States. When participants in the American Religious Identification Survey were asked, "What is your religion, if any?" the self-reported answers were divided among 65 different categories (Kosmin et al., 2001) as follows: (a) 76.5% of all U.S. adults identified with 35 different Christian religious groups; (b) 3.7% identified with 21 other religious groups (Jewish, Islamic, Buddhist, Hindu, Native American, Taoist, etc.); (c) 14.1% identified with no religious groups (atheist, agnostic, humanist, secular, or no religion); and (d) 5.4% refused to answer the question.

One striking finding is that 95% of married parents in the United States report having a religious affiliation (Mahoney, 2000). Given this level of identification, it is not surprising to note that a vast majority of American men (85%) say that religion is important in their lives, either "very important" (55.6%) or "somewhat important" (29.4%).

*One of every five adult men reports that he is more secular than religious.* The flip side of the preceding section is worth highlighting. Not every father is religiously affiliated. The American Religious Identification Survey asked, "When it comes to your outlook, do you regard yours as... Secular, Somewhat Secular, Somewhat Religious, or Religious?" (Kosmin et al., 2001, p. 17). Just under one-fifth (19%) of American men chose one of the secular options.

Researchers are tracking a strong trend toward secularism and away from religious identification that began in the early 1990s. The American Religious Identification Survey found that the number of adults who reject any religious identification more than doubled during the decade of the 1990s (Kosmin et al., 2001, p. 10, 11). Put another way, secular identification of the U.S. adult population increased from 8% to 14% in just 10 years. A closer look reveals that the proportion identifying as Christian declined from 86% to 77% of the population, while the number of non-Christians increased from 5.8 million to 7.7 million (Kosmin et al., p. 10).

*Half of all adults who identify with a particular religion are official members.* Men vary in reporting the strength of their identification with religious groups. A General Social Survey question about the strength of a person's religious preference (Davis & Smith, 2004) found that among men, only 41.3% said their preference was "strong" or "somewhat strong." Perhaps this helps to explain the finding that not every adult who *identifies* with a religious group actually *belongs* to one. In examining the 22 largest religious groups (which comprise 92% of the adult population who identified with a group), the American Religious Identification Survey found that only 54% were official members of a specific church, temple, synagogue, or mosque that engaged in sacred rituals (Kosmin et al., 2001). Turned the other way, the above proportion indicates that a very large proportion of those who identify as religious (46%) do so in a private, noninstitutional way. These figures give credence to Luckmann's earlier concept of an "invisible religion" in the United States (Luckmann, 1967).

Men also may make a distinction between religiosity and spirituality (Richards & Bergin, 2005). Specifically, the word "religious" typically describes an active membership or affiliation with an organized religious group, including participation in various rites and activities with other members. The word "spiritual" is usually a broader term and refers to something more inclusive, more transcendent. It does not include active identification with a particular group, but rather focuses on the awareness of a personal sense of connection with a transcendent experience, being, or power (c.f., Richards & Bergin, 1997). Spiritual interests and views, therefore, tend to be more fluid, flexible, and experiential. Americans generally seem to understand and use this distinction. Among men, 51.2% say they are religious, while an additional 33.5% say they are "spiritual, not religious." Only 11.1% say they are neither religious nor spiritual (Greenberg & Berktold, 2005).

*One in five religiously affiliated men lives with a spouse or partner with a different religious affiliation.* Most religiously affiliated men (59%) are married (Kosmin et al., 2001), and a substantial number of these men (about one-fifth) report living with spouses or domestic partners who do not share their religious views. The range is between 12% of Mormon men living in "mixed" religious homes to the highest levels for Episcopalians (42%) and Buddhists (39%).

*A strong majority of men accept specifically religious beliefs.* Most American men accept at least some religious teachings about the universe and engage in religious practices in their daily lives. The Baylor Religion Survey found that the vast majority of American *men* believe in the existence of a place called heaven (77.1%), the existence of Satan (67.6%), the existence of angels (73.4%), the existence of demons (60.8%), and have "no doubts that God exists" (59.2%; Bader, Froese, Johnson, Mencken, & Stark, 2005). The General Social Survey adds that most men believe in "life after death" (67.5%), and less than half believe in evolution (43.8%; Davis & Smith, 2004).

With regard to religious experiences, most American men readily acknowledge having various feelings and encounters. The General Social Survey (Davis & Smith, 2004) reported that very high percentages of men agree with the following statements: find strength in my religion or spirituality (86.5%), find comfort in my religion or spirituality (83.3%), feel guided by God in the midst of daily activities (82.3%), feel God's presence (81.1%), feel God's love for me through others (78.2%), feel God's love for me directly (77.4%), desire to be closer to God (76.7%), pray at least once a week (68.8%) or daily (45%).

The Baylor Religion Survey adds other findings about the religious activities of men, noting that many personally read the Bible, Koran, Torah, or other sacred book at least once a month (36.9%) and participate in table prayers before or after meals (88.7%; Bader et al., 2005). The Faith and Family in America Study (Greenberg & Berktold, 2005) found that many men (38.4%) view the holy book of their faiths (Bible, Koran, Torah) as "the actual word of God" and that it "is to be taken literally, word for word."

## Benefits of Religious Affiliation for Fathers

In this section, research will be cited indicating that religious affiliation is associated with higher levels of father involvement, more opportunities for male-to-male friendships, higher rates of marital satisfaction, fewer problems with substance abuse, and improved mental and physical health.

*Father involvement.* Several studies indicate that religious affiliation increases father involvement. Data has shown that fathers are more involved with their infants in the Early Head Start Program when they have the support of spiritually involved friends and are more active in a religious group (Roggman, Boyce, Cook, & Cook, 2002). Other research has shown that religiously affiliated fathers (both married and divorced) are more involved fathers and report higher quality relationships with their children (King, 2003). Wilcox (2002) found that a father's religious affiliation predicted more one-on-one activities with his children, more frequent participation in dinner with his family, and more involvement with youth activities. Theoretical explanations for this pattern include religions' emphasis on responsible fathering, moral persuasion, and social support (Dollahite, 1998). In fact, there is some evidence that merely becoming a father leads some men to make a commitment to religion (Palkovitz & Palm, 1998).

*Male-to-male friendships.* A study of men who attend male-only spiritual retreats (Castellini, Nelson, Barrett, Nagy, & Quatman, 2005) found that the principal reason men give for attending such retreats is male bonding. Additional reasons for attendance were variations on the same need to connect with other men: to reduce isolation or emptiness, to be part of a faith community, to address father-son relationships, and to work with fears or grief. Other studies have found that church congregations provide a context for men to gain significant social support and a place to share comfortably their emotions (McFadden, Knepple, & Armstrong, 2003), and further provide settings for the development of status-bridging friendships with public officials, scientists, corporate executives, and other influential persons in the community (Wuthnow, 2002). This connection between religion and male friendships has been found among several ethnicities, including African American men, for whom higher levels of subjective religiosity predict higher levels of perceived support from male friends (Mattis et al., 2001).

*Marital satisfaction.* Given the likelihood that men in satisfying marriages are able to focus more freely on fathering activities, studies about the connection between religiosity and marital satisfaction become noteworthy. Several reviews of the literature have shown that higher levels of involvement in religious activities, such as attendance at religious programs, are related to increased marital satisfaction and decreased divorce rates (Gartner, 1996; Larson, 1985; McCullough, Larson, & Worthington, 1998). These benefits hold for persons in ethnic minority communities, such as African American couples who report that spirituality is a core theme in marital satisfaction (Speed, 2005), and among Chinese American couples who report that religious experiences and practices influence their shared values, their daily activities, their organization of family life, and their commitment to each other (Ing, 1999).

*Substance abuse.* It has long been known that men are more likely than women to use and abuse alcohol (Kessler, McGonigle, Zhao et al., 1994; Robins & Regier, 1991). Clearly, a father who abuses substances takes greater risks with regard to his fathering. However, among religiously affiliated men, there is evidence of higher rates of abstinence from the use of alcohol and lower rates of abuse or dependency for alcohol or illicit drugs (Gartner, 1996; Merrill, Salazar, & Gardner, 2001). These findings are consistent with the central role given to the use of a Higher Power in Alcoholics Anonymous, and to the emphasis on religiouslike activities, such as admitting personal inadequacies, the use of the Serenity Prayer, making amends, and the focus on inner peace (Thoresen et al., 1998).

*Mental and physical health.* Other potential benefits of religious affiliation and practice include improved recovery from relationship problems (Centore & Clinton, 2008); reductions in trait-anxiety, perceived stress, and trait-anger (Bormann, Shively, Smith, & Gifford, 2007); lower levels of suicidal ideation (e.g., Bascue, Inman, & Kahn, 1982; Minear & Bruch, 1980–1981; Reynolds & Nelson, 1981); better cardiovascular health related to various forms of Christian, Buddhist, and Hindu meditation (H. Benson, 1996; Ornish, 1990; Propst, 1988); and even increased longevity among men (Larson, 1985).

## Religious Teachings About Fathering

Congregations in many faith communities have a strong interest in parenting issues. The National Congregations Study (Chaves, Konieczny, Beyerlein, & Barman, 1999) found that 61.7% of all congregations had presented "groups, meetings, classes, or events" to members on the topic of parenting during the previous year. The content of these workshops and lectures addresses a father's understanding of his role in the family, his disciplinary practices, and his values.

One important distinction helps interpret the religious teachings that are summarized in the following paragraphs. Religious identification or membership does not necessarily predict an individual father's views or practices. Large religious groups are pluralistic, not monolithic. Religions develop fundamentalist, moderate, and liberal traditions, each with different views of fatherhood.

Following scholarly reviews by experts in the study of 14 different fundamentalist traditions, Marty and Appleby (1991) found nine fundamentalist tendencies that cross religious lines: (1) religious idealism is the basis for personal and community identity; (2) truth is revealed and unified; (3) truth is intentionally scandalous; (4) adherents believe they are part of a cosmic struggle—historical events are defined and reinterpreted in light of this struggle; (5) opposition is demonized and adherents are reactionary; (6) adherents are selective in which parts of their heritage they emphasize; (7) groups are led by males; (8) strict and exclusive boundaries are constructed to keep adherents loyal; (9) adherents envy modern cultural hegemony and try to change the distribution of power.

These views, when couched in religious statements of belief, can be very powerful in influencing a man's views of his duties as a father.

Moderate and liberal traditions also exist in most major world religions. These groups tend to be more focused on underlying conceptual themes and overarching values, and emphasize commonalities over differences (c.f., National Council of Churches, USA, 2008). They pay more attention to time, place, and culture. Their views tend to be influenced more by individual differences, cross-cultural compassion, and respect for other faith communities. They are interested in commonalities among religious traditions, such as the similarities in Jewish hospitality to strangers, Christian love for neighbors, and Buddhist compassion, called "metta." They are more willing to grant credibility to nonreligious authorities, such as scholars in medicine, geology, and history. The findings of social science regarding effective fathering, for example, are more credible to them than they are for fundamentalists.

The following religious concepts have an especially important impact on fathering for religiously affiliated men.

*Father as head of family.* The idea that a father is the head of his family appears to be related closely to another concept: the metaphor of God as father. The Baylor Religion Survey found that a high percentage of adults in the United States find the word "father" describes their view of God either "very well" or "somewhat well." This is true both for men (70.7%) and women (80.1%). This use of the word "father" to describe God has roots in both Judaism (Jeremiah 31:9) and Christianity (Romans 1:7). Islam generally does not use the notion of father to describe Allah. Many religious men believe that, in the same way that God is head of the universe, the father must be head of his family. Most American men (70.0%) regard themselves as the "heads" of their households (Greenberg & Berktold, 2005). Fundamentalists across religious lines can cite quotations from their religious authorities that support this view. (e.g., Colossians 3:18 for Christians; Sura 4:34 for Muslims). As a result, some fathers in religiously fundamentalist traditions think they should have "the final say" in their families. The Young Adolescents and Their Parents study (P. L. Benson, Williams, & Johnson, 1987), sponsored by 11 different religious bodies, found that about 16.6% of men and 15.4% of women have this view of family decision making.

Older studies found a positive correlation between religious orthodoxy and authoritarianism, defined as the expectation of strict obedience to authority (Argyle & Beit-Hallahmi, 1975). Fundamentalism has been shown to have further associations with dogmatic thinking, the inability to handle ambiguity, and a generally rigid approach to life (Hassan & Khalique, 1981; McNeel & Thorsen, 1985).

It is equally important, however, to recognize other trends in these same religious traditions that take quite different views of fatherhood roles, emphasizing egalitarianism, equality of authority, and feminist approaches to the roles of fathers. These more feminist-oriented comments appear in Jewish thought (e.g., Berke, 1996; Fuchs, 2000), in

Christian scholarship (e.g., Miller-McLemore, 2004; Van Leeuwen, 2004), and in Islamic writings (Afshari, 1994; Barlas, 2002), among others.

*Corporal punishment.* Although corporal punishment does not receive much support from the social sciences (Donnelly & Straus, 2005; Schwartz, Hage, Bush, & Burns, 2006), many fundamentalist fathers believe the practice receives support in sacred scriptures. Jews and Christians can cite several such quotations (e.g., Proverbs 13:24), and Christians find further support from their New Testament (Hebrews 12:6,7).

Several empirical studies have linked religious fundamentalism or conservatism with greater use of corporal punishment (Danso, Hunsberger, & Pratt, 1997; Ellison, 1996; Mahoney, Pargament, Tarakeshwar, & Swank, 2001). The variable most predictive of corporal punishment among fundamentalist parents is biblical literalness as opposed to personal religiosity or views of God (Grasmick, Bursik, & Kimpel, 1991).

Not all religious parents believe in corporal punishment. Studies have shown a difference between fundamentalist and moderate/liberal parents. Using the notion of "sanctification" (the degree to which parenting holds spiritual significance), researchers found that high levels of sanctification predicted *less* use of corporal punishment for parents with liberal theological beliefs, but *more* use of corporal punishment among conservative parents (Murray-Swank, Mahoney, & Pargament, 2006).

*Personal code of conduct.* Many religious groups of men develop codes of conduct for themselves. For example, Promise Keepers, the conservative Christian organization for men, has defined Seven Promises of a Promise Keeper (Promise Keepers, 2007). In addition to promising to engage in religious activity, men must commit to building a strong family based on "biblical values." Similarly, Jewish men may consult a "how to" manual that discourages various forms of ethical misbehavior that affect fathering, including arrogance, gossip, abuse of power, adultery, and so forth. (Olitzky & Sabath, 1996). Islamic fathers may consult the Sharia, the code of conduct that contains rules and regulations based on the Qur'an, many of which speak to the roles of fathers. The more moderate Muslim community in Britain has offered a 10-point code of conduct designed to hinder extremism and foster women's rights (Burns, 2007).

## The Role of Masculine Ideology

In 1982, O'Neil argued that men experience internal conflict when they attempt to conform to traditional social constructions of masculinity. Silverstein, Auerbach, and Levant (2002) found evidence for this strain in their study of several groups of fathers, including a sample of conservative Christian men who belong to Promise Keepers. Men in this study reported feeling trapped in their fatherhood roles by an "over-emphasis on work outside the home" and "a sense of emotional isolation from the family" (Silverstein et al., 2002, p. 362).

Based on data from the study noted above, Silverstein et al. (2002) recommend a new model for fathering that includes two concepts. The first is the normalizing of the dual earner family, thereby reducing the strain that fathers experience by assuming that the provider role is theirs alone. The second is the development of emotionally open and expressive relationships with children, thereby "elevating the father-child dyad to the same theoretical importance as the mother-child dyad in the emotional development of children" (Silverstein et al., 2002, p. 363). In effect, this model degenders parenting, leaving fathers free to negotiate various house-care and child-care tasks and responsibilities with their wives.

Other new family arrangements have tended to marginalize the role of the traditionally socialized father. Major social changes in North American culture have occurred as a result of world wars, the liberation of women from traditional roles, the rise of philosophical feminism, and the rising divorce rate. Now fathers are functioning in a variety of new family settings, including single parenting, step-father parenting, divorced co-parenting, gay parenting, and distance fathering (cf., Mander, 2001).

For religiously affiliated men who wish to "do it right" in their roles as fathers, the strain can be difficult and complicated to sort out. A man may listen to a religious teacher preach the importance of adhering to more traditional expectations of fathering, yet find himself drawn to some aspects of newer models. He may be facing his spouse's expectations of traditional masculine role behavior, while internally preferring a more egalitarian distribution of responsibilities. These demands seem mutually exclusive and can lead to significant levels of stress. If he tries to expand his role to include mutuality, emotional expressivity, and dual earner responsibilities, he may be challenging his religious heritage or officials or his extended family. Yet if he remains loyal to a more traditionally masculine perspective, he must live with the burden of feeling constrained and dissatisfied.

## CLINICAL ISSUES IN WORKING WITH RELIGIOUSLY AFFILIATED MEN

### *Presenting Issues*

In addition to the usual concerns of fathers (e.g., paying the bills, getting good medical care for their children, etc.), religiously affiliated men have more specific worries. For example, 26.7% worry "a lot" about "maintaining the religious tradition" their children are "brought up in" (Greenberg & Berktold, 2005). Other common issues have a similarly religious cast to them.

*Division of labor.* Who should do the housework? The Faith and Family in America study found that, when it comes to doing household chores, 61.2% of U.S. women say they do more (and 19.8% of men agree with them). The study also found that women say they do more of the child-care tasks (56.9%), and 26.3% of men agree with that assessment. Just over a third (37.5%) now say that they share parenting tasks equally. (Greenberg & Berktold, 2005). Views about who should be responsible for these tasks may be influenced by the father's religious beliefs.

Should mothers work outside the home? Many religiously affiliated fathers think that when a mother works outside the home, her ability to connect emotionally with her children is harmed. Specifically, 29.2% of all American men *disagree* with the statement that "a working mother can establish just as warm and secure a relationship with her children as a mother who does not work," and further believe that "a family suffers when the woman has a full-time job" (41.1%; Greenberg & Berktold, 2005).

*Discipline questions.* Fathers have a poor reputation when it comes to disciplining their children. When a national sample was asked to agree or disagree with the statement "fathers excel in disciplining their children," many respondents *disagreed* with the statement either "somewhat" or "strongly." This was true for both men, 40.7%, and women, 56% (Greenberg & Berktold, 2005).

Most U.S. adults agree with the statement "it is sometimes necessary to discipline a child with a good hard spanking." Both men (72.5%) and women (57.5%) either "somewhat" or "strongly" agree with this view. Again, the gender difference points to a potential issue brought to therapy. Mothers may be quite unhappy with their spouses along these lines (Greenberg & Berktold, 2005).

*Superfathers.* Another issue is how involved fathers are with their child's school or other programs. Most men say they are *not* very active in their child's school or other "program" activities (49.3%), and another 10.6% say they "don't have a chance" to "get as involved as I'd like to be" with a child's education (Greenberg & Berktold, 2005). The pressures to be more involved can influence mood, marital relationships, and behavior.

*Religion and public school issues.* A father sometimes struggles with how involved to become when the public school presents material with which he disagrees. Most fathers say they are "somewhat" or "very" certain they would *not* trust the teacher and therefore say nothing (75.9%). Results are comparable for several religious categories, including Protestants (81%), Roman Catholics (77.6%), and Jewish (71.5%). Members of the Muslim/Islam faith community are notably less likely to object (33.3%) to the teacher.

*Religious instruction of children.* Many men (35.2%) believe that they should encourage their children to accept their own religious faith (Goldberg & Berkhold, 2005) and believe that their own children will be "as religious" (30.9%) or "more religious" (18.4%) than they themselves are, and that it is "very" or "somewhat" likely (74.7%) that their children will belong to the same religious group they do. Of course, children may have different views than their parents, and conflict can result between the father and a child.

*Divorce.* When a religiously affiliated father's marriage becomes intolerable, what is he to do? If he is conservative, it may not matter if his partner is aggressive, absent, or characterologically impaired. Many religious men (43.2%) *disagree* with the statement that "divorce is usually the best solution when a couple can't seem to work out their marriage problems." Further, many men in the population at large think that "God's plan for marriage is one man, one woman, for life," (72.2%) and that "divorce is a sin" (25.1%; Greenberg & Berktold, 2005). If a father espouses these beliefs and belongs to a religiously based social support network that opposes divorce, he may be under immense strain as he walks into the counselor's office.

## Professional Guidelines

Clinicians can benefit from examining the American Psychological Association's set of guidelines that define multicultural competencies and responsibilities (APA, 2002). More recently, APA passed a resolution indicating that *religious identity* also warrants the application of multicultural competencies (APA, 2007). These guidelines and resolutions give professional weight to earlier independent attempts to offer constructive recommendations along these lines (e.g., Maples & Robertson, 2000). With this background, the following perspectives will influence clinical approaches to religiously affiliated fathers, regardless of the clinician's theoretical orientation.

*Recognize that religiously affiliated fathers qualify as a special population.* A father's religious affiliation is critical information for a therapist to have and to use. In fact, not knowing about a father's religious views may be a violation of APA's multicultural standards (APA, 2002, p. 25). Academic definitions of culture generally include religious systems, as well as linguistic, educational, political, legal, and economic elements (Triandis, 1972, 2002). A particular religion's view of proper human behavior often includes very specific teachings about the responsibilities of fatherhood.

*Look for religious blinders.* Historically, mental health professionals have been significantly less religious than their clients (Bergin & Jenson, 1990). Compared with the general population, smaller proportions of psychologists have believed in God (28%), or have agreed with the statement that they live life according to their religious beliefs (33%; Bergin & Jenson, 1990). That difference continues. Large proportions of mental health professionals still say they have not attended any religious worship programs in the previous year (55%), do not believe that religion is important in their lives (48%), and do not believe in God (28%; Delaney, Miller, & Bisono, 2007).

These therapist-client differences may partially explain the documented reluctance of professional psychologists to incorporate multicultural competencies into their work with clients, even when they know they should actively do so (Hansen et al., 2006), and, in fact, do not ask assessment questions about the religious or spiritual aspects of their client's lives (Hathaway, Scott, & Garver, 2004).

On the other hand, recent research suggests that a strong majority of psychologists now believe that religion is beneficial (82%) rather than harmful (7%) to overall mental health (Delaney, Miller, & Bisono, 2007), a finding that may be related to the literature cited earlier demonstrating the benefits that religion has for some people. Further, there is now evidence that the differences in belief may not be overtly biasing clinicians in their work with religious clients (Ferrand, 2005).

This dissimilarity between clinicians' beliefs and clients' beliefs must not become a barrier to effective treatment. The APA resolution on religious prejudice indicates that "psychologists are careful to prevent bias from their own spiritual, religious or non-religious beliefs from taking precedence over professional practice and standards or scientific findings in their work as psychologists" (APA, 2007, p. 4). When clinicians respect, address, and incorporate the worldview of the religiously affiliated father into psychotherapy or consultations, they will be practicing in ways consistent with these guidelines.

*Develop a working knowledge of a client's belief system.* Gathering useful information about a religiously affiliated father's beliefs is not as daunting as it may seem. A few questions during the assessment process can reveal significant assumptions, beliefs, values, and perspectives. Sample questions are offered in the following section. This client-led learning may be supplemented with easily available empirical findings about the interaction of psychology with religious or spiritual beliefs. APA's PsycINFO is a convenient and thorough resource that can be consulted from any clinician's desk. The importance of learning about a client's belief system is noted in the APA resolutions on multicultural guidelines (APA, 2002, p. 27) and religious prejudice (APA, 2007, p. 3).

*Refer theological questions to appropriate religious officials.* It can be tempting to engage in a theological discussion about particular religious propositions and assertions. This may be appropriate when the focus is on ways these views influence psychological matters, such as fathering behavior. On the other hand, when the father is focused on a technical understanding of theological or religious propositions, referral is likely the best response. Clinicians are mental health professionals, not religious experts, and must act with "full sensitivity to the profound differences between psychology and religion/spirituality" (APA, 2007, p. 3).

*Actively respond to religious prejudice directed at fathers.* APA's resolution on religious prejudice reaches beyond the counseling room and "encourages all psychologists to act to eliminate discrimination based on or derived from religion and spirituality" (APA, 2007, p. 3). Exactly what actions to take will be determined by careful reflection within a given situation, but it does not appear permissible to take a general stance of avoidance or minimization.

## Clinical Assessment

It is no longer novel for physicians and other medical professionals to ask questions about a patient's spirituality or religious resources. The Joint Commission on the Accreditation of Healthcare Organizations (2004) has recommended a set of questions to be asked of patients in medical settings, including such queries as, Who or what provides the patient with strength and hope? What type of spiritual/religious support does the patient desire? and, What does suffering mean to the patient?

Assessing the significance of a father's religious views is essential and can begin during the intake interviews. Many questions lurk just below the surface. Does he believe that his word on parenting is final, or does his religion emphasize equal regard and equal roles in decision making? Does he believe that corporal punishment is a divine requirement? Were his own parents authoritarian in religious ways? (Research shows that children who grow up with authoritarian and abusive fathers move into their own adult lives with decreased religiosity, whereas children abused by persons outside the family tend to increase their self-ratings of spirituality; Bierman, 2005.) What values is he teaching his children? Which religious programs will they attend? Does he simply identify with a religious or spiritual tradition, or is he an involved member?

Although these questions are critical to address, many men may feel reluctant to address these issues openly in an intake interview. Therefore, it may be more helpful to conduct an assessment in broader terms, at least at the outset. Some clinicians find it possible to conduct a spiritual assessment as part of a formal and standardized set of interviews, such as the SCID I and SCID II (Structured Clinical Interview for the *DSM-IV*; First, Spitzer, Gibbon, & Williams, 1996; First, Gibbon, Spitzer, & Williams, 1997). Others prefer a more inductive approach, following leads as they develop.

*Available spiritual assessment tools.* The literature offers a wide range of instruments, questionnaires, and surveys designed to elicit spiritual/ religious information. Many of these devices are not supported by standardized validity and reliability data, but are more demographic and exploratory in nature. Religious assessment tools have been developed for many specific client populations: eating-disordered women (Richards, Hardman, & Berrett, 2007); patients with AIDS (Feingold, 2007); patients with chronic illness, surgery, or terminal illness (O'Connell & Skevington, 2007); clients who wish to use spirituality to promote mental health (Eichler, Deegan, Canda, & Wells, 2006); hospice patients (Maue-Johnson & Tanguay, 2006); African Americans (Waller & Sori, 2006); families with depression and anxiety (Prest & Robinson, 2006); substance abuse patients (Korinek & Arredondo, 2004); and many other groups.

At a theoretical level, religious assessment is now conceptualized to include multiple domains. Richards and Bergin (2005) have summarized several years of theoretical development by numerous scholars and outlined their understanding of nine principle domains: metaphysical worldview, religious affiliation, religious orthodoxy, religious problem-solving style, spiritual identity, God image, value-lifestyle congruence, doctrinal knowledge, and religious health/maturity. Examples of instruments that can be used for multiple populations include the Assessment of Spirituality and Religious Sentiments (French & Piedmont, 2005), the Spiritual Behavior, Attitude and Sensitivity scale (Ozaki, 2005), and the Spiritual Strengths Assessment (Eichler et al., 2006).

*Kansas Spiritual Assessment.* As a general practice, the present author/clinician has found it useful to ask men a series of questions about religious or spiritual views that might affect their fathering beliefs and practices. Over time, these questions have been refined with colleagues at the Professional Renewal Center (an intensive day treatment facility for impaired professionals), and these questions have become a structured interview that lasts an average of 30–45 minutes. Called the Kansas Spiritual Assessment (KSA; Robertson, 2007), the instrument is designed to be heuristic rather than measurement focused. Although the questions are about explicitly religious or spiritual themes, it has become evident through the administration of the KSA by multiple clinicians that the questions elicit information that also addresses psychological issues. The approach of the KSA questions is qualitative rather than quantitative. It is a structured interview conducted face-to-face, with the clinician following leads as necessary. As the following vignette illustrates, portions of such a spiritual assessment can uncover underlying beliefs that may hinder a man's willingness to share important psychological information with his psychotherapist.

## A CASE HISTORY: MR. O'TOOLE'S CATCH-22

Luke, a sixth grader, was anxious about many things in life, but he was especially troubled by forecasts of severe weather. After watching television pictures of a tornado near his home, Luke had become afraid of any threatening weather pattern—thunder, lightening, even dark and cloudy skies. His anxieties became problematic at school. If he heard the sound of thunder outside his classroom, he would become nauseous and ask to see the school nurse. He would then demand that his father come and take him home. No amount of reassurance by his teacher or the nurse assuaged his fears. The faintest sound of distant thunder led to somaticizing and the plea for his father's rescue. Eventually, the school called his parents in for a conference. This discussion, in turn, led to a recommendation that Luke's parents take him to a psychologist to address this issue.

Reluctantly, Luke's father, Mr. O'Toole, accompanied his wife to the office of Dr. Greenberg (a pseudonym), a local psychologist. It was clear that O'Toole did not want to be there. As they settled into their chairs for the first session, O'Toole started the conversation, "Please don't be offended, but I want to know if you are a Christian man." Recognizing that this question was about credibility and emotional safety, Dr. Greenberg replied, "That's an excellent question. It sounds like your faith can be an important part of our discussions. Am I right?" O'Toole nodded. "I welcome that," Greenberg continued. "I am very interested in talking with you about ways in which your faith has been helpful to you and how it might help us address your concerns. Would you be open to that?" At this, O'Toole seemed relieved. He did not press the question about Greenberg's religious affiliation, perhaps because the underlying suspicion had been addressed.

This led to brief inquiries about the family's membership in a local church and a description of various church activities attended by Luke. With the importance of the parents' religion acknowledged, the conversation shifted to the reason the parents had called Dr. Greenberg. In talking about young Luke's fear of tornadoes, it became clear that Mr. O'Toole was struggling with some underlying religious questions. He believed that resolving his son's problem was his Christian duty, and that asking someone outside his local church for assistance may have represented a failure for him, both as a man and a Christian father. He also thought that prayer should have been able to take Luke's fears away. These concerns needed to be expressed and normalized. Then the focus could move to Luke's worries. What did Luke need? What had the parents tried already? What did they think might be helpful?

Despite these reassurances, Mr. O'Toole remained cautious and skeptical. Dr. Greenberg then decided to conduct a more thorough assessment of O'Toole's religious views. "I'd like to know more about your personal convictions, so that we can make use of these beliefs in developing a plan for Luke." O'Toole readily agreed, and Dr. Greenberg then conducted a spiritual assessment that revealed much helpful information. For example, he learned that an influential teaching in Mr. O'Toole's own early life had been that "you must trust God for everything. If you have fears, you ask God to remove those fears." O'Toole told him that being a father was the "most sacred duty I have, before God," and that trusting a psychologist was taking a "secular" approach that made him uncomfortable.

Given these concerns, Dr. Greenberg addressed the dilemma directly. "Mr. O'Toole, let me see if I understand what you are saying. On one hand, you really want to help Luke get over his fears about thunder. You want him to stay in school rather than call you every time the skies get dark. On the other hand, you want to make sure that whatever approach we take with Luke does not harm his faith in God. Am I right?" In effect, Greenberg was making explicit the implicit catch-22 in O'Toole's thinking. If he employed the psychologist's techniques, he might be turning to secular ideas rather than his faith. But he also knew that Luke's problem had not improved by relying only on prayer.

Somehow, identifying the dilemma reduced its power for Mr. O'Toole. The parents were then able to collaborate on the development of a systematic desensitization plan. This approach was described as a "skill" that would enable Luke to control his own body's responses, similar to other skills he was developing in playing baseball and the piano. In this way, with the value of his religion acknowledged, Mr. O'Toole's faith became a strong motivation and helped him comply with the application of psychological principles to Luke's fear of thunder. In the process of pursuing these objectives, of course, many other questions about parenting emerged, and these could be addressed without the tacit resistance present when treatment began.

## SUMMATIVE COMMENT

Data cited above demonstrate that men in North America are *heavily* religious, and their views are *highly* diverse. Their views on the use of corporal punishment, the likelihood of seeking help, the appropriateness of divorce, the definition of proper gender role behavior, and many other daily concerns are affected.

To fully address presenting issues brought to the counseling room by religiously affiliated fathers, effective clinicians will ask about underlying religious or spiritual values that drive those issues. These questions will be asked routinely. They will be respectful, facilitative, explicit, and nonjudgmental. This approach now has the full weight of both the American Psychological Association (2002, 2007) and the Joint Commission on the Accreditation of Healthcare (2004).

The recommendations offered here describe a clinical approach to religiously affiliated fathers that reduces the likelihood of getting caught in the dilemma noted at the beginning of this chapter. When the counselor is not silent about the major resource for a father's values, the ensuing discussions move to a deeper level. The father feels free to discuss critically important motivations, ideals, and standards that underlie the presenting issue. The counselor discovers ideas, practices, and sources of social support that can be useful in fostering insight and change. As a result, religiously affiliated fathers are more likely to find the assistance they seek.

## REFERENCES

Afshari, R. (1994). Egalitarian Islam and misogynist Islamic tradition: A critique of the feminist reinterpretation of Islamic history and heritage. *Critique: Journal of Critical Studies of Iran and the Middle East*, (4), 13–33.

American Psychological Association. (2002). *Guidelines on multicultural education, training, research, practice, and organizational change for psychologists.* Washington, DC: Author.

American Psychological Association Council of Representatives (2007). *Resolution on religious, religion-based, and/or religion-derived prejudice.* Washington, DC: Author.

Armacost, M. (2001, December 18). The role of religion in public life (Washington). Event Transcript. The National Press Club. Retrieved from http://pewforum.org/events/?EventID=20

Association of Religion Data Archives (ARDA) (2007). Religious preference. Retrieved from http://www.thearda.com/quickstats/qs_28.asp

Bader, C. D., Froese, P., Johnson, B., Menchken, F. C., & Stark, R. (2005). *The Baylor Religion Survey.* Waco, TX: Institute for Studies of Religion, Baylor University.

Barlas, A. (2002). *"Believing women" in Islam: Unreading patriarchal interpretations of the Qur'an.* Austin, TX: University of Texas Press.

Bascue, L. O., Inman, D. J., & Kahn, W. J. (1982). Recognition of suicidal lethality factors by psychiatric nursing assistants. *Psychological Reports, 51*, 197–198.

Benson, H. (1996). *Timeless healing.* New York: Scribner.
Benson, P. L., Williams, D. L., Johnson, A. L., (1987). *The quicksilver years: The hopes and fears of early adolescence.* Search Institute. San Francisco: Harper & Row.
Bergin, A. E., & Jensen, J. P. (1990). Religiosity of psychotherapists: A national survey. *Psychotherapy, 27,* 3–7.
Berke, M. (1996). God and gender in Judaism. *First things, 64,* 33–38.
Bierman, A. (2005). The effects of childhood maltreatment on adult religiosity and spirituality: Rejecting God the father because of abusive fathers? *Journal for the Scientific Study of Religion, 44*(3), 349–359.
Bormann, J., Shively, M., Smith, T. L., & Gifford, A. L. (2007). *Emerging evidence on relationships between spiritual practices and health.* APA 115th Annual Convention, San Francisco, August 17–20, American Psychological Association.
Burns, J. F. (2007, November 30). British Muslim leaders propose 'Code of Conduct.' New York Times. Retrieved December 12, 2007, from www.nytimes .com/2007/11/30/world/europe/30britain.html?partner=rssnyt&emc=rss
Castellini, J. D., Nelson III, W. M., Barrett, J. J., Nagy, M. S., & Quatman, G. L. (2005). *Journal of Psychology & Theology, 33*(1), 41–55.
Centore, A. J., & Clinton, T. (2008). Benefits of religion on recovery from relationship problems. In J. D. Onedera, (Ed.), *The role of religion in marriage and family counseling* (pp. 181–196). New York: Routledge.
Chaves, M., Konieczny, M. E., Beyerlein, K. & Barman, E. (1999). The National Congregations Study: Background, methods, and selected results. *Journal for the Scientific Study of Religion, 38*(4): 458–476.
Cole, A. (2006). Buddhism. In D. S. Browning, M. C. Green, & J. Witte, Jr. (Eds.), *Sex, marriage, & family in world religions* (pp. 299–366). New York: Columbia University Press.
Danso, H., Hunsberger, B., & Pratt, M. (1997). The role of parental religious fundamentalism and right-wing authoritarianism in child-rearing goals and practices. *Journal for the Scientific Study of Religion, 336*(4), 496–511.
Davis, J. A., & Smith, T. W. (2004). *General Social Survey.* Storrs, CT: The Roper Center for Public Opinion Research.
Delaney, H. D., Miller, W. R., & Bisono, A. M. (2007). Religiosity and spirituality among psychologists: A survey of clinician members of the American Psychological Association. *Professional Psychology: Research and Practice, 38*(5), 538–546.
Dollahite, D. C. (1998). Fathering, faith, and spirituality. *The Journal of Men's Studies, 7*(1), 3–15.
Donnelly, M., & Straus, M. A., (Eds.). (2005). *Corporal punishment of children in theoretical perspective.* New Haven, CT: Yale University Press.
Eichler, M., Deegan, G., Canda, E. R., Wells, S. (2006). Using the Strengths Assessment to mobilize spiritual resources. In K. B. Helmeke & C. F. Sori (Eds.), *The therapist's notebook for integrating spirituality in counseling: Homework, handouts and activities for use in psychotherapy* (pp. 69–76). New York: Haworth.
Ellison, C. G. (1996). Conservative Protestantism and the corporal punishment of children: Clarifying the issues. *Journal for the Scientific Study of Religion, 35*(1), 1–16.
Feingold, A. (2007, Spring). All that is sacred: A primer on spiritual assessment. *Mental Health AIDS, 8*(3), 6. Washington DC: U.S. Department of Health and Human Services.

Ferrand, J. L. (2005). Effects of clinical psychologists' religious beliefs on the assessment and treatment of extremely religious patients. *Dissertation Abstracts International: Section B: The Sciences and Engineering.* 65(7-B), 3704.

First, M. B., Gibbon, M., Spitzer, R. L., & Williams, J. B. W. (1997). *Structured Clinical Interview for DSM-IV Axis II Personality Disorders (SCID-II).* Washington, DC: American Psychiatric Press.

First, M. B., Spitzer, R. L., Gibbon, M., & Williams, J. B. W. (1996). *Structured Clinical Interview for the DSM-IV Axis I Disorders.* Washington, DC: American Psychiatric Press.

French, A. C., & Piedmont, R. L. (2005). *Psychometric evaluation of the ASPIRES Short Form.* Poster Session presented at the annual convention of the American Psychological Association, Washington DC.

Fuchs, L. H. (2000). *Beyond patriarchy: Jewish fathers and families.* Hanover, NH: University Press of New England.

Gartner, J. (1996). Religious commitment, mental health, and prosocial behavior: A review of the empirical literature. In E. P. Shafranske (Ed.), *Religion and the clinical practice of psychology* (pp. 187–214). Washington, D.C.: American Psychological Association.

Goodstein, L. (2005, August 31). Teaching of creationism is endorsed in new survey. *New York Times.* Retrieved June 7, 2008 from http://www.nytimes.com/2005/08/31/national/31religion.html?_r=1&ex=1125633600&en=cc135bc65420aa67&ei=5070&oref=slogin

Goolsby, K. A. (2006, August 20). Faith, culture are factors in paddling. *The Dallas Morning News.* Retrieved from http://www.dallasnews.com/sharedcontent/dws/news/localnews/stories/DN-paddlingside_20met.ART.State.Edition1.3e922ce.html

Grasmick, H. G., Bursik, R. J., & Kimpel, M. (1991). Protestant fundamentalism and attitudes toward corporal punishment of children. *Violence and Victims, 6*(4), 283–298.

Greenberg, A., & Berktold, J. (2005). Faith and family in America, 2005. Summary reported in Association of Religion Data Archives (ARDA). Retrieved November 25, 2007, from http://www.TheArda.com/Archive/Files/Descriptions/FAITHFAM.asp

Grossman, C. L. (2007, July 9). Religious bonds divide some parents, kids. *USA Today.* Retrieved from www.usatoday.com/news/religion/2007-07-08-kids-parents-religion_N.htm?csp=34

Hansen, N. D., Randazzo, K. V., Schwartz, A., Marshall, M., Kalis, D., Frazier, R., et al. (2006). Do we practice what we preach? An exploratory survey of multicultural psychotherapy competencies. *Professional Psychology: Research and Practice, 37*(1), 66–74.

Hathaway, W. L., Scott, S. Y., & Garver, S. A. (2004). Assessing religious/spiritual functioning: A neglected domain in clinical practice? *Professional Psychology: Research and Practice, 35,* 97–104.

Ing, D. S. F. (1999). The relationship between religiosity and marital satisfaction in Protestant Chinese-American couples. *Dissertation Abstracts International: Section B: The Sciences and Engineering.* 59(9-B), 5088.

Joint Commission on the Accreditation of Healthcare Organizations (2004). *Spiritual assessment: Does the Joint Commission specify what needs to be included in a spiritual assessment?* Retrieved June 8, 2008 from http://www.jointcommission.org/AccreditationPrograms/HomeCare/Standards/09_FAQs/PC/Spiritual_Assessment.htm.

Kessler, R. C., McGonagle, K. A., Zhao, S., Nelson, C. B., Hughes, M., Eshleman, S. Wittchen, H., & Kendler, K. S. (1994). How prevalent are psychiatric disorders? Results of the National Comorbidity Survey. *Clinician's Research Digest, 12*(6), 5. Washington, DC: American Psychological Association.

King, V. (2003). The influence on fathers' relationships with their children. *Journal of marriage and family, 65*(2), 382–395.

Korinek, A. W., & Arredondo, Jr., R. (2004). The Spiritual Health Inventory (SHI): Assessment of an instrument for measuring spiritual health in a substance abusing population. *Alcoholism Treatment Quarterly, 22*(2), 55–66.

Kosmin, B. A., Mayer, E., & Keysar, A. (2001). *American religious identification survey.* New York: The Graduate Center of the City University of New York.

Larson, D. B. (1985). Religious involvement. In G. Rekers (Ed.), *Family building* (pp. 121–147). Ventura, CA: Regal Books.

LeBlanc, S. (2007, October 17). Parents use religion to avoid vaccines. *The Associated Press.* Retrieved June 7, 2008 from http://www.washingtonpost.com/wp-dyn/content/article/2007/10/18/AR2007101800244.html

Lindner, E. W. (2006). *Yearbook of American & Canadian churches.* New York: National Council of Churches.

Luckmann, T. (1967). *The invisible religion.* New York: McMillan.

Mahoney, A. (2000). *U.S. norms on religious affiliation, self-reported importance, and church attendance of mothers and fathers of children and adolescents: Secondary analyses of 1995 Gallup poll.* Unpublished manuscript, Bowling Green State University.

Mahoney, A., Pargament, K. I., Tarakeshwar, N., & Swank, A. B. (2001). Religion in the home in the 1980's and 1990's: A meta-analytic review and conceptual analysis of links between religion marriage and parenting. *Journal of Family Psychology, 15*(4), 559–596.

Mander, G. (2001). Fatherhood today: Variations on a theme. *Psychodynamic Counselling, 7*(2), 141–158.

Maples, M. R., & Robertson, J. M. (2000). Counseling men with religious affiliations. In G. Brooks & G. Good (Eds.), *The new handbook of psychotherapy and counseling with men: A comprehensive guide to settings, problems, and treatment approaches.* San Francisco: Jossey-Bass.

Marty, M., & Appleby, R. S. (Eds.). (1991). Fundamentalisms observed. *The Fundamentalism Project, Volume 1.* Chicago: University of Chicago Press.

Mattis, J. S., Murray, Y. F., Hatcher, A. A., Hearn, K. D., Lawhon, G. D., Murphy, E. J., & Washington, T. A. (2001). Religiosity, spirituality, and the subjective quality of African American men's friendships: An exploratory study. *Journal of Adult Development, 8*(4), 221–230.

Maue-Johnson, E. L., & Tanguay, C. L. (2006). Assessing the unique needs of hospice patients: A tool for music therapists. *Music Therapy Perspectives, 24*(1), 13–20.

McCullough, M. E., Larson, D. B., Worthington, E. L., Jr. (1998). In D. B. Larson, J. P. Swyers, & M. E. McCullough (Eds.), *Scientific research on spirituality and health: A consensus report* (pp. 129–152). Rockville, MD: National Institute for Healthcare Research.

McFadden, S. H., Knepple, A. M., & Armstrong, J. A. (2003). Length and locus of friendship influence church members' sense of social support and comfort with sharing emotions. *Journal of Religious Gerontology, 15*(4), 39–55.

Merrill, R. M., Salazar, R. D., & Gardner, N. W. (2001). Relationship between family religiosity and drug use behavior among youth. *Social Behavior and Personality, 29*(4), 347–358.

Miller-McLemore, B. J. (2004). A feminist theologian looks (askance) at headship. In E. Blankenhorn, D. Browning, & M. S. van Leeuwen (Eds.), *Does Christianity teach male headship? The equal-regard marriage and its critics* (pp. 49–62). Grand Rapids, MI: Eerdmans.

Minear, J. D., & Bruch, L. R. (1980–1981). The correlations of attitudes toward suicide with death anxiety, religiosity, and personal closeness to suicide. *Omega Journal of Death and Dying, 11*, 317–324.

Murray-Swank, A., Mahoney, A., & Pargament, K. I. (2006). Sanctification of parenting: Links to corporal punishment and parental warmth among biblically conservative and liberal mothers. *International Journal for the Psychology of Religion, 16*(4), 271–287.

National Council of Churches (2008). *NCC at a glance: Who belongs, what we do, how we work together.* Retrieved June 9, 2008 from http://www .ncccusa.org/about/about_ncc

New American Standard Bible, (1995). La Habra, CA: The Lockman Foundation.

O'Connell, K. A., & Skevington, S. M. (2007). To measure or not to measure? Reviewing the assessment of spirituality and religion in health-related quality of life. *Chronic Illness, 3*(1), 77–87.

Olitzky, K., & Sabath, R. T. (1996). *Striving toward virtue: A contemporary guide for Jewish ethical behavior.* Jersey City, NJ: Ktav.

O'Neil, J. M. (1982). Gender role conflict and strain in men's lives. In K. Solomon & N. Levy (Eds.), *Men in transition: Theory and therapy* (pp. 5–44). New York: Plenum.

Ornish, D. (1990). *Dr. Dean Ornish's program for reversing heart disease.* New York: Random House.

Ozaki, M. (2005). Development of an assessment tool on spirituality explained by three domains, will, joy and sense: From a holistic educational approach. *Journal of International Society of Life Information Science, 23*(2), 364–369.

Palkovitz, R., & Palm, G. (1998). Fatherhood and faith in formation: The developmental effects of fathering on religiosity, morals, and values. *The Journal of Men's Studies, 7*(1), 33–51.

Prest, L. A., & Robinson, W. D. (2006). Special section introduction: Advancing a systems view in the treatment of depression and anxiety. *Journal of Systemic Therapies, 25*(3), 1–3.

Promise Keepers. (2007). Seven promises of a promise keeper: Calling men to a higher standard. Denver, CO: Author. Retrieved on December 12, 2007, from http://www.promisekeepers.org/about/7promises

Propst, L.R. (1988). *Psychotherapy in a religious framework: Spirituality in the emotional healing process.* New York: Human Sciences Press

Reynolds, D. K., & Nelson, F. L. (1981). Personality, life situation, and life expectancy. *Suicide and Life Threatening Behavior, 11*, 99–110.

Richards, P. S., & Bergin, A. E. (2005). *A spiritual strategy for counseling and psychotherapy* (2nd ed.). Washington, DC: American Psychological Association.

Richards, P. S., Hardman, R. K., & Berrett, M. D. (2007). Religious and spiritual assessment of patients with eating disorders. In *The treatment of women with eating disorders*, pp. 111–131. Washington, DC: American Psychological Association.

Robertson, J. M. (2007). *Kansas Spiritual Assessment*. Unpublished manuscript. Lawrence, KS: Professional Renewal Center.

Robins, L. N., & Regier, D. A. (1991). *Psychiatric Disorders in America*. New York, Free Press, 1991.

Roggman, L. A., Boyce, L. K., Cook, G. A., & Cook, J. (2002). Getting dads involved: Predictors of father involvement in Early Head Start and with their children. *Infant Mental Health Journal, 23*(1–2), 62–78.

Schwartz, J. P., Hage, S. M., Bush, I., Burns, L. K. (2006). Unhealthy parenting and potential mediators as contributing factors to future intimate violence: A review of the literature. *Trauma, Violence, & Abuse, 7*(3), 206–221.

Silverstein, L. B., Auerbach, C. F., & Levant, R. F. (2002). Contemporary fathers reconstructing masculinity: Clinical implications of gender role strain. *Professional Psychology: Research and Practice, 33*(4), 361–369.

Simon, S. (2005, October 20). Parents cast fight as sexual vs. religious tolerance. *Los Angeles Times*. Retrieved June 9, 2008 from http://www.pewforum.org/news/display.php?NewsID=5558

Speed, M. C. (2005). Heterosexual African American couples' perception of being happily married. *Dissertation Abstracts International: Section B: The Sciences and Engineering, 66*(4-B), pp. 1975.

Triandis, H. C. (1972). *The analysis of subjective culture*. New York: Wiley.

Triandis, H. C. (2002). Subjective culture. In W. J. Lonner, D. L. Dinnel, S. A. Hayes, & D. N. Sattler (Eds.), *Online readings in psychology and culture* (Unit 15, Chapter 1). Bellingham, WA: Center for Cross-Cultural Research, Western Washington University. Available from http://www.wwu.edu/~culture

U. S. Census Bureau (USCB). (2001). *Statistical Abstract of the United States: 2001*. Washington, DC: Author.

Van Leeuwen, M. S. (2004). Is equal regard in the Bible? In D. Blankenhorn, D. Browning & M. S. Van Leeuwen, (Eds.), *Does Christianity teach male headship? The equal regard marriage and its critics* (pp. 13–22). Grand Rapids, MI: Eerdmans.

Waller, B., & Sori, C. F. (2006). Assessing African-American spiritual and religious orientation. In K. B. Helmeke & C. F. Sori (Eds.), *The therapist's notebook for integrating spirituality in counseling: Homework, handouts and activities for use in psychotherapy* (pp. 129–140). New York: Haworth.

Wilcox, W. B. (2002). Religion, convention, and paternal involvement. *Journal of Marriage and Family, 64*(3), 780–792.

Wuthnow, R. (2002). Religious involvement and status-bridging social capital. *Journal for the Scientific Study of Religion, 41*(4), 669–684.

# 9

# Increasing Clinical and Contextual Awareness When Working With New Fathers

## ROD BERGER

The birth of a man's first child has frequently been seen as complementary to that of the mother and not as a separate event for the male. Pregnancy and birth of a first child can leave men hesitant to associate stressors with the birthing journey, further complicating the symptomatic profile often associated with aloofness and distance out of respect for the physical obligations of pregnancy for the mother. The clinical focus of fathers has often been placed on traditional male experiences such as employment and financial status. These variables have often precluded examining the life-altering effects of first-time parenthood by professionals working in mental health settings.

Research focused on fathers has increased significantly in recent years (Condon, Boyce, & Corkindale, 2004; Draper, 2003; Henwood & Procter, 2003; Zelkowitz & Milet, 1997). However, historically, research on first-time fathers has centered on their abilities to parent their children and to support their spouse both emotionally and financially (Condon et al., 2004). Gradually, the medical and mental health communities have begun to recognize that new fathers experience a range of physiological and emotional changes (Berg & Wynne-Edwards, 2001; Storey, Walsh,

Quinton, & Wynne-Edwards, 2000). These findings may shed light for practitioners into the scope of experience both emotionally and physiologically, further aiding first-time fathers' care in health-care settings.

The increased demands of fatherhood incorporated with the social construction of what it means to be both a man and a father can leave men confused about what they are experiencing and what is expected of them as new fathers. To date, research on the emotional experiences of first-time fathers has focused, singularly, in terms of paternal depression and its effect on the family unit (Condon et al., 2004). Men not only experience depression or unpleasant affect, but also pleasant feelings such as joy at the birth of their first child (Draper, 2003; Henwood & Procter, 2003; Zelkowitz & Milet, 1997). The complexity and range of feelings that first-time fathers may experience have been addressed by only a handful of studies (Condon et al., 2004; Henwood & Procter, 2003; Kaitz & Katzir, 2004).

Becoming a parent signifies a transition for men that challenges predisposed notions of what being a first-time father means both emotionally and socially (Condon et al., 2004; Henderson & Brouse, 1991). In fact, the reproductive year has been shown to be a period when men are particularly at risk for psychological problems (Zelkowitz & Milet, 1997). This time frame incorporates changes in the spousal relationship and potentially increases financial strain as well as heightens opposing demands of family and work on new fathers (Zelkowitz & Milet). Assessing how first-time fathers view themselves before and after the birth of their child is imperative for understanding their psychological well-being, their involvement with their newborn, and their motivation for role change (Condon et al., 2004; Strauss & Goldberg, 1999).

Clinical implications of the lack of information on the impact of becoming a father greatly reduce a professional's ability to address effectively this unique population of men. Throughout this chapter, an examination of the available literature will provide indicators of possible intra- and interpersonal challenges for first-time fathers and methods for successful intervention. The chapter will also examine the positive experiences associated with fatherhood and the utilization of healthy coping strategies through existing gender strengths. The intention of this chapter is to better inform clinicians of the underlying symptomatology for a population of men often missed by well-intentioned professionals and to highlight the range of experiences unifying this transitional period. Throughout the chapter, the terms *first-time fathers* and *new fathers* will be used interchangeably based on their use within the given literature.

## PSYCHOLOGICAL REPRESENTATION

Often the literature pertaining to first-time fathers isolates depression as the main affective state pertinent to the male experience of parenthood

(Draper, 2003; Shapiro, 1987; Zelkowitz & Milet, 1997). Though important conceptual and empirical findings about men's depression have emerged, few have included the paternal domain or have been effectively disseminated throughout the community to provide needed intervention (Rochlen, Whilde, & Hoyer, 2005). As recently as 2003, the National Institute of Mental Health examined the role depression played in men's lives. Fathers, as a group, were notably absent from this public campaign (Rochlen et al.). The danger for first-time fathers lies in the fact that the communal outreach falls under the rubric of male depression and not paternal depression or affective dysregulation of both positive and negative experiences, thus ignoring a significant population of a specific group of men. Barring gender differences, depression is the fourth leading cause of disability in the United States, and the global burden of depression will be second only to cardiovascular disease by the year 2020 (Rochlen et al., 2005). Further, indications are that paternal experiences of depression are not momentary (Zelkowitz & Milet, 2001).

Much of the literature on first-time fathers examines traditional masculine ideology in the context of work and financial strain while disregarding the internal experience (emotional states) of first-time fathers. Studies conducted on paternal experiences have focused on fathers' caretaking abilities and self-efficacy skills (Manlove & Vernon-Feagans, 2002). Specifically, focus has been on the action of fathering (e.g., caretaking skills, financial means, and work strain) rather than on new fathers' affective experience.

There is a need for new empirical approaches to represent accurately and effectively the affective experience of first-time fathers. Fitzgerald, Mann, and Barratt (1999) have called for a shift in 21st century research. They assert that empirical studies pertaining to fatherhood should focus on direct assessment of fathers without relying on maternal report. Furthermore, research has failed to examine first-time fathers' affective experiences beginning at confirmation of pregnancy, often assessing experiences from the second trimester forward. Research has examined first-time fathers' experiences at 23 weeks prenatally (Condon et al., 2004), 3 weeks postnatally (Henderson & Brouse, 1991), and through the first year after birth (Kaitz & Katzir, 2004; Seimyr, Edhborg, Lundh, & Sjogren, 2004).

An examination of the popular press yields similar results of the marginalization of first-time fathers. Fleming and Tobin (2005) examined images of fatherhood in popular child-rearing books. A sample of 23 books found that of 56,379 paragraphs, only 4.2% were representative of fathers. The authors concluded that child-rearing books were predominately written for mothers, overwhelmingly emphasized mothers, and negatively portrayed fathers. Depictions of the fathers' subjective role were categorized by stress, a need to change, work/finance issues, and a lack of positive emotional states or behaviors (Fleming & Tobin). Abell and Schwartz (1999) believed this limited view of men significantly impacts a father's social emotional development across the lifespan:

For a man to make a long-term commitment to the care of his children may be regarded by many as a moral duty or point of honor, but little has been said about the importance of fathering in a man's healthy emotional growth and development. (p. 221)

The literature's failure to adequately address first-time fathers' affective range of experience may have important consequences on the emotional and physical health of the father, the family unit, and the transgenerational processes for men (Ahlborg & Strandmark, 2001; Condon et al., 2004; Jacob & Johnson, 2001). Garnering a more complete understanding of first-time fathers' affective experiences will allow for further understanding of paternal behaviors that have long influenced family development (domestic violence, alcohol and drug abuse, interactive play, loyalty, energetic approach, economic support, acquisition of appropriate boundaries, social rules, etc.). The result, clinically, impacts intervention strategies and conceptualizations of presenting problems.

## PHYSIOLOGICAL CHANGES IN FATHERS

Before the establishment of a baseline of first-time fathers' emotional experiences, it is important to have a working knowledge of physiological factors that may impact a father's mood states and alter his biochemistry. The clinical findings highlight the physiological changes and emotional experiences of first-time fathers, which often parallel those of their female counterparts. Nearly 20% of men with pregnant wives experienced symptoms related to pregnancy (Storey et al., 2000). While studying four hormones associated with nurturing behaviors (prolactin, cortisol, estrogen, and testosterone), researchers found evidence that male secretions and reactions mirrored that of their partners (Berg & Wynne-Edwards, 2001). Storey et al. (2000) found that for soon-to-be fathers, cortisol levels were twice as high in the three weeks prior to birth than at any other point during the pregnancy. Prolactin, which promotes lactation, rose by approximately 20% in males during the three weeks prior to birth (Berg & Wynne-Edwards). Biologists Berg and Wynne-Edwards posited that cortisol may help parents prepare for parenthood.

Testosterone was also found to alter during the pre- and postpartum periods. Testosterone levels fell 33% in fathers from 3 to 7 weeks postpartum (Berg & Wynne-Edwards, 2001). It is believed that this reduction in testosterone may set in motion a more cooperative, compassionate form of parenting. Berg and Wynne-Edwards discovered that fathers' levels of estrogen increased 30 days prior to birth through 12 weeks postpartum. Animal studies revealed that estrogen induces nurturing behavior in males (Berg & Wynne-Edwards). These findings may indicate a correlation between hormone levels and depressive presentations in men following the birth of their child (Storey et al., 2000). Collectively, this area of study has begun to establish that significant biochemical changes in fathers during pregnancy and postpartum can inform clinical conceptualizations of new fathers.

## EMOTIONAL EXPERIENCES IN THE TRANSITION TO FATHERHOOD

The transition to parenthood often impacts men more than any other point of fatherhood (Areias, Kumar, Barros, & Figueiredo, 1996; Ballard, Davies, Cullen, Mohan, & Dean, 1994; Edhborg, Seimyr, Lundh, & Widstrom, 2000; Goodman, 2004; Lutz & Hock, 2002; Matthey, Barnett, Ungerer, & Waters, 2000). During the reproductive year (conception through birth), men are particularly at risk for psychological problems, often beginning with the announcement of pregnancy (Draper, 2003; Shapiro, 1987; Zelkowitz & Milet, 1997). Shapiro hypothesized the transition to fatherhood can occur so suddenly that it often shocks new fathers into trying to cope with important life alterations.

A theoretical analysis of a man's passage to fatherhood found significant emotionality initiated at the public announcement of the impending birth (Draper, 2002, 2003). Draper's research established that during pregnancy men speak of isolation, feelings of redundancy, and ineffectiveness at engaging in the reality of the pregnancy process. First-time fathers often feel out of place and in limbo because they do not show physical signs of a maturing pregnancy as do their partners. Further, during labor, most fathers felt out of place, powerless, and unsure of what to do. As a result, these men felt emotionally vulnerable. Moreover, fathers felt a sense of disorientation between their previous life and their new roles as provider and parent (Draper). For first-time parents, the focus of attention lies with the baby and the new mother, often at the expense of the father, who may feel emotionally rejected (Barrows, 2004).

Men are encouraged to participate fully in the pregnancy and birth of their children, but are simultaneously given to understand that they are outsiders. Shapiro (1987) called this the cultural double bind for new fathers. It is made clear that while their presence is requested, their feelings are not, particularly if those feelings might upset their wives. Anger, anxiety, fear, and sadness are thought to be unwelcome in the maternity ward (Shapiro). Often, first-time fathers are torn between staying with their spouse and escorting the baby to the infant care unit (Draper, 2002). Additionally, Draper (2003) found first-time fathers to be more susceptible to feeling like an outsider in their own homes. First-time fathers can often experience low self-efficacy and dissatisfaction with parenting roles during the early transitional period of parenthood (Kaitz & Katzir, 2004). Kaitz and Katzir indicated that fathers' positive feelings toward their spouse decreased significantly from prepartum to 3 months postpartum, and feelings about themselves were at the lowest point at 6 months postpartum. The indication of such research is that new fathers are experiencing fluctuation in emotional expression and experience.

## *Depression*

The new role of fatherhood can instill a feeling of disorder in a man's life and cause significant stress regardless of a father's age, education, or socioeconomic class (Henwood & Procter, 2003). First-time fathers are at higher risk of depression from 3 to 12 months postpartum. Risk factors for these fathers included a prior history of depression and if their partners were depressed in pregnancy or during the first 3 months postpartum (Edhborg et al. 2000). The most researched area of paternal depression has centered on the impact of the depression on the fathers' ability to provide support to their spouse and child (Edhborg et al., 2000; Goodman, 2004; Lutz & Hock, 2002). First-time fathers in their 20s and 30s were particularly at risk for depressive symptomatology, with a higher incidence of depressive disorders than women of the same age group (Lutz & Hock, 2002). The greatest predictor of paternal depression was the affective states expressed by their spouses. Successful transition to parenthood for fathers was found to be determined in the prepartum period and predominately based on whether or not their partners were happy (Van Egeren, 2004). Lutz and Hock (2002) found that employment variables, quality of the marriage, and fear of abandonment and loneliness explained 43% of the variance in a father's depressive symptomatology following the birth of their first child.

Zelkowitz and Milet (1997) examined the significant risks associated with the reproductive year for men whose spouses experienced postpartum depression. Further questions in their study ascertained the level of stress experienced in multiple areas (family relations, finances, work, and health). The level of support fathers experienced from their own parents, in-laws, other relatives, friends, and professionals was also examined. The study found that 24% of the index sample (fathers with a spouse experiencing postpartum depression) had psychiatric diagnoses including depression, anxiety, somatization, and adjustment disorders (Zelkowitz & Milet). The onset of diagnosis was associated with the number of stressors reported by the father.

## FAMILY UNIT

### *Marital Relationship*

Depression in first-time fathers was found to be influenced by the perceptions of their spouse about their overall ability to parent their young

(Ahlborg & Strandmark, 2001; Corwyn & Bradley, 1999; Dudley, Roy, Kelk, & Bernhard, 2001). Empirical observations suggest that men had a propensity to rely emotionally on their partners, whereas women depended on other women for emotional support (Dudley et al). The marital relationship served as an important foundation for positive paternal experiences (Ahlborg & Strandmark; Corwyn & Bradley; Kaitz & Katzir, 2004). Mothers may be unaware of the impact they have on paternal investment and emotional health by exclusively bonding with the child, often at the expense of their spouses, implicating the role of the spousal relationship on fathers' sense of well-being (Ahlborg & Strandmark). Corwyn and Bradley discovered that fathers' perceptions of marriage and fatherhood are one and the same. Additionally, paternal investment, knowledge, and sensitivity were related to the overall quality of the marriage (Corwyn & Bradley). It appears that fathers' feelings toward the marriage mirror their feelings and subsequent interactions with their children.

## Parenting Practices

There are a limited number of guidelines pertaining to normative standards of various caretaking activities for fathers (Frascarolo, 2004; Manlove & Vernon-Feagans, 2002; Montague & Walker-Anderson, 2002). Researchers believe that parents who learn new behaviors and skills are better equipped to care effectively for their young and to achieve satisfaction with the parenting role (Feldman, 2000; Hudson, Elek, & Fleck, 2001). Increased parental involvement has been related to lower levels of depression, less avoidant behaviors, less ambivalence toward parenting, and greater feelings of control during parenting activities (Roggman, Benson, & Boyce, 1999). Furthermore, men who were involved in basic caretaking skills (diapering, bathing, feeding) demonstrated increased levels of sociability (Frascarolo, 2004).

In addition, fathers who were free of depressive symptomatology were more likely to seek support and/or intervention from third parties, including professional and social support (Roggman et al., 1999). In a study examining first-time fathers, those who received information on infant development scored higher competency scores at posttest than the control group who did not receive the information (Pfannenstiel & Honig, 1995). Self-efficacy skills often influence the quantity and quality of father-child activities.

Some studies illustrated father-child involvement and resulting infant behaviors based on the quality of interactions (Feldman, 2003; Montague & Walker-Anderson, 2002; Morman & Floyd, 2002). When presented with pictures of their fathers, infants whose fathers were involved 50% of the time in caregiving tasks looked almost 100% of the available time at their fathers' sad and happy expressions (Montague & Walker-Anderson). Additionally, the authors noted that limited participation from fathers hindered healthy infant social-emotional development (Montague & Walker-Anderson). Further, Feldman examined father-infant microlevel synchrony: a father's ability to understand the infant's baseline needs (food, comfort, diaper change, etc.). Results of the study found that fathers were equally capable as mothers in affective sharing and arousal regulation. In fact, the father-son dyad showed the highest degree of synchrony, based on interactive play (Feldman).

## Gender Strengths

It can be easy for the mental health professional to view men through stereotypical attitudes and perceptions associated with men in general. Though men can be challenging to work with, they possess a multitude of strengths, both clinically and personally, that benefit both the family unit and the professional relationship (energy, loyalty, an ability to synthesize experiences into language, and commitment to action plans). Clinically, it is imperative that the professional acknowledge not only the challenges and mood states associated with parenting, but also the positive attributes that men often contribute to the parenting dynamic. Traditionally, men are loyal to those who minimize shame and enhance personal strengths, aiding in therapeutic attendance and degree of rapport. A conscious effort on behalf of the practitioner allows for deep collaborative work to be completed on the terms of the first-time father. An approach centered on the positive attributes of first-time fathers' contributions further establishes a solid foundation with which to conduct mental health services.

Henwood and Proctor (2003) investigated the transition to first-time fatherhood by interviewing 30 men. The authors' findings presented a model of fathers that encompassed presence, involvement, putting children's needs first, approachability, nurturing, and caring (Henwood & Proctor). Research has demonstrated that men, on average, are spending more time per week with their children; there are increased numbers of stay-at-home fathers (Rochlen, McKelley, Suizzo, & Scaringi, 2008); and involved fathers decrease antisocial behavior in their youth (Henwood & Proctor).

Furthermore, fathers of boys can provide additional strengths and support for social-emotional development from the moment of birth. As gender research expands, it has been determined that infant boys' eyes are constructed for and attracted to movement (Sax, 2005). A father's propensity for active game play and movement is supportive and necessary for proper development of the young boy. This strength aids the rapport building and comfort between father and son through the inherent utilization of gender components formerly conceptualized as detrimental to growth and development. This strength opens the door clinically to explore a first-time father's experiences as a young boy himself, further promoting a more expansive understanding of a father's own interpretation of gender and parenthood.

## Clinical Work

The ability to provide first-time fathers with a timeline of expected emotional experiences will aid in normalizing their subjective emotional experiences. The mental health professional can inform fathers of physiological research findings. Further, clinicians can examine the tasks performed by the individuals' own fathers when they were growing up. This exploration may validate fathers' initial feeling states of paternity while also correlating them to experiences they had with their own fathers when they were young. The ongoing challenge, though, is that first-time fathers often expect clinical work to focus on traditional male gender roles. The constant ebb and flow between the expressed internal experiences of first-time fathers and the social construction of men as a whole require deft attention to detail and process to increase a father's help-seeking behavior and maintenance.

Traditional male gender-role norms have been found to increase a man's level of emotional distress, thus decreasing the likelihood that he will actively seek psychological help (Hudson, Campbell-Grossman, Fleck, Elek, & Shipman, 2003; Katon, Kleinman, & Rosen, 1982; Rochlen et al., 2005). Gender-role norms suggest that seeking help from a primary care physician is more acceptable than from a mental health professional. The likelihood of appropriate diagnosis for men declines even when they access health care. In a study examining maternal depression, 25% of the male spouses refused to answer questions about whom they themselves turned to for encouragement and emotional support (Seimyr et al., 2004).

Moreover, males learn to mask their feelings states early in development and often receive negative messages pertaining to help-seeking behaviors (Simon & Nath, 2004; Zeman, 1997). Katon et al. (1982) found that primary care physicians missed more than 95% of cases of depression when depression was not self-reported. "These fathers seldom ask for help with parenting issues and are often overlooked by the health care system" (Hudson et al., 2003, p. 218).

Research over the past two decades has focused on the behavior of emotional expressiveness to study men's emotional experiences (Wong & Rochlen, 2005). The primary focus has been on men's difficulty expressing themselves in a healthy manner (Ahlborg & Strandmark, 2001; Condon et al., 2004; Jacob, 2001). Extensive literature provides evidence of the negative outcomes associated with male inexpressiveness (O'Neil, 1981; Seimyr et al., 2004; Wong & Rochlen, 2005). Wong and Rochlen claimed that inexpressiveness of feelings in men may lead to (a) low self-esteem, (b) difficulties in intimacy, (c) negative affective states such as anxiety and depression, and (d) negative view of help seeking. The challenge most often faced by clinicians is helping to guide a first-time father through the emotional landscape of his own experiences and validating the presence of affective states among surface issues of employment, anger, and the like.

# INTERVENTIONS

## *Therapeutic Modalities*

As the clinical population of first-time fathers increases with social acceptance and exposure, so too will the modalities utilized to assist this population. A growing trend has been to reframe the linguistic portrayal of therapeutic work by including the word *coaching*. Therapeutic rationale for using this term has centered on the transcending language of coaching that utilizes goal attainment, decreases stigma often associated with mental health, and emphasizes skill building (McKelley & Rochlen, 2007). McKelley and Rochlen report that coaching may initiate buy-in for clients due to its linguistic alignment with male role socialization norms and practices. Therapy, on the other hand, may be viewed as an overall opposing approach to variables of competition, power, and success.

For group work centered on general male issues, the coaching vernacular may aid in overall participation and retention rates among men. The addition of fathering experiences and principles can enhance the normalizing aspects of adulthood for men while expanding their knowledge base about a fundamental time in their overall development. Therapeutic groups that have solely offered a focus on first-time fathers have had limited success, often due to first-time fathers' struggle to find merit in their own subjective experiences of pregnancy. Continued exposure to informed clinicians would greatly enhance initial selection of groups as resources and overall retention of fathers over time.

## *Assessments*

The use of assessment measures for first-time fathers may gain viability as the clinical population expands, but of more importance is its place in the continued effort to explain and interpret the broad emotional experiences of first-time fathers. The utilization of assessment results may result in the establishment of benchmarks to be reviewed mutually by both the clinician and client. Collaborating on the range of symptom expression can be a powerful tool in normalizing and rapport building efforts. The acknowledgment that becoming a first-time father can and does invoke both positive and negative emotional responses provides a client with a baseline from which to explore himself.

With that stated, there is a lack of assessment batteries to assess adequately the experience of first-time fathers. Ongoing and more thorough assessment is needed to capture first-time fathers' emotional experiences through self-report (independent of their partners' opinions), emotional states other than depression, and the different time periods significant in the emotional experiences of first-time fathers (Hudson et al., 2003; Katon et al., 1982; Rochlen et al., 2005). Further, practitioners should conduct a thorough clinical intake of family history and current stressors that includes spousal psychological presentation and its impact on the new father.

## Diagnostic Considerations

Though diagnostics are an important aspect to treatment planning, the problems presented by first-time fathers can change throughout therapy, often clouding diagnosis for the practitioner. One diagnosis that may be appropriate to consider throughout the course of treatment is the role of an adjustment disorder. This diagnostic category allows for flexibility and assists practitioners in conceptualizing clients who are experiencing paternity for the first time. A working hypothesis of an adjustment disorder further aids practitioners from falling victim to social stereotypes and from focusing primarily on overt negative behaviors and coping strategies (e.g., substance use, irritable mood). Depending on the symptom cluster, clients may be better suited to a diagnosis of an anxiety or mood disorder. Regardless of diagnosis, the benefit of an adjustment disorder diagnosis is that it helps providers maintain attention on process and its effect on clients. Parenthood is fluid and can alter subjective feelings about self, children, and the family's experience of the father. Like parenthood itself, subjective feelings about self, children, and the family's experience of the father are fluid. Mental health providers' approach to diagnosis should parallel this dynamic because symptom clusters vary both with expected and unexpected circumstances related to parenting.

## Psychoeducation

As research continues to expand in men's studies, it becomes of paramount importance to disseminate this information to our clients. Mental health providers' ability to provide substantive information (e.g., variables attributed to depressive states during pregnancy and following birth) gives first-time fathers information that normalizes experiences and feeling states. With the assistance of their clinician, clients can begin to reframe their experiences with language reflective of an "us" rather than an "I." This shared approach demonstrates that first-time fathers are not isolated in their experiences, but rather indicative of the greater male experience of parenting.

Psychoeducation couched in the therapeutic relationship can provide new fathers with a safe environment to explore isolative tendencies. Additionally, clinicians can enhance their client's ability to examine coping strategies and rationale for action in relation to common misperceptions and stereotypes of fathers. This paradigm exhibits itself through the case of John, a 36-year-old first-time father. John's presentation is similar to many new fathers in that his portrayal of himself is limiting and seen as inconsequential in relation to his child and spouse.

## CLINICAL VIGNETTE: JOHN

Like most first-time fathers who enter therapy, the presenting problem for John had little to do with his new role as a parent. John, 36, was a moderately successful architect who had been married for 7 years. John and his wife recently had their first child, a boy named Christopher. John had entered therapy on the request of his spouse to work on organizational skills at home and work, a possible career move, and a reported lack of interest in the daily activities of the family.

John's initial presentation in therapy was of a very affable individual who sought clarity and understanding about the pressures he experienced at home and work. John had begun working at a small firm, and through trial and tribulation had steadily moved up the career ladder, now making a six-figure income. The reported problem for John and his wife was that the income did not meet the needs of their budding lifestyle. John often reported that he did not fully understand his wife's wishes nor her approach to parenting. Further, he stated this was the first time he had voiced this concern, saying that he often recoils when his wife voices her opinion about finances and parenting practices. The following is an excerpt of a session with John that focused on the confusing messages being sent to him from the environment and how his parental status may have affected his mood state.

*John:*  Sorry I am late. It was really busy at work today and you know how I can get overwhelmed. But today was nothing compared with this past weekend. Once again I felt like the fool, and Susan is still talking about it...Do you remember last week how I told you about our "friends" who have "everything?"

*Clinician:*  I do...

*John:*  Well, they had a birthday party for their son, and we had to go. I really do not like spending time with them, because I always have to hear how well they are doing, and Susan and I inevitably argue on the way home because she will talk about how Christopher has to go to the same private school and do the same activities as their son when he grows up....it really is frustrating...I never know what to say...but I can say that my billable hours on my latest proposal just went up.

## CLINICAL CONSIDERATION

John's pervasive concern for a level playing field with his contemporaries is demonstrated by his initial question to the therapist regarding whether or not he remembered his busy schedule and "those" neighbors. This exchange is vital to rapport building and for normalizing, verbally, the residual effects of maintaining responsibilities without having emotional and practical support. John's last sentence supports his underlying, subjective conceptualization of himself that he is ultimately rated by the number of billable hours he can supply. These initial exchanges provide the portal for the clinician to dispel stereotypes associated with men and to normalize and reframe experience into thoughtful vocabulary.

It is critical that the clinician be aware of the shame quotient associated with a given client. Though new fathers, like John, request that we practice mind-sight (ability to think of others when they are not present) by asking if "we remember," we must make ongoing assessments of their rationale. Gender role stereotypes often reflect isolated thought ("I am the only one") and behavior ("I am upset so I will work alone and leave the parenting to my spouse"), and it becomes imperative that mental health providers continue to evidence shared understanding without shaming our clients for desiring the connection.

| | |
|---|---|
| *Clinician:* | It sounds like your experience of the party has been on your mind all week. |
| *John:* | It is the worst...well in my mind it has... |
| *Clinician:* | ...you are keeping it to yourself? |
| *John:* | ...well...I haven't exactly talked about the party with Susan, because I only focus on the fact that Christopher is 7 months old and we have to worry about budgeting for designer sneakers, sunglasses, and private schools that are unbelievably expensive... |
| *Clinician:* | I hear a lot of pressure in your voice...and I noticed that your posture has tightened up since you started talking about the party...can you tell me about that? |
| *John:* | Now you know why I end up with a headache most evenings...I am not exactly sure how to answer your question, but what comes to mind is how I thought being a kid used to be...I mean he is only 7 months old and I almost feel pressure to start flashcards and career mentoring with him so that he might be able to be as successful as "Mr. Rich's" prodigal son... |

## CLINICAL CONSIDERATION

It is important to note the items John has reported that indicate a strong sense of responsibility for providing for his family. John's frustration illustrates many men's difficulty with limited time and the pressure for success. Often this commitment to provide is seen as impatience and poor communication instead of forethought and rigor. A clinician's ability to aid first-time fathers in this area can often provide a balanced understanding about the level of destructiveness associated with negative gender role stereotypes in relation to those attributes that positively enhance the success of the family unit.

| | |
|---|---|
| *Clinician:* | You know, John, as I listen to you today the word "compare" keeps coming to mind....how do you experience that? |
| *John:* | (pauses)...Yeah, I know what it is like to be compared to at the firm and at home, and I want my son to have some peace and quiet and not feel like every day is a job interview... |
| *Clinician:* | It sounds like you can relate your experiences to this feeling. |
| *John:* | ...Yes, yes I can....my day is filled with not only work but with that ever-so-sneaky feeling that I am being assessed and judged... |

*Clinician:*  Judged? Any idea as to who might be judging you?
*John:*  You mean an actual person?
*Clinician:*  (silence)
*John:*  I don't know…I…(pauses)…I guess when I actually think about it there really isn't one person who says that they are judging or assessing me or for that matter who confronts me in that fashion other than if I falter on a specific task.
*Clinician:*  I wonder how you know if the judgmental feeling or assessment is directed to you or if you are coming to that conclusion on your own without verification…
*John:*  Good question (smiles). I have never thought about it in that manner… I just assume most of the time.


## CLINICAL CONSIDERATION

Providing first-time fathers with a venue for safe exploration requires attention to detail on the part of the clinician. For many men, just engaging in conversation can elicit various response styles and opinions. Often this lability results from limited exposure to self-reflection due to the belief that they are the only ones experiencing the emotion/frustration. Additionally, the concept of judgment may have been born from the assumption that male value rests in the production of completed tasks.

The above premise indicates the level of negativity often attributed to new fathers in relation to their ability, or perceived lack thereof, to effectively manage emotional states associated with interpersonal communications between their child, themselves, and their spouse. This becomes the challenge therapeutically because the focus of research has been on examining depressive symptomatology while mostly excluding other internal states (e.g., joy, insecurity, fear; Draper, 2003; Shapiro, 1987; Zelkowitz & Milet, 1997). Many first-time fathers also experience feelings of jealousy, exclusion, sadness, ambivalence, helplessness, and frustration (Henderson & Brouse, 1991). Because of the socially imposed challenges to clinical intervention and research, it is the responsibility of the treating clinician to provide continuous feedback to the client and with ongoing dialogue pertaining to the impact negative stereotypes can have on self-perception of abilities and worth.

*John:*  At the end of the day I would like to be, at least, thought of like a good worker…Like a nice guy who is trying hard…
*Clinician:*  Trying hard?
*John:*  Working as hard as I can to maintain my employment, pay the mortgage, and have a family…
*Clinician:*  It sounds like you have given this some thought…I wonder if you have shared these thoughts with Susan.
*John:*  No…not at all in fact…(pauses)…do you think I should?
*Clinician:*  I don't know what's best…(pauses)…what I hear is that you have placed a lot of attention and energy into not burdening those you care for.

| | |
|---|---|
| *John:* | How could I...I mean I need to keep my job and yeah I want the best for Christopher...and I am not sure if I have the right to say anything... |
| *Clinician:* | Is there room for you to succeed at those things and share today's thoughts with Susan? |
| *John:* | I...it just seems odd and that she would not be happy with me.... |
| *Clinician:* | If I can, John, I'd like to make an observation... |
| *John:* | Sure. |
| *Clinician:* | I have noticed that when you are telling me these things directly you speak with conviction and posture, but when you transition to sharing these thoughts with others I almost feel like you are apologizing... |
| *John:* | (long pause)...I know...I mean I see what you're saying...I get that way at work too, and Susan has even said that to me in so many words about work issues...basically stand up for myself. |

## CONCLUDING WITH JOHN

John presented with familiar themes (gender role conflict, work-home-life balance, etc.) for men, and yet he was also appreciably more expressive than most. This expressive ability was wrought with traditional challenges associated with an overall detachment from his own feeling states and an inability to make thoughtful connections of his subjective experience. John vacillates between being an apologetic man and a man with internal conviction of his value system. Additionally, the value system he also attempts to protect is that of his son. It becomes important to be aware of the subtleties first-time fathers present. If we were to edit John's usage of his son and replace his son with John, we might find a portal for exploration rich with content and within close proximity to John's conscious awareness of feeling states.

In subsequent sessions, John discussed his pent up fear that his wife would leave him over dissention in value systems. John began to slowly identify and separate his goals and values from those he believed to be expected both from society and his spouse. This untangling further aided John's ability to communicate his feeling states to others, both positive and negative. As a clinician, my ongoing battle was to provide an environment that supported his stated efforts without falling victim to socially established stereotypes that often govern our subconscious (e.g., Was John acting in a self-deprecating fashion? What secondary gains were being achieved?). I came to discover that my own gender (male) and open discussions of the above challenges helped to cultivate a therapeutic environment that minimized shame and provided space for John to share openly. When dialogue was exchanged that spoke to the male experience, a door opened for deeper and more connected content.

## CONCLUDING REMARKS

Clinical work with first-time fathers needs to focus on the inclusion of the man's experiences of the parenting process. Specifically, it should be communicated that the practitioner is curious about their experiences and welcomes concerns and questions. It is common for this population of men to divert such inquires, believing that it was only the mother who was a part of the pregnancy. This therapeutic opening invites professional validation of the man's experiences followed by psychoeducation about the emotional and physiological changes first-time fathers may experience.

Just as working with first-time fathers may be new to the practitioner, bridging these issues with clients will be new to them as well. Client education, one of the primary interventions with new fathers, stems from the clinician's increased knowledge of the social-emotional and physiological alterations men experience throughout and after the pregnancy. Once informed, the clinician will be better equipped to provide interventions suited to the individual needs of the client.

The therapeutic experience, grounded in sound exploration and rapport building processes, allows clinicians to provide a safe environment for the discovery of dormant attitudes and beliefs central to a new father's overall health and ability to parent. Counselors that strive to validate this exploratory process model the overall appropriateness of including first-time fathers into the fabric of the pregnancy, birthing, and parenting conversations.

# REFERENCES

Abell, S., & Schwartz, D. (1999). Fatherhood as a growth experience: Expanding humanistic theories of paternity. *The Humanistic Psychologist, 27,* 221–241.

Ahlborg, T., & Strandmark, M. (2001). The baby was the focus of attention-first-time parents' experiences of their intimate relationship. *Scandinavian Journal of Caring Sciences, 15,* 318–325.

Areias, M. E. G., Kumar, R., Barros, H., & Figueiredo, E. (1996). Comparative incidence of depression in women and men, during pregnancy and after childbirth. Validation of the Edinburgh postnatal depression scale in Portuguese mothers. *British Journal of Psychiatry, 169,* 30–35.

Ballard, C., Davies, R., Cullen, P., Mohan, R., & Dean, C. (1994). Prevalence of postnatal psychiatric morbidity in mothers and fathers. *British Journal of Psychiatry, 164,* 782–788.

Barrows, P. (2004). Fathers and families: Locating the ghost in the nursery. *Infant Mental Health, 25,* 408–423.

Berg, S. J., & Wynne-Edwards, K. E. (2001). Changes in testosterone, cortisol, and estradiol levels in men becoming fathers. *Mayo Clinic Proceedings, 76,* 582–592.

Condon, J. T., Boyce, P., & Corkindale, C. J. (2004). The first-time fathers study: A prospective study of the mental health and wellbeing of men during the transition to parenthood. *Australian and New Zealand Journal of Psychiatry, 38,* 56–64.

Corwyn, R. F., & Bradley, R. H. (1999). Determinants of paternal and maternal investment in children. *Infant Mental Health Journal, 20,* 238–256.

Draper, J. (2002). 'It's the first scientific evidence': Men's experience of pregnancy confirmation. *Journal of Advanced Nursing, 39,* 563–570.

Draper, J. (2003). Men's passage to fatherhood: An analysis of the contemporary relevance of transition theory. *Nursing Inquiry, 10,* 66–78.

Dudley, M., Roy, K., Kelk, N., & Bernhard, D. (2001). Psychological correlates of depression in fathers and mothers in the first postnatal year. *Journal of Reproductive and Infant Psychology, 19,* 187–202.

Edhborg, M., Seimyr, L., Lundh, W., & Widstrom, A. M. (2000). Fussy child-difficult parenthood? Comparisons between families with a 'depressed' mother and non-depressed mother 2 months postpartum. *Journal of Reproductive and Infant Psychology, 18,* 225–239.

Feldman, R. (2000). Parents' convergence on sharing and marital satisfaction, father involvement, and parent-child relationship at the transition to parenthood. *Infant Mental Health Journal, 21,* 176–191.

Feldman, R. (2003). Infant-mother and infant-father synchrony: The coregulation positive arousal. *Infant Mental Health Journal, 24,* 1–23.

Fitzgerald, H. E., Mann, T., & Barratt, M. (1999). Fathers and infants. *Infant Mental Health Journal, 20,* 213–221.

Fleming, L. M., & Tobin, D. J. (2005). Popular child-rearing books: Where is daddy? *Psychology of Men & Masculinity, 6,* 18–24.

Frascarolo, F. (2004). Paternal involvement in child caregiving and infant sociability. *Infant Mental Health Journal, 25,* 509–521.

Goodman, J. H. (2004). Paternal postpartum depression, its relationship to maternal postpartum depression, and implications for family health. *Journal of Advanced Nursing, 45,* 26–35.

Henderson, A. D., & Brouse, A. J. (1991). The experiences of new fathers during the first 3 weeks of life. *Journal of Advanced Nursing, 16,* 293–298.

Henwood, K., & Procter, J. (2003). The 'good father': Reading men's accounts of paternal involvement during the transition to first-time fatherhood. *British Journal of Social Psychology, 42,* 337–355.

Hudson, D. B., Campbell-Grossman, C., Fleck, M. O., Elek, S. M., & Shipman, A. (2003). Effects of the new fathers network on first-time fathers' parenting self-efficacy and parenting satisfaction during the transition to parenthood. *Issues in Comprehensive Pediatric Nursing, 26,* 217–229.

Hudson, D. B., Elek, S. M., & Fleck, M. O. (2001). First-time mothers' and fathers' transition to parenthood: Infant care self-efficacy, parenting satisfaction, and infant sex. *Issues in Comprehensive Pediatric Nursing, 24,* 31–43.

Jacob, T., & Johnson, S. L. (2001). Sequential interactions in the parent-child communications of depressed fathers and depressed mothers. *Journal of Family Psychology, 15,* 38–52.

Kaitz, M., & Katzir, D. (2004). Temporal changes in the affective experience of new fathers and their spouses. *Infant Mental Health Journal, 25,* 540–555.

Katon, W., Kleinman, A., & Rosen, G. (1982). Depression and somatization: A review. Part I. *The American Journal of Medicine, 72,* 127–135.

Lutz, W. J., & Hock, E. (2002). Parental emotions following the birth of the first child: Gender differences in depressive symptoms. *American Journal of Orthopsychiatry, 72,* 415–421.

Manlove, E. E., & Vernon-Feagans, L. (2002). Caring for infant daughters and sons in dual-earner households: Maternal reports of father involvement in weekday time and tasks. *Infant and Child Development, 11,* 305–320.

Matthey, S., Barnett, B., Ungerer, J., & Waters, B. (2000). Paternal and maternal depressed mood during the transition to parenthood. *Journal of Affective Disorders, 60,* 75–85.

McKelley, R. A., & Rochlen, A. B. (2007). The practice of coaching: Exploring alternatives to therapy for counseling-resistant men. *Psychology of Men & Masculinity, 8,* 53–65.

Montague, D. P. F., & Walker-Anderson, A. S. (2002). Mothers, fathers, and infants: The role of person familiarity and parental involvement in infants' perception of emotion expressions. *Child Development, 73,* 1339–1352.

Morman, M. T., & Floyd, K. (2002). A "changing culture of fatherhood": Effects on affectionate communication, closeness, and satisfaction in men's relationships with their fathers and their sons. *Western Journal of Communication, 66,* 395–411.

O'Neil, J. M. (1981). Patterns of gender role conflict and strain: Sexism and fear of femininity in men's lives. *Personnel & Guidance Journal, 60*(4), 203–210.

Pfannenstiel, A. E., & Honig, A. S. (1995). Effects of a prenatal "information and insights about infants" program on the knowledge base of first-time low education fathers one month postnatally. *Early Child Development and Care, 111,* 87–105.

Rochlen, A. B., McKelley, R. A., Suizzo, M, & Scaringi, V. (2008). Predictors of relationship satisfaction, psychological well-being, and life satisfaction among stay-at-home fathers. *Psychology of Men & Masculinity, 9*(1), 17–28.

Rochlen, A. B., Whilde, M. R., & Hoyer, W. D. (2005). The real men, real depression campaign: Overview, theoretical implications, and research considerations. *Psychology of Men and Masculinity, 6,* 186–194.

Roggman, L. A., Benson, B., & Boyce, L. (1999). Fathers with infants: Knowledge and involvement in relation to psychosocial functioning and religion. *Infant Mental Health Journal, 20,* 257–277.

Sax, L. (2005). *Why gender matters: What parents and teachers need to know about the emerging science of sex differences.* New York: Broadway Books.

Seimyr, L., Edhborg, M., Lundh, W., & Sjogren, B. (2004). In the shadow of maternal depressed mood: Experiences of parenthood during the first year after childbirth. *Journal of Psychosomatic Obstetrics and Gynecology, 25,* 23–34.

Shapiro, J. L. (1987). The expectant father. *Psychology Today, 21,* 36–42.

Simon, R. W., & Nath, L. E. (2004). Gender and emotion in the United States: Do men and women differ in self-reports of feelings and expressive behavior? *American Journal of Sociology, 109,* 1137–1176.

Storey, A. E., Walsh, C. J., Quinton, R. L., & Wynne-Edwards, K. E. (2000). Hormonal correlates of paternal responsiveness in new and expectant fathers. *Evolution and Human Behavior, 21,* 79–95.

Strauss, R., & Goldberg, W. A. (1999). Self and possible selves during the transition to fatherhood. *Journal of Family Psychology, 13,* 244–259.

Van Egeren, L. A. (2004). The development of the coparenting relationship over the transition to parenthood. *Infant Mental Health Journal, 25,* 453–477.

Wong, Y. J., & Rochlen, A. B. (2005). Demystifying men's emotional behavior: New directions and implications for counseling and research. *Psychology of Men and Masculinity, 6,* 62–72.

Zelkowitz, P., & Milet, T. H. (1997). Stress and support as related to postpartum paternal mental health and perceptions of the infant. *Infant Mental Health Journal, 18,* 424–435.

Zelkowitz, P., & Milet, T. H. (2001). The course of postpartum psychiatric disorders in women and their partners. *Journal of Nervous and Mental Disease, 189,* 575–582.

Zeman, J. (1997). Preschoolers as functionalists: The impact of social context on emotion regulation. *Child Study Journal, 27,* 41–68.

# 10

# Working Therapeutically With Stay-at-Home Fathers

## AARON B. ROCHLEN AND RYAN A. MCKELLEY

In my life, I never pictured myself as a stay-at-home dad. I thought of myself as a rugged individualist, totally self-reliant, dependent on none. Yet this seems to be the most natural thing to do, which is quite a paradox. It is one of the easiest things to fall into which I never would have thought in a million years.

—Steve, 42, father of two

Men in this country are playing an increasingly active role in the raising of their children. One area in which this trend is particularly apparent is the increasing number of stay-at-home fathers (SAHFs). The U.S. Census reports an 18% increase from 1994 to 2001 in the number of fathers who stay at home with their children (U.S. Census Bureau, 2002), with 40% of the households having an annual income of $50,000 or more. The census (2006) estimates that 159,000 men have remained out of the work force for more than a year to take primary responsibility for their children while their wives or partners worked.

Perhaps more important than the increasing numbers of SAHFs is the influence these men may have in shaping future gender role norms and expectations of fathers. SAHFs are becoming increasingly visible in the community, online, and at the playground. This increased visibility may directly challenge how others view these men and the role of fathers more broadly. For example, a 2007 survey conducted by CareerBuilder.com found that 37% of working dads would stay at home with their children if their spouse or partner made enough money to support the family. Further, one in four of these men reported that their work negatively impacts their relationships with their children, with 25% spending less than 1 hour per day and 42% less than 2 hours per day with their children.

While there is a long way to go, it does seem that more men are finding ways to renegotiate traditional role expectations and become full-time caregivers for their children. As will be reviewed in this chapter, SAHFs appear to be happy, satisfied, and pleased with the decisions they have made in their lives. In addition, the active role SAHFs have in their children's lives provides all fathers with positive examples of how men can be more nurturing, present, and involved with their children.

Of course, as one SAHF described, "It ain't all sunshine and puppy dogs." The parenting literature has consistently demonstrated that the decision to have children places significant strains on both parents as well as on the marital relationship. Marital satisfaction for new mothers and fathers can decrease for up to a year following the birth of a child (Elek, Hudson, & Bouffard, 2003; Perren, Von Wyl, Burgin, Simoni, & Von Klitzing, 2005; Schulz, Cowan, & Cowan, 2006). Further, Soliday, McCluskey-Fawcett, and O'Brien (1999) demonstrated that 25% to 39% of both fathers and mothers showed elevated depressive symptoms one month postpartum, and parenting stress of either member of the couple correlated with reduced marital satisfaction. More generally, the transition to parenthood has been shown to amplify existing marital difficulties (Cowan & Cowan, 1998).

While research is limited, one could argue that SAHFs may be susceptible to additional stressors. First, there is a social stigma surrounding this nontraditional role. Brescoll and Uhlmann (2005), for example, showed that employed fathers were evaluated more positively than SAHFs (i.e., employed fathers viewed as better parents and contributors to family well-being), whereas working mothers were viewed more negatively than stay-at-home mothers. Second, while feelings of isolation can be common for all new parents, men in these roles might be particularly susceptible to feeling isolated, primarily due to the fewer number of men sharing similar family roles. Finally, as reflected in the quote shared at the beginning of this chapter, the shift to being a SAHF is almost always an unexpected one.

In light of the challenges SAHFs face, this chapter has two primary objectives. The first is to provide an overview of the practical implications of our two recent projects on SAHFs, one a study on 211 SAHFs (Rochlen, McKelley, Suizzo, & Scaringi, 2008) and the second an in-depth interview-based project (Rochlen, Suizzo, McKelley, & Scaringi, in press). In doing so, we hope to communicate some of the most central themes shared from men currently in this role. The second objective is to provide clinicians with a useful set of clinical suggestions for working with SAHFs.

## THE DECISION TO BECOME A SAHF

In our research, we have not met one father who grew up with the plan or dream of becoming a SAHF. In essence, the decision to become a SAHF represents a considerable shift in how men view their roles, responsibilities, and even their identities. Familiarity with the reasons underlying the decision to transition into this role will assist counselors in providing appropriate and effective therapeutic interventions for SAHFs. Our research has found several primary factors influencing this decision. Below we review what we have found to be the most common factors men (and their partners) consider for this decision. Included are representative quotes from fathers who have been part of our research projects. (For a detailed review of the methodology used to collect interview data see Rochlen et al., in press).

Frequently the decision to become a SAHF is based largely on economic and pragmatic reasons, including timing of having children, significant job transitions, and partners (i.e., wives, girlfriends) earning more money than the father. These factors often lead to a collective decision that it makes sense for the male to be the primary caregiver for the child(ren). Most often men noted that this decision took place over time, involving many frank and open discussions. Further, the practical reasons driving a decision were frequently combined with a strong belief shared by both parents in the importance of one parent staying at home with the child, as expressed by one father who said,

> Well, first and foremost, we both believe that we wanted one of us to raise our children, ideally both of us, but we didn't want someone else raising our kids.

Many of the SAHFs we interviewed emphasized they wanted to be the one to instill values in their children and did not want others, such as day-care workers, to be the ones taking on this responsibility.

Another common explanation for why men decided to become SAHFs was the strong work identity they attributed to their wives. Men described their wives as having strong work-related identities, achieving high levels of work satisfaction and success. One extreme example of this was described by a man who noted,

> ... it consumes her and she will work till nine or ten o'clock at night. She will work every hour of the day possible, go home and sleep, and get up and do it again. And she has no life, no interests, no hobbies, nothing. If she is not at work, she has no sense of self whatsoever.

Importantly, over half of the men interviewed in our project described the decision to become a SAHF as being influenced by their perceptions that they were a better fit for being the stay-at-home parent. Participants expressed having various traits and skills well-suited to full-time parenting, such as being more of a "homebody," being "patient," and having "a lot of kid in me." Several fathers contrasted their own parenting skills and abilities to the perceived lower parenting abilities or skills of their wives. One man stated: "I have found I'm better at taking care of M. than my wife is." Another man in our research noted,

> I always knew I would make a better parent than my wife. Just because of the ways that she handled things and reacted versus how I did. I think she realized that too. I think it has worked out well. As much as our society would want to make it, not every woman makes a good parent.

## Early Impact of the Decision

In discussing the impact that becoming a SAHF has had on their lives, men shared a considerable range of both positive and negative emotions. Fear was at the top of this list. One father, commenting on how he felt after making the decision, said:

> Scared as hell. You have no training, you have very basic ideas, but until your spouse leaves and shuts the door and drives away, you are looking at these two little orbs with appendages and they're demanding things and you have no idea what they are demanding. It is very frightening.

In commenting on their reactions, many men recognized that their own socialization experiences often did not include caring for infants or young children, and with the new role came the need to develop an entire new set of skills. Despite the initial fear reported by some men, all soon found themselves fully equipped to handle the day-to-day needs of raising children as the fear gave way to feelings of competence and confidence.

Positive emotions most often reported were excitement and relief. Excitement often came in the form of an eagerness to be more present in their children's lives or the challenge of taking on a new role. In discussing relief, one father said,

> There's that sense of relief as well as joy that I knew I was going to be home…when they really start to learn and communicate…to actually be there to witness it and influence it and bring it along is really cool.

## Adjustment to the Role

Although the initial reaction to being a SAHF was described by some men in our sample as a frightening time, the overwhelming majority of men talked about feeling highly satisfied and content with their decision. None expressed regrets. In contrast, fathers spoke with great enthusiasm and emotion about the time they spend caring for and interacting with their children. For example, one father stated:

> The best thing I can say is just how rewarding it is when, like my 8-month-old laughs, giggles, whatever, she just smiles at you from across the room: "Hey dad, so good to see you!" That's all she can give me right now, and that's great.

Another man reflected on how being a SAHF compares with his working days:

> There is not a day that it ever feels like I go to work. I still feel like I'm getting away with something. There's sweetness to that... These are very pleasant days.

These qualitative comments relevant to the positive adjustment to the role of SAHF have been further supported in quantitative research. In a study of 211 SAHFs across the United States, men reported being happy overall both in life and in their relationships. In comparison with other published data, SAHFs reported similar or higher levels of relationship satisfaction, psychological well-being, and life satisfaction than other men (Hendrick, Hendrick, & Dicke, 1998; Mitchell & Bradley, 2001; Pavot & Diener, 1993). In addition, the current sample of SAHFs had similar levels of confidence in their parenting skills and equal levels of support from partners as other non-SAHF parent samples.

These findings support additional earlier research, most notably the work of Robertson and Verschelden (1993), who conducted a mixed methods study with 12 couples where the man was a "voluntary male homemaker." In this project, one of the central findings was that the men were psychologically healthy and well-adjusted.

Despite the overall positive tone of the research on SAHFs to date, not all men are adjusting well to the role of SAHF. Although more research is needed, three factors appear to have a significant role in predicting positive and negative adjustment: (1) conformity to traditional masculine norms, (2) perceived social support, and (3) parenting self-efficacy. A familiarity with these factors may be helpful for mental health providers and educators who find themselves working in various clinical contexts with a SAHF or a man considering the role.

First, the degree to which a man conforms to traditional masculine norms appears to be important in predicting life satisfaction, with high degrees of conformity (representative of traditional gender role norms) related to low levels of life satisfaction (Rochlen et al., 2008). Gender role norms are rules and standards that provide guidance for men and women about how they should think, feel, and act, and constrain them from certain behaviors that violate notions of masculinity or femininity (Gilbert & Scher, 1999). American notions of masculinity and traditional male norms have been associated with independence, dominance, feelings of control, restriction of emotional expression, and high value of work role (Gilbert & Scher; Levant & Kopecky, 1995; Levant & Pollack, 1995; O'Neil, Helms, Gable, David, & Wrightsman, 1986; Pleck, 1995; Rabinowitz & Cochran, 2002). Hence, clinicians who work with men who are considering a decision to become a SAHF may want to engage in a discussion of their gender beliefs and how this may impact adjustment and/or expectations of engaging in a norm-challenging role. This suggestion fits in well with more recently discussed models of Gender Aware Therapy (GAT) and other approaches to working with men, such as psychoeducational workshops or outreach programs (Blazina & Marks, 2001; Robertson & Fitzgerald, 1992; Vogel & Wester, 2003), support groups (Blazina & Marks), and online therapeutic interventions (Hsiung, 2000; Rochlen, Land, & Wong, 2004).

Our research also found that social support is important in predicting life and relationship satisfaction as well as psychological distress. This finding is consistent with other research literature demonstrating the importance of a strong social support network for parents (Dehle, Larsen, & Landers, 2001; Purdom, Lucas, & Miller, 2006; Speechly & Noh, 1992). Men in the role of SAHF who perceived themselves as having a strong support network reported lower levels of distress and higher levels of life and relationship satisfaction than men with low levels of social support. The practical importance of social support warrants speculation about therapeutic work with SAHFs (or men considering this role). Clearly, it is important for these men to develop a solid network of support from their partners, family, and community. The availability of SAHF support groups in communities might be a particularly important factor. Therapists working with SAHFs may find it helpful to solicit information from their clients about past and present sources of social support and work together to strengthen the network if necessary.

Finally, we found evidence that the amount of confidence SAHFs endorse in terms of their parenting skills seems to be a salient predicting variable in positive adjustment to the role. Men who are more confident in their overall parenting skills reported higher levels of life satisfaction and less psychological distress (i.e., higher overall psychological well-being). Further, men who expressed confidence in their ability to foster independent behavior in their children reported higher levels of psychological well-being. These results also suggest the importance of parent training interventions for this population, found to be particularly useful for a range of parenting subgroups (Dishion & Stormshak, 2007). Such parenting training should be sensitive to the unique considerations of SAHFs as well as the recognized stigma men may face in this role.

## HOW OTHERS RESPOND

### *Positive and Mixed Support*

Another critical factor in working with SAHFs or, more broadly, men in nontraditional roles, is recognizing how others respond to these decisions. Many of the men in our study indicated overall positive support from others, with few to no negative responses. Strong support appeared to be expressed mostly by immediate family members, in-laws, and close friends. For example, one father stated: "My wife's family has been very supportive. I can't think of anybody that has done anything but be supportive." Another father stated: "I can't think of any response I've gotten except just acceptance and helpfulness." Some men, however, expressed that they had received mixed support in response to their roles. On closer examination, it appeared that these instances of mixed support came mostly from people who were neither friends nor family members. Interestingly, the men interviewed in our project frequently expressed they were not particularly concerned or impacted by others' views. Further, several men noted that their past nontraditional experiences and roles may have accounted for others' lack of surprise in response to hearing about their decision. One father expressed, "I'm sure I've been a mystery to my family, or at least my parents, for many years."

However, fathers shared frequent stories that indicated the confusion, negative attitudes, or awkwardness of others. One participant stated: "I think maybe they got the impression I'm somehow freeloading off of my wife." In some of these cases, discovering that a man was a SAHF seemed to shut down conversation. For example, upon meeting a stranger at a social function and being asked the customary, "What do you do for a living?" one father noted that after saying he was a SAHF there was an awkward silence followed by an uncomfortable transition to another topic.

## *Joking*

Also common in our interviews were stories of how frequent jokes about SAHFs were expressed by others, often with familiar themes. Fathers described hearing frequent "Mr. Mom" references or were teased about not working or not being "real" men. For example, one father stated that his grandfather would call him on the phone and jokingly ask to speak to "the man of the house." One father recalled being asked by friends, "What's on the soaps today?" When asked about how these jokes impacted them, the majority of men said they were not particularly affected or bothered by such comments. Rochlen et al. (2008) speculated that while it is easy to dismiss the jokes from others and even between SAHFs as harmless, they may reflect representations of unconscious material as originally noted by Freud (1989). Although the reasons underlying the jokes from others were not studied, it may be that they serve as a means for other men and women to voice safely a certain degree of discomfort or reflection of the violation of more traditional societal standards. Teasing is often considered "a form of releasing aggression in a non-threatening way among intimates and in a threatening way among those who are status unequals as a show of power" (Boxer & Cortés-Conde, 1997, p. 279). Sue and Sue (2003) noted that jokes often serve as a way of reinforcing discrimination in reference to minority populations, which is more recently framed as *microaggressions* or subtle exchanges seen as "put downs" (Sue et al., 2007).

## *Stigma*

Finally, it is important to gain a sense of how SAHFs recognize and deal with potential stigma. In our study, over 65% of the sample acknowledged possible judgments and potential stigma from others. However, these men expressed feeling secure in themselves and proud of their decision to stay at home. At times this security in self came across in a direct and assertive manner, as one father expressed, "If someone's judging me, they're wasting their time." Another man stated: "I'm not trying to change what people think about it [the SAHF role]." One father expressed his strong views against stigmatizing attitudes by noting, "If someone is judging me, then they better be ready to judge themselves. If someone tries to pull that crap on me, they're about to be tangled with."

In general, men in our study speculated about different factors that may account for a lack of personal experiences with stigma in their lives, including geographic location, educational background, occupational status, political beliefs, generational status, and historical era. Speculating on how peoples' occupation or socioeconomic status might affect their judgments of SAHFs, one participant said: "If you were a welder, your welder buddies would think it was weird." Another man stated that the stigma may be less strong today than in previous decades:

> I got out of high school in the '70s. If I told someone I was getting married and was going to be a stay-at-home dad, then yeah, I would just be the circus event of the town. But through the '70s, '80s, and '90s...

## *Negative Reactions*

We also heard a number of fathers who got negative reactions from women, frequently on the playground when playing with their kids. One father noted,

> They instinctively get together and they form playgroups and those sorts of things, and you will get this "stink-eye" from the moms, this sort of, "Who the hell are you and what are you doing here?" And in the back of your mind you think, "Oh, they think I'm a child molester."

Another man referred to women's reactions when he takes his son to the park:

> I think the moms there are a little confused about what this long-haired guy with no wedding ring is doing at the park with these kids. "Is it dad's visitation day?" and all that, and again, I'm just projecting. No one has said anything. That's how I feel that I'm perceived in that group of stay-at-home-mothers.

Rochlen et al. (2008) speculated that these negative responses may be associated with opposing gender roles between nontraditional men and traditional women who tend to be stay-at-home mothers. The playground may be one of the most common places for this conflict to play out as it joins more traditional women (stay-at-home mothers) with men who are taking on a nontraditional gender role.

## NEW DEFINITIONS OF MASCULINITY

Another area of importance in working with SAHFs involves recognizing the unique identity they have carved for themselves in terms of defining self-identity and masculinity. With a man's sense of identity frequently being connected with his career and career-related success (Axelrod, 2001), men who choose to be SAHFs may have to generate their own markers of success as men. Consistent with this premise, our research has found that men have thought quite deeply about how their own masculine identity has been shaped and at times challenged by this role. Several themes emerged relevant to how being a SAHF has shaped or influenced the men interviewed in our project.

### *Redefining the Role of Provider*

One common theme was that many SAHFs used traditionally masculine terms in different ways. For example, the notion of males as "breadwinners" or "providers" is a fairly commonly accepted masculine stereotype (Levant, 1996; Mahalik, Good, & Englar-Carlson, 2003; Thompson & Pleck, 1995) in which men work and provide financially for their families. Interestingly, one father used this notion but redefined the term to suit his personal meaning, in essence rewriting the script: "It doesn't mean I'm any more or any less of a man. I'm just providing for my family. That's what my family needs; they need me here. So that's where I am."

### *Boys Will Be Boys*

A second common thread in our findings was that, while the sample overall had more flexible notions of masculinity, they shared interests and hobbies historically connected to traditional masculinity. Men told passionate stories about their interests in a range of hobbies including fixing cars, participating in sports, fishing, and hunting. Overall, the message was that these men continued to hold on to attitudes and enjoy behaviors commonly linked to traditional or norm-conforming masculinity. This was best summarized by one participant who noted, "When you change those roles you don't change those responsibilities. So I still maintain the car, mow the grass, do all those masculine things." It seems that assuming the role of stay-at-home parent does not mean giving up traditionally masculine interests and ways of being. Instead, the new role allows SAHFs to complement these interests with new skills in nurturing and deepening relationships with their families.

## Meaningful Changes to Identity

Another theme that emerged in our interviews was the meaningful changes that had happened in SAHFs' lives and identities. Many of these changes seemed associated with exhibiting more traditionally feminine characteristics, such as being more affectionate, expressing more emotion, being feelings-oriented, having greater interpersonal awareness, feeling more responsible, nurturing, and being connected to their community. One man stated, "I think I've become a lot softer and a better listener...I've become more civilized. It changes you." Another man said: "I feel like I'm more open to having feelings than I was before."

Many of the men interviewed discussed changes in feeling more connected to and having more authentic relationships with others. One father stated: "I feel more attachment to my friends, and my guy friends' wives, than I did before." Several men shared that they had become more involved in community activities (e.g., school committees, neighborhood groups), whereas they did not have the time or interest while working full-time. One man reflected:

> I'm more connected to my community and neighborhood being at home because I have the time. I'm very involved in what will be my child's future elementary school. I'm a member of the campus advisory council.

Many men reported developing closer relationships with their children as one of the most salient benefits they perceived to being a SAHF. For example, one father stated: "I'm hopeful that it will make for a longer, stronger relationship with her when she's older." This recognition of the importance of deeper connections among men with their children is reflected in results from a recent survey of fathers conducted by Minnesota's Department for Families and Children's Services (Minnesota Fathers and Families Network, 2007). Of the 600 fathers surveyed, most men considered child care to be more important than a paycheck, with "showing love and affection" ranked as number one and "financial care" ranked last.

## Flexible Masculinity

Perhaps the clearest theme we observed in our interview study was that all of the men shared definitions of masculinity that were personal and flexible, often emphasizing it was not important to them how others defined masculinity. They acknowledged the presence of stereotyped perceptions of masculinity but did not feel limited or influenced by these norms or expectations. Several SAHFs emphasized that behaving in ways that are traditionally feminine makes them feel no less masculine. One father stated:

> I've always been great in the kitchen. I figured out how to do laundry, do the bed, figured out how to use the vacuum, shampoo the carpet. There has not been any male-threatening thing I've done.

Several emphasized the lack of utility of the concepts and societal distinction between feminine and masculine.

> I don't think there should be a huge distinction between masculinity and femininity. Yes, there are distinctions, but they don't need to be as black-and-white or as divisive as people make them to be... I mean the stereotype is that masculinity is strong, feminine is weak, pretty. You know that stuff is all bunk.

A few men rejected these stereotypes quite strongly, even expressing an aversion to the traditional symbols of masculinity: "I don't play those macho mind games, I don't want to fight, I don't want to get into those sorts of things, but I don't consider those things to be what makes me a man."

## A PRELIMINARY THERAPEUTIC FRAMEWORK

> I think there should be a course or some form of counseling available for parents who make the decision that the male is going to be the primary caregiver, because it changes the whole dynamics of the male/female relationship within the house...dramatically. (Jeff, father of one)

Ideally, the research reviewed in this chapter should provide the clinician with a heightened sense of some of the strengths and challenges many SAHFs may face in their daily lives. Further, we hope this review has reflected the positive picture of the lives of SAHFs, as the limited research to date has suggested a very hopeful and promising look at their adjustment. Yet, there are some men who have or are considering the SAHF role who struggle with the decision, adjustment, or other issues that might bring them into counseling. Below, we provide a set of clinical suggestions that may be helpful when working in a clinical setting with SAHFs. However, we would like to emphasize that the integration of these suggestions will depend largely on the theoretical approach of the mental health provider. Moreover, it is critical to keep in mind that when working with a SAHF, this role is obviously only one aspect of a client's identity. Therefore, being a SAHF may or may not have relevance and/or influence the client's presenting concerns. Finally, while these are research-informed recommendations unique to this sample of men, readers are also encouraged to consult the rich literature currently available on working with men in therapy (Englar-Carlson & Stevens, 2006; Levant & Pollack, 1995; Rabinowitz & Cochran, 2002) and with the more limited literature on working with fathers (e.g., Fagan & Hawkins, 2001; Shapiro, 2007; other chapters in this book).

## Clinical Suggestions

1. *Check your expectations and biases.* As with your work with any population, it is important to be aware of your own biases and preconceived notions of what you expect a person to be like as a client. SAHFs are no exception. Our research team had many interesting discussions about how these men have occasionally challenged what our own biases were in terms of how these men would present. A counselor might assume that a male client who chooses to pursue a nontraditional role may identify with more non-normative notions of masculinity or reject some of them entirely. Men in our research illustrate how complex gender role identity can be. For example, some men may exhibit traditionally masculine attitudes and behaviors in addition to providing nurturance and emotional support in their role as stay-at-home parents. SAHFs come in all shapes and sizes and will share the full spectrum of views about politics, women, children, and parenting styles. Failing to recognize the nuances and complexity of male clients' masculine identity may result in a counselor missing particular strengths and/or areas of struggle that may be present in their lives.

2. *Be aware of the career transition.* As noted earlier, most SAHFs had full-time employment and many have plans to re-enter the work force or work on a part-time basis from home. Additionally, the socially reinforced perspective that men "should" work and be the primary breadwinner may not impact all SAHFs, but could be a considerable barrier to overcome for others. Men may need to consider a perspective that some have noted in our research where they are working and providing for their families in a central or arguably more important manner than paid employment. As one man in our study noted, "I work full-time. I just don't get paid." Several participants noted that the growth of the Internet has allowed for remote project work and the ability to maintain part-time work identities during evenings/weekends. Some men identify as full-time SAHFs; others see themselves as a combination of full-time SAHF and part-time freelancer. Counselors are encouraged to explore the full range of work identities and be open to a broad spectrum of definitions of "work." As a counselor working with a SAHF, it is also important to explore the decision not only to become a SAHF, but also the transition out of and back into the work force. Explore with your clients how others responded, what they miss most and least about work, and concerns they may have regarding re-entering the work force. Similar to many women who have left the workplace to raise children, many SAHFs noted that the transition out of the work force was much easier than what they expect to find when they return (e.g., "How am I going to explain the hole in my resume?"). However, there are significantly

fewer role models in men's lives who have negotiated this path, and opportunities for mentorship in this area may be nonexistent. Anticipating some of the issues with stigma around returning to work in the future may allow your clients ample time in the present to find suitable solutions.

3. *Explore social support and isolation.* While evaluating social support should always be a part of a clinical intake, it may be even more crucial to evaluate with SAHFs. Social support seems to play a critical role in the adjustment process, and men may be more susceptible to isolation and depression given the shortage of other SAHFs as well as the still-prevalent stigma toward men in nontraditional work and family roles. Many of men's friendships grow out of working relationships with colleagues, and the lack of structure and daily contact of the workday can be missed. This can be an especially important issue to address if you are working with a client considering the role, as many SAHFs are caught off-guard after changing roles. Giving men time to process and negotiate their relationships with family, friends, and colleagues may help alleviate some of the isolation reported by many SAHFs. Moreover, clinicians should be aware of resources in the community that may be able to provide support for SAHFs (e.g., most large cities have SAHF playgroups) as well as parenting training groups to increase men's confidence in the tasks and responsibilities of full-time parenting.

4. *Normalize the fear and obstacles.* Many authors have noted the difficulty men may experience in counseling when they feel vulnerable or exposed to weaknesses (e.g., Cusak, Deane, & Wilson, 2006; Rochlen, 2005). In all likelihood, this ambivalence to engage in therapy also holds true for SAHFs. Yet there are concerns, fears, and anxieties many of these men face both in becoming fathers and in negotiating the uncharted terrain of being a full-time parent. It is important to recognize that these men often leave behind jobs or careers where they felt a strong sense of self-confidence and moved to a role where they feel utterly inexperienced. For a significant number of men, the first infant they have ever held is their own. Normalizing the feelings associated with the change can help men meet the challenge of learning new skills with less anxiety and fear. More generally, while many men in these roles reject and seem unaffected by jokes or stigmatized attitudes, others might be deeply impacted by negative perceptions.

5. *Don't ignore the money talk.* Talking about money has been a long-standing taboo in U.S. society, and discomfort with the topic often extends to the therapy room (Shapiro, 2007). Do not shy away from talking about how money influences the family. Our research shows that financial considerations often top the list of factors influencing a couple's decision to have the male partner stay home to raise children. For most couples, the partner who

earns the higher income remains in the workplace and the other assumes the role of full-time child-care provider. While data from our large sample of SAHFs show a trend toward higher annual incomes than the average U.S. household, be sensitive to the fact that many families are on the other end of the spectrum. One common issue to consider is the difficulty some men may feel with a lack of financial self-efficacy. One SAHF in our research captured it well when he said, "I miss not having the satisfaction of my paycheck, my money...so every dollar that comes in is because of her. So that's definitely been a transition." Starting a candid discussion about potential feelings of loss related to previous financial contribution may help create an atmosphere of trust and sensitivity in counseling. However, also consider the possibility that some men may find relief in breaking free of the "breadwinner" expectation and welcome the new role. Some practical ways men have navigated this issue is by doing freelance work and managing the family's investments and bank accounts.

6. *Provide decision-making help.* Your role as counselor may also be to help with the decision-making process of becoming a SAHF. Keep in mind this can be an enormous and stressful decision for the man and the couple. Be patient in such discussions and try to bring out both the cognitive and emotional aspects of the decision. Gestalt exercises, including the empty chair, may be useful in terms of allowing your client (or clients) to talk through the pros and cons of a decision. It might also be useful to recognize any cognitive distortions (e.g., all-or-nothing thinking, catastrophizing) that might be impacting their perceptions of the reality of this decision. Clearly, it is important to keep in mind that there are no right or wrong answers, and it is not the counselor's role to provide directive advice. However, therapists can help clients work through such decisions, become fully informed of the complexity of their new role, as well as educate clients of factors that might be helpful to know related to their decision or adjustment.

7. *Consider a strengths-based approach.* Seligman and Csikszentmihalyi (2000) called for a change in the focus of psychology from "preoccupation only with repairing the worst things in life to also building positive qualities" (p. 5), and suggested a focus on human strengths and virtues. They also noted that much of the best work practitioners already do is to amplify client strengths rather than repair weaknesses. A positive source of meaning and identity for many men is a sense of responsibility and accountability beyond the self to include family and community (Hammond & Mattis, 2005). Clinicians can work together with clients in developing useful strategies for their struggles based on strengths such as a feeling of responsibility, courage to take on a new role, ability to learn new skills, and so forth. Wong (2006) suggested that an explicit focus on character strengths and virtues is congruent with many

people's conceptualizations of human flourishing and solutions to life's challenges. Taking this approach with men in or considering the role of SAHF appears to be an ideal way to support their goals of growth and to help find solutions to potential problems they may encounter.

8. *Practice Gender Aware Therapy.* Good, Gilbert, and Scher (1990) first introduced the idea of Gender Aware Therapy (GAT) where counselors are "encouraged to facilitate the development of women and men through exploration of their unique gender-related experiences" (p. 376). Principles of GAT include (1) regarding gender as an integral aspect of counseling, (2) considering problems within a societal context, (3) actively addressing gender injustices, (4) emphasizing collaborative therapeutic relationships, and (5) respecting clients' freedom to choose. This last point can be particularly salient for SAHFs and involves helping the client raise awareness of past, present, or future gender messages from others, as well as a sense of what is right for oneself (Good et al.). Men may not necessarily present with stress or anxiety about their gender role identities, but bringing it into awareness in session can allow for its exploration. For example, we heard from several SAHFs about the frustration they encounter in many restaurants and public places that do not have equal access to child-care facilities (e.g., changing stations in men's restrooms), and how they feel bombarded by parenting advertising targeted mainly at mothers. Openly acknowledging and exploring these issues can create a therapeutic environment where it is safer to address deeper concerns. Consistent with strengths-based recommendations noted above, SAHF clients would also likely benefit from recognition of their flexible and broad gender role identities. Counseling should be a place where they can process their frustrations, but also celebrate the many strengths they have as men, husbands, partners, friends, and fathers.

9. *Consider alternative treatment approaches.* Recent research in the men's help-seeking literature suggests that treatment options other than individual counseling may be more appealing or effective for men, such as support groups (Blazina & Marks, 2001), psychoeducational workshops or outreach programs (Blazina & Marks; Robertson & Fitzgerald, 1992; Vogel & Wester, 2003), and the practice of personal or professional coaching (McKelley & Rochlen, 2007). In identifying participants for our research studies on SAHFs, we found a large presence of online support groups, discussion boards, chat rooms, and blogs dedicated to men in this role. We also found that most large U.S. cities and smaller regional areas have local SAHF groups. Clients looking to expand their support networks should be encouraged to investigate these possibilities while recognizing that some groups or options may fit better than others based on personalities, purpose or goals of the group, and

so forth. Another promising alternative to traditional counseling that may be useful is the practice of coaching as it parallels a positive, strength-based approach to purposeful change in nonclinical populations (Grant, 2003). Several aspects of coaching may fit particularly well for working with SAHFs. First, coaching models are often focused on skill building and align well with clinical evidence that some men prefer framing the benefits of professional help in terms of developing new skills. Whether the clinician identifies as a certified coach or simply uses coaching language in his/her practice, central goals of coaching often focus on building skills (e.g., listening, communication, interpersonal skills) and sustained behavior change (Frisch, 2001). The International Coach Federation (2006) highlights other goals of coaching that include learning new perspectives on personal challenges and opportunities, enhanced thinking and decision-making skills, improved interpersonal effectiveness, and increased confidence in work and life roles. Clinicians are encouraged to consider how these goals may help a SAHF client negotiate new relationships and roles with family, friends, and coworkers.

## CLINICAL VIGNETTE

To understand how the trends in this chapter may emerge in the presentation of a SAHF for therapy, following is a clinical vignette. In reading the overview of this client, reflect on what might be similar or dissimilar to some of the findings in the reviewed research as well as how you might work effectively with this client given your own theoretical orientation. Also, consider what might be the overt versus covert issues or concerns for the client and how these issues might be relevant for the therapeutic work. Finally, think about what types of countertransference themes, biases, and expectations about fathering might emerge for you in this type of clinical work.

## CLIENT OVERVIEW

Steven (a pseudonym) is a 42-year-old former web designer from Texas, who has been married to his second wife for 3 years. Steven is the primary caregiver for their two children, Jason and Amanda, ages 5 and 1, respectively. Steven also has a 9-year-old daughter from his first marriage, whom he sees infrequently because she lives in the Pacific Northwest and his relationship with his ex-wife is "strained." Steven lost his job during the fallout from the technology bust in 2001, around the time his wife, a successful attorney, became pregnant. Steve noted that he did not have much of a choice in deciding to become a stay-at-home father because neither he nor his wife wanted day care as an option, and they could not afford an in-home child-care provider on one salary.

Steven recently noticed that "things weren't quite right" and went to his primary care physician for a check-up. His physician prescribed him an antidepressant, but it did not seem to be helping much with his concerns. He said that he did not consider himself depressed—"just in a funk"—and struggling more in his forties than at any other point in his life. He eventually came to therapy after an old college friend suggested he talk with someone about his recent changes.

Steven has never been in therapy and noted being skeptical of the process, sharing that his dad would "laugh his ass off" if he knew he was going to a "shrink" for help. His father has also made jokes about Steven being "Mr. Mom" and (jokingly) consults him when he needs help with laundry or ironing. Despite these slight "digs," Steven notes a generally supportive relationship with most of his immediate and extended family. However, Steven has found himself spending less time with both his friends and family, and misses his "old life." Steven also noted he has been not sleeping well, has gained some weight, and often finds himself bored when the kids are napping and his wife is at work.

Steven describes his relationship with both children and his current wife as quite positive and says his kids are "what help him make it through the day." He said he struggled some at first with the role of being a stay-at-home father but "quickly got over it." He has since been amazed that fathering has come easier to him than he originally expected. He did note that he knows of no other SAHFs and often feels like he does not fit in with others on the playground, and even recalled a few times getting some "nasty looks" from mothers at the park. He used to spend his spare time riding motorcycles and repairing old cars, but finds it difficult to pursue those hobbies given his parenting responsibilities.

## RELEVANT MASCULINITY AND FATHERING THEMES TO EXPLORE

Although much remains unknown about Steven based on this vignette, there are a few central areas pertaining to his identity as a father and as a man that we would consider to be in need of further exploration. Below are a few preliminary areas to consider, including ideas about how we might approach these areas of inquiry in counseling. Importantly, the points and suggestions offered are generated irrespective of theoretical orientation. We recognize there are many different areas to explore and therapeutic interventions to consider. However, we believe there are themes and approaches relevant to fatherhood and masculinity that cross many different theoretical orientations.

First, it is important to establish rapport with Steven given his reported hesitation about being in therapy. One way to accomplish that could be to identify Steven's strengths and positive coping mechanisms by pointing out the many positive aspects of his life and fathering skills. Rabinowitz and Cochran (2002) stress the importance of recognizing and honoring men's courage and strength to seek professional help. One very immediate way to build rapport with Steven is to acknowledge this in his own life he has taken a positive step to get out of his "funk." One way to combine Gender Aware Therapy with a strength-based approach would be to bring attention to the fact that many men are not socialized as boys and men to be at-home parents yet still manage to raise healthy and well-adjusted children. Steven could be encouraged to consider all the parenting skills, tips, and tricks he was able to learn (and possibly teach himself) in meeting the needs of an infant and young children. A therapist should be encouraged to examine with Steven the different ways he has been impacted by gender messages and the way he and others "see" him in the role of SAHF.

Second, from this initial presentation, it seems there are many, yet unexpressed, feelings connected to being a father and the decision to become a stay-at-home father. These feelings may be a combination of positive, negative, and/or conflicted based on what we know about Steven. Given his ambivalence about being in therapy, it would be critical to provide enough time during the first couple of sessions to establish trust and rapport before asking him to go deeper into his story. However, it is clear he has a powerful tale to tell about how becoming a father has influenced his life.

For example, Steven describes a positive and meaningful connection with his children from his second wife, but we do not know much about his relationship with his daughter from his first marriage other than he sees her "infrequently." It seems important to explore his thoughts and feelings about this relationship and how it relates to his ideas about fatherhood. A counselor might want to explore with Steven how he integrates or compartmentalizes his experiences as a father in two different family systems. If he expresses concern about his relationship with his first daughter, it could be useful to be practical and behavioral in helping him to reconnect with his daughter from his first marriage, as he clearly has the potential to be a positive father figure. A therapist may even find that Steven has a need to grieve some loss regarding his first daughter and should consider a strength-based approach that recognizes his positive contributions in the past in addition to regrets he may (or may not) have. In general, the emotions relevant to a man's experiences of fatherhood can be quite powerful and based in part on societal norms of men not expressing their feelings and fears. A therapist's encouragement to Steven and other men to talk about this transition and related emotions can be particularly helpful as they may not have similar outlets. Further, it may be possible that Steven may have his own conflicts in regard to his own relationship with his father. On the one hand, he describes a positive relationship with his father. Yet, his dad appears to be the one making the most jokes about his role as a primary caregiver. Subsequently, an exploration of some of his true feelings in regard to this relationship and how it may interfere with his own acceptance of his role seems warranted.

Third, there are themes surrounding isolation and lack of acceptance of Steven's new role that need to be explored. For example, he noted having no other SAHFs in his social network and described neutral (at best) responses from other stay-at-home mothers. Therapy can be one place where an "objective" person, like a counselor, can provide room for acceptance and normalization with the hope that Steven can begin to find others to fulfill that role. It will be important in working with him to gain a more substantive understanding of the precise nature of his support system and how this can be related to feelings of isolation, depression, and other related distress. A counselor could begin by examining the quality and nature of his friendships prior to becoming a stay-at-home father, encourage him to reflect how they have changed since transitioning to his new role, and problem solve concrete steps to make desired changes that may include reaching out to men in similar roles. Again, helping Steven in practical terms to establish relationships with men and women in the primary caregiving role may be paramount. This same process could also be applied to his reported regret about not spending as much time with his hobbies and finding possible opportunities to reconnect with them. Finally, his decision to share the jokes directed toward him likely has significance and reflects a lack of full acceptance and support from some family members. He could be encouraged to role-play how he might have a constructive dialogue with his father or others who make bothersome comments about his role.

Fourth, it seems critical to explore the role of work in Steven's life, including the impact of losing his job 6 years ago. Despite seemingly embracing the role of becoming a father, the loss of gainful employment may have been a salient one with lingering frustrations. Using the Gender Aware Therapy consideration of problems within a societal context, a therapist could raise the issue of identifying with work as a salient male norm in this society and invite Steven to consider how (or even if) this plays a role in his current concerns. In addition, although not expressed directly in the vignette, work may have been a source of social support and friendships. The sense of isolation Steven seems to be expressing may be related in part to this loss of contact with peers he had at work. Additionally, while his wife appears to be doing well with her career, he could be given the chance to explore both positive and negative feelings regarding his loss of employment and her continued success. Finally, it could be useful to engage Steven in a discussion about whether he has ideas about returning to web design on a part- or full-time basis at some point in his life. It is not uncommon for SAHFs to find part-time project work as an important component of their identity and a way to maintain some connection with that aspect of their lives. Alternatively, it might be that Steven, like many SAHFs, may have already shaped or altered the way in which he conceptualizes work and employment in his life. As noted earlier in the chapter, many SAHFs seem quite content with their new and rewarding "work" as fathers and caretakers.

Finally, Steven's recognition that "things weren't quite right," plus his belief that he is not "depressed," is an opportunity for a counselor to explore with him the meaning around his symptoms and the concept of depression. Some might take a traditional approach and educate him about depression by normalizing the experience, teaching him to identify common signs and symptoms, and separating the person from the illness. Another approach might be to consider talking with him about the concept of male depression suggested by Real (1997) and Cochran and Rabinowitz (2000; 2003), and discuss what having depression (versus being depressed) means to Steven. Others may want to consider the possibility that using the term *depression* itself may not be helpful and instead honor Steven's own conceptualization of his changes in behaviors, recognize his ability to notice them, and support his sense of self-agency to make changes. Regardless of the therapist's approach, this is an opportunity to socialize Steven to his experience and give him the chance to use his strengths in taking on the new role and applying them to his current concerns.

# SUMMARY

Our hopes for this chapter were to communicate some of the most central themes of our research on SAHFs and provide clinicians with a useful set of clinical suggestions in their work with SAHFs or men considering this unique, challenging, and rewarding role. The vignette illustrated a few ways that clinicians could approach similar clients, and we recognize there are many other useful approaches to this work. Clearly, more research and clinical guidelines are needed as increasing numbers of men choose to take on the primary caregiver role in their families. SAHFs are an important and growing segment of fatherhood, and there is still much to learn about this population with respect to important dimensions, such as age, sexual identity, varying levels of socioeconomic status, disability status, and a multitude of other important factors. We encourage clinicians and researchers to continue working toward understanding the experiences, background, and world views of SAHFs and finding ways to support those men inside and outside of the counseling room.

# REFERENCES

Axelrod, S. D. (2001). The vital relationship between work and masculinity: A psychoanalytic perspective. *Psychology of Men and Masculinity, 2,* 117–123.

Blazina, C., & Marks, L. I. (2001). College men's affective reactions to individual therapy, psychoeducational workshops, and men's support group brochures: The influence of gender-role conflict and power dynamics upon help-seeking attitudes. *Psychotherapy: Theory, Research, Practice, Training, 38*(3), 297–305.

Boxer, D., & Cortés-Conde, F. (1997). From bonding to biting: Conversational joking and identity display. *Journal of Pragmatics, 27*(3), 275–294.

Brescoll, V. L., & Uhlmann, E. L. (2005). Attitudes toward traditional and nontraditional parents. *Psychology of Women Quarterly, 29,* 436–445.

Cochran, S. V., & Rabinowitz, F. E. (2000). *Men and depression: Clinical and empirical perspectives.* San Diego, CA: Academic Press.

Cochran, S. V., & Rabinowitz, F. E. (2003). Gender-sensitive recommendations for assessment and treatment of depression in men. *Professional Psychology: Research and Practice, 34,* 132–140.

Cowan, P. A. & Cowan, C. P. (1998). Changes in marriage during the transition to parenthood: Must we blame the baby? In G. Y. Michaels & W. A. Goldber (Eds.), *The transition to parenthood: Current theory and research* (pp 114–154). New York: Cambridge University Press.

Cusak, J., Deane, F. P., & Wilson, C. J. (2006). Emotional expression, perceptions of therapy, and help-seeking intentions in men attending therapy services, *Psychology of Men and Masculinity, 7,* 69–92.

Dehle, C., Larsen, D., & Landers, J. E. (2001). Social support in marriage. *American Journal of Family Therapy, 29*(4), 307–324.

Dishion, T. J., & Stormshak, E. A. (2007). Brief parenting interventions. In *Intervening in children's lives: An ecological, family-centered approach to mental health care.* (pp. 125–139). Washington, DC: American Psychological Association.

Elek, S. M., Hudson, D. B., & Bouffard, C. (2003). Marital and parenting satisfaction and infant care self-efficacy during the transition to parenthood: The effect of infant sex. *Issues in Comprehensive Pediatric Nursing, 26,* 45–57.

Englar-Carlson, M., & Stevens, M. A. (2006). *In the room with men: A casebook of therapeutic change.* Washington, DC: American Psychological Association.

Fagan, J., & Hawkins, A. J. (Eds.). (2001). *Clinical and educational interventions with fathers.* Binghamton, NY: Haworth Press.

Freud, S. (1989). *Jokes and their relation to the unconscious* (James Strachey, Trans.). New York, NY: Norton.

Frisch, M. H. (2001). The emerging role of the internal coach. *Consulting Psychology Journal: Practice and Research, 53,* 240–250.

Gilbert, L. A., & Scher, M. (1999). *Gender and Sex in Counseling and Psychotherapy.* Needham Heights, MA: Allyn & Bacon.

Good, G. E., Gilbert, L. A., & Scher, M. (1990). Gender-aware therapy; A synthesis of feminist therapy and knowledge about gender. *Journal of Counseling and Development, 68,* 376–380.

Grant, A. M. (2003). The impact of life coaching on goal attainment, metacognition and mental health. *Social Behavior & Personality, 31*(3), 253–264.

Hammond, W. P., & Mattis, J. S. (2005). Being a man about it: Manhood meaning among African American men. *Psychology of Men and Masculinity, 6*(2), 114–126.

Hendrick, C., Hendrick, S. S., Dicke, A. (1998). The love-attitudes scale. *Journal of Social and Personal Relationships, 15*(2),147–159.

Hsiung, R. C. (2000). The best of both worlds: An online self-help group hosted by a mental health professional. *Cyber Psychology & Behavior, 3,* 935–950.

International Coach Federation. (2006). Retrieved on April 23, 2006, from http://www.coachfederation.org/ICF/For+Coaching+Clients/What+is+a+Coach/

Levant, R. F. (1996). The new psychology of men. *Professional Psychology: Research and Practice, 27*(3), 259–265.

Levant, R. F., & Kopecky, G. (1995). *Masculinity reconstructed: Changing the rules of manhood—at work, in relationships, and in family life.* New York: Penguin Books.

*Levant, R. F., & Pollack, W. S. (1995). A new psychology of men.* New York: Basic Books.

Mahalik, J. R., Good, G. E., & Englar-Carlson, M. (2003). Masculinity scripts, presenting concerns, and help seeking: Implications for practice and training. *Professional Psychology: Research and Practice, 34*(2), 123–131.

McKelley, R. A., & Rochlen, A. B. (2007). The practice of coaching: Exploring alternatives to therapy for counseling-resistant men. *Psychology of Men & Masculinity, 8*(1), 53–65.

Minnesota Fathers and Families Network (2007). Do we count fathers in Minnesota? Searching for key indicators of the well-being of fathers and families (MFFN Publication ISBN-13: 978-0-9792624-0-1). St. Paul, MN: Author.

Mitchell, J. Bradley, C. (2001). Psychometric evaluation of the 12-item Well-being Questionnaire for use with people with macular disease. Quality of Life Research: An International Journal of *Quality of Life Aspects of Treatment, Care & Rehabilitation, 10*(5), 465–473.

O'Neil, J. M., Helms, B., Gable, R., David, L., & Wrightsman, L. (1986). Gender role conflict scale (GRCS): College men's fear of femininity. *Sex Roles, 14*, 335–350.

Pavot, W. & Diener, E. (1993). Review of the satisfaction with life scale. *Psychological Assessment, 5*(2), 164–172.

Perren, S., Von Wyl, A., Burgin, D., Simoni, H., & Von Klitzing, K. (2005). Intergenerational transmission of marital quality across the transition to parenthood. *Family Process, 44*(4), 441–459.

*Pleck*, J. H. (1995). The gender role strain paradigm: An update. In R.F. Levant & W.S. Pollack (Eds.), *A new psychology of men* (pp. 11–32). New York: Basic Books, Inc.

Purdom, C. L., Lucas, J. L., & Miller, K. S. (2006). Couple type, parental status, and the mediating impact of social support. *North American Journal of Psychology, 8*(1), 1–12.

Rabinowitz, F. E., & Cochran, S. V. (2002). *Deepening psychotherapy with men.* Washington, DC: American Psychological Association.

Real, T. (1997). *I don't want to talk about it: Overcoming the secret legacy of male depression.* New York: Fireside.

Robertson, J. M., & Fitzgerald, L. F. (1992). Overcoming the masculine mystique: Preferences for alternative forms of assistance among men who avoid counseling. *Journal of Counseling Psychology, 39*(2), 204–246.

Robertson, J. M., & Verschelden, C. (1993). Voluntary male homemakers and female providers: Reported experiences and perceived social reactions. *The Journal of Men's Studies, 1*(4), 383–402.

Rochlen, A. B. (2005). Men in (and out of) therapy: Central concepts, emerging directions, and remaining challenges. *Journal of Clinical Psychology, 61*, 627–631.

Rochlen, A. B., Land, L. N., & Wong, Y. J. (2004). Male restrictive emotionality and evaluations of online versus face-to-face counseling. *Psychology of Men and Masculinity, 5*, 190–200.

Rochlen, A. B., McKelley, R. A., Suizzo, M., & Scaringi, V. (2008). Predictors of relationship satisfaction, psychological well-being, and life satisfaction among stay at-home fathers, *Psychology of Men & Masculinity, 9*(1), 17–28.

Rochlen, A. B., Suizzo, M., McKelley, R. A., & Scaringi, V. (in press). "I'm just providing for my family": A qualitative study of stay-at-home-fathers' views toward their roles, reactions from others, parenting values, and masculine identities. *Psychology of Men & Masculinity.*

Schulz, M. S., Cowan, C. P., & Cowan, P. A. (2006). Promoting healthy beginnings: A randomized controlled trial of a preventive intervention to preserve marital quality during the transition to parenthood. *Journal of Consulting and Clinical Psychology, 74*(1), 20–31.

Seligman, M. E. P., & Csikszentmihalyi, M. (2000). Positive psychology: An introduction. *American Psychologist, 55*(1), 5–14.

Shapiro, M. (2007). Money: A therapeutic tool for couples therapy. *Family Process, 46*(3), 279–291.

Soliday, E., McCluskey-Fawcett, K., & O'Brien, M. (1999). Postpartum affect and depressive symptoms in mothers and fathers. *American Journal of Orthopsychiatry, 69*(1), 30–38.

Speechly, K. N., & Noh, S. (1992). Surviving childhood cancer, social support, and parents' psychological adjustment. *Journal of Pediatric Psychology; 17,* 15–31.

Sue, D. W., & Sue, D. (2003). *Counseling the culturally diverse* (4th ed.). New, York: John Wiley and Sons.

Sue, D. W., Capodilupo, C. M., Torino, G. C., Bucceri, J. M., Holder, A. M. B., Nadal, K. L., & Esquilin, M. (2007). Racial microaggressions in everyday life: Implications for clinical practice. *American Psychologist 62*(4), 271–286.

Thompson, E. H., & Pleck, J. H. (1995). Masculine ideologies: A review of research instrumentation on men and masculinities. In R. F. Levant & W. S. Pollack (Eds.), *A new psychology of men* (pp. 129–163). New York: Basic Books.

U.S. Census Bureau. (2002). Children's living arrangements and characteristics: March 2002. Current population reports, P20-547. Washington, DC: Author.

U.S. Census Bureau. (2006). *Current Population Survey, 2006 Annual Social and Economic Supplement.*

Vogel, D. L., & Wester, S. R. (2003). To seek help or not to seek help: The risks of self-disclosure. *Journal of Counseling Psychology, 50*(3), 351–361.

Wong, Y. J. (2006). Strength-Centered Therapy: A social constructionist, virtues-based psychotherapy. *Psychotherapy: Theory, Research, Practice, Training, 43*(2), 133–146.

# 11

# Counseling Teen Fathers
## A Developmentally Sensitive Strength-Based Approach

FERDINAND ARCINUE AND JUDY L. PRINCE

## WHO ARE TEEN FATHERS?

According to Planned Parenthood (Weiss, 2006), the rate of teen pregnancy has declined in the United States in recent years; however, a significant number of unplanned, and usually unwanted, teen pregnancies
occur every year. The United States has the highest rate of teen pregnancy among the most developed countries at an estimated cost of $7
billion annually. In 2004 there were 41.1 births per 1,000 women aged
15–19, which represents a decline by one-third since a recent peak of
teens births in 1991 (Martin, Hamilton, Sutton, Ventura, Menacker, &
Kirkmeyer, 2006). Birth rates also vary by state, ranging from 18.2 per
1,000 births to mothers ages 15 to 19 in New Hampshire in 2004, to
66.7 per 1,000 to mothers ages 15 to 19 in the District of Columbia.
Information pertaining to fathers is often missing from birth records in
cases where the birth mother is under 25 years of age and/or unmarried.
For example, in 2004, the father's age was not available for 36% of births
to unmarried women and for 24% of births to women under 25 years
of age. With adjustments made for these limitations in the data, it is

estimated that in 2004 there were 17 births per 1,000 teen males aged 15–19. To state this latter statistic in a different way, approximately 1.7% of all males aged 15–19 have fathered at least one child. However, the National Center on Health Statistics (2006) estimates that closer to 15% of males have fathered a child before the age of 20 years. This large discrepancy in the data may be due to a number of factors including under-reporting by both teen mothers and fathers, as well as other methodological problems in the data collection.

Teenage fatherhood has been cited by experts as an area of "empirical neglect" (Robinson, 1988). Research pertaining to teen pregnancy and parenting has focused largely on teen mothers (Luker, 1996), with much less understanding about teen fathers. Interestingly, it is estimated that about 70% of the male partners of teen mothers are not teens themselves at 20 years of age or older. Teen fathers are regarded as a highly misunderstood group, perhaps in part due to impressions drawn and conclusions made from research that has often focused on adult men who have fathered children with teen mothers (Beymer, 1995). In their review of the literature, Coley and Chase-Lansdale (1998) summarize the apparent profile of teen fathers. From the available information, the authors conclude that teen fathers tend to be an average of 2 to 3 years older than teen mothers. This is an age difference consistent with overall trends in the United States indicating that the partners of mothers aged 20–39 are also an average of three years older than the mothers. Further, teen fathers tend to be poor, from low-income neighborhoods, and have completed fewer years of school than male teens who are not fathers. While teen fathers appear to work more, and therefore initially earn more than non-parent teens, the fact that they tend to achieve less education puts them at a disadvantage in the labor market, resulting in lower earnings and lesser job opportunities in the long-term. Many teen fathers are from families who experienced teen childbearing and are therefore continuing an intergenerational pattern.

## Common Myths and Stereotypes

In general, our society views teen parenthood with disapproval. Limited data combined with general societal disapproval has led to the stereotyping, even demonizing, of teen fathers. Beymer (1995) comments that teen fathers are "victims of massive misunderstanding and discrimination...they are simultaneously rejected and ignored, disparaged and excluded, condemned and punished" (p. 26). Robinson (1988) suggests that the development of certain myths about teen fathers can be traced to the war and post-war eras of the 1940s when social service agencies were utilized by large numbers of unmarried mothers. The author describes five historical myths pertaining to adolescent fathers:

Super-Stud Myth: Portrays the teen father as "worldly" and knowing more about sex than his typical peer

Don Juan Myth: Views teen fathers as exploiting and taking advantage of more naïve teen females

Macho Myth: Views the teen father as combating feelings of inadequacy and a need to prove his masculinity

Mr. Cool Myth: Sees the teen father as engaging in a casual relationship with the teen mother with little emotional reaction to the pregnancy

Phantom Father Myth: An absentee father who leaves the teen mother and child to fend for themselves

## *Debunking the Myths*

Miller (1994) and Mazza (2002) note that teen fathers have often been depicted as distrustful, irresponsible, and uninvolved in parenting, and society tends to believe that teenage boys neither can be nor want to be responsible fathers. While some teen fathers fit these stereotypes or myths, society's beliefs about teen fathers may be overly harsh. On an individual basis, cases of each of these scenarios surely exist, but recent research is showing that these are largely generalizations and misinformation. Rhoden and Robinson (1997) highlight recent findings that refute these commonly held myths about teen fathers. For example, teen fathers do not appear to be "studs" who are more sophisticated or informed about sex than teen mothers. "Failing to use birth control and making comments such as, 'I did not think she would get pregnant because we only had sex once a week,' seem to indicate these young men were as uninformed about sexuality as their female partners" (p. 108). Further, the myth that teen mothers are the naïve victims of teen fathers is challenged by evidence that the teen parents are generally close in age, from similar socioeconomic backgrounds, have about the same level of education, and are often involved in a meaningful relationship with one another. A longitudinal study by Glikman (2004) dispels the myths about teen fathers even further. Glickman found that 84% of the couples were still together after a year, the young fathers reported feelings of joy and happiness in response to the births of their children, the majority of young fathers reported seeing their children regularly and being active in their care, and the fathers found value in providing for their children emotionally. As stated by one young father, "You have to love your child. Teach your kids the right way. Give them love" (p. 201).

Numerous other authors (Johnson, 2001; Lerman, 1993; Marsiglio, 1987; Rhoden & Robinson, 1997) found that teen fathers are more involved with their children than generally thought. A more accurate picture may be that the large majority of teen fathers are involved and committed to supporting their children both financially and emotionally. In one clear example, Roy (1999) found that low-income, young fathers provide financial support, are employed, and engage in child caregiving activities. Rhoden and Robinson (1997) found that many teen fathers report fatherhood as a central event in their lives. Additional researchers (Allen & Doherty, 1996; Coley, 2001) have noted that fatherhood becomes life changing for many teen fathers, sometimes guiding new behaviors and leading to even drastic life changes. For such young men, fatherhood becomes a significant new part of their identity, with parental obligations bringing a new sense of responsibility and purpose to their lives. Teen fathers who experience such changes are likely to put great effort into being involved and loving fathers.

The authors of the current chapter emphasize the importance of therapists rejecting the myths and stereotypes ascribed to teen fathers and remaining mindful that many, if not most, teen fathers would like to be involved and effective parents. The teen father experiences fatherhood as a meaningful and life-changing event, and he is likely motivated to become an involved and central figure in his child's life. The therapist's task is to help the teen father negotiate the barriers he will inevitably encounter, such as interruptions in education, financial and employment difficulties, relationship issues with the mother, and alienation from peers.

## PROPOSED PARADIGM FOR THERAPY WITH TEEN FATHERS

The remainder of this chapter offers the clinician a new lens for conceptualizing and working with teen fathers. It is beyond the scope of the current chapter to elaborate on the multitude of issues related to a teen father's race, ethnicity, and other dimensions of diversity that are being addressed in other chapters of this text. Instead, this chapter focuses on the developmental factors relevant to teen fathers. The proposed paradigm emphasizes the positive motivation and capabilities of teen fathers and how the clinician can help the teen father negotiate the multiple barriers that he may encounter. Rhoden and Robinson (1997) point out how a "deficit" perspective on teen fathers tends to exclude them from being successful parents from the start. Professionals who carry this attitude are guided unwittingly in ways that exclude and demean teen fathers from involvement. The same authors proposed a generative model that shifts from a focus on inadequacy to a perspective of teenage fathering as premature but potentially positive. These authors propose a strength-based perspective when working with teen fathers. While positive in its tone, this approach includes an honest and realistic inventory of the individual's personal and external resources and limitations. This approach incorporates three overarching values, which can be briefly summarized as follows:

Counselor's awareness of own biases and stereotypes pertaining to
   teen fathers
Counselor's and client's active involvement in therapy
Focus on client's strengths and acceptance of limitations

Assuming that the teen decides to participate in fatherhood at any level,
the following additional tasks would be expected to become the emphasis of therapy:

Developing an identity as a father
Early and consistent participation in fatherhood
Maintaining an effective relationship with the child's mother

For a more detailed and extensive review of specific counseling issues
that teen fathers face, a number of authors (Hendricks, 1981; Kiselica,
2006; Kiselica & Pfaller, 1993; Lane & Clay, 2000) have written broad
overviews of the service needs of young fathers, including personal
counseling, educational services, employment counseling, relationship counseling, assistance with housing, parenting skills, pregnancy
prevention, and life skills training. The intention of this chapter is
to focus on the clinician's work with teen fathers in the context of
counseling.

## Awareness of Own Biases and Stereotypes of Teen Fathers

According to Kiselica (1999), teen fathers fear that they will be judged
by care providers and are therefore unlikely to utilize programs designed
for them. To offer adequate assistance to teen fathers, it is essential
that mental health providers be aware of their personal reactions to
this population. Kiselica and Pfaller (1993) called upon counselors to
clarify their own attitudes about teen fathers as a means of divesting
themselves of the stereotypes and false judgments often made about
this group. In the present chapter, *countertransference* is used in general
terms to include the entirety of the therapist's feelings and reactions to
the client. The current authors write with the bias that countertransference is a natural, expected, and potentially useful guide to inform
therapy.

## Case Examples

The reader is invited to consider the following vignettes. As you read,
imagine that both young men, Joey, age 19, and Mike, age 16, have presented to you for counseling services. Assume this is your first meeting
with each, and reflect upon your initial thoughts and feelings as you
hear their stories.

## JOEY, AGE 19, WHITE

When my girlfriend told me she was pregnant, I couldn't believe it. I assumed she was on the pill. I mean, I thought the girl was supposed to take care of that. I want her to have an abortion, but I don't think she'll do it. I don't want to be a father. I mean, not now. Maybe someday, but not now. I'm just not ready. And I have a lot I want to do. After college I want to travel, and maybe go on to medical school or law school. There's no way I can get tied down. It just wouldn't be fair to me. I'm angry that this is happening to me.

## MIKE, AGE 16, AFRICAN AMERICAN

My girlfriend is six months pregnant. I didn't think it could happen to me, but it did, and now I have to deal with it. I know I have to accept responsibility. I really want to do the right thing. I want to take care of my girlfriend and the baby. I want to be there for them. My dad wasn't around when I was growing up, and I don't want that for my kid. I'm looking for a job right now because the baby needs stuff, but it's tough because I can only get minimum-wage jobs. The hardest part is that I kind of feel left out. I'd like to have a say in things, but I don't. My girlfriend and her parents are making all the decisions. Just the other day I wanted to take her to her doctor's appointment, but her mom wouldn't let me. If I'm going to be the father, shouldn't I have a say in things?

### Reflection Questions for the Clinician

What were your initial reactions to Joey? to Mike?

Is there one young man you feel greater empathy for?

Do you think you could work equally well with either client? Why or why not?

What do you anticipate would be rewarding about working with Joey? with Mike?

What would be the most challenging aspect of working with Joey? with Mike?

How do you think you might feel and react if your own son were in a similar situation?

Think about your own beliefs and values pertaining to fatherhood in general. How might these beliefs and values shape your reactions to clients like Joey and Mike?

How might your feelings and reactions to these young men be shaped by your own cultural background and values?

As you reflect upon the two vignettes and imagine yourself face-to-face with each young man in your counseling room, you may notice both positive and negative countertransference elicited. Clearly, therapists are individuals who are as unique as the clients they serve. As unique individuals, counselors bring their own backgrounds, world views, life experiences, opinions, values, and beliefs to each client encounter. Still further complicating reactions to teen fathers are the ever-changing societal views and expectations pertaining to the role of fathers in general. As summarized by Coley (2001), social changes of the past few decades, including greater financial power for women, declining fertility, increased rates of divorce and remarriage, and increased childbearing outside of marriage, have contributed to the removal of many men from the traditional fathering roles, and sometimes even from their children's households. Therapists who anticipate working with teen fathers are encouraged to be aware of their own values and biases related to teen parenting, as well consider the ever-changing roles of fathers in modern society.

## ACTIVE INVOLVEMENT IN THERAPY

### *Rapport With Teen Fathers*

Because the teen father is often blamed or judged by others, he may present in counseling as unengaged or defensive (Kiselica, Stroud, Stroud, & Rotzien, 1992). Teen fathers often perceive service providers as unsupportive and as additional barriers to their paternal involvement (Bunting & McAuley, 2004). Therapy, in general, may be a difficult and foreign process for many teen fathers, as it may be for men in general (Levant, 1996). Due to gender role expectations and the socialization process, men with traditional beliefs about masculinity may have difficulty seeking help and sharing their emotional needs (Addis & Mahalik, 2003). In the same vein, Goodyear, Newcomb, and Allison (2000) found that teen fathers in general have a more difficult time in identifying and expressing their feelings. Therefore, it is important to establish rapport, discuss the process of counseling, and dispel myths or stigma the teen father may have regarding counseling.

Teen fathers may initially seek counseling due to the crisis of early parenthood and may need guidance for several immediate concerns. Possible areas of focus for counseling include decisions pertaining to the pregnancy itself, educational planning, employment concerns, and relationship issues with the baby's mother and others. Kiselica et al. (1992) stated the counselor must establish him- or herself as an "advocate" for the teen father. Similar to what Sue and Sue (2007) discussed when working with minority clients, it is helpful for the counselor to provide a "gift" by assisting the teen father with an immediate, concrete need or skill, such as providing the father with information or referrals for services or by teaching the teen father a new skill or strategy that would be of immediate help. This immediate and concrete benefit will help to establish a therapeutic alliance with the teen father.

Developing trust and rapport with the teen father may require a deliberate effort from the clinician. In general, the process of seeking help, disclosing one's problems, and placing trust in others can be a difficult process for men (Mahalik, Good, & Englar-Carlson, 2003) and adolescent boys. The teen father may view the clinician as an authority figure or may have preconceived ideas of what a therapist is like. The therapist may have to use careful and deliberate self-disclosure and "small talk" for the teen father to open up. For example, talking about the teen's hobbies or recent sporting events may be a way to normalize the relationship. The therapist should also consider deliberate use of alternative environments that might put the teen at ease (Kiselica, 2006), such as conducting therapy while taking a walk or playing basketball. In addition, the clinician must realize that the teen father, like many adolescent boys, may not have the skills or ability to recognize and express his emotions, and the clinician may need to help the teen develop these skills.

The teen father may not have positive role models for parenting, and the therapeutic relationship may serve as a corrective experience in this regard. Mazza (2002) hypothesized that the therapeutic relationship may show the teen a model for consistency and nurturing—character traits important for involved fathering. The professional relationship between clinician and client can show the teen father how "being there" might be like with his own child.

## *Role of Counselor*

The current paradigm emphasizes a collaborative relationship between therapist and client. Moreover, counselors working with teen fathers are encouraged to recognize when therapeutic boundaries may need to be more fluid than would perhaps be advisable in therapies with other clients. For example, allowing significant others, such as the baby's mother, parents, and others close to the situation, to participate in the therapy as needed may serve a valuable function for the teen father, who is likely to be challenged in negotiating these relationships.

Additionally, given the broad range of needs teen fathers often present with, effective counselors will be skilled at recognizing when a particular need cannot be met by therapy alone. At times the counselor may take on the role of "case manager" and make suitable referrals to community resources. For example, the clinician may need to refer the teen father to parenting classes, medical care, or help the teen parents connect to resources such as the Women, Infants, and Children (WIC) program. Unlike working with mature adults, the clinician may need to take a more active role in helping the teen father access such resources. There are specialized curricula for in-depth parenting skills training for young fathers (Hayes & Sherwood, 2000; Kiselica, Rotzien, & Doms, 1994) that the counselor may incorporate into the therapy.

Under this paradigm, the teen father would also be expected to take an active role in the therapy process. Fatherhood propels the adolescent boy into an adult role prematurely. The therapeutic process can serve as a model for taking responsibility and showing commitment. The teen father would be expected to apply the insight and direction he has gained in therapy and to pursue the goals he set for himself.

## FOCUS ON STRENGTHS AND ACCEPTANCE OF LIMITATIONS

### *Strengths*

Society's most frequent expectation of fathers is that of financial provider (Coley, 2001), with teen fathers being held to the same standards as adult fathers. Saleh, Buzi, Weinman, and Smith (2006) found that payment of child support is considered the most important aspect of paternal involvement. A focus on the teen father's economic contributions sets expectations that a teen father may not be able to meet. Marsiglio (1987) reasoned that the inability to fulfill the breadwinner role fosters a sense of inadequacy and leads many teen fathers to dissociate themselves from their children. The current paradigm encourages and emphasizes a shift to the teen father's strengths and a realistic expectation of what he *can* successfully contribute to the situation. For the first several years of his child's life, the teen father may not be able to contribute financially. If this is recognized and expectations shift accordingly, the teen father is now poised for success rather than failure.

The focus on the traditional breadwinner role is a limited concept of fatherhood; fatherhood is much more than being the breadwinner. Coley (2001) stated that children's social and emotional functioning is affected more by their fathers' commitment to and involvement with the children, rather than their fathers' financial contributions. When making money is the standard that teen fathers are held to, they will almost always fall short. When fatherhood is conceptualized as including emotional involvement, caretaking, and interaction with their children, teen fathers are better positioned to be successful and effective parents. Several authors (Coley & Hernandez, 2006; Saleh et al., 2005; Silverstein, Auerbach, & Levant, 2002) conceptualize fatherhood in a broader framework to include interaction, availability, and caretaking. Silverstein et al. (2002) advocate that in contemporary society, fathers should be legitimized as caregivers in the same way that women have been legitimized in the workplace. This "degendered" approach allows men to become involved in caretaking and be more emotionally open and connected to their children.

Helping the teen to broaden his definition of fatherhood to include other responsibilities, such as caretaking, consistency, and emotional connection, will allow the teen a chance for success. Teen fathers consistently talk about "being there" for their child (Bunting & McAuley, 2004; Glikman, 2004), implying both their physical and emotional presence throughout their child's life. A strength-based approach would focus on the caretaking, nurturing, and emotional consistency that the teen father is capable of providing. The teen father can fulfill and be successful at this role. The capability to be a breadwinner will improve with age and opportunity, but the teen father can be a positive influence on the child and the mother immediately.

## Developmental Limitations

Rhoden and Robinson (1997) state that from a developmental perspective, adults are expected to contribute to the well-being of their children. However, the primary developmental task for adolescents is the clarification of their own identity. Teenagers face the challenges of developing autonomy and independence from their parents. Early fatherhood forces the teen to "become a man." Early parenthood can impact the need for exploration and individuation and disrupt the venues for this development, such as through peer relations, dating, school, and pursuit of career (Coley & Chase-Lansdale, 1998). Therefore, from a perspective of Erikson's (1963) psychosocial developmental model, the developmental tasks for the teen father of young adulthood (intimacy versus isolation) and middle-aged adults (generativity versus stagnation) are prematurely woven into the challenges of adolescence (identity versus role confusion).

Allen and Doherty (1996) and Applegate (1988) point out that teen fathers must attempt to negotiate their transitions into adulthood while also managing their child's development and their relationship with the child's mother. Part of the clinical work also involves the teen's own development as an adolescent. Young fathers may lack the repertoire of practical and emotional skills required to fully support their children (Saleh et al., 2005). The cognitive and emotional abilities needed to be a caring, mature parent may not be available to adolescent fathers still engaged in struggling with separation from their own parents. Being emotionally supportive, making mature decisions, and taking on significant responsibilities will be large steps for the adolescent father, and counseling can help the teen father negotiate these new domains.

## Career and School Limitations

The teen father's ability to find work and provide financial support is often an important variable related to his involvement with his children. Coley (2001) and Coley and Hernandez (2006) hypothesized that the child's mother may bar a father's access to his children because of the father's inability to provide financial support. Joblessness and educational deficiencies might reduce the mother's interest in maintaining a relationship with the father.

The lack of employment opportunities for adolescent boys is potentially devastating to their attempts at fulfilling the financial support expectations of fatherhood. Unfortunately, due to their often impoverished backgrounds and the negative impact on school and career options, teen fathers are rarely strong sources of financial support for teen mothers and their children (Coley & Chase-Lansdale, 1998). Glikman (2004) reported that young fathers consistently spoke of the need to work and were keenly aware that society expected them to be financial providers.

It is important for teen fathers not to lose sight of their long-term plans or preferred careers. The therapist should explore these options with the teen father and continue to work with them in planning long-term goals. There are immediate financial needs faced by the teen father, but pressing needs should not prevent them from also focusing on the future. Some schools offer specialized programs for teen parents to help them complete their academic programs. High schools often offer programs for teen parents to help them graduate. An example of this might be nighttime programs for teen fathers who work or focused GED programs to allow them to quickly finish their high school requirements. Many colleges and universities provide low-cost or free child-care services for students with children, thus allowing teen parents to pursue college-level education.

The therapist should also be prepared to focus on basic career issues such as job-seeking skills and professional job behavior. The counselor may also need to provide referrals for more specialized career counseling or vocational training. For example, community colleges offer semester-long training programs in administrative skills, data entry, and specific technical trades that could help teens find higher-paying entry-level employment.

## Other Limitations

One limitation of which the therapist needs to remain aware is the possibility that some teen fathers are not ready for or capable of parenting. While it is normal and expected for the teen father to feel overwhelmed or fearful of the responsibilities of parenting, the therapist may, in some situations, be helpful to the client in identifying when these reactions are at a level that parenting is not possible. Therefore, the therapist needs to remain aware that not all teen fathers will be capable of fulfilling this role, and the therapy may focus on an acceptance of these realistic limitations. While the teen may not be able to meet the responsibilities of fatherhood, the therapist and teen may be able to work toward actions that would help the growth and development of the teen client. For example, the therapist can help the teen to communicate his limitations to the mother and to open up a discussion about abortion or adoption options. Also, while the teen may not be able to take on fathering responsibilities, he may consider helping the mother with child-care payments. The main point is that, while fatherhood may be beyond the teen's own developmental limitations, the client can still learn and grow from the experience.

# DEVELOPING THE TEEN'S IDENTITY AS A FATHER

Fatherhood seems to be an ever-changing concept. Society creates expectations of fathers that govern their perceived duties and responsibilities. Silverstein et al. (2002) note that men are experiencing gender role strain as they try to meet the traditional fathering role, a role developed in a different social and historical context. The broader changes in society have led to changes in the concept of fatherhood and in the roles and expectations that society places on them. Coley (2001) noted that with less clear societal guidelines and expectations, as well as the increased economic freedom of women, fatherhood is becoming a concept that can be more individually interpreted and defined.

The current authors propose that a strength-based approach to working with teen fathers would start with helping the teen father develop his own identity as a father. Redefining the fatherhood role may start with an exploration of the parenting the teen received. Childhood experiences with his own father shape perceptions of the kind of father he might want to be or not want to be with his own child (Allen & Doherty, 1996; Bunting & McAuley, 2004; Glikman, 2004; Goodyear et al., 2000). These studies found that young men who grew up without a present father wished to do things differently. Their childhood experiences with their own fathers shaped their perceptions of the kind of father they could be, and the pain of having an absent father appears to have fostered a determination to remain involved with their own child. The therapist can work with the teen father to define the type of father he would like to be and translate this into the behaviors and actions needed to meet these goals.

Along similar lines, Coley and Hernandez (2006) hypothesized that fathers who experienced consistent and positive parenting by their own father may have a healthy cognitive model of fathering to guide their own paternal involvement. Regular and consistent contact with their own fathers may lead teen fathers to develop a model of involved fathering that they can replicate with their own children.

A number of researchers noted that the birth of their child became a defining moment in many teen fathers' lives (Coley, 2001; Glickman, 2004; Rhoden & Robinson, 1997). Their identity as "a father" changed their goals, ambitions, and behavior. Many young fathers talk about taking on the responsibility and finding motivation and drive to become good fathers. Coley (2001) reported that many fathers describe parenthood as being "a life-changing experience... [they wanted] to do better than they themselves had, not make the same mistakes, and carry on their name and their heritage" (p. 746). Therapists can help teen fathers define this new identity and sense of purpose for themselves and see how this new motivation will shape their decisions and actions.

It would also be important to discuss the teen father's conceptualization of masculinity and how this relates to fatherhood (Kiselica, 2006). The teen may subscribe to traditional beliefs or scripts about manhood

(Mahalik et al., 2003) that will influence his idea of fatherhood. For example, a teen with traditional beliefs about fatherhood may see his role only as a provider. Similarly, the nurturing and caretaking role may be counterintuitive to a teen who views manhood as being independent and stoic. The therapist and teen father can explore these ideas of manhood and masculinity, help the teen define what it might mean to "be a man," and discuss how this impacts his beliefs about fatherhood.

## EARLY AND CONSISTENT PARTICIPATION IN FATHERHOOD

Allen and Doherty (1996) refuted the empirical evidence showing that less involvement over time by most teen fathers results from teen fathers' lack of commitment or values. The authors asserted that the conflict between their strong convictions about responsibility and the inability to fulfill those responsibilities drives teen fathers out of the relationship and estranges them from their child. The same authors noted that teen fathers believe they should provide emotional support to their children even if they are unable to provide financial support, and that fathers should have continual, ongoing relationships with their children.

Assuming that the teen father is motivated to participate and is capable of healthy participation, the therapist is advised to encourage early involvement. As cited by a number of authors (Allen & Doherty, 1996; Bunting & McAuley, 2004; Glikman, 2004), the phrase "being there" seems to reflect a recurrent theme among teen fathers. More specifically, "being there" appears to refer to providing emotional support and an active involvement that the teen father is frequently motivated to offer, and is capable of offering, to his child and to the child's mother. This may be a function of the teen father's investment and commitment to fatherhood, or it may be that these actions show commitment and responsibility to the child's mother, who often serves as the gatekeeper of the relationship. In either case, early involvement, even in the prenatal period, is important.

The counselor should encourage the teen father to consider the possibility of being actively involved in the early stages of pregnancy and parenthood. At the outset, this early involvement might mean having discussions with the mother about abortion or adoption decisions, going to medical appointments together, being supportive of the mother's needs, and eventually discussions about parenting. Once the child is born, a teen father can be involved in his child's life and be of support to the child's mother in a number of ways. The opportunities include routine, daily caretaking tasks such as feeding, bathing, diapering, and interacting with the child. Assistance with household chores such as cleaning and grocery shopping are additional ways that a teen father can contribute to the maintenance of a household suitable for a child. Therapists encouraging early involvement may find it useful to educate their client that new feelings are often preceded by new behaviors. By participating early in these child-rearing responsibilities, the teen father who may be ambivalent or overwhelmed about parenting may find that this early and successful participation reinforces his confidence and nurtures the emotional attachment to the child.

## MAINTAINING AN EFFECTIVE CO-PARENT RELATIONSHIP WITH THE MOTHER

While this chapter has focused primarily on the teen father, the mother of the child plays a central role in the teen father's relationship with his child. Coley and Hernandez (2006) noted that a cooperative and low-conflict relationship appears central to fathers' continued paternal involvement. In an earlier study Coley (2001) also found that a courteous or close relationship predicted greater involvement by the teen father. Fathers who are supportive to mothers during the pregnancy and birth may create a sense of co-parenting and cooperation that leads to positive patterns of engagement in the future. A greater show of commitment and participation during pregnancy and birth enhances the sense of cooperation between parents, decreasing later conflict and helping to support continued father involvement (Coley & Hernandez).

Bunting and McAuley (2004) found that about two-thirds of teen fathers are still associated with the teen mother after 2 years. Marsiglio (1987) reported that around 50% of teen fathers live with their children for some time after the birth. However, both studies note that these relationships appear to deteriorate over time. A popular term found in the literature (Saleh et al., 2005) and the media is "baby momma drama," used to describe the conflict fathers have with the mothers of their children. A strained relationship with the mother seemed to be the most significant barrier for teen fathers because of the mother's ability to manage the time spent with the child and the quality of father-child interactions (Allen & Doherty, 1996; Chambers, Schmidt, & Wilson, 2006).

Multiple factors such as child characteristics, maternal and paternal characteristics, resources, and social contexts predict the level of father involvement directly and indirectly through the quality of parental relationship (Coley & Hernandez, 2006). That is, the various factors appear to have an effect on the relationship between parents, and this relationship determines the level of involvement that the father can have with the child. Bunting and McAuley (2004) stated that a mother may interpret the father's lack of involvement as disinterest, but they hypothesize that the father's lack of involvement might be more reflective of his inability to contribute financially or his discomfort or lack of skills related to child care. Thus, father-mother relationships appear to mediate the relationship between father and child.

The therapist can help the teen father establish a healthy relationship with the mother as parents to their child. Even if the two are no longer involved in a romantic relationship, they need to be able to work together as parents. It is again important to note that developmental limitations and a lack of experience and maturity may exist because both parents are adolescents. The therapist should help the teen father gain awareness about himself and his own reactions and how he may be impacting the relationship with the mother. When appropriate, the counselor can arrange to have a joint session with the teen parents to address communication issues or ongoing conflict.

Relationship issues with mother and both sets of grandparents have a large impact on the teen's success as a father. Anderson (1993) indicated that the paternal grandmother, the mother of the teen father, plays an important role in pressuring young fathers to accept responsibility for their children. Bunting and McAuley (2004) also note that paternal grandparents are often a source of practical, financial, and moral support for teen fathers, with the grandmothers often instigating the first contact between fathers and their children.

## CASE VIGNETTE

To illustrate this therapeutic approach, we will continue with a vignette from earlier in the chapter. Mike is a 16-year-old African American who is accepting responsibility and would like to be a good father to his child. The following case example will show how therapy might evolve with this client. It is important to note that our approach to working with teen fathers is not meant to be a manualized treatment plan, but rather a set of guidelines that a therapist can use within his own theoretical orientation.

Mike is eventually referred to counseling by his football coach, who is aware of the situation and can see that Mike is in over his head. Although Mike appreciated his coach's assistance in finding counseling, Mike reported being devastated when his coach told him that he was "very disappointed" in Mike. When Mike presents for counseling, the initial shock of learning about the pregnancy had passed, and the decision to keep the child has already been made. Mike is overwhelmed and scared, but seems to have a genuine desire to meet his obligations in the most positive way he can. He had experienced the expected disapproval of important elders in his life (mother, football coach), as well as sentiments of blame and anger from his girlfriend's parents (the Super-Stud and Don Juan stereotypes are probably good descriptions of how Mike is currently viewed by Jeanette's mother and father). At the present, Mike views lack of access to his girlfriend, to decisions that are being made, and to the situation in general as his greatest challenges and concerns.

*Establish rapport and set the tone for the work.* To establish good initial rapport with Mike and to accomplish the multiple tasks of the therapy, therapeutic boundaries needed to be more fluid than usual. For example, Mike found it easier to talk to his therapist if conversations took place over a cup of coffee or while taking a walk together, rather than always in the clinician's office. "Small talk" before and following initial therapeutic contacts were a means of establishing rapport, as well as putting Mike at ease. For example, Mike and the therapist shared a passion for the Los Angeles Lakers basketball team and would often discuss reactions to the last game played as a means of beginning each session. From the onset, the therapist prepared Mike that including significant figures (his mother, Jeanette, Jeanette's parents) would most likely be a part of the work they would be doing together.

*Counselor's awareness of his own biases and stereotypes.* The counselor found it easy to empathize with Mike and experienced him as an appealing client. Mike is a young man who wants to "do the right thing," which the counselor found commendable. Mike wanted to take responsibility and seemed to be trying, but he also had many obstacles in his path. The counselor's feelings of positive regard and empathy for Mike sometimes escalated to feelings of protectiveness. In addition to positive feelings of liking and protectiveness toward Mike, the therapist also noted negative reactions of judgment toward the client. For instance, he sometimes viewed Mike as naïve, without a realistic understanding of the challenges he was facing. Thus, while the therapist found it easy to generate feelings of positive regard for Mike, he also found himself frequently feeling skeptical that Mike would be able to meet the responsibilities of fatherhood. The therapist's task from the outset was to remain aware of these personal reactions and attempt to use them in a creative manner to inform the therapy, but also to keep them in balance. The therapist found it helpful to discuss the countertransference material in his weekly peer supervision group. This helped the counselor maintain a healthy and positive advocacy for Mike without escalating into overprotectiveness that might fail to appropriately empower the teen to eventually become his own best advocate.

*Early and consistent participation in fatherhood.* At the start of counseling, Mike's girlfriend Jeanette was 6 months pregnant. The decision had already been made by Jeanette and her parents that the pregnancy would be carried to term and that Jeanette and the baby would remain in the family home. Although Mike was relieved that the pregnancy was not terminated, he informed the counselor that it bothered him that he was not involved in the decision. "She just told me one day that she had decided. I thought we should at least talk it over, but she only wants to talk to her parents. I feel like I keep getting shut out." Mike explained that Jeanette's parents were supportive of her and willing to help raise their grandchild, but were very angry at him and blamed him for "getting our little girl pregnant." Mike described feeling that they were trying to push him out of the picture altogether. In the first counseling session, Mike talked about feeling frustrated that he was not involved and acknowledged being intimidated by Jeanette's parents, who were keeping a watchful eye over the situation.

As an advocate for the client, the therapist viewed Mike's desire for involvement in the situation as legitimate and attempted to help Mike by assisting in bridging the gap with Jeanette's parents. The counselor invited Mike to organize a family session, including Mike's mother, Jeanette, and Jeanette's parents. Mike's planning and organizing of the group session was a deliberate effort toward changing the perception Jeanette's parents had of Mike. Prior to this event, Jeanette's parents had viewed Mike through the Phantom Father stereotype, as one who would leave their daughter and grandchild to fend for themselves. Mike's efforts in helping to organize the family session was useful in that it showed Jeanette and her parents that Mike was genuine in his desire to be involved and responsible. Although the group session was successful in changing the perception of Mike's intentions, there were still concerns about his ability to parent. As an outcome of this family session, the therapist was able to help Mike negotiate for more involvement, with an agreement made that Mike would now be allowed to accompany Jeanette to her doctor's appointments. This was a small but significant step toward Mike's broader goal of being a fully involved father.

*Focus on strengths and acceptance of limitations.* Mike came to counseling with the plan of finding full-time employment and helping Jeanette with financial support. Mike viewed this as his duty, as well as a means of proving to Jeanette's parents that he can accept the responsibilities of fatherhood. Mike was so determined to earn money and "be a man" in the situation that he was considering leaving school to be able to work full-time. At this point the counselor facilitated an exploration of the feasibility of Mike's plan. The counseling helped Mike to see that while his plan might be helpful in the short-term, his long-term career options would be profoundly limited without an education. Mike's discoveries in this segment of the counseling were also supported by his unsuccessful attempts to find employment. Without a high school diploma, Mike found that his options were limited. The counselor and Mike began to work on a plan that would allow him to provide some degree of financial support in the short-term but would also be more focused on providing nonfinancial types of support such as child care and active involvement in the baby's daily life. This plan for the near term would allow Mike to remain in school, which he agreed would enable him to be a primary source of financial support for his child in the longer term. Mike found that a part-time job would allow him to contribute to smaller expenses (such as diapers and toys) while also remaining in school and continuing to prepare for the best possible future. Mike's natural sense of responsibility and desire to be a good father would also lend itself to being a good caregiver. Mike may discover that he has more to offer as a provider of child care than as a provider of material resources at this time. This portion of the therapy included a family session that involved Mike presenting his plan to Jeanette and her parents. This session was effective in beginning to change her parents' view of Mike's intentions and sense of responsibility. They also understood the importance of his long-term education and career planning, and therefore felt comfortable supporting his plan. As a show of support, Mike's parents offered to provide some financial support until Mike was more financially stable. Following a strength-based approach, the therapeutic focus shifted to Mike's role as a caregiver and involved father.

*Developing an identity as a father.* During this portion of counseling, many of Mike's sessions focused on his experience of growing up without a father in the home. Mike often talked about being determined to be a good parent to his own child, yet also feeling overwhelmed with the challenges he faced. The therapist assisted Mike in exploring his feelings and experiences associated with growing up without a father and helped Mike examine how this history would impact his own newly emerging identity as a father. The focus shifted to assist Mike in identifying important "father figures" in his life. Mike was able to talk about his relationship with a maternal uncle who was affectionate and consistent during his childhood. In addition, Mike's football coach was also identified as playing a significant role in recent years by providing structure, guidance, and discipline. By exploring his lack of a father growing up and how this has shaped his desire to be a good parent to his own child, as well as by identifying other male figures who have served an important role in his life, Mike was slowly beginning to define his own unique identity as a father.

Another type of intervention the therapist employed was to process the "here and now" of the therapeutic relationship and how it also was serving as a model for a reliable, nurturing, and intimate connection with an older male figure. Over the course of therapy, the goals and aspirations of being a good father needed to be translated into specific attitudes and behaviors. For example, once the child is born, Mike plans to accept daily child-care responsibilities and work out a schedule with Jeanette and her parents to put this commitment into action. This would not only be beneficial in allowing Mike daily contact with his child, but also be effective in beginning to establish a co-parenting relationship with Jeanette that would remain important in the years to come.

*Maintaining an effective relationship with the child's mother.* Mike and Jeanette did not last as a couple. Once Mike became more involved with the prenatal process, there was a temporary period of time in which they began to plan their lives together as a family. However, Mike and Jeanette began to experience more conflict. Jeanette became increasingly angry at Mike, partly due to her frustration with having to delay graduation from high school and becoming isolated from her friends. Jeanette blamed Mike for her unhappiness and became resentful as Mike continued to go to school and see friends. As this tension increased, Jeanette began to push Mike away. Eventually Mike and Jeanette realized that their fantasy of forming a family was not becoming a reality, and they decided to end their romantic relationship. This turn of events was utilized by the counselor to open a dialogue with Mike about his relationship with Jeanette. The therapist helped Mike work through the end of the relationship as it was, but also helped Mike accept that forming a new type of relationship with Jeanette would be key to his future success as a father. Mike's goal to be a good father could still be realized if he maintains an amicable and cooperative working relationship with Jeanette.

*Termination.* Counseling with Mike ended just prior to the birth of the child. The 3 months of counseling were successful in laying the groundwork for Mike to be a successful young father. Two years later, Mike sent the counselor a holiday card indicating that he was enjoying his 2-year-old son, Coby. In his note, Mike added that he and Jeanette were both in new relationships but had remained friends and were able to work together as parents. The relationship with Jeanette's parents was said to be improving little by little over time.

## CONCLUSION

The current authors propose a new paradigm for working with teen fathers. Therapists working with this population are encouraged first to examine their own biases and judgments about teen fatherhood. Moreover, active involvement on the part of the therapist, with therapeutic boundaries remaining fluid to accommodate the multifaceted needs of this clientele, is highly recommended. The therapist can facilitate a meaningful dialogue to assist the teen father in identifying both strengths and resources for parenting as well as a realistic appraisal and acceptance of limitations. Rather than focusing on the limitations of teen fathers, this approach asks the therapist to help the teen father redefine his identity as a father and focus on his motivation, strengths, and abilities to be a successful parent and to maintain the critical relationship with the child's mother.

## REFERENCES

Addis, M.E. & Mahalik, J.R. (2003). Men, masculinity, and the contexts of help seeking. *American Psychologist, 58*(1), 5–14.

Allen, W., & Doherty, W. (1996). The responsibilities of fatherhood as perceived by African-American teenage fathers. *Families in Society, 77*(2), 142–155.

Allen, W., & Doherty, W. (2004). Being there: The perception of fatherhood among a group of African-American Adolescent Fathers. *The Prevention Researcher, 11*(4), 6–9.

Anderson, E. (1993). *Streetwise: Race, class and change in an urban community.* Chicago: University of Chicago Press.

Applegate, J. (1988). Adolescent fatherhood: Development perils and potentials. *Child and Adolescent Social Work Journal, 5*, 205–217.

Beymer, L. (1995). *Meeting the guidance and counseling needs of boys.* Alexandria, VA: American Counseling Association.

Bunting, L., & McAuley, C. (2004). Research review: Teenage pregnancy and parenthood: The role of fathers. *Child and Family Social Work, 9*, 295–303.

Chambers, A. L., Schmidt, K. M., & Wilson, M. N. (2006). Describing differences among a sample of low-income fathers: A glimpse into their romantic relationships. *Psychology of Men & Masculinity, 7*(3), 144–152.

Coley, R. L., & Chase-Lansdale, P. L. (1998). Adolescent pregnancy and parenthood. *American Psychologist, 53*(2), 152–166.

Coley, R. L. (2001). Invisible men: Emerging research on low-income, unmarried and minority fathers. *American Psychologist, 56*(9), 743–753.

Coley, R. L., & Hernandez, D. C. (2006). Predictors of paternal involvement for resident and nonresident low-income fathers. *Developmental Psychology, 42*(6), 1041–1056.

Erikson, E. H. (1963) *Childhood and society* (2nd ed.). New York: Norton.

Glikman, H. (2004). Low-income young fathers: Contexts, connections, and self. *Social Work, 49*(2), 195–205.

Goodyear, R. K., Newcomb, M. D., & Allison, R. D. (2000). Predictors of Latino men's paternity in teen pregnancy: Test of a mediational model of childhood experiences, gender role attitudes, and behaviors. *Journal of Counseling Psychology, 47*(1), 116–128.

Hayes, E., & Sherwood, K. (2000). *The responsible fatherhood curriculum.* New York: Manpower Demonstration Research Corporation.

Hendricks, L. E. (1981). *An analysis of two select populations of black unmarried adolescent fathers.* Washington, DC: Howard University Institute for Urban Affairs and Research.

Johnson, W. (2001). Paternal involvement among unwed fathers. *Children and Youth Services Review, 23,* 513–536.

Kiselica, M. S. (1999). Counseling teen fathers. In A. M. Horne & M. S. Kiselica (Eds.), *Handbook of counseling boys and adolescent males: A practitioner's guide* (pp. 179–198). Thousand Oaks, CA: Sage Publications.

Kiselica, M. S. (2006). Helping a boy become a parent: Male-sensitive psychotherapy with a teenage father. In M. Englar-Carlson and M. Stevens (Eds.), *In the room with men: A casebook of therapeutic change* (pp. 225–240). Washington, DC: American Psychological Association.

Kiselica, M. S., & Pfaller, J. (1993). Helping teenage parents: The independent and collaborative roles of counselor educators and school counselors. *Journal of Counseling and Development, 72,* 42–48.

Kiselica, M. S., Rotzien, A., & Doms, J. (1994). Preparing teenage fathers for parenthood: A group psychoeducational approach. *Journal for Specialists in Group Work, 19,* 83–94.

Kiselica, M. S., Stroud, J., Stroud, J., & Rotzien, A. (1992). Counseling the forgotten client: The teen father. *Journal of Mental Health Counseling, 14,* 338–350.

Lane, T. S. & Clay, C. M. (2000). Meeting the service needs of young fathers. *Child and Adolescent Social Work Journal, 17*(1), 35–54.

Lerman, R. I. (1993). A national profile of young unwed fathers. In R. Lerman & T. Ooms (Eds.), *Young unwed fathers: Changing roles and emerging policies* (pp. 1–27). Philadelphia: Temple University Press.

Levant, R. F. (1996). The new psychology of men. *Professional Psychology: Research and Practice, 27*(3), 259–265.

Luker, K. (1996). *Dubious conceptions: The politics of teen pregnancy.* Cambridge, MA: Harvard University Press.

Mahalik, J. R., Good, G. E., & Englar-Carlson, M. (2003). Masculinity scripts, presenting concerns, and help seeking: Implications for practice and training. *Professional Psychology: Research and Practice 34*(2), 123–131.

Marsiglio, W. (1987). Adolescent fathers in the United States: Their initial living arrangements, marital experience, and educational outcomes. *Family Planning Perspectives, 19,* 240–251.

Martin, J. A., Hamilton, B. E., Sutton, P. D., Ventura, S. J., Menacker, F., and Kirmeyer, S. (2006). Births: Final data for 2004. *National Vital Statistics Reports, 55*(1). Hyattsville, MD: National Center for Health Statistics.

Mazza, C. (2002) Young dads: The effects of a parenting program on urban African-American adolescent fathers. *Adolescence, 37,* 681–693.

Miller, D. B. (1994). Influences on parental involvement of African American adolescent fathers. *Child and Adolescent Social Work Journal, 11*(5), 363–377.

Rhoden, J. L., & Robinson, B. E. (1997). Teen dads: A generative fathering perspective versus the deficit myth. In A. J. Hawkings & D. C. Dollahite (Eds.), *Generative fathering: Beyond deficit perspectives.* Thousand Oaks, CA: Sage Publications.

Robinson, B. E. (1988). *Teenage fathers.* Lexington, MA: Lexington Books.

Roy, K. (1999). Low income single fathers in an African-American community and the requirements of welfare reform. *Journal of Family Issues, 20,* 432–457.

Saleh, M. F., Buzi, R., Weinman, M. L., & Smith, P. (2006). The nature of connections: Young fathers and their children. *Adolescence, 40*(159), 514–523.

Silverstein, L. B., Auerbach, C. F., & Levant, R. F. (2002). Contemporary fathers reconstructing masculinity: Clinical implications of gender role strain. *Professional Psychology: Research and Practice, 33*(4), 361–369.

Sue, D. W., & Sue D. (2007). *Counseling the culturally different* (4th ed). New York: Wiley.

Weiss, D. (2006). Pregnancy and Childbearing among U.S. Teens. Retrieved January 1, 2006, from http://www.plannedparenthood.org/issues-action/sex-education/reports/teen-pregnancy-6239.htm

# Counseling Gay Fathers
## Stepping Into the New Frontier

DANIEL J. ALONZO

The nature and composition of families has undergone dramatic changes in the last half-century in the United States. For many years, in the most traditional cultural presentation, the word "family" conjured up mental pictures of two White heterosexual parents in a long-standing, culturally approved, religiously and civilly sanctioned relationship with their biological offspring, usually two, a boy and a girl for ideal balance (Okun, 1996). However, this idyllic picture of the American nuclear family has been forced to change. The rising divorce rate, the increase in two-income households, the growth of feminism, the larger number of single-parent households, and the changing ethnic landscape of American society have necessitated new ways of thinking about families (Goldenberg & Goldenberg, 2002). These changes have also necessitated new ways of seeing parenthood—the skills required, the approaches taken, even the players themselves.

Increasingly, there is a growing awareness of gay male parenting, although it is difficult to arrive at an accurate estimate of the number of gay men who are parents in the United States. For the first time, the 2000 U.S. Census made it possible for people to report if they were living with a domestic partner (Schneider, 2005). Less than 1% of U.S. men (602,000) identified themselves as living in a gay male household (Schneider). However, it is assumed that the number is larger, because many gay men and gay couples may not have felt safe to admit this to Census Bureau authorities. It is not known how many gay households have children. Most researchers assert that the number of gay fathers is between 1 and 3 million (Ariel & McPherson, 2000; Ritter & Terndrup, 2002; Silverstein & Quartironi, 1996). Approximately 20% of gay men have been married and are parents of at least one child (Bigner & Jacobsen, 1992; Ritter & Terndrup, 2002). One estimate states that 12 to 15 million children live in homes with either a gay or lesbian parent in the United States (Goldenberg & Goldenberg, 2002).

The truth is that gay men have been fathers in the United States and other countries for many years (Ritter & Terndrup, 2002). For centuries, men who had a primary sexual attraction to other men did indeed become fathers, but they did so as a part of their culturally sanctioned heterosexual relationships and marriages (Bozett, 1989). Now, almost 40 years after the gay liberation movement, gay men who are open about their sexual orientation are choosing to parent for the same reasons chosen by heterosexual men: desire to bring forth and nurture human life in the context of a romantic and sexual relationship with a loving partner, and desire to make a better world by nurturing a child.

Currently, gay male parenting is a highly divisive and politically charged topic in the United States (Ritter & Terndrup, 2002). Notions persist that children are at risk for developmental or sexual-identity problems if they are not raised in a two-parent, opposite-sex household (Goldenberg & Goldenberg, 2002; Silverstein & Quartironi, 1996). However, two decades of empirical research have shown that children raised in same-sex households are at no more risk for developmental, psychological, or sexual problems than children raised in opposite-sex households (Patterson, 2006; Shiller, 2007). Children of gay fathers do not differ from the children of heterosexual parents along the lines of gender identity development, sexual orientation, sex role behavior, intelligence, or general mental health (Armesto, 2002).

Although research verifies the health of children raised in same-sex households, very little research has been conducted on the parents themselves, their developmental processes, their negotiation of sociocultural obstacles, and their unique competencies. Most of the research that does exist has been focused on lesbian mothers rather than gay male fathers (Patterson, 2006). Ritter and Terndrup (2002) cited women's socialization toward relationships and an empirical bias equating parenting with motherhood as possible explanations for the limited research on gay fathers. Furthermore, most of the research on gay fathers is older, conducted in the 1970s, 1980s, and early 1990s. With this in mind, it is important to summarize what is known about gay fathers so that mental health providers and educators can work effectively with this population.

## GAY FATHER FAMILY CONFIGURATIONS

Gay men have always been a part of families—nuclear families, extended families, families of creation, and nonrelated families of choice. They have conceived and parented children in heterosexual relationships; they have had children with surrogate mothers; and they have fostered, adopted, and raised other children. To avoid stereotyping gay fathers, it is important to keep in mind the particular family constellation of which a gay father may be a part.

It is also important to remember that many gay fathers remain in heterosexual relationships and marriages. Many choose to remain in this situation for fear of hurting their female partners, losing their children, alienating their families, or feeling exposed in the community. Some of these men are quite accepting of the choices they have made, but many of these gay fathers are conflicted, torn between a desire to stay in the heterosexual relationship and a desire to come out (Bigner & Bozett, 1989). Some men elect not to act out their attraction to other men, while others seek out sex with other men secretly (Miller, 1987). These fathers often experience deep ambivalence and shame (Johnson & Connor, 2002; Ritter & Terndrup, 2002).

Fathers who are separated or divorced from their heterosexual partners have a variety of fathering roles with their children (Ritter & Terndrup, 2002). There are situations where fathers have not reached satisfactory custody agreements with their ex-wives. For these men, the stress of divorce and separation continues (Miller, 1987). Many times the ex-wife or her new partner may be uncomfortable with the father's gay identity, creating new tensions within the family (Ritter & Terndrup, 2002). Some divorced fathers continue to struggle with their sexual identities, keeping their sexual orientations, dating experiences, and romantic partnerships hidden from their ex-wives and/or children (Bigner, 1996). These fathers often experience considerable stress as they invest energy in compartmentalizing the relationships in their lives (Bigner). However, many gay fathers come out to their wives and children, develop a stable gay identity, negotiate custody agreements with the best interest of their children in mind, move forward with their lives, and set up loving relationships with other men (Bigner). If the new partner becomes a steady presence in the gay father's life, then a stepfamily is created, whether the new partner lives with the father or not. Nonbiologically-related close friends are also sometimes considered part of the alternative stepfamily (Ritter & Terndrup, 2002). Of course, many of the same challenges that exist for heterosexual stepfamilies exist for gay father stepfamilies (Crosbie-Burnett & Helmbrecht, 1993).

Increasingly, gay men, either individually or in committed relationships, are choosing to foster-parent or adopt children. More courts within the United States are willing to allow gay fathers to adopt children, but often these adoptees are considered "hard to place" (Patterson & Chan, 1996). That is, these children have been passed over by heterosexual adoptive parents because of the child's ethnicity, age, disability, or history of delinquency (Patterson & Chan). Some gay fathers use adoption agencies, attorneys, friendship networks, or resources within the gay community either to identify children who are available for adoption or to identify pregnant mothers who are willing to give up their children for adoption once they are born (Mallon, 2000). Gay men face difficult obstacles even in the most carefully arranged adoptions, such as prejudicial agency attitudes, lack of policies around gay male adoption, and fears and uncertainty on the part of the birth parents (Patterson & Chan, 1996). To bypass these risks, some gay fathers adopt children from orphanages outside the United States, a process that requires considerable patience and substantial financial resources (Matthews & Cramer, 2006).

Finally, some gay men, either alone or as part of a couple, may choose surrogacy as the pathway to fatherhood (Ritter & Terndrup, 2002). There are a variety of surrogacy options: artificial insemination with one male partner's sperm; both members of a male couple donating sperm so that the actual father is not known; the use of the same surrogate for conception and gestation; the use of two different surrogates, one for conception and one for gestation; a single gay man or two gay male partners entering into a parenthood agreement with a single lesbian or a lesbian couple; or one of the men donating the sperm and one of the women being designated the birth mother, who will experience the non-sexual insemination process (Ritter & Terndrup). It must be stated that adoption, surrogacy, and sperm donor options require significant time and financial resources, thereby making these choices available to a small group of relatively privileged men (Berkowitz & Marsiglio, 2007).

By the early part of the 21st century, U.S. society began recognizing parenthood arrangements not previously considered. The current definition of family has expanded. Many gay fathers are no longer hiding but instead are being themselves in a variety of family constellations. Gay stepfamilies are offering children new bases of support. More gay men are choosing to adopt or have children through surrogacy. On the other hand, as diverse as these new opportunities are, most gay men who desire to become parents outside of a heterosexual relationship must still expend significant time, effort, and expense to reach the desired status of fatherhood (Matthews & Cramer, 2006). The challenges for gay fathers do not stop there.

## SOCIETAL OBSTACLES TO GAY FATHERHOOD

On a daily basis, gay fathers confront Western society's basic assumptions about family, gender, masculinity, and sexuality (Berkowitz & Marsiglio, 2007). In the U.S. culture, fatherhood is seen as the sole province of heterosexual men. To suggest otherwise is to challenge several culturally dominant beliefs: Fatherhood is a reflection of virility and strength; only heterosexual men can be strong and masculine; and women are the primary caregivers to children, not men (Mallon, 2000). These societal attitudes continue to influence the psychologies of gay men, contributing to an internalized, shame-based idea that fatherhood is not an option if one lives an openly gay life (Berkowitz & Marsiglio, 2007).

The obstacles are not all internalized, as gay men still encounter institutionalized prejudice and discrimination. Most institutional policies do not recognize same-sex relationships or same-sex parenthood (Garnets & Kimmel, 2003). Insurance coverage, inheritance benefits, tax credits, legally sanctioned marriages, hospital and day-care visitation rights, educational content, school regulations, and religious choices, to name a few, are privileges for heterosexual couples and families, not for gay partners and fathers (Garnets & Kimmel). Gay male couples are denied the right to foster or adopt children in most states (Garnets & Kimmel). Some states do not allow second-parent adoption, the process whereby the nonbiological parent in a blended family adopts the child (Garnets & Kimmel). Rarely are nonbiological parents (such as gay stepfathers) legally recognized if the primary gay father dies or if the gay male partners separate (Patterson, 1994).

Therefore, gay men must exert tremendous energy to move past societal barriers to parent children. Societal and cultural stigma forms the background for gay male parenting in the United States. It is against this background that gay men must negotiate several developmental tasks as they face the tasks of parenthood.

## DEVELOPMENTAL TASKS FOR GAY FATHERS

The early literature on gay male development focused on stage models of how gay men come to an acceptance of their identities (e.g., Cass, 1979). However, much less attention was paid to experiences after coming out that might lead to successful integration of sexual orientation into one's adult life (Alderson, 2003). In fact, gay men must grapple with several developmental challenges to arrive at an identity of a "gay father."

One of the most salient developmental tasks faced by gay men desiring fatherhood is the arrival at an acceptance that one has a right to be a parent. Berkowitz and Marsiglio (2007) found that the coming-out process for many gay men included a simultaneous thought that they would never be fathers. It can take years to reverse this belief and allow the natural procreative consciousness to develop—that is, "the cognitive and emotional awareness and expression of self as a person capable of creating and caring for life" (Berkowitz & Marsiglio, 2007, p. 368). For many gay men there are turning points, such as a weekend spent babysitting one's nephews or nieces, or a discovery of a gay adoption agency. Even with such turning points, gay men quickly learn that any possible fatherhood is going to be affected and shaped by other people and outside institutions, such as birth mothers and fertility agencies.

Another important developmental task for gay fathers is the coming-out experience itself. Gay youth often push themselves through heterosexual dating experiences until it becomes intolerable. Many young gay men marry opposite-sex partners in an attempt to convince themselves and others that they are "normal" and similar to everybody else. Many men first become fathers and later arrive at a gay identity (Miller, 1987). Research on gay fathers has shown that whether or not a father in a heterosexual marriage decides to hide his gay identity, just the consideration of the question itself is stressful, leading to compartmentalization, distance from wives, distance from children, and increased isolation (Armesto, 2002; Bigner & Bozett, 1989; Bozett, 1981; Miller, 1987). Overall, gay men who come to terms with their gay male identities before parenthood tend to have less internal stress than those who are parents before they come to terms with their sexual orientation (Armesto, 2002).

However, it is important to note that internalized shame and homophobia can continue to affect parenting throughout fatherhood, even after coming out. Some men continue to feel guilty, worrying about the effects on their children (Miller, 1987). Many gay fathers who were heterosexually married feel they are developmentally "off-time"; that is, they worry about lagging behind the developmental course of gay men who came to an acceptance of their same-sex attractions earlier in their lives (Bigner, 1996). Even gay fathers who have children after they come out still need to be vigilant for internalized shame and oppression. This is true because all gay men are exposed to the dominant cultural antihomosexual attitudes when they are young, and, to some extent, all gay men internalize these attitudes until they are able to cast them off (Ritter & Terndrup, 2002). This internalized shame has the power to affect new relationships, including those between a gay father and his child, unless the gay man can be proactive in working through this self-doubt (Armesto, 2002; Bepko & Johnson, 2000; Canarelli, Cole, & Rizzuto, 1999; Kurdek, 1997). Research has shown that children tend to handle the stresses of growing up in a gay family better if the parent has worked through many of his early shaming experiences (Armesto, 2002; Bigner & Bozett, 1989; Chernin & Johnson, 2003).

As a gay man works through internalized shame, he must also move away from compartmentalization and move toward integration of identities as a gay man and as a father (Bigner & Bozett, 1989). Silverstein, Auerbach, and Levant (2002) use the term "heterosexist gender role strain" to capture the stress that gay fathers experience in their attempts to fit into a role they have been told does not belong to them. A gay father must find ways to bridge the two identities of *gay* and *father*, to find appropriate ways to disclose his gay identity to heterosexuals and the heterosexual parenting community (day-care situations, schools, soccer leagues, etc.) and also to disclose his parenthood to other gay men and the larger gay community. Closeted, heterosexually married gay fathers may avoid this integration for years, often falling in love with heterosexual men, often being disappointed with unrequited love, and thereby confirming for themselves a view of gay life as being unremittingly lonely (Miller, 1987). Some gay fathers practice selective disclosure, coming out to a trusted few friends but avoiding conversations with other heterosexual parents in the child's community.

On the other side, gay fathers sometimes have difficulty integrating their parenthood into the larger gay community (Armesto, 2002). The political and social gay community in larger metropolitan areas continues to expend considerable resources toward the support and advertisement of attractions that appeal to younger, single gay men (Bigner, 1996). Men who are fathers sometimes feel discouraged and unwelcome (Bigner). Many fathers, especially those who were once heterosexually married, may have entertained romantic fantasies that sustained them through difficult divorces and custody battles (Miller, 1987). Now, after finally coming out, they may feel awkward and disillusioned when they meet the realities of dating in a new community, a community where they lack social skills and where they may feel "off-time" compared with others (Miller). They may hide their parenthood for fear that other gay men will dismiss them as "unavailable" for dating and relationships.

Gay fathers must learn to manage this multiminority status, being in the minority both in the heterosexual parenting world and the gay community (Armesto, 2002). Even today, when more and more gay men are adopting children and having children through surrogacy, gay fathers can feel as if they are caught between two worlds. Because openly gay parenting is a new development in society, the gay community is only beginning to develop social structures, clubs, organizations, and institutions that can support the gay father and his family. Most gay social organizations and businesses continue to cater to the young, single male to survive in a competitive market. However, such a focus may not be meaningful or appealing to a gay father in search of support for his parental responsibilities.

## PARENTING ISSUES

Gay fathers may be searching for support in their endeavors, but there is no evidence to support the stereotype that gay fathers are incapable of parenting effectively. No differences have been found between heterosexual fathers' and gay fathers' effectiveness in problem-solving, involving children in recreation, fostering autonomy, and setting limits (Allen & Burrell, 1996; Armesto, 2002; Bigner & Bozett, 1989; Bigner & Jacobsen, 1992). Gay fathers seem to use verbal communication more than heterosexual fathers, and they are found to be more responsive to the needs of their children than heterosexual fathers (Bigner & Bozett). There is no evidence to support the widely held fear that gay fathering will interfere with a child's gender identity development (Armesto).

The U.S. legal system has had a long history of being unfriendly to gay fathers (Ariel & McPherson, 2000). Most gay fathers worry about the permanence of family arrangements (Bigner & Bozett, 1989). Foster and adoption policies have traditionally seen gay men as unfit to be parents (Ricketts & Achtenberg, 1989). Surrogacy agreements are complicated and detailed, and sometimes the birth mother changes her mind (Ricketts & Achtenberg). These factors leave gay fathers vulnerable in a way that most heterosexual fathers in an ongoing marriage are not.

Gay fathers also continually monitor a potentially unfriendly environment for the protection of their children (Armesto, 2002). Gay fathers keep a watchful eye on their children's education, their children's playmates, and the messages their children receive through the media. Although most parents are vigilant, a gay father must take on additional roles of translator, mediator, and soldier for his child. Under this stress, gay fathers may experience a resurgence of internalized homophobia, bringing about questions such as, "Have I made my child's life more complicated? Is my sexual orientation a stressor for my children?" (Armesto, 2002). Guilt and shame can resurface in the form of toxic self-doubt (Miller, 1987).

One of the most frequently mentioned parenting issues in the literature is disclosure to children (Ritter & Terndrup, 2002). If gay fathers avoid disclosure, they are likely replaying the same distance and isolation between themselves and their children that they experienced with their own parents when they were young (Ritter & Terndrup). Children, of course, realize something is amiss, but not having the words to understand their experience, they may blame themselves for their fathers' distance and odd behavior (Ritter & Terndrup). Some children of closeted fathers know their fathers are gay, but they collude with the silence rather than making their fathers uncomfortable. Some fathers ask their children not to tell their ex-wives, the grandparents, or other relatives (Ritter & Terndrup). This creates pressure on the children, who eventually feel isolated from peers, their neighborhood friends, their mothers, and other relatives.

Miller (1987) stressed the importance of planned disclosure. Forced disclosure, which often takes place after a child accidentally discovers the father in an intimate situation or overhears a telephone conversation, is usually a recipe for confusion, anger, and panic. Ritter and Terndrup (2002) suggest that children handle a planned disclosure much better than most gay fathers would have predicted. Children may have a variety of questions to such a disclosure (Bigner & Bozett, 1989; Miller, 1987; Ritter & Terndrup, 2002). Some children may wonder why they are being told, and many different fears may fuel this confusion. Depending on a child's development and maturation, a child may think that the parent is preparing the child for an upcoming loss. Some children might wonder if the father's disclosure means that she or he will grow up gay too. Some children may wonder if they have to be gay in order for their father to love them. Some children ask if the father hates women, and, in a divorced family, the child may be wondering if the father hates the mother. The child may also be asking this question because it represents an unconscious fear that the mother and father will never be reunited.

Miller pointed out that this question about hating women, coming from daughters, may really mean, "Do you hate me?"

Another major parenting issue is the gay stepfamily configuration. A gay stepfamily may be created when a gay father enters into a committed relationship with another man and this new person takes on the role of the father's partner (Crosbie-Burnett & Helmbrecht, 1993). This new man usually occupies a central place in the father's new household. Children may either reside within or visit the father and stepfather's home. Ariel and McPherson (2000) explain that the gay male stepfamily encounters many of the same challenges as heterosexual stepfamilies: How do loyalties to the biological parents play themselves out? How can the child come to see the stepparent as a legitimate, protective person in the child's life? How is discipline handled in the new household? The difference, of course, is that the father has a male partner, a sex difference to which the heterosexual community may react with hesitation or prejudice. Children become aware of society's reaction, and some children become concerned about how peers will see them (Patterson & Chan, 1996).

Many gay stepfamilies navigate the new landscape with a fair amount of ease, especially as gay couples and families are acknowledged more readily than they were one generation ago (Patterson, 2003). However, it is also true that different stepfamily configurations create different challenges. In one configuration, a gay father who has divorced his wife may enter into his first relationship with another man. This father may have high expectations of this relationship, which he hopes will be the balm for the heartache he has suffered in his closeted years (Miller, 1987). In romanticizing this relationship, the gay father may be disappointed that the children are cautious or mistrusting of the gay stepfather. To some extent, the ease with which a gay stepfamily makes a smooth transition into a new identity will depend on the father's comfort with himself (Crosbie-Burnett & Helmbrecht, 1993).

Sometimes children are able to accept their father's gay identity "in theory," but it is quite another matter when they meet the actual man with whom their father has fallen in love. Young children seem to make the transition more easily than older children (Ariel & McPherson, 2000). If the child is in the pubescent or early adolescent years and is coming to terms with his or her own sexuality, the child may be judgmental about alternative sexual expressions (Ariel & McPherson). Some children may blame the stepfather for "making Dad gay," an attitude that may represent the child's wish that the original family would reunite and life would return to normal (Miller, 1987). Some older children who have been exposed to homophobic messages in the media may not want to find a gay relationship in the center of their living rooms (Miller). Adolescents who are trying to fit into a peer group might be embarrassed about what they perceive as a conspicuous difference (Armesto, 2002; Chernin & Johnson, 2003). However, it is also true that many older teenagers who are close to being launched from the family may have suspected the father's sexual orientation for a long time (Miller, 1987). They may be relieved and delighted that their father has found someone to love and someone with whom to share a residence. Still, no matter what age, some children may be embarrassed by the new family configuration, and they may attempt to control the situation by controlling their father's behavior (asking their father not to bring the gay stepfather to an event, or telling the father that they are embarrassed by the stepfather's effeminacy), controlling their own behavior (distancing themselves from the gay household), or controlling the outside environment (lying to friends or refusing to bring friends home to the gay household; Bigner & Bozett, 1989). The heterosexual parent's attitude may be one of the strongest factors in the child's acceptance of the father's sexual orientation and the gay stepfather (Ritter & Terndrup, 2000). This is often a difficult road for ex-wives to walk, as they are going through their own process of grief and mourning (Miller).

Gay stepfathers have their own paths to forge. They may experience disappointment or impatience, expecting to find their new relationships charged with sexual excitement, only to discover that once again they have to delay sexual pleasure in their lives, this time because their partners are tending to their children (Bigner, 1996). Sometimes gay fathers introduce the stepfather in a disguised way, and the stepfather can feel cheated, angry, and betrayed. Crosbie-Burnett and Helmbrecht (1993) found that the best predictor of happiness within a gay family was the extent to which the gay father welcomed and made a place for the gay stepfather.

In a second configuration, a new gay stepfamily may result if the gay father ends a relationship with one man and then later creates a relationship with another man. This is not uncommon, as gay men who come out later in their lives, after having children in the context of a heterosexual marriage, may not make good relationship choices initially; they may rush into intimacy with a man without evaluating long-term compatibility (Miller, 1987). For the newest stepfamily, the issue is the family's adjustment to the changes. How does the father handle the changes with his children? What attitudes do the children have toward a second gay stepfather? What has happened to the first gay stepfather, and what is his access to the children? The first gay stepfather may have forged a close bond with the children, and most courts do not recognize visitation rights for gay stepfathers (Patterson, 1994, 2003).

In yet another configuration, a single gay father may enter into a relationship after having adopted the child as a single man. Gay adoptive fathers complain about the difficulties of dating in a minority community that is not yet family-centered. They report that other gay men do not want to date them if they have children (Armesto, 2002). When a dating relationship actually begins, there are necessary adjustments all around: The father may initially be torn about entering into a relationship after having given so much of his focus and energy to the child up to this point; the child is not used to sharing the father with an outsider or additional parent; and the new stepfather may have to revise his expectations as he may never have envisioned himself dating a parent or becoming a parent himself (Bigner, 1996).

A few additional points must be mentioned in this discussion of parenting. First, gay fatherhood may stimulate a number of reactions with one's family of origin and extended family (Ritter & Terndrup, 2002). Sometimes the father's parents become welcoming, active grandparents, but other times the father's parents have not worked through their own internalized homophobia. The father's parents may love their gay son, but gay fatherhood may challenge long-standing religious or cultural beliefs. Gay fathers can feel confusion and deep disappointment when their parents do not feel the same level of excitement that they do. The very act of raising children may remind gay fathers of the loneliness, secrecy, and shame they experienced as children (Bigner, 1996).

Second, there are some gay families in which the gay father has either tested positive for the human immunodeficiency virus (HIV) or has an AIDS diagnosis (Shuster, 1996). This is not an uncommon situation for two reasons: Gay men continue to be heavily impacted by the AIDS epidemic, and many of the newer medications have made AIDS a more manageable disease, extending the lives of many who are infected (Chernin & Johnson, 2003). The father may have contracted the virus if he was seeking same-sex contacts in secrecy before he left the heterosexual marriage, or he may have contracted the virus after he left the marriage and started dating other men. It is also possible that a gay man with an HIV-positive diagnosis may decide that he wants to adopt children. Furthermore, there are situations where a father's new dating partner is HIV-positive. All of these situations require careful consideration of issues around disclosure of HIV-status to children (Kadushin, 2000).

Finally, diversity considerations must be taken into account with the treatment of every family and parenting issue. There is a dearth of research on diversity factors in gay male parenting within diverse cultures, although several writers (Ariel & McPherson, 2000; Armesto, 2002; Mays, Chatters, Cochran, & Mackness, 1998) remind counselors that sensitivity must be exercised before drawing broad conclusions about culturally diverse families. Armesto (2002) noted that culturally diverse gay fathers may feel further isolated from their cultures if they need to keep their same-sex attraction a secret due to cultural beliefs about homosexuality. This isolation may rob the gay family of nurturing experiences in the extended family and the ethnic community.

## CLINICAL IMPLICATIONS

As mentioned previously, the literature on gay fathers is sparse and dated. Most of the literature discusses divorced gay fathers who had children in the context of a heterosexual marriage and then came out, not gay men who first achieved a stable gay identity and then decided to have children. Furthermore, there is very little literature on empirically

supported approaches and interventions with gay fathers. Nevertheless, it is important to consider the clinical implications of the existing
literature and general directions for counseling with gay fathers. The
following discussion of clinical implications is supported by the literature and drawn from more than 18 years of working with gay men and
gay fathers across a variety of circumstances.

## General Implications

As a review of the literature has shown, gay fathers are a heterogeneous
group. They come to their parenthood in a number of different ways,
and their responses to the challenges of fathering are varied. However,
as discussed above, they choose to parent for reasons similar to those
stated by heterosexual parents—they want to create a continuous link
to the future and they want to nurture young life in the context of family and community. They sense that they have initiated a process that
is larger and more important than their own lives. They fulfill their
parenting responsibilities with the same purpose and dedication that
heterosexual parents do.

The literature is also clear that gay fathers face numerous challenges,
obstacles, and complications that heterosexual parents do not face. Gay
men often confront institutional homophobia, bureaucratic resistance,
and familial ignorance in their attempts to become parents and in their
efforts to raise children. It is a testament to the strength and resilience
of gay men that many are able to persevere and create safe, stable, and
loving homes for their children. It is clear, however, that the stress and
strain of such an endeavor in the face of societal prejudice can exact a
psychological price. Mental health providers who work with gay fathers
should recognize their clients' gifts and strengths but also monitor their
clients' reactions to prejudice and discrimination. Through treatment,
clients can find their voices and be sources of strength necessary to
champion their children. Clients can learn to identify and transform the
emotional and cognitive distortions that can interfere with free and loving attachments to their children. A caring and empowering counselor
may be the first person in the gay father's life who has listened to his
story and has expressed confidence that he can be an excellent parent.
This is a significant role for the counselor working with gay parents.

A corollary to this role clarification is the recognition that gay fathers
are not necessarily disturbed or disordered. Of course, there are some
gay fathers who have diagnosable conditions causing significant impair-
ment in their functioning, just as there are heterosexual fathers who
have mental disorders. Mental health providers must proceed in their
assessment of the client and family system without an expectation of
psychological illness. They should understand that a gay father's emotional confusion or poor judgment might be due in part to the pressures
of raising children in a dominant culture that continues to devalue his
right to parent. As a result, therapeutic approaches that help clients

identify their feelings, normalize their frustrations, validate their experiences, and commit to change are likely to be the most helpful. Therapeutic stances that are positive, affirming, inquisitive, active, and collaborative are more likely to be helpful than approaches that are neutral, distant, passive, and hierarchical, approaches that run the risk of replicating the client's alienation in a homophobic culture.

## Clinical Considerations

To provide the most informed, sensitive, and skilled interventions, counselors must perform a thorough assessment of the father's history and present situation. One of the first steps in this assessment is to learn about the father's family configuration. How was the family created, and who are the major figures in the father's current family constellation? When and how did the father decide to become a parent? Are there other families—divorced, extended, or created—that have an impact on the functioning of the father's current family? These are important questions to consider so that the mental health provider can proceed with a clear picture of the father's psychosocial development and current circumstances.

As part of the collaborative investigation into the client's history, it is important to gain an understanding of how the client negotiated developmental tasks in becoming a parent. How was this gay man able to arrive at the knowledge that he has as much right to be a father as anyone else? Has he come out, and, if so, what were the major markers of that experience? How much residual internalized shame remains, and how much shame has the client worked through? This last question is especially important, because a gay father's feelings of shame impact his relationship with himself, his child, and his partner, if he has one. Related to this question is the client's ability to integrate *gay-* and *father-*identities. What decisions has he made about disclosing his gay identity to the school- and parenting-systems with which he interacts? Has he been able to be himself and represent his parenting life to the larger gay community? How does he manage his multiminority status?

It is also important for the counselor to assess the client's interpersonal world. What are the patterns of interaction among family members— gay father and child, gay father and partner, child and gay stepfather, gay father and family-of-origin members, gay father and ex-wife, and so forth? What decisions has the client made about disclosure to others, including his child? If there is a new gay stepfamily, to what extent has the father welcomed and made a place for the gay stepfather? If the father is single, what does he think about dating and entering into a new relationship with a man, actions which will likely elicit reactions from his child? To what extent has the child accepted the father's gay identity?

As a final part of the assessment, the counselor must gain a clear understanding of the client's support system. On which nuclear family, extended family, and nonbiological alternative family members (e.g., close friends) is he able to depend? Does he have friends who are also gay fathers? Has he been able to find friends within the heterosexual parenting community? Has he been able to find and access support in the gay community? If he or his partner is HIV-positive, is he availing himself of the support offered by community organizations that help individuals and family members affected by this virus? Counselors may find the act of reviewing and discussing support systems is enough to help the gay father realize that he could use more help than he acknowledges.

As the counselor works through this assessment and begins treatment, the counselor should stay aware of the intersection of diversity and clinical considerations. Counselors must be careful not to assume that ethnically, culturally, and religiously different gay fathers will make the same choices or have the same worldviews as gay fathers from the majority culture. Some fathers from minority cultures may decide not to come out or they may choose to be very discreet with disclosures to their families. Counselors can help fathers decide which parts of their home cultures they want to retain and which parts of the larger dominant culture they want to adopt. For example, a Latino gay father may appreciate the value that his culture places on a close extended family, but he may also choose to involve his family occasionally in social events sponsored by parenting organizations in the larger White gay community. It is important for counselors to keep in mind that clients who identify with a minority cultural group have an additional identity to manage—that is, being a gay man and gay father in a non-White, ethnic community. Some clients may internalize prejudicial attitudes absorbed from messages in their minority cultures. Counselors are encouraged to work with gay fathers to examine internalized shame and to access ethnic community support for their unique family constellations.

## INTERVENTIONS

If one of the roles of the counselor is to be an active, affirming advocate for the health and strength of the gay father, then several themes provide the foundation for this work: (1) Counselors are encouraged to display patience with a client's process, understanding that change and self-acceptance after years of shame and self-doubt will not happen overnight; (2) counselors can confront client's self-defeating patterns of behavior; and (3) counselors should model congruence between internal feelings and external behavior. Based on clinical experience and the limited literature, this author suggests a partial list of interventions that can be helpful guideposts in the work with gay fathers.

*Help gay fathers identify internalized shame.* Shame, often a by-product of early and hurtful experiences, is insidious and far-reaching. Counselors should listen carefully for residual internalized homophobia in their clients' statements and call attention to self-hating statements from their clients such as, "I'm not like those other gays who go out to bars and only think about sex," or "I just don't want my children to feel sorry for me, because I've learned to live with my homosexuality," or "There's no need for my kids to see my friend and me kissing and hugging. Why should I shove my sexuality in their face?" Counselors can gently confront their gay father-clients to see that insistence on "normality" and protestations of "I'm just protecting the children" may really signal parts of themselves that are still ashamed of being gay. All gay men decide for themselves whether or not to come out, but to let such statements go unquestioned can be a disservice to the father by continuing to foster a fragmented self. Therapeutic silence also does a disservice, by extension, to the child, who must continue to live in a world of shadows, confusion, and fear.

*Help divorced gay fathers work through the loss and grief of not having certain experiences when they were younger men.* It is true that some gay fathers' psychosocial development does not match the trajectories of those who came out at younger ages. A gay father who comes out at 40 and now struggles through a painful divorce might have regret that he did not come out at a younger age. Mental health providers can help their clients see that everybody is on a different path, that life is not a race, and that what is important is that the father is learning how to live a congruent life *now,* for the benefit of his own growth as well as the growth of his children.

*Help clients work through guilt.* Not all guilt is inappropriate. A gay father might need to come to peace with himself by making amends to the people in his life who were affected by his earlier choices. It is important for a counselor to help the divorced gay father realize that in addition to the pain that his wife and children have experienced, he has been hurting too. Counselors can help their clients move forward with their lives by helping them gain an understanding of the circumstances that kept them closeted for many years.

*Confront self-destructive behavior.* Out of guilt, some fathers turn to alcohol, mood-altering substances, compulsive sexuality, unsafe sex, or other risky behaviors to punish themselves for the havoc they think they have created. Counselors can help clients see that such behavior prolongs the pain for the entire family.

*Help gay fathers see that they do not have to be perfect.* Many gay fathers are afraid to make a mistake, afraid that any slip-up may be used against them in future custody battles, or afraid that they will be compared to heterosexual parents and be judged as being inadequate or inferior. Many gay fathers do have to be vigilant for behavior that could be judged as inappropriate by ex-spouses or uninformed judges. But it is also important for gay fathers to realize that all parenting is imprecise— no one can do it perfectly. An insistence on perfection may be another way that the gay father is exhibiting internalized shame or penalizing himself out of guilt.

*Help gay fathers understand their fears.* Some fears may be based in reality, as in the example of a gay father who is aware that other children at his child's school may be engaging in bullying or threatening behavior. However, some fears come from a father's decision that "I must always be in control," "I can never let my guard down," and "I cannot let myself be vulnerable." A counselor can help a father learn confidence that he will be able to address most problems as a parent.

*Help gay fathers find the words to explain injustice and prejudice to their children.* To some extent, the gay father must run interference for his child until his child can do this on his or her own. However, it is also important for mental health providers to help fathers find the right words to educate the child but not scare the child. Fathers can learn to express confidence in their children. Fathers can help children know that there will always be loving people in their lives who will support them if they need help.

*Help gay fathers identify sources of strength within themselves.* Counselors can help their gay fathers develop pride in having a multiminority status. Or, to state this differently and more positively, counselors can help gay fathers feel proud of themselves and their membership in all the various communities of their lives, such as the parenting world and the gay male community.

*Help gay fathers identify sources of strength in the community.* Mental health providers can help gay fathers find gay community organizations that sponsor social events for gay, lesbian, bisexual, and transgender (GLBT) families, such as gay family bowling nights, or gay family picnics and softball tournaments. There are also excellent national support organizations with local chapters, such as Family Equality Council, Children of Lesbians and Gays Everywhere (COLAGE), and Parents and Friends of Lesbians and Gays (PFLAG).

*Help gay fathers decide how to come out to their children.* As mentioned previously, most children do better with planned disclosure, and most children handle the disclosure well. Counselors can help parents keep the message positive, reassuring, matter-of-fact, informative, developmentally appropriate, and above all, loving. Counselors can help parents see that their children are strong, too.

*Help gay fathers see that children have their own coming-out process.* In other words, some children, especially older preteens and adolescents, may need some extra time to process this disclosure. If the gay father took many years to come to an acceptance of his identity, it would be unrealistic to assume that a child would come to an immediate acceptance of this disclosure. This process may not necessarily be long, but children have rights, too. They have the right to take time to arrive at a genuine acceptance. Gay fathers should not misinterpret this process in a child as rejection.

*Help parents talk frankly with children.* Any question can be answered, but the answer and discussion must match the child's cognitive and emotional development.

*Help gay fathers steer away from compartmentalization and aim for integration.* The more that a gay father keeps important segments of his life hidden, the more he is teaching his children that there is something wrong with same-sex attraction. If the gay father leads a life that is mysterious, vague, anxious, and solitary, his children will likely experience confusion, hurt, and, perhaps, anger. Many children later ask their parents, "Why didn't you trust me enough to tell me?" or "No wonder I didn't like Bob [the name of the father's boyfriend]—you kept him hidden away, like there was something wrong with him. You would only let him in the house for minutes at a time, and I never really got to know him." For children to understand same-sex attraction, they need the opportunity to observe same-sex *affection.* Cutting off all demonstrations of affection between father and stepfather only serves to teach the child that gayness is bad, it is sick, and it must be managed carefully.

*Help HIV-positive gay fathers and stepfathers decide the best way to talk to their children about HIV-infection.* Again, children can tell when something is amiss. HIV-positive gay fathers and stepfathers can craft an explanation for their children that is informative, matter-of-fact, reassuring, and appropriate for a child's psychological development.

*Be a source of support for the gay stepfamily and help the father make a place for the gay stepfather.* Mental health providers can help the family locate organizations and resources for gay stepfamilies so that the family does not have to feel alone. For example, counselors can help clients locate gay family discussion groups, gay family therapy groups, and gay family social events.

*Help clients feel good about their identities as both a gay father and a proud member of another cultural or ethnic minority.* A counselor may be the only person in a client's life who is able to discuss and explore with the gay father the rewards and the stressors of a multiminority status, including the effects of such a status on the lives of his children. This is the power of narrative: People learn about their lives by telling stories about their lives, and, in doing so, they can decide if they want to write new stories by which to live.

## Treatment Modalities

In working with gay fathers, it is important to be flexible about treatment modalities and approaches as gay fathers may not always seek out individual treatment. Because gay fathers are often juggling multiple demands on time and resources, it may not be easy to find time for appointments. Some fathers may feel guilty carving out time just for themselves. Gay fathers may take care of everyone else's needs in the family before they take care of their own. Also, gay fathers may be reluctant to acknowledge stress from parenting, afraid that others will see it as proof that gay men do not have the maturity or emotional makeup to raise children. Asking for help may elicit feelings of shame or panic—"I should know how to do this," "Maybe having a child was a mistake," or "I'm in over my head." Gay fathers often find their way to counseling because of some crisis. It may be, to name a few, a coming-out crisis, an impending divorce, a break-up from a first relationship with another man, a relationship conflict between the father and a new dating partner, a child's difficulties in school, or a conflict within the gay stepfamily. If the crisis is more individual in nature, the father may have crossed a threshold of discomfort and be motivated to seek out treatment for himself. If the conflict lies between the gay parents, the father may be open to bringing his partner for couple's work. If the presenting issue revolves around a child's adjustment difficulties, the father may bring the child for individual or family counseling. If there is a stepfamily issue, the father may be motivated to bring the entire family for family counseling. It is most often the mental health provider who is called upon to assess the situation and make the most informed recommendations for the modality of treatment (i.e., individual, couple, or family therapy).

As a corollary, counselors will be more effective if they are flexible over time as to who "the client" is. Sometimes a father may need to do some individual exploration of sources of internalized shame. However, it may then be quite appropriate for the father to invite the stepfather for several couple's sessions to discuss how the father's new discoveries are affecting the relationship. In another example, an adolescent from a divorced family may need to talk with the counselor alone about his fear of accepting his new gay stepfather, afraid that this is a betrayal of his mother. However, it would be important after a period of time to bring in the gay father (and perhaps the mother and the mother's new partner) for a discussion of family dynamics. Of course, legal and ethical guidelines must always be observed, such as confidentiality, and there must always be clear discussions of what information can be shared with other members of the family. It is important to assess when clinical considerations and ethical guidelines necessitate referrals to a second mental health provider for couple or family counseling. The point of this discussion is that seemingly brilliant interventions proposed for a treatment plan may not be effective if the family's homeostasis is going to pull the gay father back to self-defeating behaviors. Couple and family counseling are powerful treatment modalities because they treat the familial system, allowing deeper and longer-lasting change to occur.

When possible, support groups for gay fathers can be an excellent source of therapeutic help. Groups provide universality of experience so that fathers do not feel alone. In-depth groups can help fathers identify intrapsychic barriers to same-sex parenting. Support groups can help fathers pool ideas and bolster each other's attempts to make changes. Groups for gay fathers and their partners can help the participants discuss the stresses of simultaneously raising children and maintaining intimacy in a relationship.

Finally, counselors should familiarize themselves with the gay father's larger world. Counselor referrals can include gay-affirmative lawyers, doctors, tutors, adoption agencies, and other professionals and paraprofessionals who can help the family. Counselors can reach out to schools, churches, synagogues, hospitals, and mental health agencies for purposes of building bridges and becoming available for consultation. Counselors can also contact gay community organizations and spearhead the development of resources and social groups for gay fathers.

## CASE EXAMPLE

Because there are many different types of gay families, it is impossible to present case examples illustrating all possible configurations. The following is one example of tensions within a gay stepfamily and the process by which family members sorted out their numerous challenges.

Tim, an advertising executive, and Luis, a hospital administrator, came to counseling because of an increased amount of anger and distancing at home. Tim, who is European American, and Luis, who is first-generation Mexican American, were the parents of Samantha, a 5 year-old multiracial daughter they had adopted at birth. Luis was also the father of Maria, an 11 year-old daughter whom he fathered in a previous heterosexual marriage that lasted 2 years. Luis came out to his ex-wife a year after Maria was born. The divorce was bitter and painful, not only for both parties, but also for the couple's families. Luis met Tim shortly after he divorced his wife, and Tim was his first committed relationship with a man. Luis saw Maria at least once a week, and Maria came to stay at Tim and Luis's house for a weekend once a month. Maria, for the most part, was accepting of her father's household, and she loved to play with her 5-year-old half-sister. Tim thought Maria had always been a little distant with him. Lately, Maria seemed be distancing herself from both Tim and Luis.

In counseling, it became clear that Luis was feeling guilty that he was not spending more time with Maria. He was realizing how many milestones he had missed in his first daughter's early years. As he watched Samantha grow older and enter kindergarten, he felt guilty that he had not been there on a daily basis to observe similar events in Maria's life. It also became clear that Luis' guilt was intensified by his parents' reaction to his life with Tim. Although his parents were always polite and hospitable to Tim and Samantha, he saw how they came alive when they spent time with Maria at larger family gatherings. With painful realization, he observed how his parents and extended family saw Maria as the true granddaughter, and how Samantha, who is half Asian, was not awarded the same legitimacy by Luis's traditional Mexican family.

In counseling, Tim also came to see that he was having feelings that were not being discussed. He made pointed statements that Luis was more worried about Maria than he was about Samantha. As the counselor probed these feelings, Tim was able to see that he had always felt on the outside of Luis's relationship with his first daughter. Although Maria was friendly to Tim, he always detected ambivalence in her. He was certain that Luis's first wife was disparaging of the gay fathers' household, and he bristled whenever Luis would defend his ex-wife. Tim came from a Midwestern family who were not forthcoming with their emotions. Tim acknowledged that it was difficult for him to tell Luis when he was sad, lonely, hurt, or afraid. As a result, Tim had started to pull away, and the couple had been having less sexual intimacy in the last year. Tim, who had had two serious relationships with men before he met Luis, had begun to harbor secret worries that this relationship might be in trouble.

In session, the counselor asked both men to begin to talk about the fears they were not expressing to each other. The counselor also helped both men see that feelings are not necessarily destructive and that the partner's response can begin the healing process. Luis began to explore his residual internalized homophobia, exacerbated by his parent's reaction to his new family and their lack of excitement with Samantha. He shared that a part of him still worried that maybe gay men were not supposed to be fathers. He cried as he talked about having thoughts that he failed one daughter by leaving his marriage, and now he was worried that he was about to fail his younger daughter as she grew older. Tim was greatly surprised and moved by these disclosures. He talked about how he saw Luis as an excellent father, both to Samantha and Maria, and how he actually felt jealous of Luis' natural way with children. Tim began to see that Maria's slight coolness over the years might be as much due to his lack of emotional spontaneity as it was from messages that she was receiving from her mother. Tim realized he had few models to emulate because his parents were not naturally demonstrative in their feelings.

The counselor was able to have the couple reflect on the impact of numerous circumstances on their relationship. As Tim increasingly interacted with parents from Samantha's school, he felt like an outsider among heterosexual parents. Although he had come out much earlier in his life than Luis, his interaction with these other parents reminded him of how he felt like an outsider much of his life. He was also able to express anger as he talked about other parents' reactions to him as a father of a multiracial daughter. Furthermore, Tim and Luis began to see that some of Maria's current distance might have nothing to do with them. She was entering adolescence. As she was beginning to experience new developmental challenges of her own, she was naturally pulling away from both fathers, sometimes out of shyness and self-consciousness. Two family sessions with the fathers and Maria gave the fathers an opportunity to talk about their love and support for Maria. It also gave Maria a chance to talk about how she did not always know how to explain her father's family configuration at school, fearing that such a disclosure could alienate new friends. The family brainstormed ways to talk to friends at school. The family readily committed to spending more time together. Maria and Luis were referred to a local COLAGE chapter, a support group for children with GLBT parents.

One family session with Luis's parents was more difficult. Luis' parents came to the session upon Luis' request, but the father was slightly removed from the proceedings, and the mother repeated several times that Maria needed a father in her life. Luis was able to find his voice and tell his parents that Maria did indeed have a father in her life, that she had a caring stepfather as well, and that the family was working to become closer. He told his parents that he loved them very much and that he needed their help right now, as he was learning how to raise a young daughter, Samantha, for the first time on a daily basis. He fought back tears as he talked about how strongly he wanted them to be a bigger part of Samantha's life.

The mother looked down at her hands and said that at first it was hard to accept Tim, but she could see now that Tim loved her son very much. But she also said that change was hard for her, and she did not know how many more changes she could accept. At this point Luis's father spoke up and said that Luis was his only son and that he was proud of what his son had accomplished here in America. He said that he would never turn his back on his son. The session ended with a renewed commitment to work toward greater family unity.

This case example illustrates the numerous possibilities in working with gay fathers. The lack of research into interventions with gay fathers results in mental health providers being true trailblazers, learning to advocate for their clients and helping to strengthen their clients' relationships. Counselors can help fathers deepen their bonds to children, partners, and families, while also helping fathers find solutions to daily occurrences of homophobia, heterosexism, and ethnocentrism. By honoring the experience of gay fathers, counselors honor the experience of fathers everywhere who work on a daily basis to manage multiple identities in a complex society.

# REFERENCES

Alderson, K. G. (2003). The ecological model of gay male identity. *The Canadian Journal of Human Sexuality, 12*(2), 75–85.

Allen, M., & Burrell, N. (1996). Comparing the impact of homosexual and heterosexual parents on children: Meta-analysis of existing research. *Journal of Homosexuality, 32*(2), 19–35.

Ariel, J., & McPherson, D. W. (2000). Therapy with lesbian and gay parents and their children. *Journal of Marital and Family Therapy, 26*(4), 421–432.

Armesto, J. C. (2002). Developmental and contextual factors that influence gay fathers' parental competence: A review of the literature. *Psychology of Men and Masculinity, 3*(2), 67–78.

Bepko, C., & Johnson, T. (2000). Gay and lesbian couples in therapy: Perspectives for the contemporary family therapist. *Journal of Marital and Family Therapy, 26*(4), 409–419.

Berkowitz, D., & Marsiglio, W. (2007). Gay men: Negotiating procreative, father, and family identities. *Journal of Marriage and Family, 69*(2), 366–381.

Bigner, J. J. (1996). Working with gay fathers: Developmental, post divorce parenting, and therapeutic issues. In J. Laird & R. J. Green (Eds.), *Lesbians and gays in couples and families* (pp. 370–403). San Francisco: Jossey-Bass.

Bigner, J. J., & Bozett, F. W. (1989). Parenting by gay fathers. *Marriage and Family Review, 14*(3–4), 155–175.

Bigner, J. J., & Jacobsen, R. B. (1989). Adult responses to child behavior and attitudes toward fathering: Gay and non-gay fathers. *Journal of Homosexuality, 23*(3), 99–112.

Bozett, F. W. (1981). Gay fathers: Evolution of the gay-father identity. *American Journal of Orthopsychiatry, 51*(3), 552–559.

Bozett, F. W. (1989). Gay fathers: A review of the literature. *Journal of Homosexuality, 18*, 37–159.

Canarelli, J., Cole, G., & Rizzuto, C. (1999). Attention vs. acceptance: Some dynamic issues in gay male development. *Gender & Psychoanalysis, 4*(1), 42–70.

Cass, V. C. (1979). Homosexual identity formation: A theoretical model. *Journal of Homosexuality, 4*(3), 219–235.

Chernin, J. N., & Johnson, M. R. (2003). *Affirmative psychotherapy and counseling for lesbians and gay men.* Thousand Oaks, CA: Sage.

Crosbie-Burnett, M., & Helmbrecht, L. (1993). A descriptive empirical study of gay male stepfamilies. *Family Relations, 42*(3), 256–262.

Garnets, L. D., & Kimmel, D. C. (2003). Relationships and families. In L. D. Garnets & D. C. Kimmel (Eds.), *Psychological perspectives on lesbian, gay, and bisexual experiences* (2nd ed., pp. 441–448). New York: Columbia University Press.

Goldenberg, H., & Goldenberg, I. (2002). *Counseling today's families* (4th ed.). Pacific Grove, CA: Brooks/Cole.

Johnson, S. M., & Connor, E. M. (2002). *The gay baby boom: The psychology of gay parenthood.* New York: New York University Press.

Kadushin, G. (2000). Family secrets: Disclosure of HIV status among gay men with HIV/AIDS to family of origin. *Social Work in Health Care, 30*(3), 1–17.

Kurdek, L. A. (1997). Relation between neuroticism and dimensions of relationship commitment. Evidence from gay, lesbian, and heterosexual couples. *Journal of Family Psychology, 11*(1), 109–124.

Mallon, G. P. (2000). Gay men and lesbians as adoptive parents. *Journal of Gay and Lesbian Social Services, 11*(4), 1–14.

Matthews, J. D., & Cramer, E. P. (2006). Envisaging the adoption process to strengthen gay- and lesbian-headed families: Recommendations for adoption professionals. *Child Welfare, 85*(2), 317–340.

Mays, V. M., Chatters, L. M., Cochran, S. D., & Mackness, J. (1998). African-American families in diversity: Gay men and lesbians as participants in family networks. *Journal of Comparative Family Studies, 29*(1), 73–87.

Miller, B. (1987). Counseling gay husbands and fathers. In F. W. Bozett (ed.), *Gay and lesbian parents* (pp. 175–187). New York: Praeger.

Okun, B. F. (1996). *Understanding diverse families.* New York: Guilford.

Patterson, C. J. (1994). Lesbian and gay couples considering parenthood: An agenda for research, service, and advocacy. *Journal of Gay and Lesbian Social Services, 1*(2), 33–35.

Patterson, C. J. (2003). Children of lesbian and gay parents. In L. D. Garnets & D. C. Kimmel (Eds.), *Psychological perspectives on lesbian, gay, and bisexual experiences* (2nd ed., pp. 497–548). New York: Columbia University Press.

Patterson, C. J. (2006). Children of lesbian and gay parents. *Current Directions in Psychological Science, 15*(5), 241–244.

Patterson, C. J., & Chan, R.W. (1996). Gay fathers and their children. In R. P. Cabaj & T. S. Stein (Eds.), *Textbook of homosexuality and mental health* (pp. 371–393). Washington, D. C.: American Psychiatric Press.

Ricketts, W., & Achtenberg, R. (1989). Adoption and foster parenting for lesbians and gay men: Creating new traditions in the family. *Marriage and Family Review, 14*(3–4), 83–118.

Ritter, K. Y., & Terndrup, A. I. (2002). *Handbook of affirmative therapy with lesbians and gay men.* New York: Guilford.

Schneider, R. (2005). Survey says... *Gay and Lesbian Review Worldwide, 12*(1), 17–21.

Shiller, V. M. (2007). Science and advocacy issues in research on children of gay and lesbian parents. *American Psychologist, 67*(7), 712–713.

Shuster, S. (1996). Families coping with HIV disease in gay fathers. In J. Laird and R. J. Green (Eds.), *Lesbians and gays in couples and families: A handbook for therapists* (pp. 404–419). San Francisco: Jossey-Bass.

Silverstein, L. B., Auerbach C. F., & Levant, R. F. (2002). Contemporary fathers reconstructing masculinity: Clinical implications of gender role strain. *Professional Psychology: Research and Practice, 33*(4), 361–369.

Silverstein, L. B., & Quartironi, B. (1996, Winter). Gay fathers. *Family Psychologist, 12,* 23–24.

# 13

# *Counseling Older Fathers*

RORY REMER, NEIL MASSOTH,
GWENDOLYN PUGH CRUMPTON,
CHEN Z. OREN, AND DORA CHASE OREN

Older fathers: Who are they? What are their roles and what are their needs? How do mental health providers effectively treat older fathers? Answering these questions is difficult because of the limited data on older fathers. Consequently, we extrapolated from what is known about fathering and grandfathering, relevant theories addressing both the internal and social experiences of older men, and salient issues of aging to formulate suggestions for conceptualizing and treating older fathers.

We begin this chapter by looking at how the U.S. government defines older fathers and the visibility of older fathers in our society. We then identify categories within the wide range of older fathers. A broader understanding of this population emerges when we examine underlying processes and roles of older men and specifically older fathers. After integrating recent gerontological literature on treating older men and gender-sensitive approaches, we suggest an approach for counseling older fathers. We conclude with a case study illustrating the approach.

## WHO ARE OLDER FATHERS?

Federal statistics indicate that in recent years the percentage of older fathers has been growing while the percentage of younger fathers has been declining. For example, in 2004 about 24 of every 1,000 men in the

United States aged 40–44 had fathered a child, and most of these men had become fathers for the first time. The fathering rate for this population represented an increase of almost 18% from the prior decade. By comparison, during the same time period the fatherhood rate for men aged 20 to 22 dropped 15% (Martin, Hamilton, Sutton et al., 2006).

The number of well-known men who had children during their middle and later stages of adulthood suggests the prevalence of older fatherhood. At the time of his death at age 71, the opera singer Luciano Pavarotti had a preschool-age daughter. Politicians running in the same presidential primary election (2008), including President Barack Obama, John Edwards, and John McCain, all had children after 40. Hugh Hefner fathered his fourth child at 65. James Doohan, who played Scotty in *Star Trek*, became father to his last child at 80.

While being an older father is relatively common, little has been said in the literature about this population. What is known about the millions of older fathers in the United States? To add clarity to the clinical consideration of this large and diverse population, we begin our discussion by identifying different types of older fathers.

## TYPES OF OLDER FATHERS

We have elected to take a broad view of older fathers. For this discussion, an older father is not limited to designate a man who had his children later in life. For our discussion, an older father is a man who is older and has children. As such, numerous categories emerge to identify different groups of older fathers.

### *Early Onset Fathers*

*Early onset father* refers to a man who had his children prior to age 40. While not meeting the federal definition of an older father, we believe that a discussion of counseling older fathers appropriately includes this large group of men. For these men, fatherhood is a continuous process starting at the birth of the first child and continuing across their life spans. These men experience both the joys and challenges of being fathers throughout the different stages of their lives. These fathers are likely to become grandfathers at a relatively young age and to be involved in multigenerational roles as fathers and grandfathers.

*David: early onset father.* David is a 65-year-old father of three (all of whom were sired in his 20s) and grandfather of eight. He has been married for 42 years. In session, David expresses the deep meaning of his children and grandchildren to him. He also talks about significant challenges he has faced and currently faces as a father. He retired 7 years ago. David and his wife make it a priority to carve out time to be with their family, often taking trips with various grandchildren. Within the family, David focuses on transferring his religious and traditional values to his children and grandchildren, perceiving himself both as a role model and a historian for the family.

## Late Onset Fathers

*Late onset fathers* are the post-40 group who married late, married and divorced without children and then remarried, or married early but postponed beginning a family. Subsequently, these fathers were over 40 when they had their children. Late onset fathers are less likely to know their grandchildren. The population trends suggest that fathers may be waiting longer to have children as they pursue career goals.

*Chris: late onset father.* Chris became a first-time father at 42. His 20s were focused on education. He obtained a Ph.D. in the natural sciences, served a postdoctoral fellowship, and began his career. Much of his time during his early 30s was focused on building his career. He dated extensively and had two serious relationships, neither of which resulted in marriage. He described his social life during his 30s as "living life to its fullest." He met his soon-to-be wife at 38, married at 40, and had his first child 2 years later. Chris stated, "I began to have children when I was ready to have children. Children were not on my screen until after I was 40. Thank God I had options that were not available to my parents. They were pressured to be married and to have kids by the time they were 25." To add emphasis, he stated, "I think that today's generations want to have children at a later age just as much as people in the past did. I think that people in the past probably wished that they could have waited until they were older." When asked about his experience of being an older father as compared to a younger father, Chris made reference to having more time (with his career well established), having more money, and being more tolerant.

## Second-Time Fathers

*Second-time fathers* are those who married once, had children while younger, and then purposely decided to or inadvertently became a father again when the initial children were older. This type of fathering, or "refathering," is thought to be less common, but the data are not available for this population.

*Howard: Second-time father.* Howard became a father at 24 and again at 28. When his children were in their teens, he and his wife decided to start a "second family." They had two more children after his 40th birthday. Howard died at age 83, having suffered a head injury from a fall off a ladder at work. At the time of his death, his children were 59, 55, 38, and 36 years old; he had 12 grandchildren and 2 great-grandchildren.

With just six years in age separating his youngest child and oldest grandchild, many activities included both generations. Sunday hikes with his younger children and all grandchildren were common. References to being an older father were dismissed. When his first generation of children (both boys) were adolescents, he was a vibrant, healthy man in his 30s who coached and played sports with his sons. As he grew older, he became involved with religious and charitable pursuits with his family, often volunteering his time at church. Howard is a typical second-time father in that much of his life was focused on family. For Howard, having a second family was simply a continuation of who he was and what he wanted to be. While there was no midlife crisis, there was a midlife awakening. Howard stated on many occasions that his desire to have a second family came from a realization that he enjoyed raising children and had no desire to be done with this task when in his early 40s.

## *Remarried Second-Time Fathers*

Remarried second-time fathers are those who had children from a prior marriage or marriages and began a second (or more) family later in life. This type of refathering has become more common as divorce and remarriage have become more ordinary.

*Jeffrey: Remarried second-time father.* Jeffrey was married in his early 20s, had two children, and divorced when his children were adolescents. He remarried when he was 47, and his daughter was born soon afterward. He states, with laughter, that "she only recently did the math and realized that she was kind of at the wedding." Jeffrey states that the wedding was planned before the pregnancy and their lack of contraception care was purposeful. His wife, 15 years his junior, was anxious to have a child quickly, primarily "because she was concerned about whether I could raise a child much longer." Now at 67, Jeffrey has a daughter who recently began college. The financial responsibility of her education is preventing him from cutting back on work or retiring. He states, "I wish that I could put away more money for retirement. College is expensive." But Jeffrey says that he has no regrets about his second family. Both of the children from his first marriage are married. Jeffrey has four grandchildren. He says, "I didn't mind being a little older than the other fathers. I've always been in good shape; I even coached my daughter's soccer team." He expressed that neither he nor his daughter minded an incident when another teammate made reference to "your grandpa" when referring to him. Jeffrey joked that "it was not a reflection on any lack of energy; being bald does have some drawbacks."

## *Continuous Fathering*

*Continuous fathering* refers to fathers who have children in a fairly regular pattern from their 20s through their 40s or later. Consequently, these fathers tend to have large families, to know their grandchildren, and to manage multigenerational roles.

*Paul: Continuous fatherhood.* Paul, the father of four, has had children consistently over a 13-year period. Married at age 29, he had his first child when he was 32 and the other children when he was 36, 41, and 45. He reports that he and his wife considered having a fifth child, but she was 40 when the fourth child was born and they had decided to "close shop" by the time she reached this age.

Paul was 51 at the time he was interviewed and stated that he did have "a bit less energy" for the demands of being a father to a 6-year-old. While asserting that his children are not short-changed because of his age, he stated that "my back feels it when I pick him up" (referring to his 6-year-old son). Paul mentioned that the major disadvantage of being an older father is having older parents. At age 51, his children range from 6 to 19 years old, and his parents are in their 70s and in poor health. "I don't know what we would do if my wife's parents were sick. There are only 24 hours in a day, and we are filling 28 of the 24 now." He does feel what he refers to as split demands of the two generations. While stating that he has "not one regret" about having children after 40, he worries about the impact on his children as he becomes old.

## DEVELOPMENT OF OLDER FATHERS

An understanding of the underlying processes of older fathers is appropriate when considering how to provide effective clinical work. Erikson's model of psychosocial development has proved useful and been widely employed for years (e.g., Westermeyer, 2004). Erikson described eight psychosocial stages (also called tasks or challenges) that span across life. Successful resolution of the specific demands of each stage is necessary for healthy development.

Erikson's theory suggests that older fathers are situated in one of two stages, generativity versus stagnation (approximately ages 40–65) or ego integrity versus despair, the final stage. In the first of these stages, generativity is characterized by the "concern in establishing and guiding the next generation..." (Erikson, 1963, p. 267). Not only does generative fathering meet the needs of men in this stage, but also largely defines it. Generative fathering is "a non-deficit perspective of fathering rooted in the proposed ethical obligation for fathers to meet the needs of the next generation" (Dollahite & Hawkins, 1998, p. 110). Pleban and Diez (2007) proposed that fathers demonstrate generative fathering by taking on the roles of protecting their children against risky behaviors, nurturing relationships with their children, promoting the prosocial behavior of their children, and fostering the personal mastery of their children. When fathers take on these roles, they demonstrate the characteristics of commitment, respect, the ability to listen, empathy, problem solving, flexibility, and openness. The mere fact of having or even wanting children does not guarantee a successful resolution of this stage. The unsuccessful resolution of this crisis can be seen in a "pervading sense of stagnation and personal impoverishment" (Erikson, 1963, p. 267). Stagnation brings a sense of self-absorption and self-indulgence. Adults in this stage feel little connection to others and generally offer little to society.

As older fathers age, they enter into what Erikson described as the last stage of psychosocial development, ego integrity versus despair. In this stage, people look back over their lives and resolve their final identity crisis. Acceptance of accomplishments, failures, and ultimate limitations brings with it a sense of integrity, or wholeness. Erikson noted that ego integrity "is the acceptance of one's one and only life cycle as something that had to be and that, by necessity, permitted no substitutions" (1963, p. 268). The finality of death must also be faced and accepted. A lack of ego integrity creates despair. The older adult who does not experience ego integrity knows that "time is now short, too short for the attempt to start another life..." (Erikson, 1963, p. 269).

Jung (1933) observed a tendency for men and women to become more androgynous during the second half of life. He postulated that men may become more likely to build close family ties. Older fathers tend to be more involved in child rearing and to be more nurturing (Parke, 2000). The increased financial security older men experience allows more time and money for themselves and their families, creating opportunities for generative fathering.

These ideas of developmental trends are supported by observing the roles of older fathers, the functions the roles serve, and their associated behaviors. At the broadest level, people define roles for themselves and for others. In this instance, an older father minimally has the roles of older man and father (and likely a host of others including spouse, historian, role model, nurturer, etc.). Expectations from self and others are formed about the roles that are played. Roles are subtly encouraged and are judged for their acceptability and functionality. Finally, people act within the roles they adopt. Biddle's (1979) role theory suggests the difficulty in capturing the "essence" of being a father while recognizing the increasing complexity of fathers' roles over time. For example, physical limitations due to aging often change the norms of how a father plays with his children. Also, the roles filled by older fathers in fostering and aiding the development of their children are impacted by their own engagement in the challenges of maturing.

We looked at the literature both on fathers and on grandfathers for an indication of typical roles of older fathers. However, while some roles and functions may be limited by age (e.g., being able to participate in a particular physical activity with children), more are consistent across the age spans. However, the way these roles are approached may significantly change with the growing intricacy of self gained through life experiences and maturation.

## ROLES OF OLDER FATHERS

Whereas some fathering roles are consistent through the life span (e.g. provider, disciplinarian), older fathers hold unique roles and may perceive, experience, and express some of the roles they share with younger fathers in different ways. Some of these differences are related to the developmental stages and broader experiences of older fathers. The list of roles and functions fathers manifest is both numerous and diverse (e.g., Bouchard, Lee, Asgary, & Pelletier, 2007; Bronte-Tinkew, Carrano, & Guzman, 2006; Findley & Schwartz, 2004, 2006; Masciadrelli, Pleck, & Stueve, 2006; Schwartz & Findley, 2006). The focus of this section is to highlight some of the different roles identified by the literature on older fathers and grandfathers. Awareness of these roles can guide mental health providers' understanding, conceptualization, and treatment of older fathers.

The provider role is a common role to all fathers regardless of age and remains a major role throughout a father's life (Russell, 1986; Spitze & Logan, 1992; Thomas, 1994). Most fathers, like most men, have been socialized from a young age to provide for their families (Turk-Charles, Rose, & Gatz, 1996). Consistently, the capacity to provide for one's family and children was predictive of quality of life and self-esteem during the senior years for African American fathers (Bowman & Sanders, 1998). Spitze and Logan (1992) found that children of older parents still received much assistance from their fathers and mothers. Gender mediates the type of help older fathers offer to their children and grandchildren. Thomas (1994) noted that grandfathers tend to provide more financial support and career guidance, and grandmothers provide emotional and interpersonal support. Fathers tend to assist in more traditional gender-related help such as repair and yard work.

The findings about older fathers' roles suggest that the shifts in gender roles in the last 30 years where fathers are expected not only to provide, protect, and discipline their children but also to nurture, provide moral support, and serve as role models (Barrows, 2004; Coley, 2001; Jain, Belsky, & Crnic, 1996; Marsiglio, Day, & Lamb, 2000) are true across generations. In 1997, older fathers accepted and embraced more the nurturing role and involvement with their children than did older fathers in 1971 (Taylor, Giarrusso, Feng, & Bengston, 2006). Thus, older fathers and grandfathers can experience increased stress, joy, conflict, and growth from the expansion of their paternal roles. Thomas (1994) illustrated that the current increasingly active role of grandparents corresponds to the increased rates of divorce and single-parent families. The literature on grandfathers provides age-sensitive awareness for appropriate clinical work with older fathers because both populations are older men. As such, an understanding of what is known about this subpopulation of same-aged men informs our work with older fathers.

Taylor (2007) proposed a set of overlapping roles that grandfathers fill, including the family historian, mentor and teacher, nurturer of emotional and physical well-being, role model, and playmate. In particular, the family historian role is unique both to grandfathers and older fathers and shapes children's sense of kinship and heritage. Educating, mentoring, and serving as role models through older fathers' and grandfathers' extensive life experiences are satisfying for the older man and of significant benefit for the children and grandchildren (Dudley & Stone, 2001; Pleban & Diez, 2007; Taylor, 2007). Moreover, grandfathers often mediate between children and parents regarding transgenerational values that are important to the continuity and identity of the family (Taylor). Grandfathers take the role of transferring wisdom by providing grandchildren with special skills and knowledge. Congruently, grandfathers see themselves as mentors who believe it is their role to teach their grandchildren values. Russell (1986) noted how grandfathers give high priority both to supporting their adult children socially and financially and to being available to give advice when worldly problems arise. Clinically significant, grandfathers often find themselves negotiating the balance of multiple roles. Their increased financial support of and involvement in the daily lives of their children and grandchildren persist through times of illness, divorce, and other family crises.

One of the important roles in older fathers' lives is helping their children move toward adulthood and life transitions (e.g., attending college, establishing a career, getting married). Grandfathers seem to be instrumental in helping their grandchildren transition into adulthood (Dudley & Stone, 2001). Older fathers see their role in this stage as providing practical help such as financial and moral support, advice, and shelter (Thomas, 1994). Overall, older fathers seem to be successful in this role and perceive the "launching period" as a neutral or positive stage in their lives. Whereas both fathers and mothers seem to be prepared for this step, fathers are more excited about entering into this new parenting stage than are mothers.

Older fathers and grandfathers who are able to engage successfully in these roles, to manage the conflicts between the different roles, and to be involved with their young and older children and grandchildren report significant benefits. Altfeld (1995) demonstrated that the quality of father-child relationships predicted father-child contact during a father's later years, suggesting the importance of aiding older fathers in establishing meaningful relationships with their children. Thomas (1994) reported that grandfathers' focus on their grandfathering role was associated with positive life satisfaction and morale. Taylor et al. (2006) suggested that fathers experience continuous emotional connection and shared values, as well as increased paternal satisfaction with their children, as both the fathers and children age.

Hays (1996) highlighted the importance of identifying and working with older clients' strengths. The author noted "sense of humor, personal pride, good social skills, helpful cultural beliefs, knowledge in certain areas, artistic abilities, or religious faith" (p. 192) as some possible strengths of older clients. Sprenkel (1999) added that older men's strengths include ability and courage to adapt and cope with challenging situations. Further, Hays suggested helping older clients connect with past experiences of survival through their rich lives and using the strengths and coping skills developed in survival for solving current issues. Many of the strengths identified by Hays (e.g., sense of humor, pride, and survival) were also described as strengths and characteristics of men (Kiselica, Englar-Carlson, Horne, & Fisher, 2008; Levant, 1995). Thus, we recommend for mental health providers to use older fathers' strengths as a tool to assist older fathers in adjusting to new life and paternal transitions as well as their roles as fathers and grandfathers.

The complexity of experiences and feelings integrated in the breadth of older fathers' lives should be understood and honored by mental health providers. Significantly, most of the literature on the roles of older fathers focuses on White fathers. The roles and experiences of older fathers are as diverse as older fathers themselves. As such, the roles, their functions, and the associated thoughts, feelings, and behaviors will be unique to each client. Understanding the impact of these issues on older fathers and on their relationships with their families is foundational to developing effective treatment.

## CLINICAL CONSIDERATIONS OF OLDER FATHERS

The American Psychological Association (APA, 2004) recognized both the growing need for effective treatment and interventions with older clients and the lack of current training for psychologists and other mental health providers to work with older adults. The resulting APA guidelines (Guidelines for Psychological Practice with Older Adults) identified six areas for practitioners to be aware of when working with older adults: attitudes; general knowledge about adult development, aging, and older adults; clinical issues; assessment; interventions, consultation, and other service provision; and education. In the following discussion of clinical considerations and treatment with older fathers, the literature on gender-sensitive counseling, gerontology, and older fathers and grandfathers will be integrated with the APA guidelines for working with older adults to provide suggestions for appropriate interventions.

Older adults can make significant progress toward mental health when they engage in counseling. Older adults are typically defined as 65 years and older with subgroups (representing different experiences) of ages 65–75, 75–85, and 85 and older (APA, 1998). When "older fathers" includes fathers over 40, the differences in age, developmental stage, and roles are more pronounced. However, men at all ages seek less counseling than women (Addis & Mahalik, 2003). Older men hold negative attitudes and expectations about counseling; and the older the man is, the more negative attitudes he may have about getting help (Lagana, 1995). Older adults, including older fathers, are often referred to therapy by a third party (e.g., general practitioner for depression). One of the first clinical considerations to address with older fathers is what brought them to counseling. It is important to assess an older father's motivation and expectation of treatment.

While it is standard of care to refer all clients for a full physical evaluation, it is even more critical to do so on a regular basis with older fathers because physical symptoms in older age can mimic symptoms of psychological disorders (Kaye & Critteneden, 2005). As indicated, initial counseling considerations include referrals to and consultations with an older father's physician, psychiatrist, or other health-care provider.

As suggested by the range of older fathers' roles, salient issues include retirement, social network and support, caregiving, sexuality changes and challenges, physical health changes, loss of spouse, substance abuse, depression and suicide, victimization, and economic status (Kaye & Crittenden, 2005; Kosberg & Kaye, 1997; Turk-Charles et al., 1996). Although it is beyond the scope of this chapter to examine all of these areas, we will highlight retirement, social network, and caregiving as three issues that are significant to older fathers and valuable to explore during treatment.

The data on the impact of the transition to retirement are conflicting as some studies suggest that retirement is a positive process while other studies describe it as a negative experience for older men (Monk, 1997). For older fathers, retirement is associated with increased time spent with their children (Taylor et al., 2006). Krause and Haverkamp (1996) suggested that a decline in previous life roles, such as work due to retirement, can increase an older father's involvement and interaction with his children. The transition to later adulthood and retirement enables fathers to shift attention from themselves and the provider role to focusing on their relationships with their children and grandchildren (Bozett, 1985).

Szinovacz and Davey (2001) looked at the effects of parents' retirement on their contacts with their children and found that although mothers decrease visits, fathers increase their frequency of visits with their children. Fathers' nurturing role, which may have been in conflict with the provider role, can increase due to the decrease of the working role. Thus, where retirement can be a time of loss and confusion, especially for older men who have internalized the singularity of the provider role (Kaye & Crittenden, 2005), being a father can serve as a protective variable and helps older fathers adapt to the transition out of work.

Related to retirement is the concept of social network. Turk-Charles et al. (1996) noted that for older adults social support is positively associated with increased health, psychological well-being, and length of life. Most older men are married, whereas most older women are not. Older men tend to rely more on their spouses for support, and older women tend to have a broader and more varied social support network (Kaye & Crittenden, 2005). Thomas (1994) suggested that despite strong feelings of affection for their offspring, older fathers' gender socialization can mediate their contact with their children. They are less likely to reside with their children and are satisfied with supporting their children, but do not like to count on receiving support from them. Thus, older men have less social support, less contact with children and grandchildren, and fewer male friends, yet report high satisfaction and indicate that their needs are met by their wives (Turk-Charles et al., 1996). Therefore, loss of a spouse may be critical to older fathers who receive most of their support and basic needs from their wives.

Kaye and Crittenden (2005) suggested that older men cope with loss of spouse with intellectualization, problem solving, and physical activities, strategies congruent with traditional male socialization. Mental health providers should familiarize themselves with masculine roles and patterns so they can identify internalized roles that may prevent older fathers from accessing their social network to seek support and care from their children. Older men prefer family over friends for support (Turk-Charles et al., 1996).

Because women provide the majority of care to older family members and experience more caregiving burden (Turk-Charles et al., 1996), men historically have been left out of the caregiving literature (Kaye & Crittenden, 2005). Kaye reported that many older men provide primary caregiving, mostly to their spouses, and perform a variety of caregiving tasks. Further, older fathers are more likely to provide care to their parents than to receive care from their older adult children (Kaye, 1997; Thomas, 1994). In general, older fathers tend both to provide and to receive more advice and financial care rather than emotional and nurturing care (Thomas). Overall, older men tend to receive less care than older women (Spitze & Logan, 1992). At the same time, because older men and fathers are not accustomed to the caregiving role, receive less social support, and are not aware of alternative resources, they report increased emotional stress (Kaye) and psychological disorders such as depression and substance abuse (Kaye & Crittenden).

It is also important for mental health providers to assess the grief that older fathers experience. Not only do older fathers experience loss of loved ones (e.g. deaths of parents, friends) as they age, but also lose aspects of self-identity through life transitions (e.g., retirement, empty nest) and the resulting loss of roles (e.g., businessman, coach).

We suggest that counselors process with older fathers the different roles they have had during their lives. As roles are identified, the counselor and client can examine these roles and assess how the roles helped older fathers achieve their goals, or, conversely, interfered with their ability to meet their goals. How did their roles change over time? Are the roles limited, or do they exclude other important roles that the older father may want to integrate? What roles were satisfying? What roles were more difficult? The goal of a review of roles is to help older fathers adjust to their current situation and, if needed, expand their current roles to benefit both themselves and their children. Educating older fathers about the impact of the roles on their involvement and relationships with their children as well as the meaning of the roles on their own lives as fathers is an important intervention. In fact, older adults benefit from psychoeducation (APA, 1998). The use of direct therapy, such as problem solving and psychoeducation (Fagan & Hawkins, 2001; Levine & Pitt, 1995), has been suggested as an effective and gender-sensitive intervention with fathers. It is worthy to note that all interventions must be appropriately matched to symptoms and/or the reasons that a client sought treatment.

Counseling Fathers

Both APA (1998) and Kaye and Crittenden (2005) suggested using the life review intervention with older men to facilitate a meaningful evaluation of past life events and explore new roles and activities, or adjust old roles to be more meaningful. Based on Erikson's final psychosocial stage, integrity versus despair, life review is a therapeutic intervention used by many gerontologists to help older clients reflect on significant aspects of their lives (Kaye & Crittenden, 2005). Integration of new or modified roles into older men's lives can help with resolutions of old conflicts and increase both current and future well-being.

Paternal roles and involvement of older fathers with their children and/or grandchildren throughout their lives should be reviewed in the context of the current definition of father involvement: *engagement, accessibility,* and *responsibility* (Lamb, Pleck, Charnov, & Levine, 1987; see Oren et al., this book). It is important to note that this life review should be adjusted to the father's age and the type of older father as discussed earlier in this chapter. Older fathers differ from younger fathers in energy levels and health, educational and occupational roles, frequency of play, play styles, responsiveness, and affection (Neville & Parke, 1997; Parke, 1995). Parke (2000) noted the importance of the point in time when a man becomes a father. For example, an early onset older father, like David, has been a father for many more years and likely has more roles to review and adjust to with adult children and grandchildren than Jeffrey, a remarried second-time father, who cannot cut back or retire. In each case, the different types of fathering roles can be discussed and balanced out in the context of the older father's presenting problem, goals, and role conflict.

Social expectations help older men understand their expected roles (Kaye & Crittenden, 2005). Identity theory, one type of role theory, suggests that fathers who see their role as a father as important tend to be more satisfied with fathering (Taylor et al., 2006). In treatment, it is important for mental health providers to be aware of their own biases and expectations of older fathers.

Kaye and Crittenden (2005) suggested that male-friendly interventions for older men include task-oriented activities; physical expression; structured, routine expression of emotion; goal setting and attainment; and mental engagement. These interventions take into account traditional male values and help men feel involved and in control of their treatment by utilizing structured activities and capitalizing on men's strengths. Thus, these interventions lend themselves well to working with older fathers.

Lagana (1995) suggested using family, physicians, and other external resources, such as the media, both to increase positive attitudes of older adults toward counseling and to facilitate referrals to and collaboration with treatment. Mental health providers can make their services known to physicians, other external sources (e.g. church, synagogue), and the broader community to inform older fathers of services available for them.

Finally, groups for older men have been suggested as effective interventions and strategies to help older men (Kaye & Crittenden, 2005; Sprenkel, 1999). Sprenkel stated that individual counseling can help older men work on their intrapsychic experiences, and group counseling can provide older men a social avenue for examining aging, loss of roles, and life transitions. Some of the goals of older men's groups identified by Sprenkel include exploration of the impact of aging on men's self-identity and self-esteem, discussion of nonreversible losses, and assistance in modifying future expectations in a realistic manner to improve emotional well-being. Kaye and Crittenden support the effectiveness of groups in reducing older men's stress (specifically, caregiving burden), increasing emotional well-being, and decreasing social isolation. With minor adjustments, groups can be modified to integrate older fathers' roles and experiences into older men's support groups. Although some support groups have been suggested as primary interventions for fathers (e.g., African American fathers; Franklin & Davis, 2001), there is need for more groups that address fathers across the life span (e.g., fathers of adult children, older fathers with young children). Mental health providers should be aware of the benefits of group counseling for older fathers and either offer these groups or provide referrals to other professionals who offer such services.

In the following section, a case example will illustrate how the counseling considerations and interventions we suggested are being used to work with an older father.

## CASE ILLUSTRATION

One of the authors of this chapter obtained permission from a current client, an older father, to use his story. For that, we are deeply grateful. As with any vignette that discusses and summarizes particular issues, other important pieces are left out. The particular client of this case example has been seen for over a year and a half. While some of the work has focused on his changing role as father and on his own father and stepfather, much of the work in session has centered on his role as a man, a partner, a son, and a businessman. Fatherhood is only a piece of a man's life, but a piece that should not be ignored. Exploration of father issues tapped into deeper and broader areas of self-identity. As you read this case example, we encourage you to think about your perspective of Mark's presenting problems and how you would work with him.

## DEMOGRAPHICS

Mark (pseudonym) is a 52-year-old White Jewish male and father to twin girls, Emily and Erica, who are 6 years old; he is separated from their mother. Mark is a late onset older father. Mark was raised by his mother and stepfather. Mark's mother divorced his biological father when Mark was a baby. When Mark was young, his mother told his biological father that it was better if Mark did not know him. At age 4, he met his biological father, who was introduced to Mark as his uncle. As an adult, Mark met his biological father for the first time when he was 24. Mark discovered that although his biological father wanted to be involved in his life, he had complied with Mark's mother's request. Mark described his biological father as outgoing, free-spirited, and successful. He noted that he has great social skills, is pleasure seeking, and tends to deal with consequences after the fact, such as in the case with Mark's birth. Conversely, Mark described his stepfather as passive and introverted. Mark's mother made most of the decisions at home. Further, Mark's stepfather did not express much feeling and demonstrated symptoms of depression.

I began seen Mark about 18 months ago. Mark's age situated him in the generativity versus stagnation stage. Congruently, Mark experienced stagnation in many aspects of his life. He demonstrated difficulty identifying and expressing his emotions. He reported feeling numb since separating from his partner. He perceived himself as functioning socially and in his job at about 50% of his potential. For example, Mark felt uncomfortable in social situations including going to the gym; his dating life consisted of many first dates; and he lacked the motivation and courage to initiate new business connections despite knowing the potential for success. Mark did not like to create waves, exhibited external locus of control (thinking that others' thoughts, needs, decisions, and feelings trumped his), and thought poorly of himself.

Mark used a football analogy to describe his life. He saw his life before entering therapy as standing on the sidelines (like his stepfather) and observing his family and his life from the outside, but not being an active participant. He reported seeing his father go through a personal transformation by attending therapy. Mark felt that he was left alone on the sidelines where his father had entered the game and left Mark behind. Mark was motivated to go through a similar transformation. As with many older men and older fathers, Mark saw therapy as a last chance to change his life.

Mark's initials goals included increasing self-awareness, decreasing anxiety stemming from a low sense of safety, increasing emotional expression to cope with his numbness, increasing self-confidence, increasing social skills and social support, and being a good father. Mark was concerned that he would be passive with his kids, as both his father and his stepfather were with him. Later in therapy, he realized that unconsciously he feared he would be forced out of his children's lives by his ex-partner in the same way his biological father was forced out of his life by his mother.

*Treatment Summary.* Mark presented himself as friendly and open to feedback. He was willing to change and to learn about himself and his life. He was curious about himself and the counseling process. He used his high intellectual ability and analysis skills to process new information and apply it to his life. Mark developed trust toward me, the counseling process, and different types of interventions, including interventions geared to increase his emotional expression and regulation. Mark's ability to trust was a strength that I later used to help him generalize to other social and family situations. Mark has been an engaging client to work with, demonstrating a high level of awareness and enabling deep work. He reflects on and processes the information discussed in session, applies much of the feedback, and gains awareness toward meeting his goals. Gender-sensitive counseling, an awareness of his developmental stage, working with his strengths, and looking at his roles are some of the important principles described in this chapter that guide the counseling experience with Mark.

*Gender-sensitive counseling.* In the initial stage and throughout counseling, Mark's gender socialization and experiences from his childhood as a boy have shaped his sense of self-efficacy as an older father (a more detailed description of Mark's developmental milestone that relate to gender socialization will be discussed later). Mark's seeking help and his decision to attend counseling were explored and processed as a strength from the initial session. Mark noted that being a father was an important motivating factor in seeking both physical and mental help. Mark reported visiting his physician when needed and did so a couple times throughout our work together. When Mark experienced dysphoric mood, he consulted his physician, who adjusted his thyroid medication. This ability to address his needs was an important realization for Mark as he learned to distinguish between depressed state due to emotional triggers and depressed mood due to physical conditions. Seeking regular physical evaluations will be important for Mark because he wants to lead a healthy life to be able to witness his daughters go through their own milestones.

Different modalities and interventions discussed as effective treatment with men and fathers, such as Cognitive-Behavioral Therapy (CBT) and imagery, empty chair to practice asserting needs and feelings to others, role-plays, and role review, were used throughout the sessions. Analogies related to cars, the stock market, and a football field were utilized to speak Mark's language and normalize his increased ability to experience and express feelings.

*Utilizing strengths.* Based on Hays' (1996) suggestion to identify and work with older clients' strengths, Mark's strengths were identified and used from the initial stage of counseling and throughout the process. Helping Mark identify his strengths was important in challenging Mark's diminished self-concept. For example, even when he felt numb, his commitment to his daughters was evident. He would come home, spend time with his daughters, and help with daily tasks. Before coming to therapy, Mark did not recognize that his behaviors reflected strong commitment to his daughters. Mark learned to apply his strengths to promote changes he wanted in his life, including changing his role as father. Some of the strengths identified in counseling included Mark's ability to apply and generalize information to many aspects of his life, consultation and teaching skills (used with his daughters), ability to recover emotionally and move on, problem-solving skills, being patient and open to feedback, sacrificing his own needs, and being committed. Further, Mark's ability to see the big picture, demonstrate patience and flexibility, and creatively problem solve were internalized into Mark's parenting skills. These strengths were integral parts of counseling.

In one session, Mark described activities and games he thought of to spend quality time with his daughters during drives and dinners. For example, he and his daughters put food in their mouths and say long, difficult words, such as "abracadabra." He reports that the activity meets a few goals as "they finish the food, we have fun and laugh, and they learn new and complicated words." Another example related to being creative and staying calm relates to an incident when his ex-partner was concerned that the girls would not want to leave after spending time at his house. Without much thought, Mark called out, "the first to the car wins" and reported that, to his ex-partner's surprise, "twenty seconds later they are both sitting in the car ready to go." Throughout counseling, Mark's hidden strengths were identified in different aspects of his life and helped increase Mark's self-esteem and willingness to be social.

*Timing and age-related experience of fatherhood.* As noted previously, the timing of fatherhood and the father's age are important initial counseling considerations. Mark reported that his age has had impact on his concept of fathering. A repeated theme in Mark's life has been his self-image of being different and inferior. Being an older father reinforced Mark's perception of feeling different. Mark noted that when he is outside at his daughters' affluent suburb, he feels and is treated like an older father and sometimes like a grandfather. At restaurants, waitresses who are old enough to be his daughter if he had fathered kids in his twenties tell him his children are cute. He struggles with feeling old while simultaneously being attracted to younger women and looking for a partner and a companion. Mark reported that when he goes to places with his mother (who looks young for her age) and his kids, he is often perceived as a grandfather, an experience he dislikes. A final aspect of Mark's age is an increased awareness and fear of the impact of aging on his physical ability, such as running and climbing with his children in the playground. Discussions of Mark's constructed meaning of his age bring to the surface some of the overall themes and underlying issues Mark experiences.

Conversely, Mark reported that when he spends time with his daughters where they live and go to school, Mark's age is similar to other fathers. Mark explained that most of these parents, and fathers particularly, first focused on their careers and on becoming wealthy and then decided to have kids. Currently, these affluent fathers enjoy the money they made and are able to spend time with their kids or spend a significant amount of money on their education, clothes, and luxuries. At the same time, because of his separation from his partner, Mark has started worrying about money and thinks twice before turning on the heater in his house so that he can save for his retirement.

*Childhood experiences.* Although a full description of Mark's childhood and life experiences are beyond the scope of this case illustration, a brief mention of some salient events that shaped his current self-identity as a man and a father are warranted. Mark describes himself as a short and skinny boy who, at 4, was told by his mother not to cry. That was the last time Mark cried. Mark also reported that when he was asked questions, his mother would always answer for him. Further, Mark reported not being involved in extracurricular activities, yet his sister was always taken to dance lessons and other activities, sometimes by Mark himself. From these early experiences, Mark learned that he could not express his feelings or voice his needs. This theme influenced Mark's social relationships, as he tended to perceive others' opinions and thoughts as more important than his and often compromised his needs. For example, Mark wanted to attend his daughters' first day of first grade, but noted to me that because he did not have the kids that morning, he would not be able to be involved in this activity. After asking him who was not allowing him to drive to school and share the experience with his daughters, Mark realized that he had not even considered that possibility. Upon further reflection, he added that everyone's (mother, ex-partner, father, friends, etc.) "old voices/messages" in his head often override his own desires and needs.

Another important childhood consideration is Mark's perception of his fathers' roles and involvement in his life. Mark saw his stepfather as a guide and supervisor because he always made sure that Mark had what he thought Mark needed, that he built his bike in a way he wouldn't hurt himself; however, his stepfather did not initiate conversations or activities with Mark. His stepfather had not challenged Mark to stretch himself nor encouraged him to experiment and follow his heart and passion. For example, Mark recalled in therapy that when he had brought a report card with B's and C's, his stepfather's response was, "If that is the best you can do, then it is okay." Generally, Mark did not perceive his stepfather as being very involved in his life. Mark describes his own learned helplessness as stemming from his stepfather's passive tendency and unrealistic ways of solving problems. When Mark told his stepfather about his experience being teased and hit by bigger kids, Mark's stepfather urged him to go and fight back. Mark reported knowing that he was not big or strong enough. As a result, Mark noted internalizing fear, helplessness, and passivity. He doubted his own internal experiences.

Another powerful example discussed by Mark in therapy was his experience when he was 11. Mark was pushed and dumped into a big trash can by older boys. Mark waited for them to leave, then got up, walked away, and continued with his day like nothing had happened. Mark did not feel much about it nor did he tell anyone about the incident. At another time, Mark reported that the one time he had asked his parents for tutoring to help in math, his request had been denied and he failed math. Later in therapy, Mark realized that he learned to be an observer in life. Before attending counseling, Mark stayed at home most days, feeling physical and emotional insecurity, which making it difficult for him to leave the house and to socialize.

*Adulthood developmental milestones.* Growing up, Mark had always fantasized about being married and being a father. Mark was in a 14-year relationship with the mother of his children before legally separating 2 years ago. They had never married because she did not believe in marriage. Mark found himself again feeling different, as the traditional marriage institution he dreamt of was denied. Mark, a computer consultant, helped build her business, and it became extremely successful. As a result, she and Mark were upper class and had no money difficulties. Before she became pregnant, Mark had asked her to agree that they would always raise their kids themselves. Their goal was for Mark to be semiretired and he and his partner would both work part-time and raise the children. Before separating, Mark used to stay home with his children when his partner worked, and he worked as a consultant when she was home. Similar to his parents' relationship, Mark's partner was dominant and controlling, and Mark reported being passive. Mark decided to leave her when his feelings of numbness and helplessness became unbearable. He stated that he felt like he was in prison and could not be heard. The two-year separation involved lengthy negotiations and represented one of the first times in his life that Mark asserted his needs. Mark and his ex-partner were able to agree on a financial settlement and custody arrangement of the children. Throughout the process of separation, Mark stayed involved with his young daughters.

*Transitions and issues related to older fathers.* The issue of retirement had a unique impact on Mark's life and fathering roles in a way that is not frequently focused on in the literature. Before the separation, Mark had reached his financial goals and was happy with his paternal role. He was semiretired and was able to be involved in raising his daughters the way he had always wanted to. However, although the settlement enables Mark to live comfortably, he reports a sense of multiple losses. Mark lost his dream of a traditional family where he raises his children on a daily basis. He also lost lifelong financial stability and early retirement. Mark often experiences anxiety about his future financial stability and worries about being alone in his elderly years. Another major fear Mark has been experiencing is losing his children. He believes that he will not be able to afford a court battle with his ex-partner, who he still experiences as controlling and violating the settlement agreement by making decisions about the children without consulting with him. Mark continues to be self-employed and is learning to balance work, dating, and nonresident fatherhood.

An additional loss Mark has been working on in therapy, resulting from his childhood experiences and the separation, is lack of social support. Congruent with many other older men and fathers, Mark did not develop a social support system. Mark spent most of his time with his ex-partner and, in the later stages of the relationship, raising the children. Despite not having many friends, the couple spent much time traveling and working together. Mark feels distant from his family and perceives his family as ignoring him and deserting him when he needs them. In one counseling session, Mark noted how validating it was for him to hear his father look at a family picture and say to him, "You look as if you are blended into the background." Mark reported that his father's comment captured how he had felt in his family for his whole life. An integral part of counseling focuses on increasing Mark's social support.

Through our work, Mark has practiced and learned to assert himself and his needs with his family. Initially, Mark's change was faced with some resistance. Yet to Mark's surprise, his ability to find his voice changed his family's view of him. Mark reported gaining respect and having some of his needs met. As an example, Mark was going to have his daughters for Thanksgiving and wanted to give them a traditional family dinner. As the holiday approached and his family kept postponing responding to his invitation to come to his home for Thanksgiving, Mark resisted using old coping skills, giving up, and preparing to be disappointed. In counseling, Mark had linked the helplessness he felt with his childhood experiences and was able to confront his family. They, in turn, agreed to come have Thanksgiving with him and his daughters. This expression was another turning point in Mark's transformation, as he felt empowered by enjoying a pleasant Thanksgiving with the whole family in his own home.

Additionally, Mark started to shift some social patterns related to dating. Using imagery and applying Mark's business strengths, he started to gain confidence and began to express his needs in his dating life. In contrast to previous dates where Mark focused only on satisfying his date's needs, he started to discuss his needs in a partner and to tell his own story. He found himself in new territory, with dates turning into relationships. Further, in past dating relationships, if his partner declined a romantic relationship or he wanted to end the relationship, his fear of experiencing and expressing his feelings resulted in Mark walking away and ignoring his partner and her phone calls. Currently, Mark is working on communicating his feelings to women, opening himself to nonromantic friendships, and broadening his social support.

The experience of being a caretaker is another important issue for Mark. Mark's mother was diagnosed with Alzheimer's a few years ago. Initially Mark bore the majority of the caretaking responsibility. Mark found himself feeling guilty anytime he did not include his mom when he was spending time with his daughters. To help his mother, Mark frequently compromised his work and other daily activities. He reported feeling resentment toward his mother. In his words: "My mom interrupts my interactions with my kids as she talks over me, and…she distracts my time with them and my roles with them as it is difficult to provide guidance, discipline, play, and so forth….She also disables me from just letting them play in their room with their toys I got them a long time ago…"

Mark was not sure about how to provide social support and caregiving to his mother while being a nurturing father to his children. He believes that his role as a father conflicts with his role as a caretaker to his mom. Mark recognizes the desire to protect the short time he has with Emily and Erica. He has decreased some of his daily responsibilities with his mom by enlisting his mother's brother and his sister to share the caretaking responsibilities.

The conflict between Mark's role as a father and his caretaking role, combined with the impact of Mark's separation, initiated an important intervention that helped Mark gain awareness of his paternal roles. In one of our sessions, I asked Mark to review his thoughts, expectations, and actions before and after the separation. Mark drew on a piece of paper a powerful diagram reviewing his life in the context of the separation. Although a full description of the diagram is beyond the scope of this example, a relevant aspect is Mark's fathering roles. In addition to being accessible, as he was physically there with his children, Mark perceived himself engaging in many roles before the separation including disciplinarian, role model and guide, emotional nurturer, and provider. However, Mark perceived the separation to cancel and remove all of his roles. In session, the diagram was followed by guided imagery. After a few minutes of relaxation, Mark was asked to imagine himself in his 80s, looking back on his fathering experience. He was asked to envision what it should look like for Mark to feel that he had successfully fulfilled his role as a father. Mark was able to connect with important fathering images. We spent the rest of the session discussing the three aspects of father involvement: responsibility, accessibility, and engagement. Ironically, Mark realized that he is already engaged in many of these experiences and roles with his daughters. Additionally, Mark reported that he had gained the voice, power, and skills to meet his goals to become the father he would like to be.

Using Mark's commitment to and involvement with his daughters, his inaccurate schema were challenged. Mark realized that he learned throughout his life to walk away from situations, as he did not see any other options. He internalized helplessness and the message that he is incapable, rather than seeing his behaviors and coping skills as underdeveloped. Mark used the phrase "walking away" to illustrate the theme of giving up, including not getting a tutor and settling for grades lower than he was capable of receiving, and just walking away, being pushed into a trash can and walking away, and walking away from social relationships in which he felt inferior. An important moment in counseling was when I noted that Mark did not walk away from his kids throughout the separation process. His natural inclination towards generative fathering could be seen despite obstacles. Mark has realized that he has the ability to face challenges and emotional experiences rather than walking away. Mark is currently applying this newly recognized strength to business. Throughout his life, Mark had a few creative business ideas that he never followed through with because others had rejected his ideas. A few years later, his ideas had become big business successes, yet by other people. He is currently working on taking risks, trusting his own internal processes, and believing in his ideas.

We decided to use Mark in this case example because he brings to life some of the issues that older fathers face, including changing roles, retirement, caretaking responsibilities, social support, and others. Mark is still attending counseling. I enjoy working with him and I am looking forward to our continuing journey together and his courageous transformation. To Mark, thank you for the opportunity to work with you. To the mental health providers who work or will work with older fathers, we hope that the ideas presented in this chapter will give you a useful roadmap to guide your work with this important segment of fathers.

# REFERENCES

Addis, M. E., & Mahalik, J. R. (2003). Men, masculinity, and the contexts of help-seeking. *American Psychologist, 58,* 5–14.

Altfeld, S. J. (1995). Caring for elderly fathers: The impact of family disruption on later life parent-child relationships. *Dissertation Abstracts International: Section B: The Sciences and Engineering,* Vol 56(5-B), Nov 1995. p. 2584.

American Psychological Association (1998). What practitioners should know about working with older adults. *Professional Psychology: Research and Practice, 29*(5), 413–427.

American Psychological Association (2004). Guidelines for psychological practice with older adults. *American Psychologist, 59*(4), 236–260.

Barrows, P. (2004). Fathers and families: Locating the ghost in the nursery. *Infant Mental Health Journal, 25*(5), 408–423.

Biddle, B. J. (1979). *Role theory, expectations, identities, and behaviors.* New York: Academic Press.

Bouchard, G., Lee, C. M., Asgary, V., & Pelletier, L. (2007). Fathers' motivation for involvement with their children: A self-determination theory perspective. *Fathering, 5*(1), 25–41.

Bowman, P. J., & Sanders, R. (1998). Unmarried African American fathers: A comparative life span analysis. *Journal of Comparative Family Studies, 29,* 39–56.

Bozett, F. W. (1985). Male development and fathering throughout the life cycle. *American Behavioral Scientist, 29*(1), 41–54.

Bronte-Tinkew, J., Carrano, J., & Guzman, L. (2006). Resident fathers' perceptions of their roles and links to involvement with infants. *Fathering*, 4, 254–285.

Coley, R. L. (2001). (In)visible men: Emerging research on low-income, unmarried, and minority fathers. *American Psychologist*, 56(2), 743–753.

Dollahite, D. C., & Hawkins, A. J. (1998). A conceptual ethic of generative fathering. *The Journal of Men's Studies*, 7, 109–132.

Dudley, J. R., & Stone, G. (2001). *Fathering at risk: Helping nonresidential fathers.* New York: Springer.

Erikson, E. H. (1963). *Childhood and society* (2nd ed.). New York: W. W. Norton & Co.

Fagan, J., & Hawkins, A. J. (Eds.). (2001). *Clinical and educational interventions with fathers.* Binghamton, NY: Haworth.

Findley, G. E., & Schwartz, S. J. (2004). The father involvement and nurturant fathering scales: Retrospective measures for adolescent and adult children. *Educational and Psychological Measurement*, 64, 143–164.

Findley, G. E., & Schwartz, S. J. (2006). Parsons and Bales revisited: Young adult children's characterization of the fathering role. *Psychology of Men & Masculinity*, 7, 42–55.

Franklin, A. J., & Davis III, T. (2001). Therapeutic support groups as a primary intervention for issues of fatherhood with African American men. In J. Fagan & A. J. Hawkins, (Eds.), *Clinical and educational interventions with fathers* (pp. 45–66). Binghamton, NY: Haworth.

Hays, P. (1996). Culturally responsive assessment with diverse older clients. *Professional Psychology: Research and Practice*, 27(2), 188–193.

Jain, A., Belsky, J., & Crnic, K. (1996). Beyond fathering behaviors: Types of dads. *Journal of Family Psychology*, 10(4), 431–442.

Jung, C. G. (1933) *Modern man in search of a soul.* New York: Harcourt, Brace.

Kaye, L. W. (1997). Informal caregiving by older men. In J. I. Kosberg & L. W. Kaye. (Eds.). (1997). *Elderly men: Special problems and professional challenges.* New York: Springer.

Kaye, L. W., & Crittenden, J. A. (2005). Principles of clinical practice with older men. *Journal of Sociology and Social Welfare*, 32(1), 99–123.

Kiselica, M. S., Englar-Carlson, M., Horne, A. M., & Fisher, M. (2008). A positive psychology perspective on helping boys. In M. S. Kiselica, M. Englar-Carlson, & A. M. Horne (Eds.), *Counseling troubled boys: A practitioner's guidebook* (pp. 31–48). New York: Routledge.

Kosberg, J. I., & Kaye L. W. (Eds.). (1997). *Elderly men: Special problems and professional challenges.* New York: Springer.

Krause, A. M., & Haverkamp, B. E. (1996). Attachment in adult child-older parent relationships: Research, theory, and practice. *Journal of Counseling & Development*, 75(2), 83–92.

Lagana, L. (1995). Older adults' expectations about mental health counseling: A multivariate and discriminant analysis. *International Journal of Aging and Human Development*, 40, 297–316.

Lamb, M. E., Pleck, J. H., Charnov, E. L., & Levine, J. A. (1987). A biosocial perspective on paternal behavior and involvement. In J. B. Lancaster, J. Altman, A. Rossi, & L. R. Sherrod (Eds.), *Parenting across the lifespan: Biosocial perspectives.* New York: Academic.

Levant, R. F. (1995). Toward the reconstruction of masculinity. In R. F. Levant & W. S. Pollack (Eds.), *A new psychology of men* (pp. 68–89). New York: Basic Books.

Levine, J. A., & Pitt, E. W. (1995). *New expectations: Community strategies for responsible fatherhood.* New York: Families and Work Institute.

Marsigilo, W., Day, R. D., & Lamb, M. E. (2000). Exploring fatherhood diversity: Implications for conceptualizing father involvement. *Marriage and Family Review, 29*(4), 269–293.

Martin, J. A., Hamilton, B. E., Sutton, P. D., Ventura, S. J., Menacker, F., & Kirmeyer, S. (2006). Births: Final data for 2004. National Vita Statistical Report – CDC, *55*(1).

Masciadrelli, B. P., Pleck, J. H., & Stueve, J. L. (2006). Fathers' role model perceptions. *Men & Masculinities, 9,* 23–34.

Monk, A. (1997). The transition to retirement. In J. I. Kosberg & L. W. Kaye. (Eds.), *Elderly men: Special problems and professional challenges.* New York: Springer.

Neville, B., & Parke, R. D. (1997). Waiting for paternity: Interpersonal and contextual implications of the timing of fatherhood. *Sex Roles, 37,* 45–59.

Parke, R. D. (1995). Multiple publications from a single data set: A challenge for researchers and editors. *Journal of Family Psychology, 8,* 384–386.

Parke, R. D. (2000). Father involvement: A developmental psychological perspective. In H. E. Peters, G. W. Peterson, S. K. Steinmetz, & R. D. Day (Eds.), *Fatherhood: Research, interventions and policies* (pp. 43–58). New York: Haworth.

Pleban, F. T., & Diez, K. S. (2007). Fathers as mentors: Bridging the gap between generations. In S. E. Brotherson & J. M. White (Eds.), *Why fathers count: The importance of fathers and their involvement with children* (pp. 307–318). Harriman, TN: Men's Studies Press.

Russell, G. (1986). Grandfathers: Making up for lost responsibilities. In R. A. Lewis & R. E. Salt (Eds.), *Men in families* (pp. 233–259). Thousand Oaks, CA: Sage.

Schwartz, S. J., & Findley, G. E. (2006). Father involvement, nurturant fathering, and young adult psychosocial functioning: Differences among adoptive, adoptive stepfather, and nonadoptive stepfamilies. *Journal of Family Issues, 27,* 712–731.

Spitze, G., & Logan, J. R. (1992). Helping as a component of parent-adult child relations. *Research on Aging, 14,* 291–312.

Sprenkel, D. (1999). Therapeutic issues and strategies in group therapy with older men. In M. Duffy (Ed.), *Handbook of counseling and psychotherapy with older adults.* New York: Wiley & Sons.

Szinovacz, M. E., & Davey, A. (2001). Retirement effects on parent-adult child contacts. *The Gerontologist, 41*(2), 191–200.

Taylor, A. C. (2007). Grandfathers: Rediscovering America's forgotten resource. In S. E. Brotherson & J. M. White (Eds.), *Why fathers count: The importance of fathers and their involvement with children* (pp. 91–103). Harriman, TN.

Taylor, B. A., Giarrusso, R., Feng, D., & Bengston, V. L. (2006). Portraits of paternity: Middle-aged and elderly paternity: Middle-aged elderly father's involvement with adult children. In V. H. Bedford & B. F. Turner (Eds.), *Men in relationships: A new look from a life course perspective* (pp. 127–145). New York: Springer Publishing.

Thomas, J. L. (1994). Older men as fathers and grandfathers. In E. H. Thompson (Ed.), *Older men's lives* (pp. 197–217). Thousand Oaks, CA: Sage.

Turk-Charles, S., Rose, T., & Gatz, M. (1996). The significance of gender in the treatment of older adults. In L. L. Carstensen, B. A. Edelstein, & L. Dornbrand (Eds.), *The practical handbook of clinical gerontology.* Thousand Oaks, CA: Sage.

Westermeyer, J. F. (2004). Predictors and characteristics of Erikson's life cycle model among men: A 32-year longitudinal study. *International Journal of Aging and Human Development, 58,* 29–48.

# Index